D1008997

PENGUIN HANDBOOK

A TRAVELER'S GUIDE TO EL DORADO AND THE INCA EMPIRE

Lynn Meisch became interested in Pre-Columbian cultures while camping in Mexico and Guatemala. After obtaining an M.A. degree in Latin American humanities, she made several trips to South America, in search of adventure and to collect Andean textiles and film traditional music and dance. She has traveled in Colombia, Ecuador, Peru, and Bolivia by plane, train, bus, truck, car, boat, and on foot and horseback. A spinner, weaver, writer, and photographer, Ms. Meisch lives in San Francisco when she is not doing textile research or leading treks in the Andes. Following the completion of this book, she was awarded both a Fulbright fellowship and an Institute for Intercultural Studies fellowship to research, photograph, and film indigenous spinning, weaving, and costumes in southern Ecuador. In 1981 and 1982 she had an Inter-American Foundation fellowship to document the effect of tourism on traditional textiles in Tarabuco, Bolivia, where she also collected weavings for the Museo Nacional de Etnografía y Folklore in La Paz and for the Textile Museum in Washington, D.C.

A Traveler's Guide

to El Dorado
& the
Inca Empire

Lynn Meisch

Illustrations by the author

REVISED EDITION

PENGUIN BOOKS

PENGUIN BOOKS

Viking Penguin Inc., 40 West 23rd Street,
New York, New York 10010, U.S.A.
Penguin Books Ltd, Harmondsworth,
Middlesex, England
Penguin Books Australia Ltd, Ringwood,
Victoria, Australia
Penguin Books Canada Limited, 2801 John Street,
Markham, Ontario, Canada L3R 1B4
Penguin Books (N.Z.) Ltd, 182–190 Wairau Road,
Auckland 10, New Zealand

First published in the United States of America
by Penguin Books 1977
Second printing 1978; third printing (revised) 1980
Revised Edition published by Viking Penguin Inc., 1984

LIBRARY OF CONGRESS CATALOGING IN PUBLICATION DATA
Meisch, Lynn, 1945–
A traveler's guide to El Dorado & the Inca Empire.
Bibliography: p.
Includes indexes.
1. Andes—Description and travel—Guide-books.
2. South America—Description and travel—1981-   —Guide-
books.   I. Title.
F2212.M5   1984   918'.0438   83-25689
ISBN 0 14 046.639 8

Printed in the United States of America by
Fairfield Graphics, Fairfield, Pennsylvania
Set in Palatino and Trump

Quotation on page v from Seven Voices by Rita Guibert, copyright © Alfred A. Knopf,
Inc., 1972. Reprinted with the permission of Alfred A. Knopf, Inc.

Poem on pages 247–48 from The Heights of Macchu Picchu by Pablo Neruda, translated
by Nathaniel Tarn, copyright © Jonathan Cape Ltd and Nathaniel Tarn, 1966.
Reprinted with the permission of Farrar, Straus & Giroux, Inc, and Jonathan Cape Ltd.

Song on page 411 from The Singing Mountaineers, copyright © Ruth Stephan, 1957.
Reprinted with the permission of the University of Texas Press.

Contents

v

Acknowledgments

Thanks to citizens and residents of the following countries, who helped me and the book in numerous ways: Colombia—Laney Odlum, Will Rogers, Suzanne and Mono Trujillo; Ecuador—Jeff Bertelsen, Peace Corps volunteer with *Productos Andinos* in Cuenca; Frank Keim; and especially Jill and John Ortman, Peace Corps volunteers with *Productos Andinos* in Quito, now owners with Jim and Kay Verner of *La Bodega*, one of the finest crafts and antiques stores in Quito, for extensive help with Ecuadorian folk art and crafts; Peru—Guillermo and Terry Jones; Rosa, Lito and Señor Tokunaga; Bolivia—Gabriela and Tito, managers of the *Hotel Ideal* in Cochabamba; Guido and Terry Bustillos; the Humberto Salama family, especially Sylvia; Dr. Geraldine de Caballero; and Peñaco, manager of the *Hotel Panamericano* in La Paz.

Thanks also to the following travelers who shared meals, maps, information, sunsets and horrendous bus rides: Irma and Wally Allen, the Bear, Stephen Douglas, Al Grant, Elaine and Francis Meisch, Steve Miller, Tina Rosa, Bill Schulze, Susy Silverman, Carla and Pauline Swart and Cathy Textor. Besides sharing adventures on the trip, Bob and Mary Martin, on return to the States, sent me their backpacking journal and equipment list, and Fred and Leslie Hart of *La Tienda* in Seattle shipped me books. Leslie also made suggestions and criticisms on the folk art and crafts chapter.

Other travelers, whom I talked to after my last trip, added their knowledge and experiences and helped me to update the manuscript continually, including Steve Berger, Gwen Carmen, David Isenhower, Lindy Kurle, Gail Sumner, Sally and Miguel Tirado, Christopher Wren, and especially Ann Houston and Elayne Zorn, who helped with Peruvian and Bolivian textiles.

On the home front, thanks to Brian Buckley and the many members of the moral support squad, and to Jeanette Oliver, the saintly pet sitter.

Many other people very graciously helped with this book, including Lidia R. Levy, manager of the Mission Travel Center in San Francisco, who aided with "Getting There"; Laura Tokunaga Stone, my Quechua teacher; Mary Moser, who translated from French and checked the spinning section; Joyce Heller, former consultant to the director of the Gold Museum in Bogotá, who contributed her knowledge of Colombian fiestas and crafts; Margie Cason, who shared information on Bolivian culture and weaving; Adele Cahlander, who provided textile analysis and extensive criticism of the Peruvian and Bolivian spinning, dyeing and weaving sections; Jacquetta Nisbet, who also helped with textiles; Vivian Burns and especially Arden Arnautoff of V.B.I., Inc., walking encyclopedias on Peruvian folk art and crafts; Herb Sigmond, M.D., who gave extensive time and advice on "Health"; Patricia Diaz, who checked the Spanish; and Nancy Rappolt and Richard T. Rappolt, M.D., who gave me my shots before the trip and cured my amoebas afterwards. Dr. Rappolt also read and criticized "Drugs," and many of the above people shared slides and photographs which I used in the illustrations.

I also owe a debt to the philosophy of travel expressed by Ed Buryn in his *Vagabonding* books, and by Carl Franz, Lorena Havens and Steve Rogers in *The People's Guide to Mexico*. Steve also passed along advice based on his travels in the Andes.

To *The CoEvolution Quarterly*, whose publication of my article "To South America" in the Winter 1974 issue resulted in this book: *mil gracias*.

Finally, to my typist, Richard Reynolds; my patient, meticulous editor, Linda Gunnarson; Ernest Scott of San Francisco Book Company, who provided thoughtful, steady guidance on the manuscript; Zanae Melander, who helped proofread the copy and prepare the index; Howard Jacobsen, the text designer; David Bunnett, who created the chapter numerals and initial letters; and to my publishers at The Headlands Press, Barry Traub and, especially, Andrew Fluegelman, who got this project off the ground and saw me through the "I can't write another word" stages: *taitacha pagasunki*.

LYNN MEISCH

Acknowledgments to the
Revised Edition

So many people have written to me in the six years since this book was first published that it is impossible to list you by name. I want you to know I have laughed over your letters and listened to your suggestions in revising this guide. I appreciate your interest; please continue to write.

There are several people who deserve special mention. Lawrence Carpenter and Lauren Kunkel generously turned over their dining-room tables to my typewriter, notebooks, and papers while I worked on revisions. Thanks also to Linda Muñiz; Jaime Reibel; to my compadres, godchildren, and friends in Ecuador; and to the many other people who offered friendship, encouragement, meals, and hot showers during my recent travels in the Andes, especially Patty and Charlie Eitzen, Jane and Rudy Ayora, and Leandro Romero and family.

*What sets worlds in motion is the interplay
of differences, their attractions and repulsions.
Life is plurality, death is uniformity. By
suppressing differences and peculiarities, by
eliminating different civilizations and cultures,
progress weakens life and favors death. The
ideal of a single civilization for everyone,
implicit in the cult of progress and technique,
impoverishes and mutilates us. Every view
of the world that becomes extinct, every culture
that disappears, diminishes a possibility
of life.*

OCTAVIO PAZ

Introduction

"El Dorado and the Inca Empire" refers to Colombia, Ecuador, Peru and Bolivia, the four countries in northwestern South America. These countries are connected by the Andes, the second highest mountain range in the world, which runs through them like a spine. I lived and traveled in the Andean countries for four years because I was intrigued by the Indian civilizations, the ruins of the great empires and the living cultures. These interests drew me south, and now the lands of the condor have a grip on my heart and soul.

Colombia is called the land of El Dorado, the Gilded Man, because of a custom practiced by the Chibcha, or Muisca, Indians, who lived near what is now Bogotá. At the inauguration of a new chief thousands of Indians gathered on the hills around Lake Guatavita and lit bonfires. The chief was covered from head to toe with resin, then coated with gold dust. He was rowed out to the center of the lake where he submerged himself. The gold dust was washed off as an offering to the spirit the Chibcha believed resided at the bottom of the lake, while the Indians on shore tossed golden offerings into the water. This custom gave rise to rumors of people dressed in gold and cities of gold, and brought the Spanish into the interior of Colombia.

The search for gold also brought the Spanish to Peru, which was the center of the Inca Empire, the last of the great South American Indian civilizations. Between 1438 and 1525 A.D. the Quechua Indians expanded from their capital of Cuzco as far north as what is now Pasto, Colombia, and as far south as the Maule River in Chile, a distance of 2,500 miles. They also moved eastward into Bolivia and Argentina. In 1532 Francisco Pizarro captured and killed the Inca Atahualpa and commenced the Spanish Conquest of the Inca Empire; the Quechua continued to fight for forty years.

The modern descendants of the Incas live in many respects as if the Spanish had never arrived. The twentieth century is present only in the large cities. Residents of the Indian communities still sprinkle *chicha* (corn beer) to *Pacha Mama* (Mother Earth) as they have for centuries, till the soil as their families have for generations, weave textiles almost identical to ones found in thousand-year-old tombs and wear a combination of Pre-Columbian and Spanish Colonial dress. When I travel among these people I feel I am in touch with something beautiful and enduring beyond anything I've experienced in the United States.

As well as the Indian cultures, I'm attracted to the land itself, which is spectacularly, hauntingly beautiful. In South America you become used to stunning scenery and unspoiled countryside the way you take indoor toilets and hot water for granted at home. The continent is amazingly diverse. It has the Andes, the highest mountain range in the Western Hemisphere; the Amazon Basin, the world's largest tropical rainforest; Lake Titicaca, the world's highest navigable lake; as well as La Paz, the world's highest capital city—to list just a few of the records. Colombia alone has more than twice as many species of birds as all of North America, and the Galapagos Islands and the Amazon Basin are a naturalist's paradise.

The possibilities for adventure are limitless. Your trip can be as rugged or as easy as you want to make it, although flying from one Sheraton Hotel to the next is hardly my idea of seeing the countryside. I have friends who took a dugout canoe a thousand miles down the Amazon from Leticia to Manaus, another who took a boat down the Río Napo in Ecuador's Oriente and another who rode horseback to Macchu Picchu over the old Inca road. (You can also hike this route.) You can pretty much do what you want, although if you get into trouble in the jungle or mountains you'll also have to get yourself out. This means you are totally responsible for yourself. If this responsibility frightens you, you can stick closer to the main cities and travel routes.

Several of my friends felt that in writing this book I was contributing to the destruction of the land and cultures I love so much. My response is that I'm not encouraging people to go—they're going anyway—and most travelers would like to be more sensitive and appreciative if only they knew how.

This guide doesn't tell you where to go or what to see and buy, but tries to give you enough background information so you can make intelligent choices and discoveries for yourself. I don't recommend specific hotels, shops or restaurants; enough guide books do that. I have really tried to do two things. One is to minimize the negative impact of you, the traveler, on South America and the other is to minimize the negative impact of South America on you. I'd like to see travelers have the best possible time with the least possible evidence of their passing. This means being healthy, comfortable, centered and sensitive to local customs. If I could offer just one piece of advice it would be this—expect the unfamiliar, relax and tread gently.

We might be smart but we aren't wise. The Indians aren't smart or educated in the American or European sense, but they are wise and I believe we need their wisdom. It's a little bit embarrassing to realize that we have pillaged our own continent in only 200 years while the Indians are farming on the same terraces they've used for millennia. We travel to learn, not to teach, and you can learn a lot on the road. If you can enjoy the challenge of travel in rugged terrain and accept South America on its own terms you will have an incomparable trip.

¡Feliz viaje!

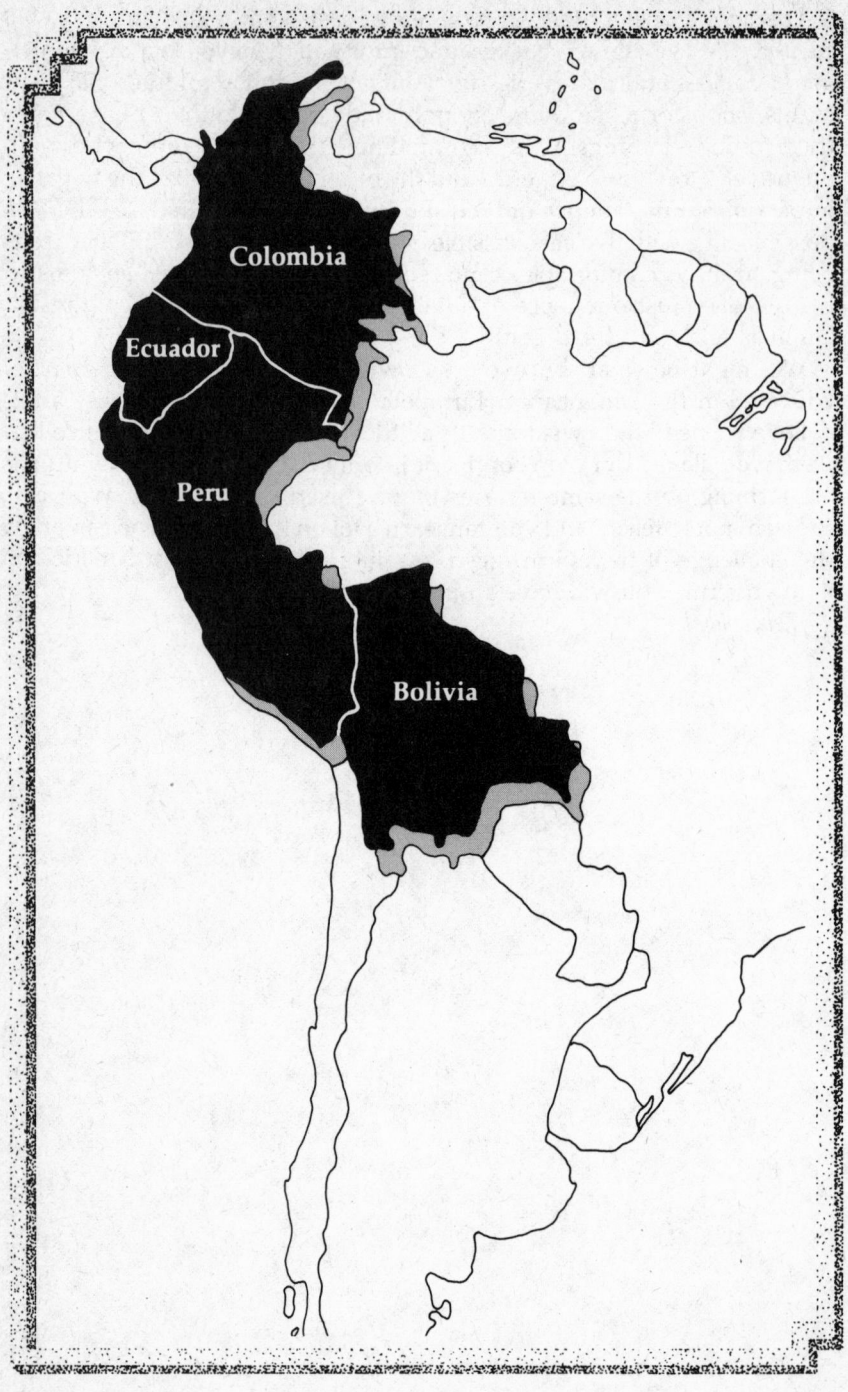

Getting Ready

s you prepare for your trip, there are a number of things to consider before you make final plans.

Where You're Going

COLOMBIA

Colombia is the only South American country with both Atlantic and Pacific coastlines. This country is astonishingly diverse geographically. The flat, grassy *llanos* and the Amazon rainforest together make up fully half the country, and there are also steamy coasts, deserts (including the Guajira Peninsula) and three Andean ranges *(cordilleras)* with fertile, temperate, river valleys in between. People have adapted to all of these environments, making good use of local materials in clothing, housing and tools.

Today, only about one percent of Colombia's population is full-blooded Indian. Mixed-blood Indians *(mestizos)* comprise fifty percent, whites *(blancos)* twenty percent, and blacks *(negros)* and mulattos about twenty-nine percent of the population.

The contemporary Indian tribes of Colombia have been pushed to the edges of the country. Spanish settlers either annihilated the Indians in the desirable, arable areas, as did the settlers of the United States and

Canada, or (unlike the North American colonists) intermarried with the native people, resulting in a *mestizo* population whose culture bears little resemblance to that of the original inhabitants. Among Colombia's small Indian population, there are only a few remaining groups of highland Indians, and all are located in the departments of Cauca, Nariño and Putumayo, near the Ecuadorian border.

ECUADOR

Ecuador can be divided into three main geographical regions: the Pacific coast *(costa);* the Andes (or Sierra), which run from north to south through the center of the country in two major ranges; and the eastern jungle (Oriente).

Unlike Colombia, nearly half the population of Ecuador is Indian, with most of them living in the Sierra and Oriente. In addition, about forty percent of the population is *mestizo,* including a few blacks and black–Indian mixtures *(zambos),* and about ten percent is white.

The two Andean *cordilleras* are linked by smaller ranges, and the Andean Indians of Ecuador live in the ten intermountain basins formed by these ranges. The long valley between the *cordilleras* is called *la avenida de los volcanes* (the avenue of the volcanoes) because of the snow-capped volcanic peaks which tower above the valley floor.

Ecuador feels very different from Colombia, primarily because of its large Indian population, many of whom speak Quechua and have retained their traditional lifestyles. These include the Otavalo, the most prosperous Indians of the Andes; the Salasaca, who were transplanted from Bolivia by the Incas and still wear black in mourning for the death of the Inca Atahualpa four centuries ago; and the Jivaro, or Shuara, who speak Shuara and are the only Indians known to have successfully revolted against the Spanish (in 1599) without having been reconquered.

PERU

Like Ecuador, Peru can be divided into three main geographical regions. The thirty-mile-wide coastal strip is a desert which is broken only by oases created by the approximately forty rivers which flow from the Andes to the Pacific. Civilizations have flourished in these river-valley oases for nine thousand years. The Peruvian coastal desert is one of the driest in the world due to the effect of the unusually cold Humboldt Current, which flows northward from Chile past the Peruvian coast. Cooled by the air above these cold coastal waters, rain clouds dump their water at sea and rarely on the coast. Because of this phenomenon, the Atacama Desert in Chile has absolutely no recorded rainfall. However, there's progressively more rainfall as you travel northward in

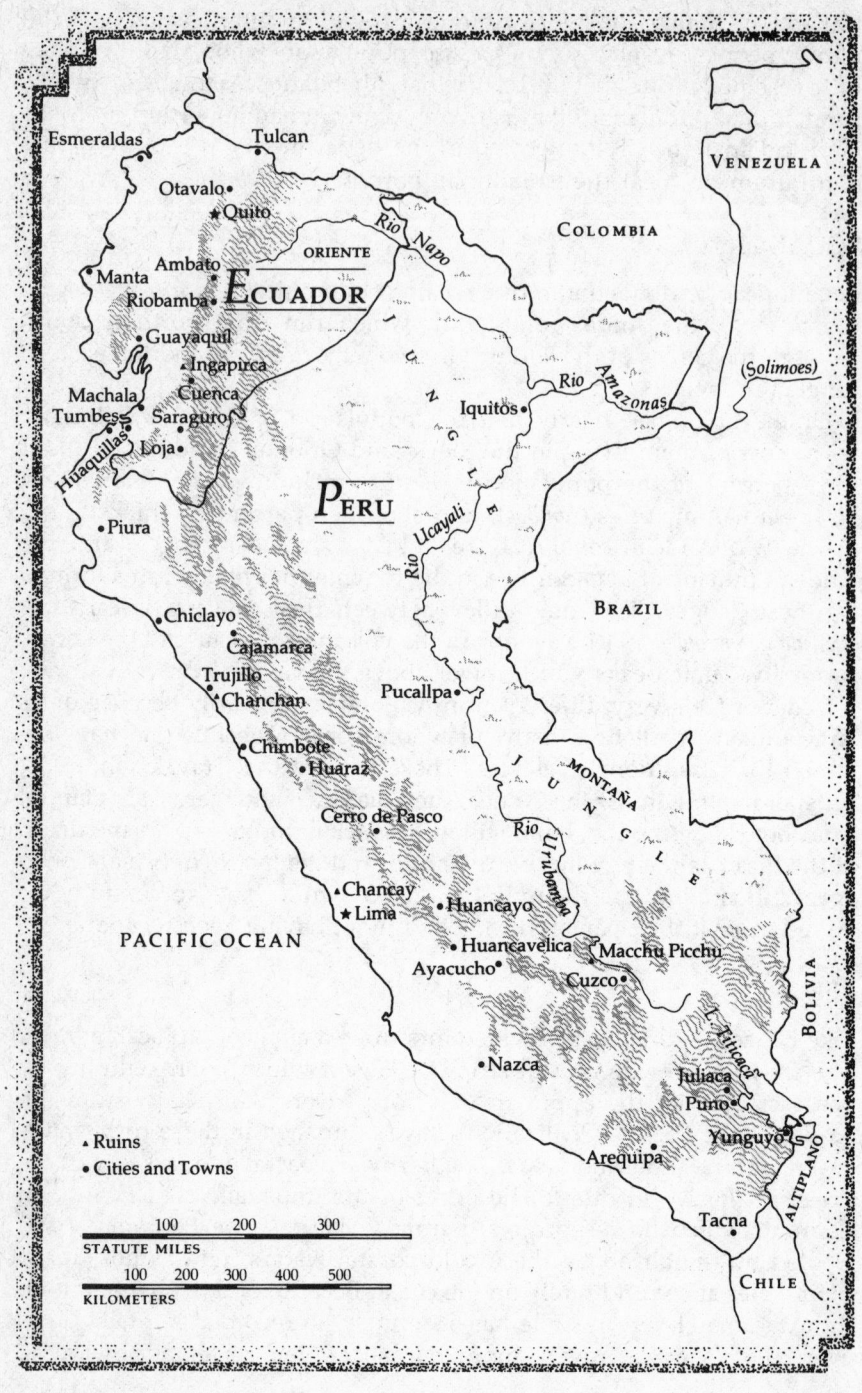

Esmeraldas
Tulcan
Otavalo
★ Quito
Ambato
ORIENTE
Manta
Riobamba
ECUADOR
Rio Napo
COLOMBIA
VENEZUELA
Guayaquil
Ingapirca
Cuenca
Machala
Saraguro
Tumbes
Loja
Huaquillas

Rio Amazonas
(Solimoes)
Iquitos

J U N G L E

Piura

PERU

Rio Ucayali

Chiclayo
Cajamarca
Trujillo
Chanchan
Pucallpa
BRAZIL
Chimbote
Huaraz

J U N G L E
MONTAÑA
Cerro de Pasco
Rio Urubamba
Chancay
★ Lima
Huancayo
Huancavelica
Macchu Picchu
Ayacucho
Cuzco

PACIFIC OCEAN

Nazca

L. Titicaca
Juliaca
Puno
Yunguyo
BOLIVIA
ALTIPLANO
Arequipa

▲ Ruins
• Cities and Towns

Tacna
CHILE

```
       100       200       300
STATUTE MILES
     100   200   300   400   500
KILOMETERS
```

Peru. Once or twice a century, a warm current known as *El Niño* flows southward and counters the effect of the Humboldt Current, dumping torrential rains on the Peruvian coast and generally making a mess. During the winter season, there's usually heavy continuous fog along the coast for weeks on end.

The second geographical region is the Sierra, or Andean highlands. The Andes become wider as you travel southward from Ecuador into Peru and Bolivia—from 60 miles wide in Ecuador to 180 miles wide in Bolivia. The Peruvian Andes run roughly from northwest to southeast in a number of ranges, such as the Cordillera Negra, the Cordillera Blanca, the Cordillera Vilcabamba and so on, with peaks reaching above 20,000 feet. The Cordillera Blanca is the highest Andean range in Peru and includes Mt. Huascarán, which reaches an elevation of 22,198 feet.

Between the *cordilleras* are the high tablelands known as the *puna* or, around Lake Titicaca, the *altiplano*. Most Peruvian Indians live in these high mountain valleys, which range in elevation from 9000 to 14,000 feet. The Callejón de Huaylas and the Urubamba Valley in the Cuzco area are two such densely populated valleys. Today the Sierra is the center of Peruvian Indian life, and it is here that most travelers spend their time.

The third and largest geographical region is the hot humid jungle known as the *montaña* or *selva*. The Sierra is separated from the *selva* by a transitional zone, *la ceja de la montaña* (the eyebrow of the jungle), where the Andes drop away into the jungle lowlands. The Yungas, the subtropical valleys where coca leaves are grown, are located in this region.

About fifty percent of the population of Peru is Indian, thirty-three percent *mestizo* (or *cholo*), twelve percent white and five percent black and Oriental. Because of cultural differentiation, the designations Indian, *mestizo* and *cholo* often refer to lifestyle and language, rather than race (see page 91, "Class Consciousness"). In the Sierra, seventy to eighty percent of the population is Indian and would probably define itself as such. Five-sixths of these Indians speak Quechua and the remaining one-sixth speak Aymara.

BOLIVIA

Most travelers enter Bolivia from Peru, crossing the high, windswept *altiplano*, or they fly into La Paz, landing at El Alto Airport, which is the highest commercial airport in the world. Bolivia can be divided into two main geographical regions: the Andean highlands, which constitute one-third of the country, and the eastern jungle lowlands, which make up the remaining two-thirds of the territory. The country has no seacoast.

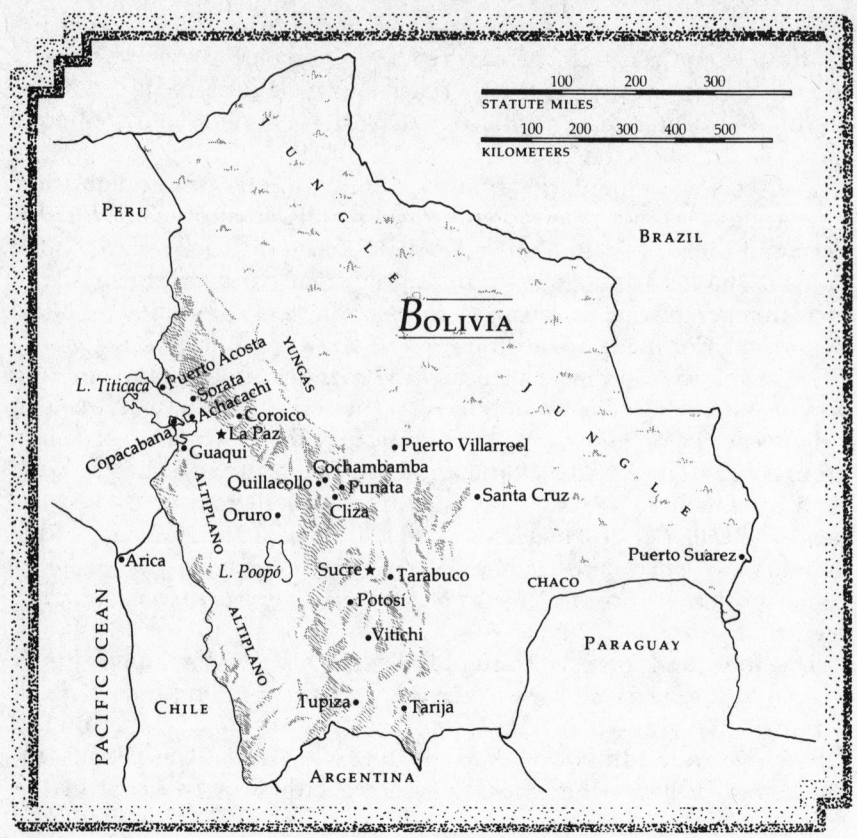

Bolivia is an intriguing country. It's the most rural, most Indian and least populated of the Andean nations. About sixty to seventy percent of the population is Indian, twenty to thirty percent *mestizo* and *cholo* (although this is misleading, since in Bolivia any person who lives in town is considered a *cholo*, regardless of race), nine percent white and one percent black.

Bolivia as a whole is not densely populated. However, most of its people are concentrated on the *altiplano*, especially around Lake Titicaca, and in the high valleys, and there's tremendous population pressure on the land in these places.

Climate

Most people think of South America as typically tropical—that is, hot and sunny. This is true for the Caribbean coast, the Colombian and

Ecuadorian coasts and the Amazon Basin. Otherwise, altitude, not lati-
tude, determines climate. This means you can freeze if you don't dress
properly in Bogotá, Quito, Cuzco, Puno and La Paz, which are all above
8600 feet in elevation. If you've ever been in the mountains you know
how cold it can be when the sun isn't shining. The Andes are beautifully
hot and sunny during the day, but as soon as the sun sets or goes behind
the clouds it's another story. Many Andean peaks are above 20,000 feet,
and the Peruvian and Bolivian *altiplanos* are at least 12,000 feet above sea
level. The air is thin and cold, and during the South American winter
months these places can be bitterly cold, especially at night. In 1911,
Hiram Bingham, the rediscoverer of Macchu Picchu, wrote, "In the
Andes, one is rarely comfortable except when the sun is shining."
Remember that and plan accordingly. (See Chapter Two, "What to
Take.")

For most Europeans and Americans, our summer months are set aside
for vacation, which isn't necessarily the best time to visit South America.
Since the seasons are reversed south of the equator, June, July and
August are winter months and can be very cold. It often goes below freezing on the *altiplano* and occasionally it snows. Lima is covered by a dismal,
damp, gray fog. Also, Peru is mobbed by tourists from June to September
and finding accommodations can be a challenge. Hotels roll out bedding
on their lobby and dining room floors, and even first-class train passengers sometimes find themselves sitting on their suitcases in the aisle.
However, if this is the only time you'll have to travel in South America I
definitely say go anyway. At least it's dry, since most rainfall in the Andes
occurs between December and April.

My own favorite months for traveling are March, April and May, and
September, October and November—that is, fall and spring in the Southern Hemisphere. The days are sunny, hot and dry, and the nights cool,
sometimes cold. When the rains begin in December they often wash out
roads and railroad tracks, rendering many places inaccessible.

The Amazon Basin is hot and humid all year, although rainfall varies,
so it doesn't matter much when you travel there. Before starting a river
trip in this region it's best to inquire locally about travel conditions.

These descriptions are very general; there are many local variations in
climate in a continent the size of South America. No matter when you
travel, bring a down jacket and a rain poncho—you'll need them.

Timing

How much time should you allow for your trip and how should you
schedule it? Be loose, because South America is loose. I've never been

able to understand people who go on vacations with every day planned. In South America your very precise plans will go very precisely wrong. Always allow for acts of God, man and military governments. Give yourself extra time. A friend got stuck in Puno, Peru, for a month because of an uprising which led to a prohibition on travel in that area. This is an extreme case, but it does happen.

When I traveled with my parents in Peru for three weeks we made an itinerary: Lima, Arequipa, Puno, Cuzco and Macchu Picchu, then back to Lima. We planned the trip carefully and had a number of things we wanted to do, but we allowed lots of leeway. For example, the trains connecting Arequipa, Puno and Cuzco run in one direction one day and in the opposite direction the next. So, if for some reason we missed a Tuesday train, we would stay in town and catch the Thursday train, which still allowed us enough time to visit all the places we planned. Losing a day or two did not ruin our plans, and believe me, you're going to lose some days! There are delays that simply can't be avoided (storms, landslides) and some that can, but if you don't have a tight schedule the delays won't matter.

If you're traveling in Peru during June, July and August, you should make all hotel and plane reservations well ahead of time (meaning two weeks to a month), since the country is jammed with tourists this time of year, particularly Cuzco. You can always find a room to rent, but the reason you can is that it's so bad no one else wants it, or you could end up sleeping on the floor in a hotel lobby. The very good, and reasonably priced, government Tourist Hotels require reservations in advance during these months, although you can always check with them in case a party doesn't show up. This often happens at Macchu Picchu. The hotel is always booked, but by two or three in the afternoon there are rooms available because people don't show.

Because my parents were traveling for only a month, they spent a few days in Bogotá, a few days in Quito and the surrounding countryside and three weeks in Peru. They didn't even attempt to visit Bolivia. On our first trip Bill (my boyfriend at the time) and I spent a month in Colombia and a month in Ecuador and then returned home. We wanted to know several countries well rather than cover a lot of ground. I think you'll find this approach fruitful. Try to plan your trip for a month minimum—three months to a year is better—and don't try to cram too many countries into a short period of time. Relax and let things flow. If you get stuck somewhere, enjoy the chance for a rest, write letters and do your laundry. Don't gripe about South American disorganization; if it's flawless efficiency you're after, visit Germany or Switzerland.

Above all, your trip should be fun. So what if you don't get to Argentina? What's the point of going somewhere just to say you've been there, at the cost of frayed nerves and a bad temper? If you do manage all your scheduled stops it's wonderful (and somewhat amazing), but there's no point in hurrying through places just to get somewhere else. Remember, too, that another traveler may introduce you to a place you've never heard of or read about, so be relaxed enough to enjoy side trips and adventures. On my last trip I saw four countries in nine months, and while I definitely plan to visit the countries I missed, I got to know a few places well.

Travel Agents and Tours

You don't need a travel agent to plan your trip, except perhaps to help with airline bookings (see Chapter Four, "Getting There"), and you certainly don't need to take a tour, even if you're timid and don't speak any Spanish. My inclination is to avoid traditional tours as I would the Black Death. You can plan the trip yourself and have a wonderful time. You don't even need to make hotel reservations in advance except for Lima, Puno and Cuzco during June, July and August.

Furthermore, even using a travel agent is no guarantee that things will go smoothly. (Understand from the beginning that if you're expecting everything to come off without a hitch you might as well stay home and wait for the Second Coming. Things are always out of whack in South America and that makes it interesting. You never know what's coming next.) My parents had confirmed reservations, in writing, for the first class Hotel Savoy in Lima, made through a good travel agency in the States. I arrived in Lima several days ahead of them and decided to check things out. No one at the Savoy had heard of them, so I went ahead and made their reservations. In Puno we had a Peruvian agency, Lima Tours, book us into a hotel in Cuzco. This was done only on the condition that we buy an afternoon tour of Cuzco, which my father did. When we arrived in Cuzco absolutely no one at the hotel had heard of us and our "confirmed reservations," and there were no rooms. (I suspected that someone arrived ahead of us and bribed the clerk to put them in our rooms. This is not uncommon.) We spent more than an hour riding around Cuzco in a taxi, feeling cold, hungry, tired and cranky, before we found a vacancy. The next day I planned to go to Lima Tours, tear up our tickets, throw them at the clerks and demand our money back—only my father actually wanted to take the tour, spoiling my opportunity for theatrics. I did tell Lima Tours that we were angry about our confirmed hotel reservations which didn't exist and asked them to reimburse us for the previous night's taxi ride, which they did. (In situations like this it really pays to speak Spanish.) Anyway, so much for travel agents and tours. We did just as well, if not better, on our own.

All right, what if you want to travel on the Río Napo or in the jungle, which you couldn't possibly do on your own unless you're really adventurous or a skilled outdoorsman? Wait until you reach a jungle town, then check out what is available. Don't be taken in by agencies offering luxury tours of the Amazon complete with a visit to a "savage jungle Indian tribe." You'll pay through the nose to see the pathetic remnants of an Indian tribe, debased and corrupted by traders, tourists, liquor and cheap goods. Tourists tend to judge by looks and often fall for slick inauthenticity. The Humphrey Bogart character with the decrepit boat may offer you an incomparable tour for half the price. Remember that nothing looks very good in the jungle for long, and don't be put off by peeling paint or a rundown exterior. Ask local people and other travelers for advice before you sign up for an expedition and agree on a fee beforehand. Bargaining is always in order.

Going with the Flow

The best trips have a rhythm that develops as the journey progresses. Make general plans, but allow for the unexpected. Here are a few suggestions for keeping things flowing:

§ Read books and *National Geographic*s to get an idea of what you want to see and do. (See "Books" later in this chapter.)

§ Buy a Roman Catholic liturgical calendar, which shows Christmas, Lent, Easter and the feast days of the various saints. Then try to arrange your trip to take in some of the many festivals and holidays. Bill and I filmed the Good Friday procession in Quito, watched the St. John's Day celebrations in Cochabamba and filmed Aymara music and dancing at Huatajata on Lake Titicaca on the Feast of Saints Peter and Paul. A list of major feast days and fiestas can be found in Chapter Seventeen.

§ Visit the cities and enjoy the restaurants, museums, shops and churches, but don't limit your trip to cities alone. Get into the countryside and visit some local markets.

§ Always ask other travelers where they've been and what they recommend. Be open enough to go off on side trips. Someone's fabulous, highly recommended spot may turn out to be a dud, but it also may turn out to be a high point of your visit. Bill and I delayed our trip to Bolivia and accepted the invitation of Bob and Mary Martin to ride with them in a rented car to the Callejón de Huaylas in Peru, which turned out to be the most beautiful place I've been in that country.

§ Ask hotel clerks and local residents about interesting places to visit, favorite restaurants and bars, etc. Don't neglect local people as a source of information; after all, who knows more about an area? However, residents often think foreigners will be comfortable only in the most expensive places, the tourist traps, so ask them where *they* eat, where *they* stay and what *they* like to do. You can also ask what you ought to pay for a poncho at the market or for a taxi ride in town. Remember, though, that you may sometimes be given wrong or misleading information, especially when you ask directions. People hate to disappoint you by saying they honestly don't know, so always ask several people about directions when heading off to an unknown place.

Traveling Companions

As a woman, I found it difficult to travel alone. South America is very much a man's world, and by South American standards a respectable woman doesn't travel by herself, although a man can. (Two or three women traveling together is acceptable.) Often, the fact that I was alone made me appear disreputable, and I was hassled. I never felt I was in any great danger, but the attempts by men to pick me up and their ugly comments got very tedious. Being alone also placed limitations on where I could go and what I could do and took some fun out of the trip. I simply could not and did not go alone to certain places, including bars and remote jungle regions.

The other side of the coin: if you start out alone and follow any of the major traveling routes, such as the Pan American Highway from Colombia to Peru, you won't be alone for long. You'll inevitably meet up with other travelers, usually men, who also are journeying alone. (Adventure, sex, romance! . . .) I've made some fine friends this way.

During eleven months in Colombia, Ecuador, Peru and Bolivia, I traveled for five months with Bill, for three weeks with my parents and for five months alone, although for short periods of time I journeyed with two Canadians, Carla and Pauline Swart; with my good friend Steve Miller; with two Americans, Cathy Textor and Susy Silverman; with a group of animal collectors and zoologists and with other adventurous souls. It's probably most enjoyable to travel with a member of the opposite sex—just say you're married. If anyone asks about the difference in your names (and no one does), say you were married after you got your passports.

GROUPS

I'm inclined to avoid traveling in groups on long trips. I get so hungry and impatient during the interminable debates on where to eat that I'd just as soon go off by myself. But groups can be fun, especially for a week or two. Bill and I had fun traveling with another couple for several weeks and I thoroughly enjoyed my travels with the group of animal collectors in Bolivia.

Whoever your companion is, you had better get along well to begin with, because things will only get worse under stress, strain and culture shock. You should also agree on the nature of the trip: are you going to visit museums and Inca ruins or rough it in the jungle? Each of you should have approximately the same amount of money to spend and be in general agreement as to how you're going to spend it. Would you rather fly sometimes and skimp on hotels, or take the second-class bus but eat at better restaurants? Or would you rather skimp on everything and spend the money on handicrafts? Do you have the same discomfort tolerance? I'll pay a bit more for a hotel with hot water because I absolutely hate being cold, while others find cold showers invigorating and would much rather spend the difference on beer. Things like these suddenly become important after a month on the road.

KIDS

Traveling with infants is quite possible. The biggest worry is health, so be sure your baby has had all the necessary inoculations (see Chapter Thirteen, "Health"). If your baby is breast-fed, a lot of the worry about contaminated food and water is reduced, although some diseases can be passed in mother's milk. Older children also require special consideration; to travel happily, you must take their interests and energies into account. It's no fun being dragged from country to country or enduring long rides in buses or trains. I know I'd mutiny.

My observation is that children (and lots of adults) adapt better to staying in one place, with short side trips. If you plan to stay in one town, you can usually find a good maid who will cook, clean and look after the children for room, board and about twenty dollars a month. (We aren't going to discuss exploitation here. This is the going rate, but if your conscience dictates you can always pay more.) Therefore, if you're planning to live in Quito for six months and travel a bit in Ecuador and Peru, a child will probably enjoy the experience. But I wouldn't recommend taking a seven-year-old on a three-month tour of six countries.

Gail Sumner, whose two daughters were born in South America, said it's very easy to travel with children. When she and her husband checked into a hotel room, they were never charged for the girls (who were both under five), even when an extra cot was provided. They weren't charged for the children on buses or trains and sometimes were charged only a partial fare on planes, if they had to pay for the girls at all.

Fair children are a curiosity in South America and receive a lot of attention and affection, which makes the parents' life a lot easier. When the family lived in a small town, Gail had an entire village of babysitters. Everyone knew where the little blonde babies lived, and she never worried when one of the girls wandered off. Someone always brought her back. In markets, people "borrowed" the kids to show to their friends—someone was always holding and caring for the girls. Gail said other travelers used to ask her if she wasn't afraid the babies would be kidnapped, but she said the idea is ridiculous. No one with six little kids of her own needs or wants another one, and besides, how would someone ever hide or disguise such an obviously *anglo* child?

This experience isn't unusual. In South America there's a tradition of familial and neighborly involvement with children that's uncommon in the United States. It's not unusual to see children as young as three caring for their even-younger brothers and sisters. Because people have taken care of their brothers, sisters, neighbors and cousins since an early age, they're comfortable with children and good with them.

PETS

There's absolutely no reason to take your dog, white rat, canary or boa constrictor with you to the Andean countries. Like children, they are unhappy when dragged from place to place. Pets also run the very real risk of dying from the effects of strange microbes or of ending up in someone's stew pot. The only exception is if you're driving. Then a large dog with a loud bark and big teeth will keep the curious and greedy out of your vehicle. The dog will have a place to stay and a sense of territory (the car). Be sure your dog has had shots for distemper and rabies within the six months preceding your trip and that you have a certificate from your veterinarian attesting to this. Contact the consulates of the countries you're planning to visit and find out exactly what papers are required. Do this about two months before you leave to give yourself and the vet enough time to complete the paperwork. Most countries simply won't let an animal across the border without the proper health papers. Before you leave you should also stock up on medicine for worms and fleas, since your dog will contract both these pests regularly. You can't buy commercial dog food in the Andean countries, except perhaps in Lima, so your pet will have to eat whatever you can buy in the market. When you return home, have your dog wormed and examined for tropical parasites by a knowledgeable vet.

Consulates

Just before your trip, you might want to contact the consulates to obtain tourist visas or travel information. My only experiences with South American consulates in the United States have been in San Francisco. I always found the personnel warm, friendly and eager to help, although in several cases I had to conduct business in Spanish, which was fun for me, but would be a real problem for anyone who doesn't speak the language well. (One consul spoke five languages, but not English, so why he was assigned to the United States is beyond me.)

If you want to write or phone a consulate, you'll find it listed in the white pages of your telephone directory under the name of the country or under "Consulates." I haven't included a complete listing of the Colombian, Ecuadorian, Peruvian and Bolivian consulates in the United States because the consulates move so frequently. In general, consulates for all South American countries can be found in major American cities.

As for the kind of information you can expect, remember that consular officials are members of the upper-class, educated elites of their countries, so you can't rely on them to help you with details concerning travel in the countryside or in remote areas, since they certainly don't spend their vacations riding around in trucks and buses with *campesinos*. As official representatives of a nation, they aren't likely to present the seamier side of things and are required to give the official position on all matters. (Don't expect them to admit that you can change money on the black market, for example.)

Although you can obtain a tourist visa in advance of your trip from either a consulate or an airline (and, in fact, you *must* apply in advance for Colombia's ninety-day tourist visa), remember that what really counts is the border (see Chapter Five, "Border Crossings, Customs and Currency"). No matter what anyone at the consulate in the United States tells you, and no matter what you have stamped on your passport, border officials can refuse to admit you for reasons ranging from local emergencies or epidemics to the fact that they don't like your looks. They might also give you less time in their country than you request. You just have to play it by ear. Remember, too, that even though the consul says you can't do something (such as take two cameras into the country), nothing like that is impossible if you're willing to pay a bribe at the border.

Introductions to South Americans

If you have South American students at your school, or have relatives or friends with relatives in South America, get their addresses, and, if possible, introductions. Perhaps someone here will write to say that you're coming to visit. Meeting South Americans and being invited to their homes are the best parts of a trip, but it can be extremely difficult for a traveler to make these friendships without an introduction of some kind. My Quechua teacher in Berkeley gave me the addresses of her relatives in Ayacucho and Lima, and these incredibly warm and hospitable Peruvians in turn introduced me to others. My friend Susy Silverman went to Cochabamba to visit the family of a Bolivian girl who had lived with her family in Seattle. I was traveling alone at the time, and Susy and the Salamas frequently invited me to have dinner with them. After months of eating in restaurants it was a treat to eat with a family at home. The Salamas also introduced us to aspects of their culture we would have missed, took us out to eat, accompanied us to markets, advised us how much to pay for handicrafts and showed us their city. Needless to say, spending time with a South American family does wonders for your Spanish.

You also might offer to take small gifts from people you know to their friends and relatives in South America. This is greatly appreciated by all, especially since the mails can't be trusted. Carrying a package ensures that you'll get in touch with people, in case you feel silly or shy about simply showing up and saying, "Hello, I knew Mario at school and . . . " If you're taking a gift from Mario to his family you'll be more likely to look them up and feel less like you're imposing. Invariably, with or without a gift, South Americans will be happy to see you and will overwhelm you with their hospitality.

Books

Although I'm a book fanatic I'll try to restrain myself and won't insist that you read enough to obtain three college credits. Still, books and

National Geographics are invaluable in planning your trip, and you'll continually find yourself saying, "I've just got to see that! " or perhaps, "No way." Most North Americans are abysmally uninformed and misinformed about South America. Often it's downright embarrassing. I can't emphasize enough the importance of learning something about the countries you're going to visit.

Before and between trips I haunt libraries, bookstores, antique shops and the Salvation Army, tracking down material on South America. My most recent treasure is a book called *Green Hell* ("Adventures in the Mysterious Inferno of Eastern Bolivia Where Four Men Walked with Death at Their Elbow"), written by Julian Duguid in 1931. Another recent acquisition is *Vagabonding Down the Andes*, written in 1917 by Harry A. Franck. What tickles me about these books is that so little has changed since they were written. I rode with death at my elbow on more than one bus trip.

Later in this chapter you'll find a list of recommended reading to get you in the mood for your trip. My own interests run strongly to Pre-Columbian art, archaeology, adventure and nature, as well as the ancient and modern Indian cultures, while I'm less interested in diplomatic and economic history. The suggested reading reflects these prejudices. I've also listed bookstores in Bogotá, Quito, Lima, La Paz and Cochabamba where you can buy maps, books and magazines in English (as well as French and German), including some of the ones on the recommended list. Throughout this guide I recommend that you buy some books (all inexpensive paperbacks) before you leave and then take them along on your trip.

I have found that the first time I read a book about an unfamiliar subject—for example, *Ancient Arts of the Americas*—the contents stay with me only vaguely. Nonetheless, on a visit to the Gold Museum in Bogotá, I found that I retained enough background information so that the exhibits of Pre-Columbian goldwork were not entirely unfamiliar. Then I went back to my hotel room and reread parts of the book and the museum experience meant more to me.

During the trip with my parents we were stuck in our hotel room in Cuzco during a week of nasty rainstorms. We passed the time by reading some of the paperbacks we had along, including *Lost City of the Incas*, Hiram Bingham's account of his search for the lost capital of the Incas and his discovery of Macchu Picchu instead. We also read Victor W. Von Hagen's *Realm of the Incas*. Our trip to Macchu Picchu meant immeasurably more because of our reading. I'll say it just one last time: the more you read and the better informed you are, the more rewarding your trip will be.

GUIDEBOOKS

I've read every guidebook I could find, including *South America on $10 a Day* and Fodor's *South America*, and think almost all of them are a complete waste of money. They just don't tell you what you need to know and in some cases lead you astray.

There is one guidebook which I do wholeheartedly recommend: the *South American Handbook 1983*, edited by John Brooks (Trade and Travel Publications, Ltd., The Mendip Press, Parsonage Lane, Bath BA1 1EN, England). I carried the *Handbook* on both trips and found it invaluable. In fact, it's so far superior to all the others that there's no comparison. In the United States the *Handbook* is distributed by Rand McNally & Company, P.O. Box 7600, Chicago, Illinois 60680. The cost is $29.95 and it's worth every penny.

The *Handbook* is crammed with information on South America, Central America, the Caribbean and Mexico, including climate, geography and maps, history, holidays, necessary documents for visitors, transportation to, from and within the countries by land, sea and air, what to see and town-by-town listings of sights, restaurants, museums and hotels. I find it most useful for finding hotels, restaurants and how to get around. For example, it tells you which Ecuadorian bus line has the best safety record—something you appreciate as you contemplate the roads. The *Handbook* is not just for *ricos*, but includes restaurants with thirty-cent meals and hotels with hot water for a dollar a night. The *Handbook* is revised yearly and is therefore quite up-to-date. Since this travel guide was designed to provide information the *Handbook* omits, between the two you should do all right.

If you can't find the *Handbook* before you leave, you can buy it in one of the South American bookstores listed on page 23.

GENERAL READING

The following are inexpensive paperbacks which you might want to buy and read before you leave or save for quiet moments on the trip.

Keep the River on Your Right, by Tobias Schneebaum (New York: Grove Press, Inc., 1969). Schneebaum went to Peru to paint on a Fulbright fellowship and ended up living in the jungle with the Akarama Indians. The book appeals to everyone's fantasy of running away from civilization to live with the Indians and reminds me of *Wizard of the Upper Amazon* (see Chapter Fourteen, "Drugs").

Living Poor: A Peace Corps Chronicle, by Moritz Thomsen (New York: Ballantine Books, 1969). *Living Poor* is one of the best accounts of a Peace

Corps experience that I've ever read. Thomsen lived in Río Verde, Ecuador, and his book is very perceptive and balanced.

The Voyage of the Beagle, by Charles Darwin (New York: Bantam Books, 1972). This is Darwin's account of his ocean voyage around the South American continent, including his visit to the Galapagos Islands, which was the catalyst for his theories on evolution. Interesting reading, especially for a visit to the Galapagos.

Latin America Yesterday and Today, edited by John Rothchild (New York: Bantam Books, 1973). This is a collection of essays on Latin America, for the most part by Latin American writers. I especially like the sections on Indians, blacks, revolution and the Latin American character.

The Human Condition in Latin America, by Eric R. Wolf and Edward C. Hansen (New York: Oxford University Press, 1972). There are good sections on South America, especially on Indians and Europeans, communities, and the role of religion.

FICTION

One Hundred Years of Solitude (New York: Avon Books, 1971), *No One Writes to the Colonel and Other Stories* (New York: Avon Books, 1968) and *Leafstorm and Other Stories* (New York: Avon Books, 1972), all by the Colombian writer Gabriel García Márquez, who won the Nobel Prize for Literature in 1982. A friend said she never understood Colombia until she read Márquez.

The Green House, by Mario Vargas Llosa (New York: Avon Books, 1973). This novel takes place in the Peruvian Amazon and in Piura, Peru, the locale of the green house in the story.

Contemporary Latin American Short Stories, edited by Pat McNees Mancini (Greenwich, Conn.: Fawcett Publications, 1974). This anthology includes stories by Márquez, Llosa, Borges and Ecuador's Jorge Icaza, as well as other Latin American greats. It's perfect reading for the airport—the later your flight the more stories you can finish.

Jorge Luis Borges, an Argentine, is probably South America's greatest living writer. Many of his works are available in English paperback editions, including *Labyrinths, The Book of Imaginary Beings* and *Other Inquisitions.*

POETRY

South America has had two Nobel-prize-winning poets, Pablo Neruda and Gabriela Mistral, both Chileans and favorites of mine.

Five Decades: Poems 1925–1970, translated by Ben Belitt (New York: Grove Press, 1974) and *The Heights of Macchu Picchu,* translated by Nathaniel Tarn (New York: Farrar, Straus & Giroux, 1966), both by Pablo Neruda. Both of these anthologies include the poem "The Heights of Macchu Picchu," which I carried with me and read in the ruins.

Neruda and Vallejo: Selected Poems, edited by Robert Bly (Boston: Beacon Press, 1971). This anthology includes poems by Neruda and by the Peruvian poet César Vallejo.

Selected Poems of Gabriela Mistral, translated by Langston Hughes (Bloomington, Ind.: Indiana University Press, 1966). Gabriela Mistral has written the loveliest poems about children and motherhood that I've ever read, although her work isn't limited to these themes.

For a listing of other paperbacks you might want to take along on your trip, as well as further recommended reading, see Chapters Seven, "How Things Work"; Thirteen, "Health"; Fourteen, "Drugs and Hallucinogens"; Fifteen, "Archaeology and Pre-Columbian Civilizations"; and Sixteen, "Native Cultures, Folk Art and Markets."

BOOKSTORES

Colombia. In Bogotá the bookstore with the best selection of English-language reading material is *Librería Bucholz,* which is located downtown on Avenida Jiménez, near the corner of Carrera 8. The *Librería Central,* located at Calle 16, No. 6–34 (next to the Avianca building), is also excellent.

Ecuador. In Quito, *Libri Mundi* has a large selection of books in English, French, German and Spanish. It's located at Juan León Mera 851, near the corner of Veintimilla, with a branch in the Hotel Colón.

Peru. Lima has many foreign-language bookstores because of its flourishing tourist trade. There's an English-language bookstore in the Hotel Bolívar on the Plaza San Martín and another good bookstore, *Librería ABC,* right next door to the hotel on Calle Ocoña. Also try the *Librería ABC* at Colmena 689.

In Cuzco almost every little shop has English-language books about the Incas.

Bolivia. In La Paz, *Los Amigos del Libro* carries books and magazines in English, French, German and Spanish. It's located at Calle Mercado 1315, in the heart of downtown.

Los Amigos Del Libro also has branches in Cochabamba, on Calle Peru at the corner of España, a few blocks from the main plaza; in Oruro, on Junín at the corner of 6 de Octubre; and in Santa Cruz, on René Moreno 21.

Many of these bookstores carry maps, so be sure to inquire.

Maps

It's difficult to find good maps of South America, especially maps of the individual Andean countries which show the little villages and towns you've read about and would like to visit.

The National Geographic Society publishes a number of fine maps. I took their map of South America along with me. You can write to the organization at the following address for a complete list of maps as well as order forms:

> The National Geographic Society
> 17th and M Streets N.W.
> Washington, D.C. 20036

Bradt Enterprises carries many good maps, some imported from the Andean countries. (See page 154 for ordering information.) Also check with the South American Explorers Club, Avenida Portugal 146, Lima (telephone 31-44-80). It is located off Avenida Alfonso Ugarte, between España and Bolivia, near the United States Embassy.

You can buy the best maps in the countries themselves. In Colombia excellent maps can be obtained from the *Instituto Geográfico Augustín Codazzi*, which has its headquarters in Bogotá—any taxi can take you there. The *Instituto* also has branch offices in Colombia's department capitals. In Ecuador the best map is available from the Military Geographical Institute, Calles La Unión y Oleas, Quito (telephone 52-20-60). In Peru good maps (called *hojas de ruta*) are available from the *Touring y Automovil Club del Peru*, Avenida César Vallejo 699, Lince, Lima (telephone 40-32-40). In Bolivia road maps are available at the *Museo de Arte Popular*, located on Calle Ingavi at the corner of Calle Genaro Sanjinés in La Paz. You also can buy very detailed maps of Bolivia from the Military Geographical Institute, located on Calle Saavedra in La Paz. These maps (called *hojas*) are especially useful if you plan to backpack.

Maps are also available in bookstores in each country.

Language Instruction

SPANISH

Except for Brazil, Surinam and the Guianas the dominant language in South America is Spanish. You'd be surprised how many people arrive unprepared for this. South America is not like Europe, where lots of people speak English as a second language. In fact, in Peru the emphasis is away from English altogether and toward making the population bilingual in Spanish and Quechua. You can't get along on English alone in South America. Generally speaking, the better your Spanish, the better your trip. Brush up on your high-school or college Spanish, take a Berlitz or adult-education class or get help from a Spanish-speaking friend—but get some background in the language.

I've checked out just about all the teach-yourself-Spanish books and recommend three, two of which I took with me to South America. The first is *See It and Say It in Spanish,* by Margarita Madrigal (New York: Signet, 1961). This book is a word–picture method that gets you started in Spanish and moves along quickly. It has a good introduction to verbs and gives you patterns rather than boring grammatical explanations. At the back of the book you'll find a traveler's reference, which lists foods, colors, numbers, etc., as well as complete conjugations of a number of verbs. A major advantage for the traveler is that the book is small and light.

An Invitation to Spanish is by the same author, Margarita Madrigal, and Ezequias Madrigal (New York: Simon and Schuster, 1943). This book is very similar to *See It and Say It in Spanish.* Buy one or the other and use it.

Spanish Made Simple, by Eugene Jackson and Antonio Rubio (Garden City, N.Y.: Doubleday and Co., 1955), is "a comprehensive course for self-study and review." This is a large workbook and takes discipline to use, but if you keep at it your Spanish improves by quantum leaps. I tried to use it for fifteen minutes every morning and when I did, the results were encouraging.

I haven't come across any phrase books I'd recommend. There are several reasons why. First, it's advisable to learn some patterns and verbs, so that you understand how the language works. That's why I recommend Madrigal's books. For example, one of the first phrases you will (and should) learn is *"¿Dónde está . . . ?"* ("Where is . . . ?") You can then tack on any number of endings: *el banco* (the bank), *el baño* (the bathroom), *un hotel barato* (a cheap hotel), *mi equipaje* (my luggage), etc. My other objection to phrase books is that they don't present the language the way it's actually spoken. For example, rather than sputtering *"Haga el favor de darme mi llave"* ("Let me have my key, please"), all you have to say is *"La llave, por favor"* ("Key, please").

Rather than taking a phrase book, I'd recommend one of the Madrigal books and a good Spanish–English dictionary. Don't take one of the very small, pocket-size Spanish–English dictionaries; they aren't comprehensive enough. The dictionary might be flat enough to fit in your shirt pocket, but it won't have half the words you need. Carry a good one. In my opinion the best traveler's dictionary is *The University of Chicago Spanish–English, English–Spanish Dictionary* (New York: Pocket Books, 1950), compiled by Carlos Castillo and Otto F. Bond. It's a paperback and costs under two dollars.

Finally, don't neglect comic books or children's books in your attempt to learn Spanish. *Condorito* is a comic book published in Chile and distributed throughout South America. You can buy it in bookstores and at newsstands. *Kaliman* is a hero similar to Superman, and you can find his adventures sold everywhere. In Bolivia I was puzzled by turban-like hats with a metal "к" in front, which I saw little kids wearing, until I came across a *Kaliman* comic book. When you're finished with a comic, you can always give it away or pass it around the train or bus.

For a list of common Spanish greetings and phrases, see Chapter Six, "Language."

INDIAN LANGUAGES

Two other languages besides Spanish are spoken by millions of people in the Andes: Quechua and Aymara. For more about these Indian languages, including where you can study them in South America, see Chapter Six.

Several universities in the United States teach Quechua or have Quechua (and possibly Aymara) language tapes which you may be permitted to use. You also might be able to find a South American student who'll tutor you in Quechua or Aymara. Be sure to get someone from the area you're planning to visit, however, as there are many different dialects, and it won't do any good to learn Ecuadorian Quechua if you're planning to live in Peru or Bolivia.

What to Take

The bare necessities for my next trip include my water colors, violin, spindle, basketry supplies, Versatex textile paints, air brush, backstrap loom and about twenty pounds of books, along with a wheelbarrow to haul it all around. (Someone should come up with a collapsible wheelbarrow that fits under a plane seat and is cleverly disguised to look like a cosmetics case.) No one ever agrees on the bare necessities and one person's must is another's toss-out; so let's forget the bare necessities until we've covered the basics and then see what room there is left.

Clothing

You need the least amount of clothing necessary to get you through climates ranging from tropical to polar, and for occasions ranging from bus rides to parties to consulate visits.

The trick to traveling in South America is to look straight. In other words, forget your favorite ethnic and outrageous clothes. I leave my Moroccan shirt and my Indian mirrored dress at home and try to look as inconspicuous, conventional and respectable as possible. In fact, after choosing the more conventional clothes from my closet, I even went so far as to make myself some special traveling clothes.

There are several reasons for looking respectable, and you all know what that means—non-hippie. If you're young, the more conventional you look, the less likely you are to be harassed by the police in any situation. Looking conventional and moderately prosperous also helps enormously when you apply for tourist cards and cross borders. Furthermore, you can broaden your range of contacts in South America. If you look respectable and non-threatening, you leave open the possibility of getting to know all kinds of people—from Indians to college students to nice, middle-class families. It's a shame to miss out on a friendship just because someone is put off by your appearance.

Not once, on entering any country, was I asked by the authorities if I had the official minimum amount of money. Peru, for example, officially requires you to have $8 for each day on your tourist card. This is an excuse to keep out undesirables (by their standards), and the rule is primarily applied to freaky types. I always got by because I looked "respectable."

Long hair on men isn't the issue it once was. In fact, it's rather a fad among young South American males. Still—you, I and the border officials know the difference between hair that comes over the collar and a bushy Afro or a midback pony tail. And a mustache is one thing, while a Santa Claus beard is something else (the Che Guevara look isn't advisable). If your entire identity depends on your hair, there isn't much I can say; but wearing your hair shorter and neater, and shaving your beard, make things a lot easier.

Older travelers, particularly women, tend to overdress and to drag too much along. Bear this in mind: pants are worn everywhere by South American women, even to church and to the office. Not jeans, but dressier pants. I wore corduroy slacks in cold weather and cotton-polyester blends in warmer climates. (The latter also wash and dry easily.) My mother brought an inexpensive pantsuit, which she wore everywhere.

Plan to dress in layers. In the Andes the difference between the sunny and shady sides of the street is as much as 30°F, and the temperature drops drastically when the sun sets or goes behind the clouds.

I recommend the following basic clothing:

§ A couple of pairs of pants and jeans. Women should *not* take jumpsuits; they are utterly worthless when traveling because you have to take the whole thing off to get at your money belt or go to the bathroom.

§ A couple of T-shirts, a cotton turtleneck, and long- and short-sleeved shirts. Pure cotton is much better than pure polyester because it breathes better, although cotton–polyester blends are okay.

§ Underwear and socks (wool or cotton). For women, a pair of tights. Women should also consider a bra. For one thing, it's warm, and for another, South Americans are provoked by nipples showing on non-Indian women. By their standards, this is lower class and immodest, and a braless traveler might just as well tattoo a sign on her forehead saying "Pinch me." Camisole tops are comfortable, warm and an acceptable solution to the modesty problem.

§ Down jacket, preferably with a hood and stuff sack. *This was the single most useful item I had along.* There is little or no heating of any kind in most buildings, and the mountains are cold, sometimes snowy. In many hotel rooms it was so cold I could see my breath in the air, and I often wore my down jacket to bed. Being cold can ruin your trip, so a down jacket is invaluable. When you're traveling in warmer areas you can stuff it in its sack.

§ Bathing suit. Nude swimming is not done in public. There are thermal hot springs throughout the Andes, and consequently you'll find swimming pools in the most unlikely places. (Don't forget about the ocean beaches.) You'll regret it if you don't have a suit along.

§ Sandals. Ones that don't have straps between the toes are more versatile as they can be worn with socks on chilly days. Sandals can double as bedroom slippers.

§ One pair of walking or hiking shoes. Bill and I brought hiking boots on our first trip and found them too heavy and hot. On our second trip Bill wore Adidas shoes and I wore canvas shoes with crepe soles. In the jungle, canvas shoes are better than leather ones because they dry out

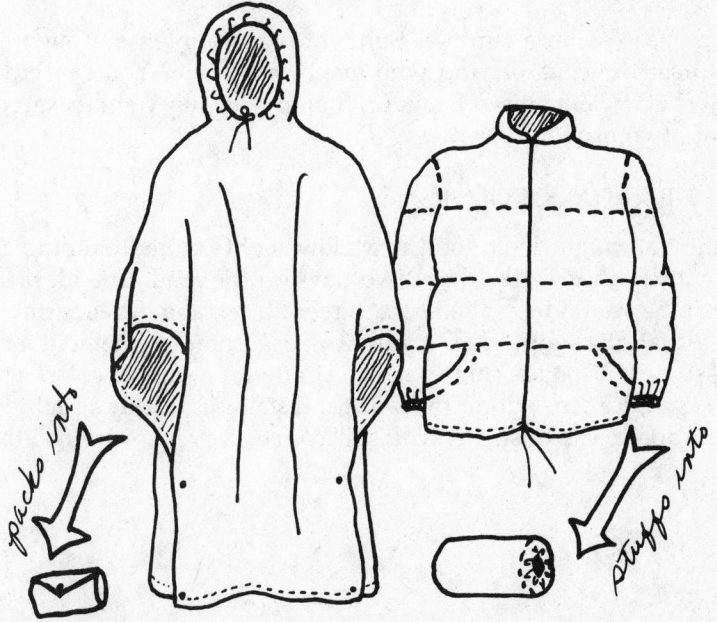

faster. If you're not going into the jungle, but plan to backpack in the mountains and have a favorite pair of hiking boots, you'll probably want to take them.

§ *For men:* one pair of pants other than jeans, a dressy shirt and maybe a tie for special occasions. I met several Americans traveling in Bolivia who had been invited to weddings and were glad they had something appropriate to wear. Your nicer clothes also can be worn at border crossings (although everyone looks like the wrath of God after long bus rides) and when you apply for tourist cards.

§ *For women:* at least one skirt or dress. It's wonderful to get out of jeans on hot, sunny days, and you'll also have something for special occasions. I brought two skirts with me and wore them often. Although I love long skirts and had one of mine along, I didn't wear it very much. Ankle-length skirts aren't worn by South American women and tend to label you as a foreigner or hippie.

§ Pajamas or a nightgown. Unheated Andean hotels aren't conducive to nude sleeping, and in most cases bathrooms are communal and are located down the hall from your room. Since standards of modesty are stricter, it's not appreciated if you dash nude down the hall.

§ Shorts or cut-offs and one sleeveless top. I wore mine, but not too often. Nevertheless, I was glad I had them along, and I plan to take them on my next trip.

§ Lightweight raincoat or poncho with hood or hat. When it rains! . . .

§ Sweater. I wore mine all the time.

§ Sunglasses and a sun hat. Sunlight is more intense at high altitudes and near the equator, and who needs sunstroke? You can buy a nice, straw hat in Colombia or Ecuador, though you may want to start out with a hat of your own.

WEARING DARK COLORS

While you might look good in yellow, light-colored clothing turns an ugly, dirty shade after about two days on the road. The ideal traveling wardrobe would be made of that green, black and brown army camouflage material—although it might cause some excitement at border crossings and police checkpoints. At any rate, darker colors are much more practical; they don't show dirt and stains as readily as lighter colors. You'll appreciate this when you spill coffee all over yourself on the train.

POCKETS

There is a modification you can make on your regular clothes that proves invaluable for traveling. This is the addition of extra pockets, especially hidden ones. Buy ready-made pockets, or make your own, and sew them into everything, even your bathing suit. If you don't feel up to this, add Velcro tape closures to the pockets in your shirts, jeans and pants, to keep things from falling out and to deter pickpockets.

One pocket should be reserved for toilet paper and another for small change, since you don't want to dip into your money belt too often in public.

Ann Houston and I compared pocket designs. For her trip to South America she made a rain poncho with enormous inside pockets, large enough to hold a notebook. She also sewed extra pockets on the inside of her boyfriend's jeans and used Velcro tape to keep them closed. Both of us made skirts with large, extra pockets.

Ann's design for a pocketed skirt is illustrated below. The skirt has inside pockets that are kept closed with invisible zippers set into the yoke. An ordinary skirt pattern with a yoke can be adapted quite easily.

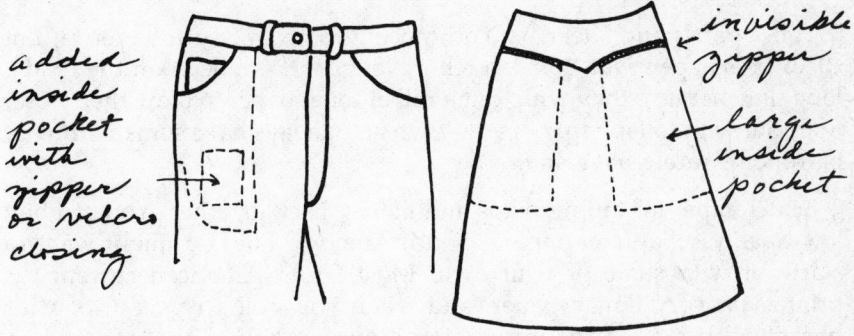

added inside pocket with zipper or velcro closing

invisible zipper

large inside pocket

WASHABLES

Don't take anything that needs to be dry-cleaned. Although you can have dry-cleaning done, it's generally quite expensive and can take a while. As for regular laundry, you can always wash clothes yourself or have the hotel launder them for you very cheaply. (Be sure to settle on a price beforehand.) Usually the manager hires a woman who washes everything by hand. Sometimes she hauls the laundry down to the river and beats it to death on the rocks. I've never had anything ruined in one washing, but after months of laundering everything becomes faded and frazzled and one day falls to pieces in your hands. For obvious reasons you shouldn't take any clothing that's precious. In fact, all clothing should be taken to South America with the understanding that it may never return.

Other Basics

These items have proven essential:

§ Swiss army knife with can and bottle opener and scissors.

§ Gallon-size Zip-loc bags. These keep bread fresh, shampoo from leaking, and your wet bathing suit from making everything else wet, too.

§ Small flashlight and extra batteries, for those occasions when there isn't any electricity or the hotel's generator shuts down.

§ Earplugs. What a lifesaver! Like the time the baby in the next room didn't stop crying all night. Or for sleeping on noisy buses.

§ Soap and towel. Most inexpensive hotels and pensions supply neither since it's customary for travelers to carry their own.

§ Toilet paper and Kleenex. You can buy both in South America, but Kleenex is expensive. You can tell travelers who've been on the road a long time because they whip out a roll of toilet paper to blow their nose. Start out with toilet paper of your own and always have some with you. Bathrooms rarely have any.

§ Scotch tape, for taping maps and money back together. You can buy low-quality cellophane tape in South America, but you might want to start out with some of your own. Most South American currency is printed on very flimsy paper, and when you pull a wad out of your pocket with a flourish, it sometimes rips in half. Shopkeepers and cashiers don't accept pieces of bills, but do accept it taped together, and undoubtedly some people think the money's counterfeit if it isn't all taped up. Indians, however, are suspicious of taped money and often refuse it.

§ Indelible magic marker, for addressing letters and packages to be sent home. There's enough trouble with mail as it is; don't compound the problem with an address that washes off in the rain.

§ Flat, rubber drain plug. Like toilet paper, this is a rarity in bathrooms.

§ Small sewing kit with a couple of safety pins.

§ Medical kit. This is important—see Chapter Thirteen, "Health."

§ Money belt. This is an absolutely essential item; it rates as high as a down jacket in terms of making the trip easier. I don't buy the kind of money belt that resembles an ordinary belt with a zipper inside. Instead, I buy a flat, nylon pouch, lined with plastic, that's made to be worn around your waist *under* your jeans. Luggage supply stores usually carry them but you may have to shop around. These money belts are large enough to hold your passport, tourist card, travelers checks, cash and plane ticket home. The belt is completely hidden, but easy for you to get at. Since most thievery in the Andes is on the order of pickpocketing or purse-slashing, oftentimes you don't discover that things are missing until later. Knowing that your money and documents are safe eases your mind and makes your trip more enjoyable.

§ Purses. A large shoulder bag is invaluable for both men and women. It's handy for carrying food, a book, earplugs, maps and toilet paper on the bus, while the rest of your luggage is thrown in the rack on the top of the vehicle. *Never carry an open-top purse or pouch.* The reason for this becomes clear the first time you dump everything out on the floor of the bus or someone picks your purse. If you have an open-top bag, sew a zipper along the top before you leave, or add ties or Velcro tape. It's also better to have a purse that isn't easily slit; carry a leather or heavy plastic bag rather than a cloth one.

§ The usual cosmetics. Women should also take plenty of tampons. They're hard to find and expensive when you do.

Sleeping Bags

You can't buy sleeping bags in South America, so go prepared. Bill and I took sleeping bags along but left them with friends in Lima. However, there are instances when you're going to need a good, light, down or polyester fiberfill bag: if you plan to do any backpacking and camping; if you want to ride river boats or if you intend to rent a house in an Indian village. Sleeping bags are also handy if you're making the entire trip overland or traveling on a very tight budget. I traveled for a while with two hardy Canadians, Carla and Pauline Swart, who often used their down bags as blankets on long, cold, overnight bus rides and in the cheaper hotels.

The longer your trip, the more likely you are to need a sleeping bag. If you're only planning to be gone for a few months and expect to stay in decent hotels, a sleeping bag isn't necessary. If you're uncertain, take one anyway, since you can always sell it to other travelers or South Americans. (However, don't expect to get full price for a seventy-dollar bag—that's just too much for travelers to spend. On the other hand, you could sell a thirty-dollar bag for what you paid for it.)

Suitcase versus Backpack

How should you carry all this stuff? As with sleeping bags, the way you choose to carry your belongings depends a great deal on the kind of trip you plan to take. I've always used a suitcase because a backpack labels you as young, foreign and impoverished, whether or not this is the case. There's a definite (rather unfavorable) stereotype attached to back-packers. In several instances, backpackers were the only travelers on a plane subjected to a Customs search.

On the other hand, you can throw a pack on your back and hike for miles—this is what backpacks were designed for. They weren't de-signed to be thrown on the top of a bus and covered with hundreds of pounds of cargo. Understand that on bus rides in the Andean coun-tries, *all* backpacks are thrown on the outside luggage rack, and the frames sometimes get bent and broken. Backpacks also get broken in the luggage racks on trains.

Although I prefer a soft canvas suitcase, on my next trip I'm also taking an interior-frame pack, also called a frame rucksack. This is a relatively new invention. Rather than having an exterior, aluminum frame, these new packs have fiberglass, steel or aluminum slats inside, allowing them to be used comfortably for loads up to forty pounds. Two good brands are the Chouinard Ultima Thule and the Kelty Tour Pack. These packs are light, can be carried in the bottom of a suitcase when not in use and give you the option of taking backpacking trips whenever you like. (Most hotels are happy to watch over the rest of your belongings.) You can also fill your pack with treasures acquired during your travels.

Duffle bags with shoulder straps are still another good way to carry your belongings.

Be sure you have locks for all duffle bags and suitcases and that you tie backpacks shut securely to prevent theft. (Thieves sometimes slit backpacks, so stuff your most valuable items deep inside.) Whatever you take, be sure you can carry it all yourself and that you can walk a mile with it if necessary, unless you've figured out a design for the folding wheelbarrow.

Optional

A number of things are optional, which is to say they're bare necessities for some people and beyond consideration for others:

§ Electrical appliances. I say don't take them. The current varies from city to city (it even varies within cities) and from country to country. Some places have no electricity at all and others have power shortages. If you insist on taking something that runs on electricity, be sure to take a transformer and a complete set of plug adapters.

§ Several rubber-covered coat hangers. This might sound strange, but I had a few and used them constantly. Most hotels don't supply any coat hangers, and I also used mine to hang up laundry. Some friends and I even used them to hold up the tail pipe and muffler on a rented car. Carry inflatable hangers if you feel the others are too heavy. A couple of clip clothes pins come in handy, too.

§ Camera and film. Be sure to bring sufficient film; it's very expensive in South America and some kinds aren't available at all. The same goes for batteries and flash bulbs. Batteries wear out quickly in cold weather. My movie camera went through batteries at roughly three times its normal rate and I couldn't find replacements (9-volt and 1.5-volt alkaline batteries). If my parents hadn't brought me new ones, my filmmaking would have ground to a halt.

Having film developed in South America is expensive, so send it home fast and have it developed there. Prepaid mailers for developing 35-mm film are useful. I also had mailers for my super-8 movie film but found that the weight of the film cartridge made postage exorbitant. All the film I mailed back (from Bolivia) arrived home in excellent condition. Also, remember the saying about putting all your eggs in one basket and don't send all your film in one package. You should always make up several packages and send them air mail. Absolutely *do not* send your film out surface mail; it's much too slow.

Until you ship exposed film, keep it sealed airtight in Zip-loc bags. Pack all exposed film with silica gel, which you can buy from a camera store before your trip. Silica gel absorbs moisture that can otherwise cause mildew or color changes on film and is also used in shipping cameras to prevent moisture damage. I stored some of my exposed movie film with silica gel for six months and the film suffered no damage.

Another way to get your film home safely is to ask a returning traveler to take the package and mail it for you when he gets back. People are good about this since anyone who has traveled in South America knows how precious those photos are.

§ Peanut butter and granola. (Perhaps protein powder, too.) If you're planning to backpack, definitely take freeze-dried food, especially high-protein dinners. Peanut butter and granola are very hard to find in South America and they were the mainstay of my on-the-road diet when I had them. Many hotels allow you to cook in their kitchen, so you can always make more granola when you run out. For more on this subject of perpetual interest—namely, what you'll be eating—see Chapter Twelve, "Food."

§ Small plastic cup and spoon. These utensils, along with fresh or canned juice and granola, allow you to eat breakfast in your room or snack late at night. The cup and spoon come in handy in any number of ways.

§ Wash 'n Dri towelettes, for washing your hands on the bus and train and for use in bathrooms with no running water (the majority).

§ Small camping or cooking stove. We met two travelers in Ecuador who had come overland from the United States on a tiny budget and with amazingly small packs. They carried a little stove and cooking kit and prepared all their own meals. It was inexpensive, they had fun shopping in the market and, as an extra bonus, they hadn't been sick at all.

The fuel most readily available in South America is kerosene, called *petróleo* or *kerosina*. It's best to ask for *petróleo para lámparas* (kerosene for lamps) to make sure you get the right kind. Kerosene is cheap—running your stove costs about two cents a day.

Optimus makes two kerosene-burning stoves, the Optimus 48 and the Optimus 00. Kerosene stoves require a separate priming fuel, such as alcohol, to get them started. Burning alcohol is called *alcohol para quemar*, and like kerosene it's cheap and readily available in South America. You should have unbreakable and leakproof plastic bottles to carry

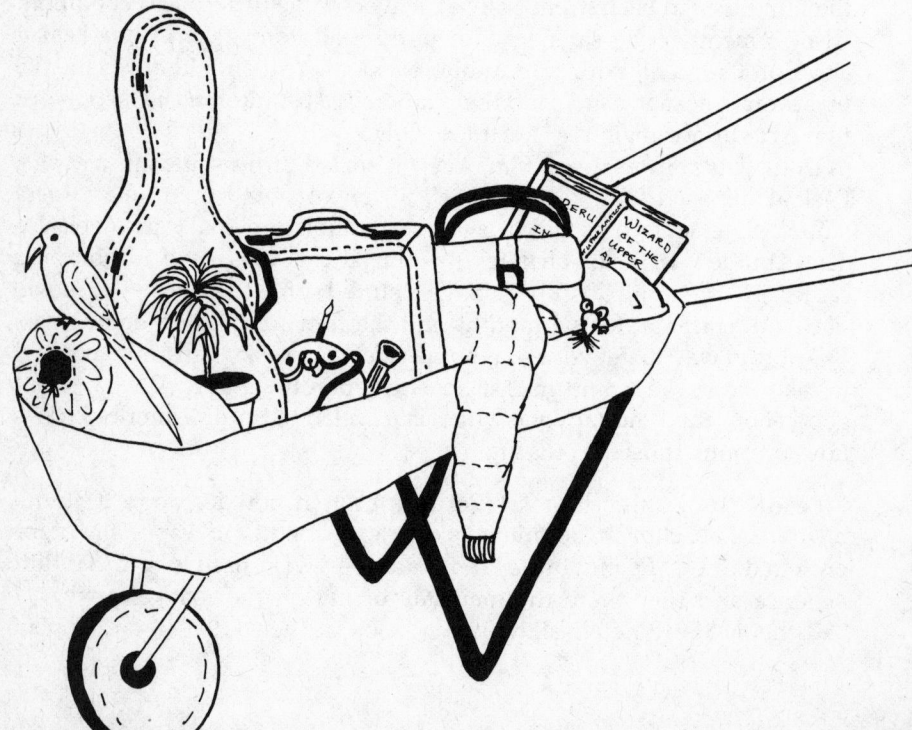

alcohol and kerosene. Obviously, if you're taking along a stove you also need a small, compact cooking kit.

If you don't want to start out with a stove you can buy one in South America. Primus (kerosene-burning) stoves and parts are sold in stores and markets all over South America. They cost between fifteen and twenty dollars, about what they cost in the United States.

§ Small day pack. I had a tiny, fold-up pack that unfolded into a nice rucksack. It was perfect for short hiking trips, and we used it to carry a picnic lunch to Macchu Picchu.

§ Tent. This is necessary only if you're planning to backpack. Two sheets of plastic with grommets also works, but you need some kind of shelter since you may run into rain or snow.

§ Canteen. Like a tent, this is necessary only if you're planning to backpack. (For more on what to take backpacking, see the "Backpacking" section of Chapter Ten.)

§ Rope. About twenty-five feet of lightweight, but strong, rope comes in handy as a clothesline, for tying bundles, etc.

§ Craft supplies. This is where I tend to let things get out of hand. Just about all the Indian men and women do things with their hands. If you spin, knit, embroider, crochet, carve wood, weave on a backstrap loom or anything similar, bring it along. It helps pass the time when the bus breaks down and is an excellent way to break the ice and make friends. Also consider art supplies, sketch pads, water colors and magic markers.

§ Writing materials, including a notebook or journal, for notes, expenses and the addresses of new friends.

§ Small musical instrument. (Not a guitar, unless it's really one of your bare necessities. Guitars are just too big and too fragile to take traveling. Wait until a pig sits on your guitar on the bus and see what I mean.) A flute or recorder is quite practical. Warren Weisbach, an accomplished flutist, earned extra money on his trip by playing in restaurants and by giving concerts. Even better, he gave free performances when the mood struck him, delighting everyone within hearing, including me.

§ Photographs. My mother came up with a good idea for anyone who has her hair set in beauty parlors. She carried a photo of herself with her hair exactly as she likes it, and took this photo whenever she went to a beauty parlor. She was able to sidestep the language barrier, and her hair looked exactly the way she liked it.

While we're on the subject of photos, be sure to carry pictures of your family, friends, pets and hometown, as well as postcards of your region.

People love to get a glimpse of how the weird travelers live. My parents sent me photos of my younger brother's wedding, and while I was looking at them in a Cochabamba restaurant I collected all the waitresses. They were fascinated, especially since the wedding took place outdoors, the bride was wearing a dress my grandmother made in the early 1900s and the groom looked somewhat like a hippie, although he'd cleaned up his act considerably for the event.

Gifts

It's always nice to have things to give away. Magic markers and postcards from home are good, as are such small tools as flashlights, fishhooks and flies, screwdrivers and cigarette lighters. Levis, rock-and-roll and jazz records, and pocket calculators are also treasured. T-shirts are great, especially ones with designs. You can give them away or trade them. On my next trip I'm taking tiny water-color sets and small dolls to give to little kids. Use your ingenuity in coming up with small, useful items.

Don't Take . . .

Don't take firearms. There's no need to carry a gun, and if you're caught with one you brought in illegally you're in big trouble. Despite all the rumors about robbers and *banditos,* I've never met anyone who was injured in a robbery attempt. Most thieves rely on stealth, not force. A money belt is your best protection. However, if you're planning a hunting trip, contact the country's consulate to find out about the necessary permits. The paperwork will probably discourage you from carrying a weapon, but maybe that's the idea. Be sure you do everything legally and follow all rules to the letter. If you still have problems at the border, it's probably because the official wants a bribe (see Chapter Seven, "How Things Work").

Don't take anything brand new on your trip. By "brand new" I mean never worn, untried and untested. Try out and use every single item before you go. You may find your walking shoes hurt your feet, your sweater itches or your backpack is missing a part or needs adjusting. The time to discover this is before you go.

Also, don't count on replacing anything in South America. What is and isn't available defies all logic and reason and sometimes all your efforts to find it. There's a brief listing of "What's Available Down There" on the pages that follow, but remember that you can't depend on finding any clothing, equipment or particular brand of cosmetics for certain. If you want it or need it, take it along.

What's Available Down There

CLOTHES

As a rule, you should take everything you need with you, including sandals and shoes. Should you need to replace something and you're either large or lanky, you're definitely in trouble. South Americans, particularly those of Indian descent, are much smaller than North Americans and Europeans. At 5'6" I'm several inches taller than many of the men and women. If you're either over 5'10" or heavy, forget about replacing clothes and shoes unless you have them custom-made. You can always have a tailor make a shirt, jacket or suit quite cheaply. In some places you can also have sandals made to fit. However, you have to hang around and wait for your order, and you may end up waiting quite a while.

There are a few exceptions to the size and fit problem and these are generally a result of tourism, since the artisans have learned to make a few things in larger sizes. Ponchos, of course, fit just about anyone. In Ecuador you can find wool sweaters and embroidered cotton shirts in larger sizes for both men and women. This is because the Peace Corps has been active in developing Ecuadorian crafts for the export and tourist market. In Peru and Bolivia you can find some alpaca vests and sweaters in larger sizes, also as a result of tourism and the export trade.

Just a note on Chile, Brazil and Argentina. These countries have sizable populations of European descent and are also the three most highly developed South American nations, which means they have clothing industries. If your last decent pair of pants is disintegrating, and by chance you're heading to one of these countries, especially Brazil or Argentina, that's where you should shop for clothes. Indeed, many Bolivians go to Buenos Aires to do their clothes shopping.

If you need something in Colombia, Ecuador, Peru or Bolivia, your best bet is always the capital city or perhaps a large port. If you can't find something in the capital (manufactured goods, that is), don't expect to find it in the interior.

One final resort before you give up hope completely: the black market (*el mercado negro*). Often the black market is a part of the regular market, and the vendors simply pay off the police so they can sell manufactured goods they've smuggled into the country. In La Paz, the Institute of Bolivian Tourism has been kind enough to include the location of *el mercado negro* on their official tourist map of the city. In other places, ask around.

SUNDRIES

Take along enough special cosmetics and sundries to last the entire trip. If you only use a particular brand, such as Bonne Bell face lotion, take plenty. The same applies for brand-name medicated make-up, soap, toothpaste, hand lotion, shampoo, Tampax, Kotex or shaving cream. Naturally there are South American brands and some North American and European sundries available, but you can't count on finding a particular brand—and if you do, it's going to be expensive. If you don't care what brand toothpaste, soap, shampoo, etc., you use, you can always find some.

Although there may be exceptions, keep in mind that for just about everything from postage stamps to sundries, Peru is cheapest, followed by Colombia, then Ecuador and Bolivia. Stock up on sundries in Colombia before heading into Ecuador, and shop again in Peru before entering Bolivia or Ecuador. Bolivia is the most expensive (for sundries, canned goods, imported items, etc.) because it doesn't have a seaport nor much manufacturing. Almost everything is imported and must first pass through other countries (Chile, Peru, Paraguay, Argentina or Brazil); consequently the prices go up.

In the larger cities in Colombia, Ecuador and Peru, you'll find TIA stores, which are the Andean version of Woolworth's. These stores carry typical dime-store merchandise, including clothing, household goods, cosmetics, food, art supplies and junk. I never leave Bogotá, Quito or Lima without a trip to the TIA, where I stock up on toothpaste, notebooks and other odds and ends.

Peru also has Sears–Roebuck and Monterrey stores, where you can buy some more of life's necessities.

Money
and
Documents

ooner or later you have to confront the hard, cold reality of money and documents. It's impossible to get very far without them.

Money

It's nice to know that the American dollar still has purchasing power somewhere. It is *the* desired currency in South America. Everyone—Canadians, Australians, Europeans, Asians—should carry American dollars in the form of cash, travelers checks or letters of credit. Don't carry Canadian dollars, deutschmarks, francs, etc. My advice is to take two-thirds of your money in travelers checks and one-third in cash. Make a list of the serial numbers of your travelers checks before you leave and keep the list with you in a place separate from your checks.

TRAVELERS CHECKS

American Express travelers checks are well known and accepted everywhere. First National City Bank and Bank of America have branches all over South America. Their travelers checks aren't as well known, and are therefore somewhat harder to negotiate, but you can always cash them at one of their branches.

The highest denomination travelers check sold by Bank of America is $100, while First National City Bank issues checks in higher sums—for example, $500. First National City Bank also offers what is known as a denominational exchange: you can have a check broken into smaller denominations free of charge at any one of their branch offices. This is probably a good idea if you're carrying a large amount of money and don't want a huge wad of checks.

I strongly advise against any phony lost-travelers-checks scams. Besides the karma involved in a dishonest act, these incidents have made it extremely difficult for those who've really had their travelers checks lost or stolen to recover their money. This hurts us all. While companies advertise instant replacement of funds for lost or stolen travelers checks, I've talked with people who waited up to two weeks for reimbursement, causing them all kinds of problems.

CASH

In some instances cash dollars are more desirable than travelers checks and bring a better exchange rate. For details on this, see Chapter Five, "Border Crossings, Customs and Currency." Carry $50 and $100 bills as well as small change, including a few quarters to use for tips, cab fare, etc., when you first arrive. The larger denominations are easily cashed in banks, money exchanges, shops and hotels.

LETTERS OF CREDIT

On our first trip Bill and I had a letter of credit from our bank. This isn't necessary but can be useful and is nice to know about. The Bank of America and First National City Bank no longer issue letters of credit to travelers because of fraud and excessive paperwork. American Express still does.

To obtain a letter of credit, you deposit money (for example, $1000) with American Express and they write you a letter of credit for that amount. The letter serves as a passbook so that you can go to any American Express office and withdraw money up to $1000. Each withdrawal is entered on your letter and subtracted from your initial deposit. The letter is designed in such a way that no one but you can use it. It must be cosigned in the presence of an American Express official and you must show some identification (your passport) before money can be withdrawn. American Express needs at least two weeks to prepare a letter of credit since the transaction is handled through their New York office. They don't handle sums less than $1000, and the money to be deposited with them must be in the form of cash or a cashier's check. They don't accept personal checks.

The letter of credit worked to our advantage when border officials checked Bill's finances. They only looked at the face of the letter, which read "Good for $1500," and not at the back, which showed the withdrawals. He never had any problem meeting a country's official minimum amount of money for entry, even though the letter of credit had been used up.

HOW MUCH?

It's tricky advising people on how much money to take because the amount you need depends on two things: your lifestyle and what you want to buy.

An example of a really inexpensive (dirt-cheap) trip is the one taken by Ann Houston and Christopher Wren. In 1973 this couple spent seven and a half months in Peru and Bolivia on $800 apiece, which included their plane tickets from Panama to Lima and from Lima back to Miami. They averaged 35 to 75 cents apiece for meals, most of which they ate in the market or on the street. Since they stayed in what are known as "hippie hotels" (the real cheapos) their hotel bills averaged 40 to 50 cents each a night. The most they ever spent for a hotel was $1.25 each and the least was 30 cents, for which they got one single bed into which they both were squished. Once they arrived in South America, they traveled mostly by bus and by truck.

Ann and Chris also cut down on expenses by staying in one place for a while. They rented part of a house for $15 a month while Chris recovered from hepatitis. In addition they spent $700 on textiles for their collection.

Since this trip was made ten years ago, you should add $900 per person, to cover inflation, mainly for air fares. The cheap hotel and meal prices still hold.

I probably spent twice what Ann and Chris did for the same length of time, about $2000 for nine months in 1974. It's misleading to consider my trip typical, though, since I did a lot of backtracking. I was researching a book and buying items to export to the United States, and I went back into Peru from Bolivia to travel with my parents, all of which increased my expenses beyond those of the average traveler. I also visited Colombia and Ecuador; Ann and Chris didn't.

Most of the time I stayed in hotels that were one step up from the cheapos—a little closer to middle class and a little more comfortable. The least I spent for a hotel was 60 cents a night and the most was about $5 (except when I was traveling with my parents, at which time my standard of living rose considerably). My average hotel bill was between $1.50 and $2 per night, and at this price you can pretty much take hot water for granted. My meals cost from 30 cents to $2, and $2 was eating really well. I traveled by plane as well as by train, bus and truck, and I, too, put additional money into folk art and textiles.

This type of trip was safe for a woman traveling alone. It's easier to endure a wretched dump when you're with someone than when you're the only woman in the place. For that reason I stayed at the better, less depressing places when I knew I'd be spending a long period of time in one place alone. I stayed at the cheapos when I was traveling with other people, or when these were the only accommodations available, which is usually the case in the countryside.

A different kind of trip entirely is that of the first-class traveler, and I had a glimpse of this when my parents visited. They stayed in first-class hotels in Bogotá, Quito and Lima, places which cost $12 to $20 per person, and ate at the better restaurants. They rented cabs to take them sightseeing (the height of luxury) and flew between cities. When they traveled with me, however, their standard of living went down since I dragged them on overland train rides and city buses. After losing our rooms in the Tourist Hotel to a tour one night, we all huddled together in the Grand Hotel Tito, which cost us $1.80 apiece—and that was high for the accommodations.

If you have money and want to spend it, you certainly can do that in South America. The first-class trip is long on comfort but short on adventure and real contact with the people (if you do the entire trip first class, that is). A first-class trip pretty much limits you to the capital cities and a few large towns, since there just isn't anything first class in the country. Yet trips through the countryside and to remote areas can be the most memorable parts of a South American trip—Inca ruins, villages, markets, mountains and more sky than you'll ever see again—and you can experience this for very little money.

HAVING MONEY SENT TO YOU

No matter how much money you take, you always seem to need more, and at some point might need to have money sent to you. Remember this: never trust the mails. Absolutely *never* have cash mailed to you, and it's wise not to have any kind of money sent by mail. (Mail is frequently lost, stolen or opened.) Instead, have a relative or friend go to a bank that can wire money to the First National City Bank or Bank of America in the city where you're staying. There is a one-percent charge for this service, taken off at your end, so if you need exactly $400, have a bit more wired. You can have your money in a few days—three to five days is average.

The transaction is quicker if the person in the United States goes to a Bank of America or First National City office. It takes a little longer if the money is wired through another bank first.

To claim your money, go to the bank (with your passport), tell them you are expecting money and approximately how much, and produce your identification. The cables come in daily, and they'll check to see if your name and the amount is on their list of incoming wires. Except for Ecuador, you can't receive your money in American cash dollars, but you can receive it in travelers checks in dollar denominations, in the local currency or in any combination. If you have money wired in this fashion, no one else can claim your funds, since you must produce your passport. Also, there's no chance of running into trouble trying to cash a money order or cashier's check drawn on some obscure Iowa bank.

Sometimes the money exchanges (*casas de cambio*) may cash money orders or even personal checks. Try them out, but don't count on it.

Put your money and travelers checks in your money belt as discreetly as possible before you leave the bank. (You could ask to use the bathroom and stash your money while you're there.) Thieves sometimes watch tourists leaving banks, hoping for the opportunity to pick someone's pocket or steal or slash a purse. This happened to a friend of mine in Bogotá, so be cautious.

Documents

PASSPORTS

A passport is needed to travel to most foreign nations, including Colombia, Ecuador, Peru and Bolivia. You can obtain a passport from certain designated post offices, county courthouses or United States Passport Offices (located in Boston, Chicago, Honolulu, Los Angeles, Miami, New Orleans, New York, Philadelphia, San Francisco, Seattle and Washington, D.C.). For further information address the following:

> Passport Office
> Department of State
> Washington, D.C. 20524

Passports are valid for ten years and can be renewed. To obtain a passport you need the following:

§ Proof of citizenship, such as a previous passport, naturalization certificate or birth certificate that has the embossed seal of the local records department. You may not present a Xerox of your birth certificate; you must have a copy that has the seal on it.

§ Identification, such as a driver's license or student ID card.

§ Two recent photos, which must be between two-and-a-half and three inches square. These must be head on, against a plain background, and can be in color or black and white. The passport office does *not* accept snapshots or photo-booth pictures. There are photo studios that specialize in inexpensive passport photos.

§ A fee of $42.00 ($35.00 for the passport plus a $7.00 "execution fee").

Allow yourself at least several weeks to get your passport and then keep it in a safe place. When traveling, keep your passport in a money belt or in a pouch around your neck. A lost or stolen passport is a serious matter and can result in weeks of delay during your travels. There is a thriving black market in American passports and the United States Department of State makes it hard to replace them, the idea being to get you to hang onto yours. Make a note of your passport number and keep this separately. If your passport is lost or stolen, report it missing to the nearest American consul immediately. (In the Andean countries the nearest consul can be a long way off.)

TOURIST VISA

A visa is a document issued by a country to a foreign citizen granting him permission to visit that country. Tourist visas to the Andean countries are very easy to obtain. You don't need to go to the country's consulate ahead of time, *except for Colombia*, nor do you need photographs. Tourist visas, also called tourist cards, are usually issued free through the airlines or at border crossings. For details, see Chapter Five, "Border Crossings, Customs and Currency."

HEALTH CARD

The International Certificates of Vaccination, or health card, is the document on which your inoculations are recorded. The health card has been approved for travelers by the World Health Organization and must be presented at all border crossings. It can be obtained from your local public health department, your doctor or the United States Government Printing Office, Washington, D.C. 20402.

Inoculations. Inoculations are extremely important and some are required for entrance into the Andean countries. Don't go to the Andes without having *all* of your vaccinations up-to-date. A complete list of inoculations and a vaccination schedule is found in Chapter Thirteen, "Health." Read that chapter carefully and make sure you begin your inoculations about six weeks before your trip since some immunizations can't be given together and others are given as a series of shots which must be spaced a week or more apart.

TRAVELER'S INSURANCE

You can buy traveler's health and accidental-death insurance, as well as insurance to cover all of your personal possessions, through various agencies. Check it out. It's worth knowing that even if your camera is stolen, you can collect insurance money to replace it.

Many homeowner's insurance policies cover travel mishaps, including theft, but if you don't have this kind of coverage obtain insurance from American Express or the Travelers Insurance Company.

REGISTERING FOREIGN-MADE GOODS

If you have foreign-made equipment, such as a camera, watch or tape recorder, be sure to register them with United States Customs before you leave. (You can do this at the airport.) Save the registration paper and present it when you re-enter the country so that Customs won't charge you duty on your possessions. After all, they have no way of knowing whether you obtained your Minolta at home in Ohio or at a duty-free shop in Panama.

Please note that contrary to the signs at United States airports, security x-rays can and do fog and ruin photographic film! If possible, you should hand-carry all your film through security checks or you should send it through in special protective pouches available at camera stores. This applies to both exposed and unexposed film.

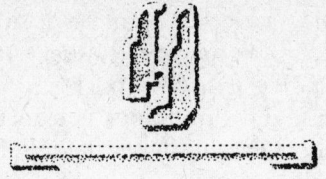

Getting There

hile some travelers prefer a slow, overland trip through Mexico and Central America, my own preference is for getting to South America fast. There are lots of possibilities and the choice is yours.

Air

Many major airlines fly from the United States to South America, including Aerolineas Argentinas, Aeroperú, American, Pan Am, Avianca, Varig, Viasa and Eastern.

Since the deregulation of air fares in the United States, the fares and departure times have changed with bewildering regularity. In addition, the competition has resulted in the bankruptcy of two old standbys (Braniff and Aerocondor), which no longer fly to South America. In 1983, outlets other than airline ticket offices and travel agencies were permitted to sell airline tickets. You can now book your flight through Ticketron, for example.

There are several airlines that have cheaper fares than the others. These airlines don't have ticket offices in most American cities, but you can call them at toll-free numbers or buy your ticket through a travel agent or outlet. (The airline will obtain your tourist card and pass it along to your travel agent or give it to you on board the plane.) Be aware that when you deal with cheapo airlines you might get cheapo service. Flights are often overbooked and depart late. Refunds are hard to obtain if you don't use your ticket.

You could also lose out if the airline discontinues service. When Braniff terminated its flights to South America in 1982, people holding tickets bought directly from Braniff were left in the lurch, while those who bought tickets through travel agencies could use their tickets on other airlines. You should watch for price wars and special offers, which can result in enormous savings for travelers. The situation is so complicated and changes so rapidly that I suggest you use a good travel agency, which will help you obtain the best fares and can also help you get a refund on any unused portions of your ticket.

Following are listings of several airlines that fly to South America, including some which don't have offices in most cities in the United States. For example, Aerolineas Argentinas has daily jets from Miami, Los Angeles and New York to Bogotá, Lima, Rio de Janeiro and Buenos Aires. Eastern flies from Miami, New York, Los Angeles and New Orleans to Panama City; Bogotá, Cali and Branaquilla, Colombia; Quito and Guayaquil, Ecuador; Lima, Peru; La Paz, Bolivia; and also to Chile, Paraguay and Argentina.

Ecuatoriana flies from Miami to Quito and Guayaquil. For further information check:

Ecuatoriana Airlines

Toll-free number: (800) 327-1337

1 Biscayne Tower
2 Biscayne Boulevard
Miami, Florida 33132
Telephone: (305) 377-8484

Miami International Airport
Telephone: (305) 526-5734

Lloyd Aéreo Boliviano (LAB) has daily round-trip flights between Miami and Santa Cruz, Cochabamba and La Paz, Bolivia. They also fly from Miami to La Paz via Panama City and Lima.

Lloyd Aéreo Boliviano

Toll-free number (except Florida): (800) 327-7407

225 S.E. First Street
Miami, Florida 33131
Telephone: (305) 374-4600

Faucett flies from Miami to Iquitos and Lima, Peru.

Faucett

Toll-free number: (800) 328-2388

3095 N.W. 77th Avenue
Miami, Florida 33122

A note on dealing with Miami International Airport: when I've called both the airlines and the duty-free shops, frequently I've been connected with people who don't speak English. This is no problem if your Spanish is good, but if it isn't you're better off letting a travel agent handle the situation.

When flying *any* airline to, from and within South America, confirm and re-confirm your reservations. Around major holidays and at the height of the tourist season (June through August) you should make reservations as early as possible, confirm them a week or two before your departure and reconfirm again 24 hours before the flight. (Then be prepared to arrive at the airport and have the airline deny that you ever called them. Be firm and polite, then scream and yell.)

Be sure to check with the airlines on their reconfirmation policy. Some will automatically cancel your reservations if you don't reconfirm 24 hours in advance. This can be tricky if you are somewhere like Macchu Picchu where you can't reach a ticket office, but usually you can work it out.

Whether you're flying the major airlines or the cheapos, it's worthwhile to buy all international airline tickets in the United States, since they're cheaper here than in South America, where countries add a ten to fifteen percent tax on international flight fares. If you know you want to fly from Quito, Ecuador, to Lima, Peru, buy the ticket in the United States and leave the date open. You can make reservations as your trip proceeds. Be careful not to lose your ticket; keep it safely tucked away in your money belt.

Except for international flights, buy all your transportation tickets as you go along. It's cheaper. For example, a plane ticket from Cochabamba to La Paz (within Bolivia) costs $20 in the United States but only $12.50 in Bolivia.

When buying your airline tickets, note that you need a ticket *out* of Colombia, Ecuador and Peru in order to enter these countries. Your return or onward ticket is requested when you check in at the airlines before your trip, and they won't let you on the flight without it. A return ticket on any kind of transportation to the United States or any other country is acceptable. It isn't necessary that you actually use this ticket. You could, for example, take a freighter home from Colombia or travel overland out of Peru and cash in your unused airline ticket for a refund, but there's a catch. A refund usually must be handled in the country in which the ticket was purchased. Aerocondor is very difficult about refunds; it takes about six months of hassle if you're both persistent and lucky, so I suggest buying an Aerocondor ticket only if you intend to use it. (Don't lose it, either, since they neither refund nor replace lost or stolen tickets.) If you're buying an airline ticket simply to comply with the mandatory return or onward ticket regulation, check with the airline you buy it from to find out their policy on refunding unused tickets. Besides having to do it in the country where the ticket was purchased, there's often a time limit on refunds. Usually the ticket must be used or refunded within a year.

The requirement that you have a ticket out of the country in order to enter wreaks havoc with travelers planning to go overland from Colombia. Rather than tie up your money in tickets from Colombia to Ecuador to Peru, which you don't plan to use, ask an airline to sell you a $50 open ticket. You can present this at each border check and say you plan to use it to fly to the next country. If anyone asks, say you left it open because you aren't sure of your exact departure date. You can use this ticket if necessary or cash it in within one year for a refund.

The usual baggage allowance for all the airlines is twenty kilos (forty-four pounds) for coach passengers, plus carry-ons (camera, purse, etc.). When planning your trip, check with the airlines for the latest information on baggage allowance, flight schedules and fares, since they're always subject to change.

SPECIAL AIR FARES AND PACKAGES

The major airlines offer special fares available for travelers to South America. These air fares and package offerings change with bewildering regularity.

If you're planning to fly to a South American country other than Colombia and want to stay longer than thirty days, your best bet is the 150-day excursion fare offered by Braniff and other members of IATA (International Air Transport Association). The round-trip, United States–Lima ticket costs about $670, depending on your departure point in the United States.

A new plan which you should be aware of is the Advance Purchase Excursion Fare (APEX). Basically, this plan allows independent tour operators to sell individual seats on overseas charter flights. You don't have to be a member of any particular club or group and you don't have to buy ground accommodations. However, you must buy a round-trip ticket thirty days in advance and stay at your destination from twenty-two to forty-five days. You can save as much as half the cost of a regular ticket! If you're able to plan far enough in advance, ask a travel agent about APEX, or variations on it, which are known as Advance Booking Charters (ABC).

If you really enjoy flying, Avianca (Colombia) offers a special ticket called *"Conozca Colombia"* ("Know Colombia"), which gives you thirty days of unlimited flying within Colombia for $100. The *Conozca* ticket *must* be bought outside Colombia. You can't go through any city more than once (except to make connections) and you have to submit a rough itinerary, which you aren't held to strictly. I'm not sure this is such a wonderful deal, considering the amount of flying you'd have to do to get your money's worth. You'd have to stay in a lot of places for short periods of time, which I don't like. However, depending on what you want to see and do, it might be worth checking out.

TRAVEL AGENTS

Although travel to South America is increasing, most travel agents aren't very familiar with this part of the world. Therefore it's best if you have specific plans in mind and then ask an agent to make the arrangements. Since Aerocondor, Ecuatoriana, Lloyd Aéreo Boliviano and other South American airlines don't have offices in most North American cities, it's easier to have a travel agent make your flight reservations and obtain the tickets. Since agents make their living on commissions from the airlines, their services cost you nothing. Be sure to allow your agent plenty of time to obtain your tickets since it's more difficult (and takes longer) to make arrangements long distance.

Travel agents sometimes misinform travelers—either out of ignorance or because they misunderstand the kind of trip their clients are planning. A friend of mine was told she couldn't go overland to Brazil through Colombia, Ecuador, Peru and Bolivia, and this just isn't true. Thousands of people, including myself, have made this overland journey (although I didn't go on to Brazil from Bolivia). Even though the agent talked my friend out of her adventure and sold her a plane ticket to Río, she subsequently returned home by the overland route, once she got the correct information.

So, if you want to fly to the middle of the Amazon and return by boat, you can do it—and don't let a travel agent tell you that you can't. Nothing is impossible in South America, although just about everything is difficult—or at least challenging—as well as exciting. Follow your inclinations.

Land

If you're taking the bus through Mexico and Central America, the *South American Handbook* is the guidebook to have because it covers Mexico and Central America as well as South America. Once you reach Panama you must make arrangements to get around the Darien Gap, the 125-mile section of jungle where the Pan American Highway doesn't exist. Most people fly to Colombia or take a boat (see the *Handbook* for details), although we met a Canadian who traveled through the Darien by jungle trail and dugout. (He said it was quite an adventure and was on his way to the hospital to get rid of his intestinal parasites when we met him.)

DRIVING

It can be done, but it isn't easy. There are several obstacles. The first is the *carnet de passage en douanes*. Basically, the *carnet* ensures that you won't sell your car in South America illegally—that is, without paying the proper taxes. Only Peru, Argentina and Chile permit you to take a car into the country without it. The catch to the *carnet* is that you must make a cash deposit of $2000 with a bank in the United States or post a letter of credit for that amount. There's also a $35 fee and another refundable deposit of $100, payable to the agency issuing the *carnet*. If you fail to return with your car or with the papers properly executed, you forfeit the $2000. Two agencies in the United States are authorized to issue the carnet: the American Automobile Association (AAA) and the American

Automobile Touring Alliance (AATA), whose main office is located at 2040 Market Street, Philadelphia, Pennsylvania 19103. Contact your local AAA or write to them at 1712 G Street N.W., Washington, D.C. 20006. AAA also supplies maps and highway guides of Mexico and Central and South America and issues traveler's theft and accident insurance to its members.

If you come up with the money and survive obtaining the *carnet*, you're faced with still more obstacles. The first trick is to get your vehicle safely through Mexico and Central America. Then you have to contend with the Darien Gap, which is impenetrable by car. Autos are shipped around the Gap from Colón, Panama, to Cartagena or Barranquilla, Colombia (the Caribbean route), or from Balboa, Panama, to Buenaventura, Colombia (the Pacific route). In Bogotá I met two American travelers, Sandy and Rudi, whose vw van made it on the *Betsy Bee* via the Caribbean. Friends of theirs weren't so lucky. Their van was being transported on a barge in the Pacific when an inexperienced crew member snapped the cable connecting the barge to its tugboat, which destroyed the tug's motor and left the barge and tug separately adrift on the ocean. I don't know what happened to the tug, but the barge carrying the van and some passengers and crew eventually washed up on a remote island off Colombia's swampy, malarial Choco coast. While I was in Bogotá an expedition was organized to recover the van. A lumber boat reputedly

visited the island twice a month, and there was hope that it could transport the van back to the mainland. I can't tell you the end of this story because no one returned before I left for Quito. The van may still be rusting on the island, its owners desperately trying to figure out some way to at least recover their *carnet* deposit.

Sandy and Rudi recommended the following paperback travel guide for people who drive to South America: *Latin American Travel Guide Including the Complete Pan American Highway Guide*, by Ernst A. Jahn (Compsco Publishing Company, 663 Fifth Avenue, New York, New York 10022, $7.95). This guide provides general travel information plus road maps, routes, mileages and auto-shipping information. By a strange coincidence, just as their copy of the book was wearing out completely, Sandy and Rudi picked up the author as he was hitchhiking in Bogotá during a rainstorm, and he gave them a brand new copy. Sandy and Rudi found the guide helpful, if a bit sensational at times. In case I haven't sufficiently impressed you with the impenetrability of the Darien Gap, I quote Mr. Jahn's lurid account:

> In 1972, a team of 33 British scientists and soldiers crossed
> the Darien which took them 99 days. They had to haul
> their two trucks by rope when the going was too rough,
> and had to raft them across rivers. At some points
> they had to hack their way tree-by-tree through some
> of the most treacherous territory on earth. The savage
> jungle has thousands of poisonous snakes lurking in
> foul swamps, enormous black ants whose sting could numb
> a man all day, and tarantulas the size of a dinner
> plate. The $260,000 expedition was supplied by airdrops
> with food and gasoline. The team lost 5 men who
> were sucked to their death in an oozing mud swamp.

The Canadian who walked through the Darien recounted none of these horror stories, but your problems are more likely to arise with shipping your car around the Darien rather than with driving through it, which you'd be insane to attempt.

The biggest difficulty with having a car is the fact that you have to watch it all the time. A vehicle with American license plates is usually loaded with goodies, so there's going to be a battle for them between you and the locals. My friend Laney Odlum, who has been living in Colombia, offers this advice: "People should really think it over before bringing a vehicle down here since it means constantly babysitting it; there is also the very real possibility that it will be stolen. Always leave vehicles with a particular person guarding it—in his yard or something—*not* with some street urchin keeping an eye on it. Parking lots are pretty safe, but *don't* leave the keys."

You should be aware that any outside trimmings on a car, such as mirrors and windshield wipers, quickly disappear. Because of this, a South American driver ordinarily removes the windshield wipers and only puts them on his car when it begins to rain.

If—after all this—you still want to drive to South America, Mexico undoubtedly will be your shakedown cruise. There's a paperback guide available that's sure to put you in a good mood, and keep you there, as it helps you with such essentials as "Preparing Your Car," "Driving in Mexico," "Basic Living Skills," "Restaurants," "Markets," "Cooking in Mexico" and more. Carl, God bless him, has even included the Spanish words for about 250 car parts and tools. The book I'm referring to is *The People's Guide to Mexico,* by Carl Franz (Santa Fe, N. Mex.: John Muir Publications, 1972). No superlatives suffice for this book. It's excellent.

Overlanding: How to Explore the World on Four Wheels, by John Steele Gordon (New York: Harper & Row, 1975), is another paperback that's quite useful to car travelers. Gordon's approach to driving in South America (and anywhere) is more positive than mine, and he includes a lot of valuable information.

If you do take a vehicle, by all means get these books. They're full of specific, useful advice. It's also worthwhile joining AAA for the travel information they provide, as well as for obtaining the mandatory *carnet.*

Sea

I've talked to several people who've taken freighters to South America from the Caribbean and from Central America. They said it was cheap and easy, and they found a ship to travel on by simply hanging around the docks and asking. You can also look for freighter schedules in the newspaper. Deck passengers hang hammocks and you should bring your own, although you can buy them on board some freighters. I don't know anyone who's taken a freighter from the United States to South America, but I'm sure it can be done. The best source of information on freighters is *The Freighter Travel Manual,* by Bradford Angier (Radnor, Pa.: Chilton Book Company, 1974). In addition, the *South American Handbook* contains a very complete listing of freighter and passenger lines with runs between Europe, England, North America and South America.

CRUISES

If you're interested in a cruise, talk to your travel agent. Since the main idea of a cruise is shipboard partying rather than seeing much of South America (there are a few port calls), it isn't something I know much about.

SAILING YOUR OWN BOAT

A word of warning if you're sailing your own boat: the United States Congressional Coast Guard Subcommittee issued a report in 1974 on the growing number of yacht and boat hijackings in the Caribbean. Small boats that have taken on crews in Caribbean and Pacific ports have been hijacked by these crews, the owners killed and the boats used for cocaine and heroin smuggling. We have a friend who disappeared in this manner in 1973. (These incidents took place *outside* the Bermuda Triangle.) While I hate to make you paranoid about meeting new people, you ought to be extremely careful about any passengers and crew you take on in the Caribbean or Pacific ports of Panama and Colombia.

Which Is Best?

If you simply want to get to South America cheaply and fast, your best bet is to fly to Colombia and then head south overland to Ecuador, Peru and Bolivia. Many, many travelers take this journey; I've done it myself. Another alternative is to fly to Bolivia now that the L.A.B. flights are reasonably cheap and make the overland trip going back north. That way, you end your trip in Colombia and can return to the United States on Aerocondor. If you have a year or two, a fair amount of money, the desire to see all of Latin America and the stamina to withstand a lot of punishing bus rides, then the overland trip from Mexico through Central America is for you. You shouldn't take this last trip thinking that it's cheaper than flying, however, since your expenses undoubtedly will add up to more than the $140 air fare from Miami to Colombia.

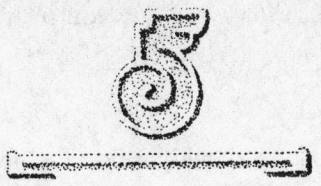

Border Crossings, Customs and Currency

The very phrase "border crossing" seems to strike terror in the heart of the traveler, particularly the young, impecunious one. It needn't. Most countries welcome tourists because they spend money. If you *look* like you have money to spend, your welcome will be warmer. Keep in mind that the hippie look doesn't go over well, especially in Colombia, where an antidrug rampage is under way as this book is being written.

The easiest, fastest entry into a South American country is by air. This also has to do with appearances. Immigration officials assume that anyone who has enough money to fly has enough money to stay. I've never been asked if I had the official minimum amount of money when I arrived by air. (In several cases I was almost broke, as I was expecting money to be wired to me.)

Official Financial Minimums for Entry

The Andean countries have official financial minimums and if you don't meet these requirements they can refuse you entry. (Don't think these minimums reflect what you'll spend; they're unnecessarily high.)

Colombia. The equivalent of $20 for every day you plan to stay.

Ecuador. The equivalent of $10 a day.

Peru. The equivalent of $8 a day.

Bolivia. The equivalent of $300. The time period to which this applies is vague.

These minimums are often used to refuse entry to young, hip travelers. The best way to get around them is by looking neat and prosperous. Another way is to explain with great earnestness that you've already contacted your family and your father has wired money to you in the capital. If they will kindly let you in, you can receive your stipend. If you're traveling with a close friend who has more money than you, you can use some of his or her money temporarily to meet the minimum. You can even try using someone else's travelers checks and hope that the officials won't notice the discrepancy in signatures. Just the sight of the wad ought to satisfy them. Work this out ahead of time so that if you're asked for proof of solvency you can each pull out some money or checks from your money belt.

Border Crossing and Entry by Air

§ A week before you leave a country buy your ticket and make sure your reservations out are confirmed. If the country you're entering requires a ticket *out* as a condition for entry, you often have to show this ticket or buy one before the airline will sell you a ticket *in*. Colombia, Ecuador and Peru require this. A ticket out to anywhere on any kind of transportation will do (see Chapter Four, "Getting There"). When you go to the airline ticket office, take your passport *(pasaporte)* and health card *(certificado de salúd* or *certificado de vacunación)* along with you. In fact, take all your documents and tickets.

§ Make sure you're straight with Immigration in the country you're leaving. In most cases, if you came in by air you were processed in at the airport, and if you're leaving by air you'll also be processed out there, so you don't need to do anything until you arrive at the airport an hour or so prior to your departure. If you're uncertain about what to do next, go to your airline's ticket counter and present your ticket. They will direct you.

If you came in by land and are leaving by air, you may have to stop at the main Immigration office in town before you leave. (This is always true for Bolivia.) Again, if you're confused about what to do, ask at the airline when you buy your ticket. The airlines are well informed about Customs and Immigration (*Aduana y Inmigración*) procedures. In any event, you may want to check with Immigration beforehand just to be sure all your papers are in order, rather than getting hung up at the airport.

§ Before you leave get rid of your local currency and pick up a little currency for the country you're entering. South American countries don't want each other's money (they want American dollars), and the exchange rates among South American currencies are low. (For a more detailed discussion, see the "Currency" section following.) Be sure, however, to save enough local money for the taxi ride to the airport, a snack and the airport departure tax. The taxes are as follows for international flights:

Colombia. Whatever works out to $8 at the current exchange rates.

Ecuador. $5 or its equivalent in *sucres.*

Peru. $10, which must be paid in American dollars.

Bolivia. $14, or its equivalent in pesos.

§ The fourth step is to obtain a tourist card (*tarjeta de turista*) for the country you're entering. A tourist card is the piece of paper you fill out, while a tourist visa is the permit to visit a country. However, I use the words interchangeably since for all practical purposes they're the same. For example, Peru says American tourists don't need a visa; all you need is a tourist card, which you get at the border. In other words, you don't need to go to the Peruvian consulate ahead of time to get permission to visit Peru. The requirements for a tourist card or tourist visa are exactly the same for all the Andean countries: a valid passport and a health card with proof of yellow fever and smallpox vaccinations. You don't need any photographs.

Obtaining a tourist visa used to be simpler than it is now. Although I've never gone to a country's consulate ahead of time to get a tourist card, you now have to do this for Colombia. You can no longer obtain Colombia's ninety-day tourist card at the border. Just to confuse you, Colombia issues two different tourist visas. One allows you ninety days and is given free, but it *must* be obtained at an airline ticket office or at any Colombian consulate *before* you reach the border. This means that if you're entering Colombia from the United States, you should obtain this card from the nearest consulate in the United States or from the airline when you buy your ticket. If you're entering Colombia by land or air from Ecuador, you should stop at the Colombian consulate in Quito and obtain this ninety-day visa *before* heading for the frontier or airport.

Here's why: Colombia has another tourist visa, one that's issued by request or at the border. It's good for only forty days and should be used only if the traveler doesn't intend to return to Colombia during that calendar year. If you accidentally get this visa, you can't get back into Colombia that year. This can be disastrous if you plan to fly to Bogotá, travel to the other Andean countries and then fly back home from Bogotá. With the ninety-day tourist visa you can stay in Colombia for up to ninety days, leave and then return to Colombia for another ninety days *if* you obtain each visa before you reach the border. If you mistakenly get the forty-day visa, try bribing the border officials. There's no guarantee it will work, but when you're in a bind try everything.

You should be aware that a visa's time period is calculated from the date you actually enter the country, not from the date it was issued, but you must use your visa within a certain amount of time. For example, you have forty-eight months in which to use Colombia's ninety-day tourist visa.

Ecuador, Peru and Bolivia issue tourist cards at the border as well as at their consulates and airline ticket offices. I've always gotten my visas at the border when I arrived by land and by air and have never had any trouble.

Remember this: while tourist cards are issued for up to ninety days, the exact amount of time you're given depends on the mood of border officials. In 1976 Bolivia started giving out fifteen-day stays to "undesirables" arriving by land. Also, *always* ask for more time than you think you'll need. If you're planning to stay for thirty days, ask for sixty. This gives you a margin of safety in case you change your plans or get delayed. I invariably ask for the full ninety days.

For some reason, writing about obtaining visas makes it seem harder and more confusing than it actually is. Except for Colombia, you can just show up at the border and get a free, ninety-day tourist visa. The straighter you look, the easier it is, although border officials are used to people arriving in somewhat disheveled condition, since land travel is rugged.

You're given your tourist card to fill out at the consulate or airline or during your flight. It's a simple form. Since you have to print through several carbons, have a ballpoint pen along with you. Write in English unless your Spanish is good. You'll be asked the following:

Nombre (name). Your last name, or surname, may be requested by *sobrenombre* or *apellido*. Don't use anything fancy, such as "James Robert Johnson, Esq." Customs officials don't like things out of the ordinary, and your name should appear exactly as it does on your passport. So "James R. Johnson" or "Johnson, James R." is the way to do it, depending on what's asked.

Estado civil (civil status). What they mean is are you single, married or divorced. Please don't write "living together." If you're traveling as a couple, write "married," even though the names on your passports are different. Your excuse, if anyone bothers to ask, is that you didn't change the passport before you left on your trip.

Edad (age).

Fecha de nacimiento (date of birth). Write out the date; for example: June 11, 1950; not 6/11/50. When a South American or European writes 6/11/50 it means the sixth of November, 1950. This discrepancy in usage can cause you lots of problems.

Nacionalidad (nationality). Citizens of the United States should write "u.s.a." rather than "American," since you run into Latin Americans who insist (correctly, but picayunely) "We're all Americans."

Lugar de nacimiento (place of birth). I give the country ("u.s.a.") rather than the city and state, since "Minneapolis, Minnesota" is confusing to Immigration officials ("What country is that?").

Domicilio permanente (permanent residence). Your home or permanent address. If you're transient use your parents' or a friend's address. As a rule, your permanent address should be in the country in which you hold citizenship—no long explanation about how you've been living in Mexico for the past two years.

Procedencia (departure point). Not where you started your entire trip, but where you boarded this particular flight.

Destino (destination). The easiest and most acceptable answer is your flight's destination, rather than "India, eventually" or "Tierra del Fuego."

Clase de visa (type of visa). The answer is "tourist."

Profesión (occupation, profession). Something nice, such as "teacher," not "unemployed" or "seeker of truth." Make up an impressive-sounding occupation if you have to (anything having to do with computers sounds good).

Fecha de llegada (date of arrival). You also may be asked for *lugar* or *puerto de llegada* (place or port of entry). This is the city the plane is landing in or near.

Fecha de salida (date of departure). Leave this blank. It will be filled in when you leave the country. Same for *lugar* or *puerto de salida* (place or port of departure).

Pasaporte número (passport number).

Nombre de la companía de transporte (name of transport company—that is, the airline). You may be asked for *tipo de transporte* (type of transport). The answer is "airplane."

Firma (signature).

There may be slight variations, but this covers the basics. You're given the same kind of card to fill out at the border outpost if you arrive by land, and the answers are the same except for the name and kind of transportation. Don't lose or throw away your tourist card; you have to show it at police checkpoints and turn it in at the border when you leave.

§ Proceed through Customs and Immigration when your plane arrives at the airport. Your passport and tourist card are stamped, your health card is examined and your luggage *(equipaje)* is opened for inspection. The luggage inspection is generally lax. No one has ever gone through my baggage thoroughly. The Customs inspector usually takes one look at the amount I'm dragging around, rolls his eyes and has me open one suitcase. He peeks into the bag tentatively, fearful that if he tears it all apart I'll detain him for hours repacking it. If the officials suspect you're carrying drugs, however, it's another story, and you can expect to be searched very thoroughly.

There are official limits on what you can take into each country for your own use: a certain number of rolls of film, so many packs of cigarettes, etc. I ignore these rules out of necessity since, for example, there's no Kodak Ektasound movie film available in South America. I've never run into any trouble. On the other hand, if Customs opens your suitcase and discovers ten pocket calculators or watches, you'd better have a good story, the proper import papers or be prepared to pay a bribe.

If you're carrying gifts for South Americans, take them out of their packages, remove the price tags and pack them among your own things. There are various obscure rules regulating the importation of new items for non-personal use, and your explanation that they're gifts won't help. Bill and I carried a wide variety of gifts, including a fifteen-pound tin of peanut butter that was a little difficult to hide among our belongings, and never had trouble with Customs. (They probably assumed we're eccentric travelers.) However, I've never tried to carry in such things as televisions or stereos; use your common sense when packing and carrying gifts.

Airport customs is fast, often a half hour from plane to taxi. The most common delay, particularly for young travelers, is the drug search. At El Alto Airport in La Paz I was pulled aside after I had passed through Bolivian Customs and Immigration and was waiting to board my flight to

Lima. A woman narcotics agent gave me a very thorough body search, completely stripping me (while the men peeked). All hand luggage was also searched. I had no contraband, but if I had been carrying even one joint or a gram of cocaine it would have been discovered. Bogotá's El Dorado Airport is also notorious for these searches; in fact, all Colombian airports are. If you're clean, you're released in time to make your flight. If not, missing your plane is the least of your worries.

Incidentally, if you're caught with drugs at an airport, try bribing your way out immediately. Most encounters with the law in South America are settled by bribes, and the fewer people involved and the sooner payment is made, the cheaper it's going to be. As the United States continues to pour more money into South America to halt the flow of cocaine, however, it becomes more and more difficult for the small-time doper to buy his way out of trouble. Steer clear altogether. Don't buy, use or even discuss drugs (see Chapter Fourteen, "Drugs and Hallucinogens").

Border Crossing and Entry by Land

Crossing the frontier by land is more exciting and unpredictable than arriving by air, and it usually takes more time. Generally there are a lot of residents returning home, as well as other South American travelers, whose papers are carefully checked and who are routinely searched for contraband. This means a delay for the entire bus, train, truck or *colectivo*. Border officials are also more likely to ascertain if young travelers have sufficient funds and are more likely to refuse them entry. It's definitely an adventure.

§ Check with Immigration in the capital city or nearest large town in the country you're leaving and make sure all requirements are met. You may have to obtain an exit stamp. This is true for Colombia, where you must be stamped out by the security police (DAS), who don't have offices at all border crossings. Also, when crossing into Peru from Bolivia via Copacabana, be sure to have Bolivian Customs stamp your papers in Copacabana. There are no facilities for doing this at the actual frontier, which is about four miles away, and you will be sent back to Copacabana if you fail to get your papers stamped there. Peruvian Customs won't allow you to enter without your Bolivian exit stamp!

§ Plan ahead and spend most of your local currency, but save a little for the ride, food and any exit fees. Bill and I were charged 50 *sucres* (about $2) each when leaving Ecuador by land. This is the only country with a land departure tax. Before you cross the border, exchange the last of your old currency for the currency of the country you're entering. Ask around and bargain because rates vary.

§ Check out with Immigration and Customs in the country you're leaving and turn in your tourist card. Check in with Customs in the next country.

If you get off a vehicle that stops at the frontier, you may have to take a taxi to cross the border or it may be close enough for you to walk. It's a taxi or bus ride between Colombia and Ecuador at Ipiales, and a bus or truck ride anywhere between Peru and Bolivia. It's a short walk between Ecuador and Peru at Huaquillas, where we were approached by a boy with a little wagon, who hauled our luggage across the international bridge for a few *soles*.

If you're riding on a vehicle that's traveling across the border, expect to get off and on a few times while papers and baggage are checked. Keep an eye on your luggage, especially if it's stored on top of the bus. Things sometimes disappear from backpacks during Customs searches.

An important warning concerning entry into Peru: as I've mentioned, you must have a ticket out of Peru in order to enter. If you come in by land you will be forced to buy a bus ticket out (unless you already have a plane ticket, as we did). You'll be sent to a *Transportes Morales* office, where they'll try to sell you a $10 ticket from Puno, Peru, to La Paz, Bolivia, or an equally expensive ticket into Ecuador. These are notorious frauds. When you arrive in Puno the ticket probably won't be honored and you will not be given a refund. It's a standing joke that *Transportes Morales* exists by selling worthless tickets, not by providing transportation. I once witnessed an angry mob at the company's office in Puno. The travelers were told there wouldn't be a bus to La Paz for a week and they'd just have to find some other ride. Sorry, no refunds.

Be smart. You can buy a $2 or $3 ticket from where you are *back* to the nearest town over the border (for example, from Aguas Verdes, the Peruvian border town, to Huaquillas, Ecuador). Even though you'll never use this ticket, you'll only lose $2. Or buy a ticket from Yunguyo, Peru (the town near the Bolivian border), to Copacabana, Bolivia (the first town over the border). Under no conditions should you buy the Puno to La Paz bus ticket from *Transportes Morales* or the equivalent ticket out of Peru into Ecuador. Remember, a ticket on any bus, plane, train or boat out of Peru satisfies the law.

If you ever decide to ride on *Transportes Morales,* buy the ticket only after you've boarded the bus or are in the ticket office and can see the bus you're taking waiting outside. Otherwise they aren't to be trusted.

While airport Customs and Immigration facilities operate at all hours (whenever an international flight arrives), this isn't true for the outlying border posts. The frontier posts for Colombia, Ecuador, Peru and Bolivia operate only during daylight hours. They're closed from 6 P.M. to 6 A.M. and from noon to 2 P.M. for lunch. If a bus arrives in the middle of the night the driver might be able to rouse an official with a bribe, but lone travelers are generally told to come back in the morning, so plan accordingly.

At each border crossing it's up to you to get the proper stamps. Sometimes Customs, Immigration and the police are in the same building, but not always. You may have to visit three different buildings on each side of the frontier. When you think you're done with all the formalities, ask if there's anything more: *"¿Algo más?"* or *"¿Necesito más?"* Only then should you head into the interior.

Once you're inside the next country, the fun is just beginning. Expect your vehicle to be stopped at least three times for Customs and papers checks. It's been my experience that officials are much nicer to North American and European travelers than they are to other South Americans. The Ecuadorian police hauled two Colombian travelers off our bus near the border, probably because they were young, long-haired males. All the other passengers argued on their behalf, hung out the windows, shouted at the police and booed loudly when the Colombians weren't allowed back on, but to no avail. No one esle was bothered.

Smuggling is rampant from Colombia into Ecuador and from Peru into Bolivia. You may inadvertently end up on a contraband special— a bus loaded with people returning to their country with illegal goodies. As we approached the border at Yunguyo, Peru, there was a flurry of activity on our bus. After clearing Peruvian Customs, the Indian women from La Paz ran around tucking boxes of Peruvian spaghetti under the seats of *gringo* travelers. They stashed ketchup bottles up sleeves and blankets in the bottom of sacks. One woman stuffed her daughter's tights with packages of jockey shorts until the child looked like a sausage and then asked each foreigner to sit on a couple of packages, which we did. When we reached the Bolivian side, the police boarded and looked at our passports, and then the Customs officials entered and tore the bus apart. As they searched, I could feel the packages of underwear beginning to slide out from under me. The boxes of spaghetti were discovered and confiscated, as were other contraband treasures. Fortunately for all of us we never had to stand up, and just when the underwear was about to fall to the floor, giving the whole show away, the Customs officials got off the bus. The Bolivians who managed to get their goods through went into hysterics with glee. There were at least three other searches, the final one taking place just outside La Paz. By that time the passengers were tired and overconfident, and Customs made another big haul. The underwear made it through, though, and the woman came around, collected it and thanked us all. She then unstuffed her daughter. The jockey shorts undoubtedly appeared for sale the next day in the black market in La Paz.

During the entire bus ride, nothing belonging to any of the young *gringo* travelers was searched; the focus seemed to be entirely on contraband coming in from Peru. As I understood it, passengers whose goods were confiscated could ransom them back from Customs by paying a bribe. How serious anyone took this was hard to determine. The passengers' goal seemed to be to get as much contraband through with as little ransom as possible, while the Customs officials looked upon the bribes or fines as a way to supplement their own meager salaries. It was an interesting diversion on an otherwise bumpy, dusty, tiring journey.

Bill and I had one of our more bizarre border encounters when we crossed from Ecuador into Peru. Let me state right away that Peruvian officials seem very strict and nasty about everything, especially in comparison with Ecuador, where the attitude is quite relaxed. After crossing the border, Bill and I caught a *comité* heading south from Aguas Verdes. Each time the driver shifted into third gear it seemed as though he had to start downshifting to stop for another police check. At each

checkpoint they demanded to see everyone's papers in a manner best described as unfriendly. A good fifty miles into Peru we ran into yet another inspection. By this time it was dark. The Peruvian police insisted that we get out of the car and, using a flashlight, checked our arms and ankles for needle marks. (I was afraid my mosquito bites were going to get me thrown out.) We didn't look disreputable, and they didn't search our clothing or luggage. It seemed more like personal harassment or an attempt by the police to prove they were hip. We never did figure it out.

Your best source of information regarding border crossings is other travelers, especially those returning from places on your itinerary. Ask them about border procedures, currency exchanges, possible problems and the best solutions, and share your own experiences.

Renewing a Visa

If you find that you want to stay in a country longer than ninety days, you can renew your tourist card for an additional ninety days. Present yourself at Immigration about five days before your visa runs out and ask for a renewal. There shouldn't be any problem, but if there is, try offering a bribe. Otherwise, leave the country and come back in again, getting another ninety-day visa at the border when you re-enter. Once again I refer you to other travelers. Ask them if they've had a tourist visa renewed and where they had it done. The travelers' grapevine is your best bet for up-to-the-minute news. Plan ahead so you'll know if the renewal can be done locally or if you have to go into the capital.

Colombia. A friend of mine who lives in Colombia described obtaining an extension on a tourist visa as a "hassle" and said you can't count on it. Officially, Colombia does permit visa renewals for up to sixty days, but actually obtaining the renewal is another story. Look respectable and have a good reason for wanting to stay longer. Try for a renewal in any large city, although you might be sent to Bogotá.

Ecuador. A ninety-day extension is sometimes refused. Check at Immigration in Quito or Guayaquil before your visa expires.

Peru. Also renewable for up to ninety days. You probably can do this in Cuzco as well as Lima, but check it out.

Bolivia. Visas are renewable for ninety days here, too, but you can anticipate some hassle and you may have to pay a $5 fee. I spent an entire day at Immigration in La Paz trying to explain that I only wanted to stay in Bolivia another month and didn't want or need a resident visa. I got a thirty-day extension but it took a lot of smiling and fast talking. You can usually renew your visa in Santa Cruz, Sucre or Cochabamba.

Currency

The currency situation is tricky. Rates change too frequently to keep up with. Any rates I mention here will be out of date by the time you read this. Your best bet is to check with travelers coming from countries you're about to enter. (We heard about the Peruvian black-market money exchange this way.)

Note: throughout South America, American dollars are often symbolized by "u.s.$" to distinguish them from some local currencies, which also use the "$" sign. In this book, the sign "$" always refers to dollars.

How to go about changing your money varies tremendously from country to country, as do the laws governing the transactions. Basically, the American dollar is king in South America; it is *the* currency to have. Carry American dollars, preferably two-thirds in travelers checks and one-third in cash. Remember, too, that South American countries don't want each other's currencies and that the farther away you get from a country, the less its currency is worth. Therefore, try not to change more money than you need.

There are money-changing facilities at every international airport and at all borders. It's a good idea to change between $10 and $20 at the airport for tips, the taxi ride to the city and so on, but don't change more than that. Airport facilities offer the official exchange rate and you can shop around later for better rates.

COLOMBIA

The basic unit of currency is the *peso,* symbolized by "$" (the same as the dollar). The rate of exchange between the *peso* and the dollar is very favorable to the dollar. You can legally change money anywhere, but don't deal with people who approach you on the street because they'll shortchange you.

Banks post the official rate, which has gone from 34 *pesos* to one dollar in 1976 to 100 *pesos* to the dollar in 1983 and will probably go up further. (What this means is that Colombia has become cheaper for travelers, since prices in the country haven't gone up as fast as the exchange rate.) Don't change your money in banks or *casas de cambio,* though. Most shops will give you a better rate and so will many hotels. There's a reason for this. Colombia doesn't allow anyone to take more than 500 *pesos* (about $15) out of the country. This includes any Colombian who is traveling abroad and means he or she must buy dollars.

Therefore dollars are in demand, and shops and hotels apparently sell dollars to other Colombians who are planning trips abroad. Check out a number of shops and see what rates they offer. If you have Colombian friends they'll be glad to change dollars, too.

In Colombia, cash dollars are more valuable and bring a better rate than travelers checks, although you might find someone who'll give you a good rate for travelers checks also. Keep in mind that when you leave Colombia you are only permitted to change $60 worth of *pesos* back into dollars, so don't change too many dollars to *pesos* while you're there.

When leaving Colombia and entering Ecuador, it's best to change your Colombian *pesos* into Ecuadorian *sucres* at the Colombian border towns, not in Ecuador. As a rule of thumb, it's always best to exchange one country's currency for another's inside the country you're leaving. The rates are better. This rule doesn't apply to buying dollars. Since dollars are always in demand, you'll always lose trying to buy back dollars; so estimate your needs carefully and never change too many dollars at any one time. Try to exchange one Andean country's currency for another's rather than converting money back to dollars at a loss.

If you have money wired to you in Colombia, keep two things in mind. First, you have to take the money in *pesos* if you want cash, although you probably can buy travelers checks in dollar denominations. But you cannot get cash dollars. Second, there is a service charge of at least one percent. If you need money wired, Ecuador is a better place to receive it.

A word about carrying money in Colombia: it's best to check all your money and travelers checks (except for a few dollars or *pesos* that you plan to spend that day) with the hotel manager. (The exceptions are the super-cheap hotels where the manager himself might not be trustworthy. Use your judgment.) Always get a receipt. Thievery and robbery are common in Colombia. Never leave money in your room (the maid might steal it) and never carry it all with you. Keep your passport and tourist card with you in your money belt, however, because you might be asked to show them.

ECUADOR

The basic unit of currency is the *sucre*, symbolized by s/. The *sucre* has been devalued sharply in recent years, even though Ecuador has oil and is the only South American country besides Venezuela to belong to OPEC (the Organization of Petroleum Exporting Countries).

Ecuador has one very nice advantage: banks give you American cash dollars when money is wired to you and when you cash travelers checks. If you're having money wired, have it sent to Ecuador (either Quito or Guayaquil). When you receive your money, insist on dollars if you want them. The bank may give you a song and dance, but if you insist they'll produce the dollars. It's also to your advantage to change some of your travelers checks into cash dollars before you enter either Colombia or Peru.

It's legal to change money anywhere in Ecuador, so shop around; check out hotels, *casas de cambio* and stores. Avoid banks, which charge a one-percent fee for money-changing transactions. If you're changing travelers checks in dollars into cash dollars, this one percent isn't charged. It only applies to exchanges between two different countries' currencies. To make things even easier, buy Bank of America travelers checks before you leave home, as there are Bank of America branches all over South America. Then, when you march into Bank of America's Quito branch with the bank's own brand of travelers checks, there's absolutely no excuse for them to give you trouble over cashing them into dollars. (It's also wise to carry some American Express travelers checks; these are more easily negotiable in certain places because more South Americans are familiar with them.)

Although I've gotten slightly more than the official rate at some shops in Ecuador, the exchange rate everywhere generally hovers close to the official rate. There's no limit to the amount of *sucres* or foreign currency you can take into or out of Ecuador. Because of recent devaluation of the *sucre*, most travelers have been changing money a little at a time as the rates sometimes change daily, with the dollar buying more *sucres*.

So—Ecuador is a good place to have money sent and to pick up those handy American dollars. Also, be sure to change your Ecuadorian *sucres* into Colombian *pesos* or Peruvian *soles* while you're still in Ecuador.

PERU

The basic unit of currency is the *sol*, symbolized by *s/.* Peru has been hard hit by inflation—between 80 and 90 percent a year. The government has been devaluing the *sol* in a series of mini devaluations at the rate of between 500 and 600 *soles* per year. The rate rises weekly, sometimes daily. If you're planning to be in Peru awhile it's best to change your money little by little, getting a higher rate each time.

The complicated exchange regulations of former years have been lifted. It is now legal to change money anywhere, and the rates vary. Dollars cash invariably bring better rates than travelers checks. Remember, however, that Peru is notorious for thievery, especially Cuzco, and that you can have stolen travelers checks replaced.

The worst places to change money are the better hotels. They not only give less than the going rate, but they also charge a commission.

Banks usually give top rates, but they charge a commission if you are changing less than $100. Furthermore, there are often long lines. *Casas de cambio* will change any amount of money, although I ran into some that would not accept travelers checks. Their rates may vary, and if you are in a large city where there are several *casas de cambio* within a few blocks it is worthwhile looking for the best rate.

Finally, many small shops have signs which say *"cambia dolares"* or *"compra dolares"* (meaning "we change dollars," or "we buy dollars"). The shops will change small, as well as large, denominations, and many accept cash or travelers checks. The best price for dollars in Cuzco was at a small shop which sold tourist items. All the shops in the arcade had a *"compra dolares"* sign, and they competed against each other to give the best rates.

Peru is not a good place to have money sent. The banks will pay you only in *soles*, usually at a low rate (which may be different from the rate at which they exchange cash dollars). Peruvian banks also charge commissions which, on top of the lower exchange rate, whittle away at your funds.

When you are ready to leave Peru, spend your *soles*. It is sometimes difficult to convert them back to dollars. The branch of the *Banco de la Nación* at the Lima airport refuses to change *soles* to dollars, so I ended up spending my *soles* in the airport shops.

If you are traveling by land to Bolivia, Chile or Ecuador, change your *soles* at the border for the currency of the country you are entering.

BOLIVIA

The basic unit of currency is the *peso*, symbolized by $b. After years of relative stability the *peso* was greatly devalued, from 30 *pesos* to the dollar in 1982 to 1500 *pesos* to the dollar by the beginning of 1984. The *peso* floats on the open market and can fluctuate wildly. Because of these fluctuations, ask travelers coming from Bolivia what rates they got and if the *peso* is rising or falling.

It is legal to change money anywhere. The best rates prevail in the large cities: Santa Cruz, Cochabamba and La Paz, with lower rates in Oruro, Sucre and Potosi (because of less demand for dollars there). It is often impossible to change money at all in the smaller towns so bring plenty of *pesos* with you on a trip to the *campo*.

The *casas de cambio*, rather than banks, are the best places to exchange money, and cash dollars usually bring a better rate than travelers checks. Even better rates are sometimes obtainable in stores that have the *"compra dolares"* signs.

In La Paz top rates are given by the dozens of people who hang out downtown on the corners of Calles Camacho and Colon, with briefcases bulging with *pesos*. These people need dollars for their businesses, or to travel, and they run a regular open-air *casa de cambio*. In Cochabamba and Sucre money changers conduct business on the main plaza. The ones I dealt with in all three cities were honest and some even took travelers checks, which I sat on the curb to sign.

Before you have money sent to Bolivia, find out if the banks are on strike and if you can receive your money in travelers checks in dollar denominations. If you must receive it in *pesos*, find out the rate. Bolivia has an official exchange rate of 500 *pesos* to the dollar, applicable to certain transactions. This rate was one-third to one-half the open market rate, so try not to get stuck with it.

Remember to spend or change your remaining *pesos* before you leave the country.

CREDIT CARDS

Major credit cards (VISA, MasterCard, American Express and Diners Club) are accepted in many airline ticket offices, hotels, restaurants and tourist shops in South America. In a pinch it's handy to charge something. However, pay attention to how the bill is written up. You want it in dollars, not the local currency. If your bill is charged in Bolivian *pesos*, for example, the bank may convert it to dollars at the official exchange rate of 500 *pesos* to the dollar (versus 1500 *pesos* to the dollar on the open market). If you charged a 20,000 *peso* bill, it would come to $40 at the official rate versus $13.30 at the going rate. Be sure to have your bill converted to dollars at the going rate and charged to your credit card in dollars. You should agree on this before a purchase is wrapped up or you've checked into a hotel.

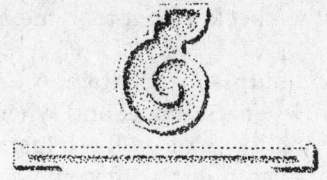

Language

The languages spoken in the Andean countries are Spanish, Quechua and Aymara. Not too many people speak English, so don't count on getting by with English alone.

Spanish

The Spanish language is called *castellano* in South America. While nothing can take the place of a good Spanish course or serious language study on your own, the following section includes a number of greetings, courtesies and idioms which, if used properly, will greatly facilitate communication. It's impossible to overemphasize their importance.

GREETINGS AND COURTESIES

As a culture the Latins are warmer, more polite and more physical than we are. Handshaking and hugging are important social courtesies, among both men and women. The bear hug men give each other is called the *abrazo*, and if you become friendly with a South American you'll be hugged. After his recent trip, Bill remarked that he got so used to the *abrazo* that he felt physically deprived in the United States. Men and women kiss women on the cheek, and it took me a while to adapt to this. Now I miss it, too.

Your first introduction to a South American will probably be accompanied by a handshake, both when you meet and when you depart. If you become more familiar you'll move on to the hugs and kisses.

South Americans begin all encounters with some form of greeting. You don't just barge into a taxi and ask how much it costs to go to the airport. You begin with:

Buenos días. ‖ Good day.

Buenas tardes. ‖ Good afternoon.

Buenas noches. ‖ Good evening. Good night.

You should greet everyone—including the little old lady in the market, the hotel clerk and the corner policeman—before you plunge into your conversation or question.

The following expressions are also commonly used as greetings, usually with someone you already know:

¡Ola! ‖ Hello!

¿Cómo está? (formal) ‖ How are you?

¿Cómo estás? (familiar) ‖ How are you?

¿Cómo le va? ‖ How's it going?

¿Qué tal? ‖ What's happening? How are you doing? (There's no literal translation.)

When you're asked *"¿Cómo está?"* you can respond with:

Bien. ‖ Well.

Así así. ‖ So so. Okay.

. . . And remember your *"gracias."*

In Mexico the *usted* form is commonly used when addressing someone, but that's the more formal, polite term. In South America my Peruvian and Bolivian friends got after me for not using *tú*, the more familiar term. They felt I was being too distant and formal, so *tú* it was. I suggest using the more formal *usted* until South Americans respond with *tú*; then use *tú* yourself.

"Adiós" literally means "with God" and comes from the phrase "Go with God." It's used both as a greeting and parting in South America, so don't be surprised if people greet you in passing with *"Adiós."* Some other words for "good-bye" are:

Ciao. (Italian) ‖ Goodbye. (Very popular with young people.)

Hasta luego. ‖ So long.

Hasta la vista. ‖ So long. Until I see you.

Hasta pronto. ‖ See you shortly.

(Que) Le vaya bien. ‖ Go well. (This has the connotation of "Good luck" and is often said to someone making a long journey.)

I remember the first time I trampled on an old lady's foot and realized I didn't know how to say "I'm sorry" or "Excuse me" in Spanish. If you find yourself in a similar situation say:

Lo siento. ‖ I'm sorry.

Perdóneme. ‖ Pardon me. (Use this when you're interrupting a conversation or moving through a crowd.)

Dispénseme. ‖ Excuse me.

(Basically the same usage as *perdóneme.*)

Discúlpeme. ‖ Excuse me. (Use this in more serious situations, such as when you bump into or offend someone.)

If you want to get through a crowd, pass in front of someone or enter a room, the polite phrase is:

Con permiso. ‖ With your permission.

The responses include:

Pase. ‖ Pass.

Pase adelante. ‖ Come in.

Ándele. ‖ Go ahead.

Siga no más. ‖ Continue. Enter. Go right ahead. (You'll hear this constantly in Ecuador.)

"Please," of course, is *"por favor."* When you say *"Gracias"* to someone, you'll hear:

No importa. ‖ It's not important. You're welcome.

No hay de qué. ‖ You're welcome.

De nada. ‖ You're welcome. (Literally, "For nothing.")

Other polite expressions you'll hear and use include:

A la orden or *A sus órdenes.* ‖ At your service. (This is usually used by waiters and clerks.)

Muy amable. ‖ (You are) Very kind.

No entiendo. ‖ I don't understand.

Buena suerte. ‖ Good luck.

If you don't understand a phrase, say:

¿Cómo? ‖ How?

¿Qué? ‖ What?

Repita eso, por favor. ‖ Repeat that, please.

If someone bothers you, say politely but firmly:

No me moleste, por favor. ‖ Please don't bother me.

Córtela. ‖ Cut it out.

If you want to express sympathy or empathy, try:

¡Qué pena! ‖ What a pain!

¡Qué lástima! ‖ What a pity!

¡Ojalá! ‖ God grant! God willing! I hope! (This interjection came from Arabic and is an adaptation of "O, Allah!")

¡Ojalá que ___. ‖ I hope that ___.

se mejore pronto ‖ you feel better soon

Further weaknesses in my Spanish came to light when I wanted to introduce people. I didn't know how to phrase an introduction. The proper phrase is:

Quiero presentarle a ___. ‖ I wish to present to you ___.

mi esposo ‖ my husband

mi amiga, Ana ‖ my friend, Ana

The proper response when you're introduced is:

Mucho gusto. ‖ Pleased. Glad to meet you.

Tengo mucho gusto en conocerle. ‖ I'm very pleased to meet you.

The person to whom you're introduced often responds with:

El gusto es mío. ‖ The pleasure is mine.

Remembering the greetings and courtesies is part of slowing down and adapting to the South American pace. If you always use these greetings, your reception will be noticeably warmer. If someone says, *"Tranquilo"* (meaning "Calm down" or "It's okay"), you're probably beginning to get overexcited. Of course, this is sometimes easier said than done, such as when an airline loses your luggage or the dry-cleaner returns your jacket in shreds. As you turn red and start to open your mouth, the clerk smiles pleasantly and says, *"Tranquilo."* There are a number of appropriate and inappropriate responses, which I leave to your imagination.

In some of the same situations that you hear *"Tranquilo,"* you'll also hear the phrases *ahora, ya mismo, al tiro* and *ya pronto,* which literally mean "right now." However, in South America "right now" includes a time span ranging from the next thirty seconds to the next few days. You'll be told the bus is arriving *"ahora"* or that your laundry will be ready *"ya pronto"* or that the postmaster is returning *"ya mismo,"* and it could be hours.

While we're on the subject of language, it's time to bring up the use of the term *gringo.* In Mexico the term may be used disparagingly, but this is not the case in South America. *Gringo* simply means "a non-Latin foreigner." An American black would be called a *gringo,* as would a Japanese, European, Canadian and white American. *Gringa* is the feminine form. I was often called a *gringita,* meaning "little *gringa,"* and the term was not meant as an insult. *Gringacha* is Quechua for "little *gringa."*

DIMINUTIVES AND ACCENTS

When you arrive in South America fresh from a Berlitz refresher course in Spanish, you can still have trouble with the language and it won't necessarily be your fault. Besides the abundance of local idioms and the incorporation of many Quechua and Aymara words into the language, South Americans do some strange things with Spanish.

One such idiosyncrasy is the frequent use of diminutives—that is, adding *"ito"* or *"ita"* to nouns and adjectives. This is very common in Bolivia. You'll be asked if you'd like some *cafecito* (a little coffee). Or if you want to buy a *bolsita chiquitita* meaning a *bolsa chica* (little purse). This is fairly easy to catch on to once you understand the code. (It reminds me of learning pig latin.)

Learning to understand local accents is a bit harder. *Calle* (street) is usually pronounced *cai-yay.* In Ecuador, however, they "zh" the *ll. Calle* is pronounced *cai-zhay. Ella* (she) is pronounced *ai-zha,* like "Asia." I had trouble with this at first.

In both Ecuador and Bolivia they also "zh" the *r's.* I noticed this most in Bolivia, where *rico* (rich) is pronounced *zhrico,* and *terrible* (terrible) is pronounced *terrzhible*. Practice these for a while and then try *ferrocarril* (railroad), which if said with a good Bolivian accent makes you sound hopelessly drunk.

SURNAMES

Last name, or family name, usage is different in South America. It's common for Latin Americans to take their mother's as well as their father's last name. One example that comes to mind is that of former Mexican President Luis Echeverria Álvarez, who is usually known as Luis Echeverria. Echeverria is his father's last name, while Álvarez is his mother's maiden name and is added on the end. The mother's name is sometimes indicated only by an initial, *e.g.*, Luis Echeverria A.

If you use first, middle and last name during your travels, you may confuse South Americans and create extra problems for yourself. When my father registered at a Bogotá hotel as Francis Roman Meisch, the hotel clerk assumed that Roman was the family name and Meisch was his mother's name, so he entered him as Francis Roman M. His card was filed under "R" for Roman. A friend called the hotel for three days trying to get in touch with "Mr. and Mrs. Francis Meisch" and was told there was no such party registered. Having lived in Colombia for several years, she finally figured out that the name had been misinterpreted.

The best bet with names, and a good habit to get into for both men and women, is to list first name, middle initial and last name on all documents—for example, Francis R. Meisch—and spare yourself and the South Americans confusion.

HAND GESTURES

South Americans use a lot of gestures when speaking. In fact, try speaking Spanish with your hands held behind your back after you've spent a morning bargaining in the market. It's nearly impossible. Several gestures have very particular meanings.

In South America, you should never point at a person with your finger. It's considered extremely rude. It's interesting to note that in Peru and Bolivia the Aymara Indians point with their chin.

Also, when indicating someone's height, never use your hand flat. This gesture is used to indicate the height of animals, not people. To show that you have a cousin who is "so tall," hold your hand as illustrated below.

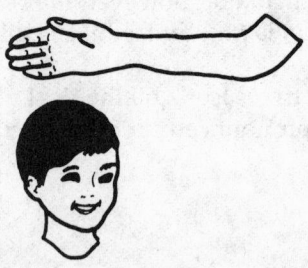

A finger pointed to the eye means *"¡Ojo!"* ("Be careful!" "Be alert!" or "Keep your eyes open!"). The conductor used this gesture on the Colombian train when he warned us about thieves.

In Colombia, if you want to beckon someone, you do so with your palm down. Another common gesture is a finger pointed to the neck, which means "bad" or "unfavorable." You ask someone the reputation of a particular restaurant and he points to his neck. Don't eat there.

TOASTS

What do you do when someone toasts you in a *cantina* or at a party? A common toast is *"Salud,"* which means "Health." If you wish to offer a toast, say, *"Quisiera brindar* (or *tomar*) *a* _____ ,' which means "I wish to toast _____ ." You can then add any number of endings: *"su familia"* ("your family"), *"el año nuevo"* ("the new year") and so on.

Indian Languages

Besides Spanish, two other major languages are spoken by millions of people in the Andes. These are the indigenous languages of Aymara and Quechua. Aymara was the language spoken by the Indians of the Colla, the area around Lake Titicaca and what is now Bolivia.

Quechua is actually a family of languages. There are, for example, at least five different Quechua languages spoken in Peru, and two different languages, called "Quichua," spoken in Ecuador. Quechua is a growing language, spoken by more groups in more areas now than in Inca times.

According to linguist Lawrence Carpenter, Quechua probably originated in the Amazon Basin, moved into the Peruvian jungle and then into the Peruvian highlands. Roughly around the time of Christ it was also spoken by a group, the Chinchay, who lived on the coast of Peru. The Chinchay spread Quechua as a trade language. When the Incas conquered the Chinchay between 1000 and 1200 A.D., they adopted Quechua and subsequently spread it throughout the Andes as they expanded their empire. Quechua means "people of the intermontane valley" but the Indians themselves refer to it as *runa simi* or *shimi* (the language of the people).

At least ten million people speak Quechua today and two million speak Aymara. Quechua is spoken in the southern Colombian Andes and jungle; parts of the jungles of Ecuador, Peru and Brazil; all through highland Ecuador and Peru; in northern Chile and Argentina; and in most of highland Bolivia. However, La Paz, the Lake Titicaca area and parts of Oruro and Potosí are Aymara speaking. In the highlands of

Peru and Bolivia it is estimated that half the population speaks Quechua *only*, so when you travel in remote areas your Spanish will be of little help.

In 1953 Quechua was made the second official language of Bolivia and in 1975 it was made the second official language of Peru. This is significant because traditionally there's been a social stigma attached to speaking Quechua—it was *indio* and therefore lower class. Peru made a start with bilingual education and bilingual announcements on radio and television but then let the program lapse. There are opportunities to learn Quechua if you are interested. The language is taught in the United States at the universities of Illinois, Wisconsin, Cornell and Texas. There is also a good language school run by the Maryknoll missionaries in Cochabamba, Bolivia, that teaches both Quechua and Aymara.

Finding Quechua–English and Aymara–English (or even Quechua–Spanish and Aymara–Spanish) dictionaries is just about impossible in the United States. You can, however, find Quechua–Spanish and Aymara–Spanish dictionaries for sale in the Andean countries.

Because Quechua and Aymara weren't written languages, they had no alphabets. They were first written using the Spanish alphabet and much disagreement has arisen over spelling. For example, the word for "baby" is the same in both Aymara and Quechua, and the simplest

spelling to my way of thinking is *wawa*. However, I've also seen it spelled *huahua* and *guagua*, the latter in Ecuador where bread-dough figures are called *guaguas de pan* (bread babies). *Wasi,* which is Quechua for "house," is also spelled *huasi* or *guasi.* And so on. If you buy a Quechua dictionary look up "baby" or "house" to get an idea of the orthography in use. Furthermore, both Quechua and Aymara have glottalized or aspirated sounds for which we have no letters. These are sometimes indicated by double letters such as *kk,* but also by a letter followed by an apostrophe such as *t'.*

In Chapters Twelve ("Food") and Sixteen ("Native Cultures, Folk Art and Markets"), I've listed the Aymara and Cuzco Quechua (as well as Spanish) names for various items whenever possible, since you'll hear the indigenous words used quite often. In addition, the knowledge of just a few Quechua words is useful and interesting, especially in Peru, where many Quechua place names are still in use.

You'll frequently encounter the following Quechua names of places, gods and goddesses on maps and in your reading about Peru and the Inca Empire:

apacheta ‖ A sacred spot, marked by a pile of stones placed by travelers at the highest point of a mountain pass as an offering. The Indians also add a few eyebrow hairs and a wad of coca leaves to the pile.

apu ‖ Master. *Apu* is a name given to sacred mountains—for example, Apu Auzangate. All snow peaks were worshipped by the Incas and were called *apus.*

cancha ‖ Enclosure. The *Coricancha* in Cuzco (partly covered by the church of Santo Domingo) is the old Inca Golden Enclosure, the Temple of the Sun, Moon, Stars, Thunder, Lightning and Rainbow. The courtyard of a house is called the *cancha,* and in Bolivia the permanent marketplace of a town is called *la cancha.*

chaca ‖ bridge

chasqui ‖ In Inca times, a relay runner or messenger.

cocha ‖ Lake, ocean. *Mama Cocha* is Mother Ocean.

cuzco ‖ Navel. The Incas considered their capital city to be the navel or center of the world.

huaca ‖ Sacred place. There are thousands of *huacas* throughout the Andes, ranging from caves and stones to magnificent temple ruins. The Spanish term *huaquero* refers to a person who makes his living digging up and selling relics from graves or ruins.

huaman ‖ Hawk. Sacsahuaman (Speckled Hawk) is the huge Inca fortress overlooking Cuzco.

huayna (also spelled *wayna*) ‖ Young man. The ruins of Macchu Picchu (Old Man Peak) were named after the peak overlooking these ruins; the smaller peak on the other side is Huayna Picchu (Young Man Peak).

Illapa ‖ The god of thunder and lightning.

inti ‖ Sun. *Inti Taita* is Father Sun, who is still worshipped in the Andes. *Inti Raymi* is the Festival of the Sun, celebrated at the winter solstice. In Cuzco *Inti Raymi* is a major fiesta and is celebrated on June 24. The Inti-huatana is the Hitching Post of the Sun. These stone monuments were destroyed by the Spanish because they were pagan, but the one at Macchu Picchu remains.

khatu ‖ market

khatuna wasi ‖ market house, store

llacta ‖ Town, city. Pikillacta, which means Flea City, is a ruin south of Cuzco. Patallacta, which means Terrace City, is a town in the Urubamba Valley.

llacta kinray ‖ street

macchu ‖ old man

mama ‖ mother

mayu (mayo) ‖ River. The Putumayo in Colombia is the Putu River.

ñan ‖ roadway, path

orgu (urco) ‖ mountain, hill

pacha ‖ Clothing; also earth. *Pacha Mama* is Mother Earth.

pampa (bamba) ‖ Desert, grassy plain. The city of Cochabamba, Bolivia, is named after the desert lake. The town of Moyabamba, Peru, means river plain.

pata ‖ Agricultural terrace (*anden* in Spanish); also square, plaza. Yucaypata and Colcompata are Inca terraces near Cuzco which were planted with corn. The Colcompata was also the Garden of the Sun. The Cusi Pata in Cuzco was the Square of Joy and was one of the plazas used for festivals and markets.

picchu ‖ peak

pirca ‖ stone wall

puca (puka) ‖ red

pucara (pukara) ‖ Fortress. Puca Pucará is the Red Fortress, a beautiful Inca ruin a few miles outside Cuzco.

punku (pungo) ‖ Door. The Puma Punku ruins near Cuzco translates as the Door of the Puma.

quilla ‖ Moon. *Mama Quilla* is the moon goddess.

raymi ‖ festival

rimac ‖ Speaker. The Apurimac River is the Talking River. Lima was derived from *rimac*.

rumi ‖ Stone. The Rumichaca at the Colombian–Ecuadorian border is the Stone Bridge.

sallca ‖ the *sierra*

sara ‖ Corn. *Mama Sara* is the corn goddess.

suyu (suyo) ‖ quarter

tahua (tawa) ‖ four

Tahuantinsuyu ‖ The Four Quarters, the name the Incas gave to their empire. It consisted of the Chinchasuyu, the northwest quarter (northern and central Peru and Ecuador); the Contisuyu, the southwest quarter (southern Peru); the Collasuyu, the southeast quarter (Bolivia, northern Argentina and northern Chile)

and the Antisuyu, the northeast quarter (the *montaña*, toward the Amazon).

taita ‖ father

tambo (tampu) ‖ Inn, roadhouse. The Incas established *tambos* every twelve to twenty miles along their highways. Various villages and sites in the Cuzco area are named after *tambos*—for example, Paucartambo, Limatambo, Pacaritambo and Tambo Machay.

uru ‖ Grubs or caterpillars. Urubamba is a plain where there are caterpillars.

Viracocha ‖ Creator God

wasi (huasi) ‖ house

In Quechua the plural of a noun is made by adding the suffix *kuna* (also spelled *cuna*). For example, *wasi* is "house" and *wasikuna* is "houses." In Aymara the plural of a noun is made by adding the suffix *naka,* except after numbers. For example, *warmi* is "woman" and *warminaka* is "women."

QUECHUA FOR BACKPACKERS

The following phrases hardly do justice to this beautiful language, but the knowledge of a few Quechua words and phrases, coupled with gestures, will help you communicate in areas where little or no Spanish is spoken. (Accents are included merely as an aid to pronunciation.)

Where is (or are) _____? ‖ *Maípi* _____?

  food ‖ *mikúna*

  drink (any liquid) ‖ *upyána*

  hotel ‖ *tambo*

  bathroom ‖ *escusádo*

How much? (price) ‖ *Imainátaq válin?*

yes ‖ *arí*

no ‖ *mána*

please ‖ *áma jína káychu*

thank you ‖ *taitácha pagasúnki* (literally, "God will pay you")

The ethical precepts of the Inca Empire were expressed in three phrases: *ama sua; ama llulla; ama quella* (don't steal; don't lie; don't be lazy). This is used as a greeting in the Peruvian Andes, and if it's said to you, the appropriate reply is *"Qampas hinallataq"* ("To you, likewise").

In Ecuador, however, the Indians may greet you with *"Alabado,"* which means "Praised be (God)." You can answer with *"Alabado."*

How Things Work

et's face it, South America's going to be different. If it weren't, what would be the point of going there? The sudden realization of just how different things are is called culture shock, which can take the form of depression, anxiety, homesickness or an acute desire for a hamburger and root beer float. You make, or hear, such comments as "It's so dirty!" "Everyone's trying to cheat me," "Why can't they do things right?" and "I can't understand a thing that's being said."

Obviously, the more you know about the culture the less it will shock you, and the less you will shock the South Americans. That's why I emphasize background reading so strongly. It's also frustrating if you don't understand the language and can't make yourself understood. (How do you say "Where's the bathroom?") A normally articulate adult suddenly finds himself with the linguistic facility of a two-year-old—"Want taxi. Go restaurant." Anyone's Spanish improves as the trip progresses, but the better you speak it to start, the easier it's going to be on you, not to mention all the South Americans who have to contend with you.

Once you're on your way there are several things that can help the transition. If you practice yoga, meditate or say your prayers in the morning, keep it up. It provides continuity and helps you stay centered. A journal or diary is another useful device. If something is strange and a bit frightening, write it down. The very act of writing helps you put things in perspective, and it's also a good way to record your adventures. I vented my feelings to my journal after a lonely or frustrating day and expressed my joys on paper when there was no one to share them with. (Reading a journal months later brings all the details, with sounds and smells flooding back!)

Remember, also, to consciously change your pace. Slow down. I often think our American habit of rushing around is a way to avoid reflection, and to South Americans we must appear incredibly hyperactive. Appreciate the three-hour siesta and don't complain because the shops aren't open. Sit in the plaza, eat a leisurely lunch, write letters or take a nap. Flow into the South American rhythms. Why not leave your watch at home? It's one less possession to worry about breaking, losing or having stolen, and a travel alarm does the trick for catching trains, planes and buses.

A common and favorite antidote for culture shock is English-language news—*Time*, *Newsweek* and the Latin American edition of the *Miami Herald*. When we were traveling, whoever got his hands on a news magazine first hogged it greedily, occasionally reading items aloud. After reading about crime in the streets, the economy and the environment, we felt assured that everything was normal back home and that California hadn't fallen into the ocean. American news serves another purpose—it tells you what's going on in South America, since the press there is so heavily censored. Although they occasionally add to your homesickness, American newspapers and magazines generally help you enjoy South America by keeping you in touch with what's happening down there as well as back home.

From my journal, Wednesday, April 24: "Still in Guayaquil . . . because our laundry wasn't ready. The only comforting fact of the day is last Sunday's *Miami Herald*. It's making me homesick." (See what I mean about losing days? We spent two extra days in Guayaquil waiting for our laundry.)

Monday, June 3, La Paz, Bolivia: "Bill flew in from Lima yesterday with a *Miami Herald*, and there were all these things I forgot existed: washing machines, vacuum cleaners, the League of Women Voters, consumer protection agencies . . . Trust the *Miami Herald* to tell me what's really going on down here, since freedom of the press doesn't exist. Velasco, in Peru, attacked a Peruvian journalists' meeting as 'subversive' and fired the Naval member of the junta who supported them."

Occasionally, American magazines and newspapers don't show up on the newsstands, and then you know they've printed something the local governments didn't like. Even if you never read *Time* and *Newsweek* at home, you'll soon become addicted to them in South America!

The rest of this chapter concerns a variety of things that are going to be different for you in South America. Some of these differences are blatant and others are subtle, but if you understand how things work beforehand, you'll be more prepared for these changes as you travel.

Time

The South American sense of time is completely different from ours. There simply isn't the same kind of emphasis on punctuality, nor is there the same aversion to waiting. It's not considered rude to be anywhere from half an hour to an hour late for an appointment or dinner date.

You'll discover, too, that there isn't the same emphasis on efficiency. To most North Americans, South Americans are dismayingly slow and inefficient. But consider things in their terms, which should become *your* terms if you don't want to have a coronary on your vacation. To begin with, why should someone knock himself out when an ulcer may be his only reward? South Americans don't necessarily advance in their jobs by working harder—they're usually locked into that position for life. It's who you know, not how hard you work, that counts. And the resulting, more relaxed pace certainly makes work days more pleasant. On another level, a bus driver may ask himself what's really more important, sticking to a precise schedule or spending a little more time at his daughter's birthday party. Everyone sitting at the side of the road knows the bus will come sooner or later, so what's the rush?

These are some of the reasons I emphasize taking off your watch or leaving it home, giving yourself extra days and not scheduling every last minute of your trip. Never make too many appointments for one day; you won't make all of them and you'll end up feeling irritated.

I've found that organizations that deal with foreigners and have international connections, such as airlines, are the most efficient in our terms (five stars for Lufthansa), and that national and local bureaucracies are the worst (minus ten for the post office). Hence you should *always* allow yourself extra time to do such things as renew a visa, pick up packages and mail parcels home.

Once again—slow down, slow down, slow down. . . .

Machismo

South America is definitely a man's world. *Macho* means "masculine," "male" or "virile" and is an adjective of approbation for a South American male. If you're a woman a man tries to show he's *macho* by making passes at you, whispering comments, perhaps pinching you and by getting you to go to bed with him if he can.

There's a definite double standard, however, because if you actually do have sex with a South American man you are then a whore and he loses respect for you. I mention this as a warning to women. Unmarried South American women are closely chaperoned and many are never permitted to go out alone or on a date unless accompanied by another member of the family. This even applies to young women who have gone to college and have dated on their own in the United States. When they return to South America they are once again chaperoned. Obviously, a lone woman traveler appears disreputable.

It's also acceptable for a South American man to have a mistress on the side while it's not permissible for his wife to have a lover. For example, in Colombia a man can divorce his wife for adultery but she can divorce him for adultery *only* if there's a public scandal.

The *macho* complex is a Latin, not an Indian, trait and Indian men don't bother women travelers. Quechua standards are different because some Indians still engage in trial marriage, a custom dating back to Inca times which is socially sanctioned and does not penalize either party. If a trial marriage works the couple goes on to a formal marriage, and if it doesn't the couple separates. Any children resulting from a trial union are accepted by the community and the woman is still considered eligible for marriage.

Travelers should be cognizant of a Bolivian custom known as *viernes de soltero*, which means "Friday single" or "Friday unmarried." The white or *cholo* men, married or not, are "single" on Friday night; they go out to drink, carouse and visit whorehouses while their wives stay home and mind the children. Women are not welcome in bars and *cantinas* on Friday nights unless they're whores. It's a good night for a woman traveler to eat in a nice restaurant, go to a movie or stay in her hotel and write letters.

Class Consciousness

While it might be "in" to be an Indian in the United States today, it's definitely not a high-status situation in South America. To most people there, being Indian means being poor and exploited—the very bottom of the socio-economic pyramid. In fact, in Ecuador, Peru and Bolivia, *indio* (Indian) is not a racial term but refers to any person who lives, dresses and speaks as the Indians do. This means you could be a full-blooded Indian but be acknowledged as a mixed blood *(mestizo* or *cholo)* if you leave the Indian community, adopt Western dress and speak Spanish rather than Quechua or Aymara. You could even be acknowledged as white *(blanco)* if you meet the social and economic criteria. Patiño, the Bolivian tin multimillionaire, was accepted as *blanco* in Oruro, Bolivia, because of his wealth. On the other hand, you could be white and be recognized as Indian if you married into that community and lived as the Indians do.

Traditionally, *mestizo* refers to a mixed blood while *cholo* refers to an Indian who's moved into town, although sometimes the terms are used interchangeably. The Indians themselves are very aware of these distinctions. For example, in Peruvian jungle towns *cholo* carries the negative connotations of poverty and ignorance. There are terms for different skin colors, too: it's better to be called *trigueño* (brunette) than *moreno*, which is used to describe a dark or swarthy person. (Blacks are called both *morenos* and *negros*.)

In Bolivia, however, *cholo* has better connotations. For example, a country woman who can't speak Spanish is called a *moterosa*, while one who moves to the city and wears *chola* dress (bowler hat, manufactured shawl and *pollera* skirt) is called a *de vestido* or a *chola decente* ("dressed" or "decent" *chola*). Black-Indian mixtures are called *zambos*, and once again the distinction is cultural and economic. I saw a black woman in La Paz dressed in a bowler hat and *pollera* skirt who was recognized as a *chola decente*.

At the top of the heap are whites, who call themselves *blancos*, *gente decente* or *gente buena* ("decent" or "good" people). This is a cultural and economic distinction, since many members of the upper class have Indian blood. Being *blanco* usually implies that you never do manual labor, even to the extent of having a maid accompany you to the market to carry your purchases, and it also implies that you don't work with your hands at all. This undoubtedly is one reason the Indians were so intrigued when they saw me embroidering or spinning. In some areas whites are proud of their *limpieza de sangre* (purity of blood), which implies descent from one of the original Spanish settlers.

There is some class and cultural animosity in the Andean countries. In Ecuador the whites call Indians *longos feos* (dirty Indians) while the Indians call the upper classes *yuraq siquis* (white assholes). In Peru and Bolivia the Indian term for whites and powerful *cholos* is *mistis,* and the Indians prefer to be called *campesinos* (meaning "country people") rather than *indios. Indio* has a bad connotation to the Indians, based on four hundred years of poverty and mistreatment.

It saddened me that in middle- and upper-class Peruvian homes there was no sign of pride in Indian heritage—no beautiful handicrafts or textiles were visible. Instead, these Peruvians endeavored to emulate middle-class Americans who buy their furniture at Sears.

If you blossom out in full Indian regalia in the Andean countries, you look ridiculous. Indians don't understand it and probably think you're mocking them, while middle- and upper-class people think you're ludicrous. Ponchos are worn more often by the middle class in Colombia, Ecuador and Bolivia than in Peru. The choice is yours, but you should be sensitive to the situation. I save my magnificent Indian ponchos for San Francisco.

It's also irritating to South Americans when a woman wears a man's hat or poncho or vice versa. Any man wearing a bowler hat in La Paz would be laughed off the street, while a woman wearing an Indian man's poncho is also thought to be ridiculous.

Camera-shyness

Many Indians are camera-shy and dislike having their picture taken. Some of this is resentment at having their privacy invaded, but it also has to do with fear of the evil eye *(mal de ojo)* or witchcraft sickness *(mal daño).* For example, the Aymara believe that humans are born with three to five souls or lives and that photographs steal their souls and therefore hasten their death.

Try to be sensitive to people's feelings. If you must photograph, do it quickly and inconspicuously. A telephoto lens is sometimes helpful. Ask yourself if the photo is really necessary. And if someone objects strenuously, put your camera away.

Beggars

Beggars *(mendigos)* strike at the guilt most of us feel because we're prosperous, well fed and able to travel when so much of the world is going hungry. I've never satisfactorily resolved this. After all, I have money and the beggars don't, and a *peso* would probably help the old couple out. On the other hand, they'll still be on the street corner tomorrow and the day after because personal charity isn't getting at the root of the problem. (Most of these countries have no social-welfare programs.)

What should you do? I developed a policy which worked for me: I gave money to old, crippled or blind beggars, but not to children, since children seemed to approach only foreign tourists and I wasn't sure they were really needy. A friend of mine feels that giving money to children encourages people to mutilate the children in order to make them more effective beggars—and horrible as it sounds, it's true. I also watched to see how many Latins gave money to beggars, and some of them actually did—usually to the old, the crippled and the blind. If you're really reluctant to give away money, share food. While I don't give money to children, I've given little kids oranges and tangerines. (Give children something nourishing, not candy.) You also could let a kid earn money by carrying a lighter bag up to your hotel room, finding you a cab or helping you in the market. Kids love to help and be involved, and you can tip them a few *pesos* for their efforts.

Tipping

I've found most South Americans who serve the general public to be courteous and helpful. Because salaries are so incredibly low, a tip is definitely appreciated. We tipped the laundrywomen, waiters and waitresses, bartenders, hired help at the hotels, cab drivers and anyone who had gone out of his or her way to be helpful. In one case we ordered custom-knit vests at the market (due a week later), agreed on the price and left a deposit. The next week the vests weren't ready by the time we were ready to leave the market, so we left a message at the stand. That evening the owner walked all the way to our hotel with the vests, after having spent a long, tiring day at the market. The vests were lovely, and when we paid the woman we also gave her a tip, hoping she would use part of it to take the bus home. We appreciated her reliability and her craftsmanship and she appreciated the tip. (For more on tipping, see Chapter Twelve, "Food.")

Bargaining

Many people are embarrassed and uncomfortable about bargaining and I don't really understand why. It's a lot of fun! Although a few shops now have "Fixed Prices" signs (to attract tourists who are afraid to bargain), you'll find yourself bargaining on everything: the cost of a dozen oranges in the market, the price of your hotel room, a taxi fare or a traffic fine. South Americans aren't about to be cheated and there's a price below which they will not go. The idea is to come close to their price.

Start by asking "¿Cuánto cuesta?" ("How much does it cost?") or "¿Cuánto vale esto?" ("What is the value of this?"). The vendor then names a price. Although it's hard to generalize, my experience has been that you settle on sixty to eighty percent of the initial price. This surprises people who are used to bargaining in Mexico and Guatemala, where you often arrive at a price equal to half the asking price. In South America people seem to name a price much closer to what they actually want, unless they think you're an idiot and will pay anything. Once a person tells you how much he or she wants, you make a counter-offer. You can start as low as one-tenth to one-quarter of the asking price. The vendor will probably laugh in your face and make a counter-offer. Sometimes this process involves elaborate stories. The vendor tells you she's the sole supporter of seventeen children, two aging parents and needs an operation. So you raise your offer a little and tell her all your money has been stolen but you can't go home without buying a present for your mother. The bargaining continues until you agree on a price. The whole transaction can be completed in a few minutes, even seconds, unless you both get carried away telling tales of destitution. If you absolutely won't go higher and no agreement has been reached, walk away. This sometimes brings the person running after you.

All of this bargaining can go on without your saying much more than numbers. How much talking you do depends on the quality of your Spanish, and the vendor's, since many Indians speak only enough Spanish to transact business. Even if you don't know the Spanish words for numbers, you can write them down or use your fingers. You'll find, too, that bargaining in South America is less voluble than in Mexico. In Indian markets bartering is sometimes carried on silently—corn is exchanged for onions without a word being said. This system is based on an unspoken agreement in the Indian community as to the worth of various items. Outsiders usually offer cash, so a certain amount of verbal communication is necessary. Remember to start any transaction with a greeting, such as *"Buenos días"* or *"¿Cómo está?"*

Never bargain by deprecating the merchandise. If you're looking at an item of clothing, don't say, "I'll only give you fifty *pesos* because it's ugly and badly made." If that's the case, you have bad taste for wanting it in the first place. It is legitimate to point out a hole or flaw (nicely). If you're buying several items you can use that as a bargaining point. You might arrive at a good price because you're buying two sweaters and three pairs of gloves. Or the woman may not come down on her price but she'll throw in an extra little purse. When you agree, say, *"Está bien"* or *"Muy bien"* ("Very well") and hand over your money.

In South America, particularly when buying food in the market, you should be aware of a custom called the *yapa*. The *yapa* is "a little bit extra." For example, you've just bargained for a couple of onions and a dozen oranges. As you close the transaction the lady throws in an extra onion, which is your *yapa*. *Yapas* are usually given to steady customers or to people who buy a lot of goods at one time.

How do you know how much something is worth? With handicrafts, one sure way is to visit the tourist shops and study the prices. These shops usually buy from the same women in the market as you do and then mark the items up. Obviously, anything in the market should be less than in the shops. You can also ask other travelers what they paid for an item and where they bought it.

When shopping at the market, it's perfectly acceptable to handle and inspect the items you're interested in purchasing. (Just ask if you may see the items, and be sure to add *"por favor."*) In fact, careful scrutiny may increase a vendor's respect for you. Because I am a weaver and have learned some textile terminology in Spanish, I made good buys in textiles because the vendors knew I understood and appreciated their goods.

It's acceptable to bargain in almost any situation; no one is offended when you try and the worst that can happen is that the vendor will stick to his or her original price. Sometimes people are so tickled that you're willing to try that they reduce the price a little. People in the United States never think of bargaining over the cost of a hotel room, for example.

Don't neglect bartering either. I met two travelers in Cochabamba who had purchased ponchos in Ecuador, but liked the Bolivian ponchos better. They wondered what would happen if they tried to trade their ponchos at the market. "Try it" was my answer, so they did, and they returned from their venture with two Bolivian alpaca vests. (I've always wondered what two Ecuadorian ponchos hanging in a Bolivian market would do to the theories of visiting anthropologists.) You can trade just about anything—your old clothes, Swiss army knife, flashlight, etc.

Bribes

Since we've just discussed bargaining, it's appropriate to discuss bribes, since you'll bargain on them, too. A bribe is called a *mordida* (literally, a "bite"), and in Bolivia it's also known as a *coima*. I see bribery as a form of tipping. A little extra money makes things go better. You don't need to pay through the nose, however. How and when to bribe? Anytime you're harassed by the police or by any official, and anytime you run into baffling obstacles. For example:

§ The police tell you that your papers aren't in order because the name on your tourist card is Brian Buckley and the name on your passport is Brian Francis Buckley, or vice versa. It really couldn't matter less, but it's an opportunity for them to make a little extra money—at your expense.

§ You arrive at a hotel (with or without reservations) and are told there are no rooms available.

§ You want to ship a small package of handicrafts home, but the local Customs officials are giving you all kinds of trouble. You can't seem to penetrate the red-tape barrier.

§ You're caught with a joint or a gram of cocaine. (Good luck—bribes are less effective in drug arrests these days.)

§ You're delayed at Customs because you're carrying twenty rolls of film into the country, a few over the official allowance.

§ You arrive at the train station to buy a ticket and are told the ticket office is just closing for the weekend. Sorry.

In these situations the problem clears up if a little money changes hands. Obviously the ticket office's closing is much less serious than the drug situation, which you might not be able to bribe your way out of anyway. Your ticket may cost you fifty cents extra, while the drug arrest may run at least several hundred dollars, if they accept the bribe at all.

There are several ways to go about making payment. You could ask, "*¿Cómo podemos arreglar esto?*" ("How can we fix [or adjust] this?") or "*¿Hay una multa?*" ("Is there a fine?"). The official names a price, and you should immediately make a counter-offer. When the "fine" is agreed upon, you pay and it's settled. In the hotel and train station situations, just slip the clerk a small sum and say, "*Para usted*" or "*Por su ayuda*" ("For your help"). Help you will receive.

If you have to deal with bureaucracies—for example, if you want to change your status from tourist to resident so you can stay and teach English or open a shop—you may run into some procedural hassles. Red tape is called *trámites* and the person you pay to see a procedure (such as obtaining your resident visa) through the legal and procedural maze is called a *trámitor*. Remember this term, as a good *trámitor* can save you hassles and headaches. Some *tramitores* are government officials, but mostly they're just people who know the ropes.

If you're involved in more serious matters—for example, you've been arrested for drugs or you'd like to obtain an import license so you can bestow the blessings of pocket calculators on Peru—you'll need a lawyer *(abogado)*. Not just any attorney will do. The key word is *palanca*, which means "leverage," "pull" or "connections." It helps a great deal if your attorney is first cousin to the judge or the nephew of the president. The scales of justice weigh connections, not evidence. Therefore you need *un abogado con palanca* (an attorney with leverage), so ask around until you find one. South Americans know the value of *palanca* and who has it, and they'll steer you to the proper lawyer. He then handles the pay-offs.

If this chapter is beginning to upset you, remember that we aren't discussing theoretical political systems. We're discussing how things work and I'm giving it to you straight. If you're inclined to feel superior to this system, just remember some of the corrupt aspects of American political campaign contributions.

Kickbacks

Like bribery, kickbacks are a part of everyday life. The boy at the train
station who offers to take you to a good, cheap hotel gets a small sum
from the hotel, as does the taxi driver who offers to drive you to a good
restaurant.

In many places, owners of handicraft shops pay taxi drivers and tour
leaders who bring them customers. In Quito many shops pay tour leaders
up to ten percent of the amount sold to a group he or she brings in. If a
shop owner doesn't want to go along with this system, the tour leader
takes his or her group shopping elsewhere. I'm not making a moral
judgment on this kind of activity, but want you to know that a taxi driver
or tour leader who recommends a place isn't necessarily unbiased, but
is recommending a place that pays him to do so.

Transacting Business

Foreigners transacting business in South America, particularly young
people involved in exporting handicrafts or opening small shops or
restaurants, should take pains to appear respectable and businesslike.
Appearance is very important. A business card is a good thing to have;
you can have them printed in the United States or in South America.
It's also advisable to disassociate yourself from the drug culture and
hippie scene, especially if you want to open your business in a small
town. Local officials are very reluctant to allow hippies to move into
their communities and put innumerable barriers in your way should
you fit that image. If you're involved in anything really complex, it's
worth hiring a good *trámitor* or a good attorney, one with *palanca*.

Politics

With few exceptions, most South American countries are run by the
military. The coups (*golpes*) you hear so much about usually consist of
power struggles within the military and neither citizens of the country
nor travelers are involved in any violence. In many countries, there's
strict press censorship and little toleration of dissent. Civil disorders,
such as labor strikes and student demonstrations, are dealt with harshly.
My advice is to stay off the streets and away from demonstrations,
particularly if you feel there may be violence. On the whole, tourists
aren't in danger, primarily because they're usually not involved in local

or national politics. In some countries you could have books confiscated—I wouldn't travel in Bolivia with *The Diary of Che Guevara*. Be discreet.

Is there anti-Americanism and, if so, how do you deal with it? The first thing to remember is that the Spanish brutally exploited both the people and their land a good two hundred years before the United States won its independence. The descendants of the *conquistadores* have continued this fine family tradition. Some of the South American university students who are the most vocal critics of the United States come from wealthy families with large landholdings—taken from the Indians—and they have no intention of giving up the servants and cheap laborers on their *haciendas*.

For the most part, the Andean countries are populated by Indians and *campesinos* who are desperately poor, have no education, subsist on less than a thousand calories a day, have a high infant-mortality rate and a low life-expectancy and in large part exist outside the money economy. Not that they've always accepted their lot with resignation; these countries have a long history of mostly unsuccessful peasant rebellions and uprisings.

Besides the ruling classes' exploiting their own populations, the South American nations have also exploited each other. Chile took away Bolivia's seaport of Arica in the War of the Pacific (1879–83), Peru annexed a great deal of Ecuador's Oriente in the 1940s and Paraguay won an enormous portion of Bolivia's Chaco in the Chaco War (1933–35). Great Britain and other European nations also have had their fingers in the South American pie.

Now, however, the single greatest foreign power in South America is the United States. Unfortunately, this country is involved in what amounts to the exploitation of resources, suppression of nativist movements and interference in the politics of Latin American countries. A prime example is the recently exposed and disgusting role of the CIA in the overthrow of the government of (legally elected) Salvador Allende in Chile.

For all this, there's amazingly little anti-Americanism—probably because the average South American is unaware of the extent of America's influence. Perhaps the political turmoil of the 1960s and the vigorous American protests against our country's involvement in Indochina have shown South Americans that there's active opposition within the United States to some of our government's excesses. The response to me as a person has been one of warmth and kindness, mixed with curiosity and envy, and I think most travelers will find this to be the case. In fact, sometimes South Americans are more pro-American than I am.

If you do run into "*Yanqui,* go home" sentiment, quietly go your way, or tell the person you agree with their criticisms of the United States (if you think they're true).

It's irresponsible not to be aware of these issues, particularly the problems involving economic exploitation and social injustice. The following paperbacks provide excellent background reading:

The Shadow: Latin America Faces the Seventies, by Sven Lindqvist, translated by Keith Bradfield (Harmondsworth, England: Penguin Books, 1972). I always recommend this book because it's such a balanced and well-researched account of the problems facing Latin America. Lindqvist turns a critical eye on both the Latins and the United States. The book begins and ends with interviews of people living in the slums of Lima. It's gripping reading, and that's not true of most socio-economic writing.

The Diary of Che Guevara. Bolivia: November 7, 1966–October 7, 1967, edited by Robert Scheer (New York: Bantam Books, 1968). Here it is, Che's diary of his experiences as a guerrilla in Bolivia. Quite a story, but don't take it along on your trip. Che may be a folk hero, but he isn't popular with officials.

Peasant Rebellions in Latin America, by Gerrit Huizer (Harmondsworth, England: Penguin Books, 1973). Although this book isn't sold in the United States and Canada, it's available in England and South America. It has the best account of the successful 1950s *campesino* revolution in Bolivia that I've ever read.

Peru 1965: Notes on a Guerrilla Experience, by Héctor Béjar, translated by William Rose (New York: Monthly Review Press, 1970). Let a native Peruvian tell you why he picked up a rifle and took to the hills.

Land or Death: The Peasant Struggle in Peru, by Hugo Blanco (New York: Pathfinder Press, 1972). Hugo Blanco is a revolutionary who organized and led peasants in the Cuzco area in the 1960s. He was eventually jailed by the Peruvian government and was exiled to Mexico in 1971. If you want to understand why people feel compelled to resort to violence, read what Blanco has to say.

Thievery

Nearly every visitor to the Andes has an encounter with thieves. You have to realize that the very fact that you're able to travel makes you richer than ninety-five percent of the South Americans, many of whom are lucky to ever get outside their own village or city. It doesn't matter that you held an extra job on weekends, saved for two years and then sold everything you owned to make the trip. The fact that you're there makes you rich. Then, too, think of all the interesting things you have along—camera, watch, travel alarm, shoes, blue jeans, a good jacket— things which many South Americans will never own (unless they get them from you). Don't take anything along unless you're willing to part with it.

Understanding that you're among poor, hungry people doesn't make it any easier when something is stolen from you, so it's best to try to keep your possessions in your own hands for as long as possible. Before you leave buy traveler's property insurance from an agency such as American Express, so that at least you'll be able to replace items if they're stolen. Many renter's and homeowner's insurance policies also cover your possessions while you're traveling. Make a note of the serial numbers and models of all equipment so that you can make a proper report to the insurance company should things disappear. Next, buy a money belt and wear it at all times, with your passport, health card, cash and travelers checks inside. (If you don't wear it, check it at the hotel and get a receipt.) Don't travel with an open-top bag or unlockable luggage and don't carry money or cameras in your pockets. Keep an eye, or better yet, a hand on your things.

The following are first-hand examples of thievery which happened to me or my friends. My purpose isn't to terrify you but to give you an idea of the kinds of situations in which theft occurs so you can take proper precautions.

A friend was sunning on the beach in Cartagena with her camera next to her. Someone came along at a run, scooped up her camera and kept running. It's a good idea to keep your camera attached to your body, preferably with an uncuttable, unbreakable strap. Another good precaution is to take out the camera only when you're actually using it. If you're at the beach, take a few pictures, check the camera at the hotel and then go back to the beach and relax.

Another friend had an Instamatic camera lifted from his back pocket on a crowded bus in Quito. A Peace Corps volunteer who should have known better had his wallet picked from his back pocket on a bus in the same city. The obvious solution is not to carry valuables in back pockets and to be especially alert on crowded city buses.

An American woman living in Colombia had her open-top purse picked on the street in Bogotá. Another American resident of Colombia was carrying two packages to the post office in Bogotá when two men came running from behind. Each man grabbed a package; then they ran off in different directions. The American chased one man and recovered a parcel but the other thief got away. I really don't know what preventive measures he could have taken in this situation. It was just one of those things.

Colombia has a well-deserved reputation for thievery. There's a lot of purse-snatching and pickpocketing in Cali, Bogotá and other large cities, usually aimed at tourists. For that reason I never carry a camera or purse in Bogotá. I tuck the equivalent of a few dollars in an inside pocket and carry a bit of Kleenex and sometimes my notebook and pen, but no purse to tempt people. Watches are often pulled right off wrists in Colombia, so wear yours high on your forearm under your shirt, or remove it and carry it in your money belt. The same goes for jewelry. Don't flaunt it. In fact, don't wear it at all. Earrings are ripped right off ears—if you have pierced ears, beware! And hang on to your camera. If you must carry it around, keep it hidden under your jacket or poncho.

Another common scam in Bogotá is for several men to approach a tourist and hastily identify themselves as plainclothes police. They say they suspect that the camera was stolen and must take it to the police station to check it out. They offer a totally worthless receipt and then disappear with the camera. For good. They aren't police. Never, never surrender your camera (or anything else) to anyone, and don't go along with them if they ask you to come to the station. Instead, step into a shop or restaurant or call a uniformed policeman. Your insistence on involving uniformed police causes the phony police to leave fast. There are variations on this routine. Always remember not to let anyone, no matter how official he appears, walk off with your things on the street. I know of no instances in which travelers' possessions have been confiscated by the real police as suspected stolen goods. In many Colombian cities, including Bogotá and Cartagena, there are uniformed tourist police who wear white armbands. If it looks like trouble, yell for one or find one quickly.

Although I'm coming down on Colombia especially hard for theft there's an historical explanation for some of this lawlessness. Beginning with the assassination of the Liberal politician Jorge Gaitán in 1948, Colombia exploded in an orgy of violence named, appropriately, *la violencia*. Initially an undeclared civil war between Liberals and Conservatives, *la violencia* claimed between 200,000 and 300,000 lives in two waves, 1948–53 and 1955–63, with isolated outbreaks since. It's difficult to find a Colombian who hasn't lost a friend or family member to *la violencia*. The last outbreak in particular was less a political feud than sheer banditry, with numerous acts of robbery, murder and savage mutilation performed by organized groups, usually led by a *capitán* with some outrageous nickname. Buses left cities only in armed convoys.

While the average traveler isn't likely to be subjected to physical violence, *la violencia* has sufficiently disrupted the fabric of Colombian society to make general acts of lawlessness, especially thievery, fairly common.

In addition to the past decade's *violencia*, there has been some leftist and Communist-led guerrilla warfare in the countryside. However, the guerrillas' target is the government, rather than travelers and poor *campesinos*. I came across no horror stories from travelers other than tales of ordinary thievery. My feeling is that Colombia's stability is tenuous, but that unless another wave of *la violencia* erupts in full fury, travelers are as safe there as in the other Andean countries.

Because Colombia is renowned for thievery many travelers go through the country in a state of intense paranoia and alertness. By the time they reach Ecuador they relax and promptly have something stolen. I've never had anything stolen in Colombia although two boys tried to pick Bill's pocket in Popayán. On the other hand, my travel alarm was stolen from an unlocked, zippered bag at the airport in Guayaquil, Ecuador. This was a classic case of ignoring my own advice. You can buy small, cheap locks in hardware and dime stores in the United States that will hardly stop a determined burglar, but will keep someone from slipping a hand into your bag. I didn't have enough locks for all my bags so I tied them shut for the rest of the trip. Always keep an eye on your things at airports. A number of people usually compete for the chance to carry your luggage to the taxi or bus, and bags can be stolen easily in the confusion.

Be extra alert in train and bus stations, especially in Peru, where there are so many tourists that thieves have easy pickings. My father's camera was stolen from the train in Arequipa, Peru. In this case we foolishly left my mother alone in the coach guarding a large pile of belongings. The camera case was on the seat across from her. As she noted later, the theft occurred when we ignored our own rule of keeping camera equipment attached to our bodies. In this case, if the strap had been looped over her shoulder (or if my father had been carrying it), the thief would have been deterred.

Conventional leather camera bags (the kind my father had) are bulky and inconvenient and aren't even dust- and waterproof. Besides, you might as well put a sign on it saying "Expensive Camera, Steal Me." I made a quilted bag for my movie camera that didn't look like a camera bag at all. It not only fooled thieves but also fooled the Indians, who are camera-shy and become wary when they see tourists approaching with conventional equipment.

There's also a lot of thievery at the train and bus stations in Huancayo, Peru. It's quite possible that the ticket-sellers are in cahoots with the thieves, since some travelers I met had the feeling that ticket agents noted where they kept their wallets and may have informed the thieves,

who picked pockets and purses during the crowding and confusion
that occur at boarding times.

While I was in the Bank of America in La Paz, a Japanese tourist had
his luggage stolen while he was transacting business. He put his suitcase
down next to him and someone quietly picked it up and walked out. No
one, including the bank guard, noticed anything amiss. A good habit to
get into is to put your luggage between your legs and grip tight. That way
you'll feel the pull if someone tries to take it. You might look like you
desperately have to pee, but you won't lose your suitcase. In restaurants
and trains, wrap luggage and camera straps around your arm or ankle.
In this case the tourist lost everything he had, including an expensive
camera and travelers checks. Not only that, but he left his list of serial
numbers attached to his checks so he was in for one hell of a time obtaining refunds.

Also be careful when you hang your laundry on clotheslines at hotels.
You won't know who's to blame for the disappearance of those precious
blue jeans, but it could easily be another traveler in need of replenishing
his wardrobe. Lots of clothing disappears this way. It's safer to hang
clothes in your room unless you give the whole load to a laundress, who
keeps an eye on them as part of her job.

The market in Cochabamba, Bolivia, is gaining a reputation for
thievery equal to Colombia's. One friend had her purse slit and another had her purse picked while we were shopping together. Again,
neither of us noticed anything wrong until it was time to pay for a shawl
and my friend realized her money was gone. I had my pocket slit in the
same market. I was buying a lot of textiles and handicrafts and couldn't
fit all the money in my money belt, so I put it in my pocket and pinned
the pocket shut. Fortunately I realized what was happening when I
started getting shoved, so I didn't lose any money. A better solution,
which I subsequently tried, was putting extra money in a small pouch
which I wore *under* my shirt so the strap couldn't be slit.

My most frightening encounter with a thief occurred one evening in
La Paz when I returned happy and high from a Bach and Beethoven flute
concert and surprised a thief in my hotel room. He had picked the lock or
used a key which fit my door and I discovered him in the act. He turned
out the light and jumped on me, and I was so startled I fought with him.
He got out of my room, I chased him through the upstairs lobby and
down the stairs and the manager finally nabbed him at the door.

Although I shook for several hours afterward, I realized something
about robbery in South America that was of some comfort. Thieves are
mainly after your possessions and are less interested in doing you bodily
harm. The thief in my room only wanted to escape. He had no weapon
of any kind nor did he seem interested in raping or hurting me. Most

thievery is of the sneaky, stealthy kind—your purse or pocket is picked or slit and the thief slips away. In most places thieves are too poor to own a weapon, and gun control is very strict. In Bolivia, for example, no citizen can own the same kind of weapon used by the army or police. This effectively rules out the average poor Bolivian's owning a gun more modern than a musket. (The middle and upper classes ignore the law.) So, although you might lose your property on your trip, you're unlikely to be personally harmed.

While you should always be reasonably cautious when traveling, be sure you take with you only things that are insurable and replaceable. Don't take something that's precious—leave it at home so you won't worry about it. If something is stolen during your trip, report this to the police and get a statement from them. (They usually prepare a very impressive document.) Then report the loss to your insurance carrier as quickly as possible. Above all, don't let the theft ruin your trip.

Traffic

Automobiles, not pedestrians, have the right of way in South America. It's another case illustrating the primacy of brute force and seems to be connected with the *macho* complex. Traffic doesn't slow down in the slightest for blind, old men or crippled ladies. While traffic lights usually help keep things somewhat under control, don't rely on them. Be alert and fast on your feet, and cross wherever and whenever you can. Don't worry about things like jaywalking—worry about being run down. It's even more exciting at night. Many people drive with their headlights off under the mistaken impression that they're saving wear and tear on the engine. Vehicles also travel at breakneck speeds on either side of the road, or right down the middle, particularly in mountainous areas where drivers try to avoid ruts.

In cities and towns many intersections are blind because buildings are set right on the street. A driver customarily announces his arrival at an intersection by honking, and then he barrels on through. I never did get used to this kind of noise pollution, the many near collisions or what seemed to be deliberate attempts on my life.

Toilets and Sanitation

Some people never do adjust to South American sanitary conditions. People there are more natural about natural functions. Pretty soon you will be, too, although it's still jolting to see a well-groomed Ecuadorian businessman urinating against the side of a bank in downtown Quito.

When you do use a toilet, you're in for more surprises. First, there's *never* a toilet seat on the toilet, although you may see one propped up against the wall. Second, *you* supply the toilet paper *(papel higiénico, papel sanitario)*, although occasionally the management throws in an old magazine or newspaper. When you're finished, you don't throw the toilet paper in the toilet. Sewage systems aren't designed to handle paper and you can really clog up the works by throwing paper in the john. Instead, you throw it on the floor or (rarely) in a wastebasket, and the maid occasionally sweeps the whole place out. It neither looks, smells, nor is very sanitary. In fact, sometimes it's downright disgusting, but that's how it works.

In more remote areas, the toilet is the pig sty. (This has done nothing to increase my appetite for pork.) By the time you're this far into the countryside you'll have learned to keep your pocket stuffed with toilet paper. Another hint—before you go to the sty, pick up a handful of pebbles to throw at the pigs so you can do your business in safety.

Elevators

South American elevators have all the usual numbers, plus "PB," which stands for *planta baja,* the ground floor. When you want to reach the main floor, push "PB," not "1." The first floor is what we usually call the second floor, and so on. Floor is *piso*—*primero piso* (first floor), *segundo piso* (second floor), *tercero piso* (third floor), etc.

Movies

I never see movies at home anymore—they're too expensive. Instead, I catch them in South America, where they cost between twenty-five and fifty cents. Besides American movies (with Spanish subtitles), European, Indian, Chinese, Japanese, Mexican and Argentine films are also shown. In Bolivian towns there's usually a bulletin board in the main plaza that lists all the local theaters *(cines* or *teatros)*. Shows *(estrenos)* start at the same time every night, usually 6:30 P.M. and 9:00 P.M. Movies change once or twice a week, and there's generally a crowd around the bulletin board checking out what film to see that particular evening.

Westerns are very popular, as are Kung Fu movies. In fact, anything violent and bloody is popular, along with religious themes. You might have a choice of such double features as *Bambi* and *Dirty Harry, The Ten Commandments* and *Superfly,* or *The Godfather* and *Beach Blanket Bingo.* The movies are preceded by 35-mm slide advertisements for such things as toilets, shoes and Pepsi, and by a newsreel sponsored by Iberia Airlines. This media barrage always left me stunned and had no connection whatsoever with anything in the lives of the average Indian audience, which was largely made up of Indian women who refused to remove their hats. I never attended a movie theater anywhere that wasn't packed, especially on weekends. It's a great way to pass time if you're stuck somewhere.

Sports

Soccer (*fútbol*) is a very popular sport in South America, and a match is a fast-paced, highly skilled event. The only problem is that soccer fans sometimes get out of hand, venting their enthusiasm and high spirits indiscriminately, and every so often mayhem and murder result. This happens most frequently during international championship matches, when national pride is involved.

Bullfighting (*la corrida de torros*) is also popular, and the best Spanish matadors appear in the capital cities. Although I'm not attracted to this sport, I'll attend a bullfight before making a judgment.

Pelota de guante (gloveball) is Ecuador's national sport and it's said to be difficult and exciting. You should be aware of it in case you have the opportunity to see a match. (Sports events aren't expensive and a ticket shouldn't cost more than a dollar.)

Peruvians and Bolivians play several dice games with a leather cup and five dice. *Cacho* is one such game and any number can play. *Cacho* and other table games are often played in the *cantinas* accompanied by lots of beer. Ask someone to teach you.

Sapo (toad) is another popular game played in the *chicherías* (chicha taverns). Metal discs or coins are tossed at the open mouth of a metal toad, and points are scored. It's easy to join these games and local residents welcome eager participants. South Americans often seem apologetic about their culture, as if they're certain it's inferior to that of North America, so when you express a genuine interest in and enjoyment of their culture and customs, they're delighted to teach you.

Tourist Offices

As with many other agencies, you have to learn how to make tourist offices (*oficinas de turismo*) work for you. Almost every city and decent-sized town in South America has one. Just ask.

I visit tourist offices primarily to obtain maps. Major cities and towns usually issue city maps free of charge. Some of these maps are printed in English as well as Spanish, and they often contain very complete listings of restaurants, hotels, museums, handicraft shops, schools, laundries, beauty salons, hospitals and clinics, banks, the post office, the long-distance telephone office and more. Once you have one of these maps, you're all set. Ask for a *mapa* (map) or *guía turística* (tourist guide).

The tourist office is designed to help travelers, and the staff is generally very friendly. The only problem is that they often misinterpret what you want, so it's best to go in with very specific questions. If you wander in and ask, "What's there to do in town?" you'll probably be sent to a tacky nightclub run by the office manager's brother. On the other hand, if you ask if there's a *peña folklórica* (folk music club) in the vicinity, you'll probably spend an evening more to your liking. When you ask about lodging, once again be specific ("A hotel with hot water that costs under a dollar a night"), or you'll be sent to the Hilton. Be sure to ask if there are archaeological sites or ruins nearby and how you can get to them by truck or by bus, or they might insist you have to hire a cab.

Don't let the tourist office tell you something is "impossible" or that "you really don't want to see that." (I got the latter response when I wanted to visit a weaving village.) South Americans often overestimate the amount of money travelers have to spend and underestimate travelers' interest in their culture. If a town is noted for its handicrafts, find out if you can watch the artisans at work. For example, in Cuenca, Ecuador, it's possible to visit workshops in which the famous, but misnamed, Panama hats are finished.

You might also want to inquire about swimming pools *(piscinas)* open to the public. Some private clubs and many of the better hotels have pools that are open to visitors for a nominal fee, usually about a quarter. I treated myself to refreshing visits at a nearby pool during a long stay in Cochabamba.

If you feel you've been gouged or overcharged, you can register such a complaint at the tourist office, but if you've enjoyed your stay or if a hotel manager or shop owner has been especially helpful, be sure to mention that, too.

The Metric System

The United States is in the process of converting to the metric system of weights and measures, which is in use throughout South America. The following table lists the conversions you're most likely to use during your trip, but you'll find it much easier to put away your slide rule and learn to think in metric terms.

1 kilometer = .62 mile

So, when you see a sign saying "100 kilometers" it's about 60 miles. I convert kilometers to miles simply by dividing by 2 and adding a bit more. On bus rides, this gives me a rough estimate in miles without using pencil and paper.

1 centimeter = .39 inch
100 centimeters = 1 meter = 1.09 yards

A meter is a little more than a yard, so when buying cloth by the meter you'll get a bit extra if you're thinking in yard measurements.

1 liter = 1.06 quarts

This is so close you can pretty much consider quarts and liters the same. A gallon is 3.78 liters.

1 kilogram = 2.2 pounds

A *libra* is half a kilogram. Roughly then, 1 *libra* equals 1 pound (1.1 pounds to be exact).

0° Celsius = 32° Fahrenheit (freezing)
100° Celsius = 212° Fahrenheit (boiling)

The formula for converting temperature from Celsius to Fahrenheit is to divide the degrees Celsius by 5, multiply by 9 and add 32. It's much easier to learn to think in Celsius. 10° C (50° F) is chilly. When it's 25° C (77° F) it's a warm, pleasant day.

Common Initials and Acronyms

A.A. ‖ *Apartado Aéreo,* an airmail post-office box.

C.I.A. ‖ Not the United States intelligence agency, but *companía,* company.

COMIBOL ‖ *Corporación Minera de Bolivia,* Mining Corporation of Bolivia.

COPISA ‖ *Companía Peruana Internacional de Aviación, S.A.,* Peruvian International Aviation Company.

DAS ‖ *Departamento Administrativo de Seguridad,* the Colombian Security Police.

EE.UU. ‖ E.U. stands for *Estado Unido,* United State. Double initials make a plural; so EE.UU. is *Estados Unidos,* United States (of America).

ENC ‖ *Empresa Nacional de Correos,* National Postal Enterprise.

ENTEL ‖ *Empresa Nacional de Telecomunicaciones,* National Telecommunications Enterprise.

FF.AA. ‖ *Fuerzas Armadas,* the armed forces.

FF.CC. ‖ F.C. is *ferrocarril,* railroad; so FF.CC. is the plural, *ferrocarriles,* railroads.

ISS || *Instituto de Seguro Social,* Social Security Institute.

LAB || *Lloyd Aéreo Boliviano,* Bolivian Lloyd Airlines.

LAN || *Líneas Aéreas Nacionales,* National Air Lines.

PCN || *Policía Civil Nacional,* National Civil Police.

S.A. || *Sociedad Anónima,* Anonymous Society, meaning an incorporated company that sells stock. It also stands for *Sud America,* South America.

SAM or SAN || *Servicios Aéreos Militares* (or *Nacionales),* Military, or National, Air Services.

SATCO || *Servicios Aéreos de Transporte Comercial,* Commercial Air Transport Services. There are several airlines with variations of these initials.

SNEM || *Servicio Nacional de Eradicación de Malaria,* National Service for the Eradication of Malaria.

SOP || *Secretaría de Obras Públicas,* Secretary of Public Works.

TAM(E) || *Transportes Aéreos Militares (Ecuatorianas),* (Ecuadorean) Military Air Transport.

YPFB || *Yacimientos Petroliferos Fiscales Bolivianos,* Bolivian State Petroleum Field Enterprise.

Communications

y now you've figured out that there's usually some catch to doing things in South America. The catch to communicating with the outside world is that it may not happen and it's impossible to predict why. Take the mails. The chances of any airmail letter getting through are no better than 70–30. The odds for any airmail letter containing a check are even worse. Packages are worst of all, although your chances depend on how interesting the contents are to whoever handles the package.

Mail

Forget surface mail for letters and postcards. Air mail takes long enough, and surface mail takes a good six months—if it makes it at all. Mail service depends on many factors, including the political situation in a country, how the mail is routed, whether or not the postal employees are on strike and how the postmaster feels that particular day. I've had an airmail letter from the United States reach me in La Paz in five days, while another airmail letter sent to La Paz was returned to the sender in San Francisco after six months in postal limbo. I've also mailed letters from Bolivia and Peru that arrived in England and the United States in a week, while another group of letters sent airmail from Ecuador took two months. Don't ask me why.

After consulting my friends when I returned home, I figured out that I received about fifty percent of all correspondence airmailed to me. Some of it has since been returned to the senders and the rest has disappeared off the face of the earth. I don't mean to discourage you from trying to communicate—I just want to alert you to the unreliable nature of the mails.

RECEIVING MAIL

There are three possible ways for the average traveler to receive his or her mail. Letters and packages can be addressed to a person in care of General Delivery (*Lista de Correos*), American Express or an embassy or consulate. To ensure (as much as possible) that a letter is delivered to its destination, tell your correspondents to print or type your name and address very clearly on the envelope and remind them to use average, unexciting airmail stamps to discourage budding stamp collectors in the postal system from swiping your letter to get the stamps.

If you have your mail addressed to General Delivery, it's best to have it sent to a large city served by air. It makes no sense for a letter to arrive in La Paz in five days and then take two months to go overland from there to Ayata. All letters in care of General Delivery should be addressed as follows:

> Your name
> c/o *Lista de Correos*
> City, Department or State
> Country
> Continent

In many cities the *Lista de Correos,* literally the "list of the mail," is exactly that—a typewritten or handprinted list of all incoming mail that's posted daily or weekly in *el correo* (the post office). A person is usually listed alphabetically by last name, but you never can tell. It's best to look under each of your initials. To avoid unnecessary confusion arising from South American surname usage (see page 80), don't have mail addressed to you with your middle name, since a letter addressed to Lynn Ann Meisch might get listed under "A."

In other cities the list isn't posted, so you have to inquire at the post office. Whether or not you get your mail depends on if and how the clerk deciphers your name. It's best to present your passport or to print your name clearly on a piece of paper. Sometimes you can watch while the postal clerk sorts through the mail; this way you can make sure he doesn't miss any letters for you. I've become very adept at reading upside-down and I always watch like a hawk, since I've caught clerks casually passing over letters for me.

To claim your mail you need to show some identification, so have your passport handy. Mail sent in care of General Delivery is held for about thirty days.

It's also possible to rent a post office box (*casilla* or *apartado*) if you're staying in a town for any length of time. It certainly beats General Delivery, since the clerks are more adept at matching the box number on a letter with the correct box than they are at deciphering names. In many cases it's a lot quicker, too, since often there are long lines at the *Lista de Correos* windows of post offices located in large cities and tourist towns.

If you have mail sent to you in care of an embassy or consulate, make sure there *is* an embassy or consulate in that city. If you choose to receive your mail this way, it works best in the capital cities of Bogotá, Quito, Lima and La Paz.

American Express also receives mail for travelers, but this service is provided free of charge only if you're an American Express client. To prove this, simply present your American Express card or travelers checks. Otherwise the charge is one dollar per letter. If you've already used up your American Express travelers checks, some proof of purchase, such as your receipt, works for claiming mail.

American Express offices keep regular business hours, but you can't just saunter in and pick up your mail any old time. Usually mail is given out at specific times, and these hours aren't flexible. If you're coming into a city to pick up mail, be sure to allow yourself an extra day to get it, in case you arrive after the mail has been given out for that day. For instance, if mail hours are from 2 P.M. to 3 P.M. daily and you walk in at 3:10 P.M., you won't get your mail, even though you have tickets on a 5 P.M. train out of the city.

American Express holds mail for thirty days and then returns it, so check with them frequently. They won't hold packages for you, however, since they don't have the space to store them. Instead, they send a package back to the post office and notify you of its arrival. It's then up to you to find the parcel in the maze known as the postal system. In La Paz, for example, there are four different buildings in which overseas packages are kept, and you have to check out all four.

The following list includes all the American Express offices located in the Andean countries:

Colombia

Mailing Address
Tierra Mar Aire Ltda.
Casilla 21–93
Barranquilla, Colombia

Office Location
Calle 35, No. 44–43
Telephone: 31933 or 317183

Tierra Mar Aire, Ltda.
Apartado Aéreo 5371
Bogotá, Colombia

Edificio Bavaria Torre B.
Locale 126, Carrera 10 #27–91
Telephone: 283-2955

Also: Calle 92 #15–63
Telephone: 257-3642 or 257-3682

Tierra Mar Aire, Ltda.
Casilla 44–64
Cali, Colombia

Carrera 3 #8–13
Telephone: 731–333 or 741–444

Tierra Mar Aire, Ltda.
Casilla 2761
Cartagena, Colombia

Carrera 4 #7–196 Bgrde.
Telephone: 43442 or 43646

Same as office

Tierra Mar Aire, Ltda.
Calle 49A #46–32
Medellin, Colombia
Telephone: 422228 or 450573

Same as office

Tierra Mar Aire, Ltda.
Carrera 4 #14–35
Santa Marta, Colombia
Telephone: 3497 or 4190

Ecuador

Mailing Address
Ecuadorian Tours, S.A.
Casilla 3862
Guayaquil, Ecuador

Office Location
9 de Octubre 1500
Telephone: 397–111

Ecuadorian Tours, S.A.
Casilla 2605
Quito, Ecuador

Rio Amazonas 339
Telephone: 528–177 or 520–777

Peru

Mailing Address
Lima Tours, S.A.
Casilla 67
Arequipa, Peru

Office Location
Santa Catalina 120
Telephone: 276–624 or 276–633

Lima Tours, S.A.
Casilla 531
Cuzco, Peru

Avenida Sol Norte 567
Telephone: 2809

Explorama Tours
Casilla 446
Iquitos, Peru

696 Sargenta Lores
Telephone: 235–471 or 235–063

Lima Tours, S.A.   Belen 1040
Casilla 4340   Telephone: 276–624
Lima, Peru

Bolivia

Mailing Address   *Office Location*
Magri Turismo Ltda.   Avenida 16 de Julio 1490
Casilla 4469   Edificio Avenida, 5th floor
La Paz, Bolivia   Telephone: 341–201 or 232–954

It's not a good idea to have letters sent to you certified or registered. It doesn't guarantee you'll receive the mail—it just takes longer. You have to go to the main post office to retrieve certified or registered mail and the red tape isn't worth it.

Nothing of value should be sent to you by mail, especially money, because there's a good chance it will be stolen. A friend living in Colombia had his mail sent to an *apartado* in Bogotá's main post office. One day he arrived at the post office and realized his key was with a friend. He could see two letters through the glass window of his box, and one letter contained a long-awaited check; so he told the clerk he didn't have his key but that he had to get the letters because he was expecting money. That was a big mistake. He watched the clerk take two letters out of his box. A short time later the clerk came to the window with *one* letter for him. He had to send a quick "stop-payment" letter to the States and wait for his money all over again.

There's no use complaining in a situation like this—everyone in the postal system probably gets some of the booty. The fact that a letter is registered makes no difference; inquiries are just thrown away. For some reason, thieves aren't deterred by the fact that they may not be able to cash a check or money order they've stolen. If they think there's any chance whatsoever of getting something out of it, they'll steal a check out of the mail, no matter what kind it is nor how difficult it is to cash.

It's not a good idea to have packages sent to you by mail either because just about anything of value gets stolen. Although some packages do get through, especially to Ecuador and Bolivia (a friend received medicine mailed to her in La Paz), you just can't count on it. For example, Colombia prohibits the importation of certain foodstuffs, but the regulations don't specify which ones. This gives postal officials carte blanche to confiscate anything that strikes their fancy. Good-bye to that package containing peanut butter and an eagerly awaited yogurt starter. The peanut butter may eventually grace some Colombian's dinner table and the yogurt starter may go to the pigs, but you can bet you won't see any of it.

I actually did receive a package of paperback books I had airmailed to me in Lima, but it took me several days of agony to retrieve it from the post office. I finally had to find some important official and do one of those disgusting, nice-young-lady-about-to-burst-into-tears numbers —which wasn't far from the truth. I was leaving Lima the next day and the two days I had allotted to reclaim my books weren't enough. The problem seemed to be that since the package was insured for $50, the postal officials couldn't believe there were only books inside—maybe they thought there were diamonds hidden in the book bindings. Even after they inspected all the books they were skeptical. One lesson I learned from this experience was never to insure packages for more than they're worth because it makes postal officials suspicious. Perhaps I could have gotten my books easily if they'd been insured for only $15, or not insured at all, or if I had offered someone a bribe at the first sign of trouble. I finally ended up paying $1.10 for the package, which outraged my Peruvian friends, who said I shouldn't have paid a cent. I guess I was lucky the books weren't stolen outright.

Besides the problem of thievery, import duties on overseas packages are high and are capriciously applied. Assuming the near impossible— that a package does get through—you can easily find yourself paying double the worth of the items in duty alone. It's best to plan ahead and carry all necessary items with you, rather than having goods sent to you later on.

SENDING MAIL

As I have stated, all letters or postcards mailed from the Andean countries should be sent airmail. They also should be sent from a major city

since the donkey carrying your letter to the main post office in the capital could take weeks to arrive there. It's a good idea to address your letters in indelible ink. If a letter is particularly vital—for example, "Send money"—I recommend mailing several copies of the same letter at weekly intervals. Better yet, send a telegram as well as the letters.

The post office is called *el correo* or *la casa de correos* and is usually centrally located on or just off a town's main plaza. In small towns the post office can be located in just about any building, from the general store to the postmaster's residence. Just ask. Usually there are booths inside or outside the post office where you can buy postcards *(tarjetas postales)*, paper *(papel)*, greeting cards *(tarjetas)* and aerogrammes *(aerogramas)*.

You can send an airmail letter from any post office, except in Colombia (see below). Sometimes there are separate windows for air mail *(correo aéreo)* and surface mail *(correo ordinario)*. Stamps are called *estampillas* or *timbres*, and special delivery is *entrega inmediata*. When sending postcards, it's always best to buy stamps and affix them to the cards *before* you write anything since many stamps are large and may only be available in small denominations, so that they cover up most of the writing surface.

Colombia has completely separate postal systems for surface and air mail, so be sure you find the correct building or use the correct mailbox. Surface mail is categorized as *correo urbano* (city mail) and *correo nacional* (national mail), and the boxes are painted green. Air mail is called *correo aéreo* and the boxes are painted yellow.

Hotels and stores throughout the Andean countries sometimes have boxes (marked *buzón)* for the collection of mail.

It's possible to mail a package home, although frequently there's an agonizing amount of red tape involved. Packages mailed out of the Andean countries seem to arrive at their destinations more regularly than packages coming in, perhaps because outgoing parcels often contain folk art and handicrafts, which the locals don't consider worth stealing. If your package is heavy and there's no need for it to arrive home quickly, you may want to send it surface mail. Although it may take months, it's cheaper than airmail.

When taking a package to the post office, be sure to leave it open so that it can be inspected. Take tape, string, paper, magic marker and your Swiss army knife along so you can wrap the package in front of the inspectors after they've checked it.

I've found air freight to be more reliable than the mails for sending packages home, although it's more expensive. However you ship things, Peru seems to present the most difficulties and persists in taxing exported animal products, which includes most handicrafts. It's best to ship your Peruvian souvenirs from Ecuador or Bolivia.

Air Freight

The airlines that fly passengers to South America also carry cargo, and I've found this to be an excellent way of shipping goods home. Air freight is fast, too—I've had packages travel from La Paz to San Francisco in just five days.

Air freight rates are determined by weight and usually get better on heavier shipments. There's also a minimum weight required—about five to ten kilos. Goods should be packed securely and delivered to the airline cargo office, unless the company advises you otherwise. You can pay when the package is shipped or send it collect. When you send a package air freight, it's a good idea to insure it. Although the airlines have never lost any of my packages, this has been known to happen. For further details regarding air-freight service, inquire at any airline office and they'll connect you with their cargo department.

The airline will handle all Customs inspections for you. Just be sure to include two invoices for Customs officials. (For information on shipping goods home or returning with them, see "United States Customs and Duty," at the end of this book.)

Toward the end of our first trip, Bill and I collected all the things we didn't think we'd need on our way back north and air-freighted them home from Quito. We labeled the box "American Goods Returned" so Customs officials would realize we hadn't bought the stuff abroad and wouldn't charge us duty on it. (Although there's no duty imposed on American goods re-entering the country, don't try to sneak foreign goods in with them—Customs officials aren't stupid.) Shipping these items home afforded us more room in our suitcases to carry our South American treasures into the United States, thus taking advantage of our $100 duty-free allowance.

Telephones

In many South American countries private telephones must be purchased by the subscriber, often to the tune of several thousand dollars, and the waiting period for a phone can be several years. In effect, each subscriber is buying stock in the system. Once purchased, a phone continues to be listed under the name of the original subscriber (even after he or she dies!), and the telephone and number come with the house. Therefore you'll save yourself a lot of trouble if you get the telephone numbers of any friends or relatives in South America before you leave since you may not find them listed in the directory (*guía de teléfonos* or *directorio telefónico*). In fact, you may not find a directory at all.

Public phones are extremely frustrating, because usually there are no directions and no directories and you have no way of knowing what kind of coin, or how many, to deposit. I find it much easier to use a phone in a restaurant or store, since the people there are often helpful and will sometimes make the call for you. There's usually a charge—about five or ten cents.

HOTEL PHONES

When you pick up the phone in your hotel room, the switchboard at the main desk lights up or rings, and the person at the main desk answers. You should respond with *"Bueno."* Unless you want room service or another hotel service, ask for *una línea* (a line), and the switchboard operator will give you an outside line. As soon as you hear the dial tone, place your call *(llamada)*.

LONG DISTANCE

Placing a long distance call isn't easy. There are generally two places in a city that are equipped to do this: first-class hotels and the long distance office *(la oficina de larga distancia)*. It's easiest to make your call at a hotel, but sometimes it's a service offered only to guests.

There are two kinds of long distance calls: person to person *(persona a persona)* and station to station *(a quien contesta*—literally, "whoever answers")*. A collect call is called *una llamada al cobrar.* However, Ecuador is the only country in which you can make a collect call to the United States from a public phone.

The long distance office is usually located in the center of the city. It's frequently located in the same building as the telegraph service, and often near the post office. In Ecuador the long distance service *(el servicio de larga distancia)* is called IETEL and in Bolivia it's known as ENTEL. The long distance service in Peru is ENTEL–Peru while in Colombia it's called TELECOM. Any telephone company *(empresa de teléfonos)* can tell you where you can place a long distance call.

A visit to the long distance office is an event not always worth repeating. Generally there's one harried woman at a desk, several dozen numbered booths and hundreds of South Americans waiting for their calls to go through. First you line up at the desk. It's best to have all the information for your call printed very clearly on a piece of paper, as follows: *persona a persona,* the name of the person you're calling, city, state, country, phone number (with area code) and *de* (from), followed by your name. The woman at the desk then gives this information to a long distance operator, who attempts to place the call. In the meantime, you wait. This waiting period can run anywhere from thirty minutes to several days, although an hour or two is about average. When your call goes through, the woman at the desk calls your name and tells you the number of the booth to enter to take the call. If you wish, you can ask the operator to inform you or cut you off after the initial three minutes are up.

If you wish to pay for a long distance call when you make it (pago ahora) rather than calling collect, pay the woman at the desk when you give her the information. If your call doesn't go through, she returns your money, sometimes minus a small service charge.

You should be aware that telephone credit cards aren't always accepted. The telephone company wants the money when you make the call or they want you to make the call collect. Our Bell Telephone International credit card was useless in South America.

Although hours vary, long distance offices are generally open in the evening since that's when overseas lines are free.

Keep in mind that phone calls to and from South America are expensive and that connections are sometimes horrible, although the situation has improved since my first trip. When calling from South America abroad you generally have to go through the operator, but you can now direct dial from the United States to all the Andean countries. This is substantially cheaper. You could call home, talk three minutes and ask the person you're calling to direct dial back. I did this from Bolivia to the United States. To my surprise, my call from the ENTEL office in Sucre reached Florida in minutes, the connection was perfect, and the return directly dialed call to me also came through within minutes. You could also write to someone and have the party direct-dial you at an arranged date, time and phone number.

Some countries also have frontier rates. It is much cheaper to call the United States from Otavalo, Ecuador, than from Quito, for example, because Otavalo is close to the Colombian frontier.

In Colombia, long distance calls to the United States can be placed at TELECOM offices at a cost of twelve dollars for three minutes. The calls go through in two hours, sometimes less. However, a collect call to the United States can only be placed from a private phone, since TELECOM offices do not handle collect calls. The problem with trying to place a collect call is that people are reluctant to allow you to use their private phones since the phone company often charges both parties for the call and it's impossible to argue with them. Therefore it's best not to count on making a collect call home from Colombia.

HELPFUL PHRASES

May I please use your telephone? ‖ *¿Puedo usar su teléfono, por favor?*

international operator ‖ *operador internacional*

Where is the long distance office? ‖ *¿Dónde está la oficina de larga distancia?*

Where can I place a long distance call? ‖ *¿De dónde puedo llamar por teléfono larga distancia?* (If you want to know where you can

I wish to call ____. ‖ *Quisiera llamar a* ____.

place a long distance call, it's probably best to phrase your question in this manner. South Americans can be very literal, and if you ask for an ENTEL office you may be told there isn't one in town, which is true, although there might be another place— *e.g.*, a hotel or company—that handles long distance calls.)

Telegrams

Telegrams *(telegramas)* or cables, which are telegrams sent by radio or undersea cable, are very effective means of communicating with countries outside South America and are much cheaper than long distance calls. It's possible to send telegrams from places where there's no long distance service. The telegraph or cable office is frequently located in the same building as the telephone service or in the post office. Ask for *la oficina de telégrafos.*

There are three classes of telegrams: urgent *(urgente)*, which goes out right away; ordinary *(ordinario)*, which is sent the day it's received; and the night letter *(carta de noche)*, which goes out the night it's received.

The night letter is the cheapest and costs about eight dollars for twenty-one words, including the address. (How many words does it take to say "Send money"?) Print your message clearly and carefully. Delivery is generally rapid (overnight for the night letter), although my friend Elayne said that it took three weeks for a cable from Lima to reach her in Berkeley, California—another one of those mysterious, inexplicable delays.

Telegrams can be sent to you at a hotel, private home, in care of American Express or in care of the post office. Telegrams are usually delivered by messenger, but I received one by phone at a hotel in La Paz. At first I thought I was listening to an obscene phone call in Aymara. As it turned out, the clerk at the telegraph office, who didn't speak a word of English, was trying to read my telegram phonetically.

In Colombia, telegrams are sent through *Empresa Nacional de Tele-*

comunicaciones (TELECOM), which has offices in all major cities and towns. In Ecuador, try *Cable y Radio Ecuador*, RCA, ITT or ENTEL. In Peru and Bolivia, try RCA, ITT, Cable West Coast or *Comunicaciones Mundiales*. Because these countries are in the process of nationalizing and consolidating their telecommunications systems, don't give up if you draw a blank when you ask for a specific company name. Instead, ask for *la oficina de telégrafos* or *el servicio de telégrafos*, or phrase your question: "*¿De dónde puedo enviar un telegrama?*" ("From where can I send a telegram?").

Telegraph offices are generally open until late in the evening, sometimes until midnight. (For information on wiring money, see page 44.)

HAM **Radio Operators**

There are amateur radio operators throughout South America who will try to get a message through to your family in an emergency or who will put a radio call through for you. The trick is finding the operators—you just have to ask around. My friend Susy Silverman found a local HAM radio operator who put a call through for her to Buenos Aires, Argentina. The person receiving the message in Argentina then reached the party in Buenos Aires by phone. You could try calling the United States this way. If you have a HAM friend in the United States, get his or her call letters before you leave, since that definitely makes things easier. You also might prearrange a specific date or night of the week for messages to be sent.

On the Road

his chapter contains an assortment
of travel rules, hints and suggestions which cover some of the situations
you're likely to encounter on the road.

Travel Rules

The following rules apply generally to travel in South America and
especially to long distance transportation. Your trip is going to be
much more pleasant if you follow them. Every time I disregarded a
rule I had reason to regret it.

TRAVEL RULE ONE

Always ask prices beforehand. You learn this very quickly, especially
in taxis. Always agree on a fare before you get in (unless the cab is metered), since drivers love to hit you for an outrageous fare if you forget
to ask first. Also try to have small change on hand so the driver can't pull
the "No change" routine. This is more likely to happen when you're
rushed—for example, when you're trying to catch a plane. You don't
have time to play around so you hand the driver a fifty-peso note for a
10-peso ride and fume when he says he doesn't have change.

The same rule applies to buses and trucks and to restaurants which don't list prices on their menus. Always agree on a price before commencing a ride or ordering a meal. It takes just one exorbitant bill for you to learn.

TRAVEL RULE TWO

Never get on any vehicle going anywhere without taking food. Trains, planes and buses often leave early in the morning, before stores or cafés open, so plan ahead and buy food the day before. Frequently your ride won't stop for meals, and if you arrive at your destination at midnight restaurants are sure to be closed. This is when your emergency supply of granola comes in handy. Long trips are also the times to break out the peanut butter you've brought from home or managed to buy on the black market. It's high in protein and non-spoilable and makes a good meal on fresh bread. Delicious homemade breads and rolls are available in markets and *tiendas* everywhere. Buy them the day before your trip. When canned fruit juices are cheap, take some of these along, too. (Your Swiss army knife supplies the can opener.)

Try to pack healthful food. On a long haul you feel much better eating tangerines, peanut butter sandwiches and fruit juice than you do eating cookies and drinking pop.

Remember that your luggage usually goes on top of the vehicle while you sit inside, so you won't have access to it. Your food, toilet paper, camera, map and perhaps a book should all be with you. Zip-loc bags are invaluable for these treks, so that you don't open your bag and discover a banana map and a peanut butter camera.

TRAVEL RULE THREE

Always have something warm to wear. Like food, this should be with you inside the vehicle, not packed away with the luggage. If it's an overnight trip you should also have your sleeping bag inside. It doesn't do you any good to have warm things and enough food for a week if you can't get at them.

This rule also applies to your initial arrival in South America. It might seem strange to have your down jacket out in Miami, but you'll be glad when you land in Bogotá.

Consider this situation: you get on a bus at nine in the morning on a hot, sunny day, wearing shorts, sandals and a short-sleeved shirt. To your surprise there's no stop for lunch and you didn't bring anything to eat. At about two in the afternoon the bus breaks down, putting you three hours behind schedule. At sunset you realize that you're climbing high into the Andes. You're hours late, hungry, and as snow begins falling in the pass, miserably cold—freezing to death, as a matter of fact. Suddenly a tire goes flat and the driver shoos everyone off the bus while he tries to change it. You now understand why all the Indians got on the bus that morning wearing shawls, ponchos and wool hats, and you wonder if there's a hospital at your destination that knows how to treat frostbitten toes.

Before you have a chance to climb on top of the bus and hunt for your pack amidst the hundreds of pounds of cargo, the bus driver hollers, "¡*Vamos!*" ("We're going!") and herds everyone back on the bus. He can't wait while you look for your warm clothes because he has to make up for lost time. Why, you wonder, did you ever leave Chicago?

I've been in situations like this often enough to have learned that, no matter what, even on a ten-mile trip to the market, my down jacket (if not a sweater or poncho) is a must. Not optional, but a must.

Anytime you cross a *cordillera* of the Andes you'll run into extremely cold weather. Take a good look at your map and realize that no matter how hot the weather when you start, it gets viciously cold in the mountains.

I repeat, if you're traveling at night, carry your sleeping bag and poncho with you inside the vehicle. Many people have told me it was so cold at night they survived only by crawling into their sleeping bags. Ponchos, sweaters, down jackets and sleeping bags can also be wadded up and used as pillows or head covers, especially if noise and lights keep waking you up. If you're tired as well as cold and hungry, you have all the ingredients for a really bad experience, and it's *all preventable* with a little planning.

TRAVEL RULE FOUR

Have your passport and tourist card with you at all times. If you have a money belt, the papers should be in it and the belt should be worn. You may be asked to present your passport when buying a bus, train or plane ticket. Buses usually have passenger lists which are presented to the police at routine checkpoints. Don't be alarmed if the police or military enter the bus and have everyone get off. This happens more frequently near borders. In general, the authorities aren't very interested in the average traveler; they're searching for arms, contraband, subversives and illegal immigrants. Nevertheless, be sure to have your papers ready and present them when asked. Incidentally, these checks are a blessing if you need a bathroom. There's usually one in or around the check station and (especially if you're a woman) you'll be shown to it with great courtesy.

If there's political unrest in the area, it's all the more important to have your papers in order. I was in Bolivia during two attempted military coups, and a state of emergency *(estado del sitio)* was declared. This meant that all travel was even more strictly controlled than usual. Anyone going farther than about five miles from home was required to obtain a safe-conduct pass *(salvoconducto)* from his local police station. The police checked to see that my name was not on their list of wanted subversives, looked at my passport and tourist card and then issued my *salvoconducto,* which was my permission to travel. I had to tell them when I was leaving, where I was going and why, and the mode of transportation. The Bolivian airlines would not sell me a ticket to La Paz until I had my *salvoconducto.*

When you're told to do something like this, don't ignore the instructions. Later on you might not be permitted to board a vehicle or you could be hauled off because your papers aren't in order. It was a bore going down to the police security office in the *prefectura,* but the military government was calling the shots. The *salvoconducto* was issued to me free, and all I lost was a half hour of my time.

TRAVEL RULE FIVE

No recriminations when it all falls apart. Sooner or later you're going to have a bad day. The trip will be sheer hell. As you sit in the stinking, broken-down bus, hungry, tired and cold (because you disregarded the preceding rules), it's not the time to say, "I *really* just wanted to stay on the beach in Mexico," or any of the variations on that theme. Don't become one more negative factor; consider the event an adventure and think of how it's going to read in your autobiography or in letters to friends. Imagine how disappointed everyone will be if you write "Having an uneventful trip" and how much more interesting the letter will be describing your present circumstances—"And then the driver hit a llama and the bus went into a ditch and . . ." You might even catch up on your letter-writing while you sit there.

Other Travelers

Naturally you'll be meeting other travelers. It's an opportunity to make new friends, and fellow travelers are an excellent source of information, especially if they're returning from places you plan to visit. However, travelers can also prevent you from making real contact with local people. The latter occurs when you get into a "scene."

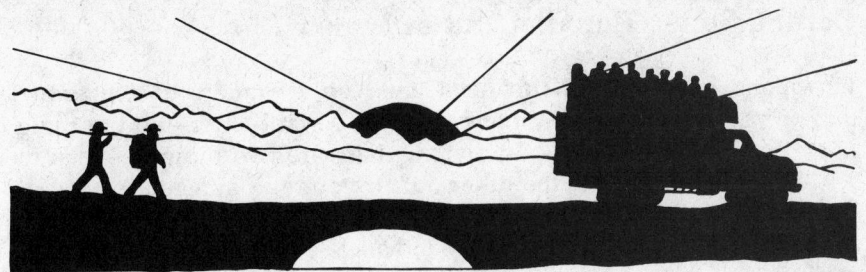

A scene develops when a number of *gringo* travelers begin hanging out together, perhaps renting a house in a village. Two things generally attract people to scenes: sex and drugs. Sometimes there's so much sex, dope and socializing that you hardly know you're in South America—until the police come along and arrest you. When you come down in a Colombian jail you suddenly realize you are indeed in a foreign country.

I'm off to South America to meet South Americans and experience their country and culture. So I try to avoid scenes. Besides, it's safer. Scenes are *always* getting busted. It's sad but true that a congregation of young foreigners (read "hippies") in a town *invariably* brings the police.

When you do meet other people on the road, get their home address or, if they're transient, get their parents' or a friend's address. Do this the first time you meet, even if you're planning to meet again (in case you don't). Eventually you'll want to get in touch. I really enjoy meeting, living and traveling with other people, and we always stay in touch long after we've returned to our respective homes. Some of my friends from the road have helped with this book, adding their perspectives and information.

Always talk with other travelers. You can help each other by trading maps, exchanging names of good hotels, restaurants and places to change money, and warning each other about nasty border officials or police crackdowns. Other adventurers have unique experiences to share and can sometimes alert you to places and adventures you might otherwise miss. Hooking up with other people and traveling together for a while is rewarding, if only because there's so much to assimilate that two or three sets of perceptions are better than one. But don't let your delight at discovering people who speak your language and share your values blind you to what you really came to see: South America. Realize that one traveler alone, or two, are much more likely to meet South Americans and be invited to their homes. If you find that most or all of your contact is with people from home and that you're speaking English almost exclusively, you're missing out on the essence of your trip, which is meeting South Americans and gaining an understanding of their lives.

Getting Stuck, Running Out of Money . . .

It happens sometimes. It happened to me. You're planning to meet some-one or you're waiting for money or an important letter—and nothing happens. You're stuck. At this point, there are two things to keep in mind. The first is to get the news out. If you're in immediate need of money, send a telegram or make a collect phone call home (see Chapter Eight, "Communications"). If you send a telegram, also send out an air-mail letter containing the same information. I sent an urgent telegram from Cochabamba to San Francisco that was never delivered. I never learned what the problem was, but I waited and waited for money that never came until communication was re-established. If your need is ur-gent, have the money wired to you, not sent by mail (see Chapter Three, "Money and Documents").

The second thing to keep in mind is how best to stretch the funds you have left and divert yourself while you wait. Be sure to check into a hotel with its own restaurant so you can have your meals put on the bill. This way you're sure to eat. What little money you have left can be used to entertain yourself—movies are very cheap. Always be prepared to wait a long time for your money, since things don't necessarily happen on schedule in South America. That way, if your money arrives in only five days, rather than two weeks, you'll be pleasantly surprised.

If you find yourself settling down for a long wait, there's one diversion open to you besides museums, art galleries, etc.—and it's free. This is your country's cultural center, which usually can be found in the larger cities. It's a good place to meet people, so whether you're stuck or just have a few days to spend in a large city, you should check it out.

In Bolivia the American cultural center is known as the *Centro Boliviano Americano,* and there are *centros* in Bolivia for other foreign countries as well. The American *centros* sponsor free programs and musical events in English and Spanish, offer English-language classes and also have fairly extensive bilingual lending libraries. Most of the books in the libraries were collected in hands-across-the-sea drives, so the collections are rather spotty: Hawthorne, Poe and other American classics, more books on American history than anyone would want to read in two incarna-tions, 1950s junk novels and some real treasures. There's enough good reading to satisfy anyone. I decided to read women authors during the month *(month!)* I was stuck in La Paz, so I read all the novels the *centro* had by Pearl S. Buck, Willa Cather, Shirley Jackson and more. Unfor-tunately, since the library's emphasis was on American culture, there were very few books about Latin America, which was disappointing. I'd find myself sitting on the Prado in La Paz reading a book about Navajo weaving when I really wanted to know more about the shy Aymara women who were walking by me with babies on their backs. *Centros* also carry periodicals ranging from *Good Housekeeping* to the Sunday edition of the *New York Times*.

In La Paz, the *Centro Boliviano Americano* is located on Avenida Arce 2142, just outside the downtown area toward the Hotel Crillón. The Cochabamba *centro* is located on Calle 25 de Mayo 5698, three blocks north of the main plaza. There's also a *centro* in Santa Cruz. Hours vary.

In Peru, there's a cultural center in downtown Lima called the *Instituto Cultural Peruano–Norteamericano*, located at Jirón Cuzco 446, as well as one in the suburb of Miraflores outside Lima. In Bogotá, Colombia, there are three branches of the *Centro Colombo Americano*, and these are located at Calle 19, No. 3–05; Carrera 15, No. 76–86; and Carrera 12, No. 82–11. Undoubtedly there are other cultural centers throughout South America. Ask at your country's embassy or consulate or look in the white pages of the local telephone directory under "*Centro*."

Staying Longer

It just might happen that you want to stay longer—perhaps a year or two. If so, the problem of earning a living immediately comes to mind. Probably the easiest job to get is one teaching English. Apply to all public and private schools, from grammar through university levels, and to the *centros* and any other institutions that teach languages. If you're hired, your employer will help you convert your tourist card to a resident visa.

There are also American schools throughout South America that teach classes in English for the children of Americans living there and for any residents who want their children to have a bilingual education. These schools usually hire their staffs well in advance of the academic year and recruit teachers in the United States. Sometimes, however, if you show up in the right place at the right time, you can land a job. I met an American woman in Cochabamba who applied at the American school there in time to secure a job teaching math and social studies and thereby managed to stay in Cochabamba for two years. Although salaries are lower than those in the United States, the cost of living is somewhat lower also. Besides, your purpose is to earn enough money to stay in the country, not to get rich.

It's also possible to spread the word that you're available as a tutor, perhaps by putting up signs at schools and other educational centers. Although this kind of freelance teaching won't qualify you for a resident visa, you can earn enough to live in a country for a while longer.

Such jobs as waiting on tables pay so poorly that they aren't worth it. A Bolivian girl told me she worked ten hours a day, six and a half days a week, for thirty dollars a month. You should also be aware that by accepting this kind of job you're taking work away from residents in countries that have high unemployment rates.

If you have specialized skills—for example, you're a nurse or an engineer—you could be hired by a local concern or by a foreign firm doing business in the country. However, most of the people I met who were staying in South America for an extended period of time had lined up their jobs before they left home. For example, Charlie and Jean Farkas, who taught at the American school in Lima; Ron Ninnis, who taught physics at the university in Cochabamba; and Cathy Textor, who worked through her church, all arranged their jobs before they left their own countries.

Other friends of mine who've managed to live in South America have been involved in projects requiring substantial outlays of funds, such as raising bees or opening a handicrafts and antiques store. I also met travelers in several countries who had opened natural-food restaurants that earned them enough money to live on.

Overall, I'd say that teaching is the most likely way for most of us to earn money. However, if you really want to stay in a country longer, you'll find a legal, honest way to make money.

Of course, if you want to stay longer without finding employment, you can always settle down in one place and live for as long as the money you brought with you holds out. Indian huts are cheap—ten dollars a month would be high. Expenses vary from place to place. In general, living in the country is much cheaper than living in the city. If you buy your food at the local market and cook it yourself, you could live like a king or queen on fifty dollars a month, depending on your other vices. Dependencies on cigarettes, beer and lots of movies obviously raise your cost of living.

Common Geographical Terms

Throughout your travels, whether you ride the bus or train, hitchhike or backpack, you'll find the going a lot easier if you understand some basic geographic terminology and travel designations. The following list is designed to familiarize you with some of the more common Spanish terms:

abra ‖ pass

acequia ‖ Irrigation canal. Many Inca and pre-Inca canals are still in use along the coast of Peru.

altiplano ‖ High (13,000 feet) tablelands of southern Bolivia and the area surrounding Lake Titicaca.

Amazonas ‖ The name of a province

or department in several countries· also used generally to refer to the Amazon rainforests.

autopista (Colombia) || freeway

avenida || avenue

bahía || bay, harbor

barriada, barrio || neighborhood, city district

bosque || woods

cachuela (Bolivia) || Rapids found in a river.

caleta || little bay

calle || street

camino || road

cañon || canyon, gorge

carrera (Colombia) || street

carretera || highway

    carretera pavimentada || paved highway

    carretera afirmada || gravel road

    carretera sin afirmada || Dirt road which is probably quite rough and rutty; it can be a muddy mess in the rainy season.

    carretera de huella o trocha || Foot highway—in other words, a footpath. Don't count on taking a car on it.

    carretera no relevada || This means that the roadbed isn't obvious.

ceja de la montaña (Peru) || The "eyebrow of the jungle," the area where the eastern slopes of the Andes fall off into the Amazon rainforest, above an altitude of 8000 feet.

centro poblado || populated center, inhabited area

cerro || hill

Chaco (Bolivia, Paraguay, Argentina) || Lowland, grassy, tropical plains.

ciénaga || swamp, marsh

cima || peak, summit

ciudad || city

colina || hill

cordillera || mountain range

costa || coast

cuenca || river basin, narrow valley

cumbre || summit, top

desierto || desert

dunas || sand dunes

estero || swamp

finca || farm

gasolina en grifo || gas (from gas pumps)

gasolina suelta || gas (in barrels)

golfo || gulf

isla || island

jirón (Peru) || street

jungla || jungle

lago, laguna || lake

llanos (Colombia) || Lowland, tropical plains toward the Amazon, similar to the Chaco.

loma || Small hill. In Peru, *lomas* are areas of vegetation on the coastal desert; the plants get their water from the winter mists and dry up in the summer.

mar || sea

médanos || Shifting sand dunes of the coastal deserts.

mesa, meseta || plateau

montaña || Mountain. In the Andes *montaña* refers to the eastern slopes of the Andes where the tropical rainforests begin.

monte || uninhabited jungle

nevada || snowfall, snowy

nevado || snowcapped peak

océano || ocean

Oriente || East. In Ecuador this term refers to the Amazon lowlands east of the Andes.

pampa (Quechua) || Desert, prairie, field. This term is used in Argentina to describe the great plains.

pantano || swamp

páramo || High, cold tablelands in the Andes.

parque || park

pascana || inn

paso || pass

paso a nivel sin barreras || Railroad crossing without barricades or signs.

pasto || pasture, grasslands

pico || peak

playa || beach

pongo (Quechua) || Door; also narrow, dangerous ford.

pueblo || town, village

puente || bridge

puerto || port

puesto || station

puna (Quechua) || Basically the same as *altiplano* and *páramo* —the high, cold tablelands in the Andes.

quebrada || ravine, gorge

riachuelo || brook

río || river

ruinas || ruins

sabana || savanna, treeless plain

selva || jungle

sendero || path

serrano (Peru) || mountain-dweller

sierra || mountain, mountain range

sitio || place, spot, location, site

trocha || footpath

túnel || tunnel

urbanización || housing area, urbanization

valle || valley

volcán || volcano

Yungas (Peru, Bolivia) || Subtropical valleys from 3000 to 8000 feet on the eastern slopes of the Andes. (Probably a Quechua word.)

Transportation

traveler's first impression of the South American continent is that it appears to be a vast automobile graveyard—only graveyard isn't exactly the right word since most of the vehicles are still running. Geriatrics ward is more like it. Every vehicle in the Western Hemisphere that has been put out to pasture, honorably retired or irreparably damaged in an accident makes its way to South America, where it gets another thirty-year lease on life. These vehicles are resurrected and kept running with infinite patience and mechanical ingenuity.

Since the Andean countries don't have factories burping an unlimited number of new playtoys annually, an automobile is a precious thing. Imported vehicles are heavily taxed. For example, in Colombia the tax is $8000 on a new American sedan and $20,000 on a sports car—that's 250 to 350 percent tax on the cost of the vehicle! One reason for the prevalence of jeeps, even in cities, is that four-wheel-drive vehicles are considered farm implements and are not taxed as heavily, making them more affordable. Once a car does find its way onto the roads it's treasured and kept there, long after more wasteful countries would have laid it to rest.

Because private cars are not as common as in the United States and Europe, public mass-transit systems are heavily utilized, although calling the bus and truck lines "systems" puts a strain on the word. Once you get over the visual shock of seeing a truck composed of the front end of a 1953 Studebaker and the body of a 1920 Ford pickup and called a trans-Andean transport, you're faced with figuring out how these lines connect with each other and actually move goods, animals and people from place to place. It all works, if somewhat more slowly than you're used to.

The *South American Handbook* (see page 21) provides excellent information on trains, buses, planes, boats, *colectivos* and every other kind of transportation for all the Andean nations, including fares, departure times, driving times and recommended lines. Consult the *Handbook* or local tourist bureaus for exact information.

A warning on bad times to travel: there are some really terrible times to travel and this is when a Catholic calendar and your list of fiestas (see Chapter Seventeen) come in handy. Anytime there is a major fiesta, transportation in the area is completely messed up. Buses and trucks are jammed with people who are either drunk or hung over, and it can take you several days to get a ride. Once you're in a vehicle it takes three times as long as usual to make the trip because of all the people getting on and off and partying and carrying on. The overcrowding and general inefficiency reach mind-boggling levels.

To give you just a few examples: travel around Lake Titicaca during *Todos Santos* and *Día de Los Muertos* (November 1 and 2) is horrendous, as is travel in and around Popayán, Colombia, during *Semana Santa*. At one point we were hung up in Quito for five days, unable to get a plane to Bogotá, because all flights were booked solid with people going to Bogotá for the South American soccer championship matches. The list goes on and on, so be alert to major fiestas along your route and try not to get mixed up in the travel chaos accompanying them.

Buses

There are many ways of getting around in South America, most of them cheaper than their counterparts to the north. The most common form of cheap transportation is the bus. Try as you might to avoid it, sooner or later you'll spend a lot of time on the bus. It helps to be prepared and to know what to expect.

Are all those horror stories you've heard about the buses true? The answer is yes. Buses (and trucks) always seem to be going off cliffs, breaking down or running into each other. However, considering the staggering number of ancient and decaying vehicles that daily ply the Andean roads, the number of fatalities is amazingly low. Statistics are on your side. I've never talked to a traveler who died in a bus accident.

In Colombia, Ecuador and Peru the bus is called a *camión, micro* or *autobús*. In Bolivia it is called a *góndola, ómnibus, micro* or *autobús*, and *camión* refers to a truck. In all four countries the bus company or line is called a *flota* or *transporte*—for example, *Flota Copacabana* or *Transportes Morales*.

In most towns there's no central bus station; instead, there's a small station/office for each line. When you want to find out where to catch the bus, ask, "*¿De dónde sale el camión (autobús, góndola) a ____?*" ("Where does the bus leave for ____?"). This is better than asking for the *estación de camiones* (bus station) because sometimes there isn't a bus station at all; the bus simply stops in the plaza, loads up and departs from there.

The average *camión* is a Bluebird school bus that's been outfitted with a luggage rack on the roof, overhead racks inside, a couple of Che Guevara decals and a shrine to the Blessed Virgin. You soon grow used to riding under the protection of Mary and Che. Since the buses and roads (and sometimes the drivers) are usually in a state of disrepair, an uneventful trip is indeed a miracle. As the bus starts up, the passengers make the sign of the cross and offer a short prayer. You may want to join them or (Bill's method) take three Valium and drift into unknowing bliss. The bus may or may not have such amenities as window glass, springs in the seats, a door, muffler, headlights and working brakes.

It's a rare bus (I've been on just one) that has a bathroom on board. Rest stops are catch as catch can, often with the occupants hopping out to pee by the side of the road, so plan for this. (I plan for this by not drinking on bus trips and by finding a restroom before I get on.) Sometimes I just get off and join the rest of the travelers, although one friend peed in his boot and dumped it out the window.

Buses don't always stop for meals, so when a bus pulls into a town vendors rush to the windows with their wares. Unless you take food along, this may be your only chance to eat. Since you can't be sure that vendors are going to show up, it's best to have food with you.

Bus tickets are usually sold in the bus line's combination station/office, and seats are chosen by signing your name in a box representing a seat on the bus. This gives you a chance to sit next to your traveling companion, if you have one, or to choose a window seat. The wheel humps are usually found in the fourth or fifth row from the back, so try to avoid them. Also avoid the first seat near the door or you'll be battered and bumped by everyone getting on and off, and don't choose the seats farthest in the back since the noise can be unbearable if the bus has no muffler and the drifting fumes can make you sick. A seat somewhere in the front half of the bus is best. Occasionally seats aren't assigned and you have to scramble for a comfortable one (or any one) when the bus loads. This includes people making assaults through the windows. Sometimes the bus departs when it's full rather than at a scheduled time.

Bad news: eventually you're going to hear the words *"Se fue"* or *"Ya salida,"* meaning "It's gone" or "It already departed." Good luck.

In parts of the Peruvian Andes the roads are regulated so that traffic goes in one direction on Mondays, Wednesdays and Fridays and in the opposite direction on Tuesdays, Thursdays and Saturdays. (I've never figured out what happens on Sunday—a free-for-all?) Anyway, you only have a chance to catch the bus out of town every other day. The arrival time for the bus is uncertain, and the bus company won't sell you a ticket until it shows up. When it does, forget about buying your ticket. There will be an attack on the bus similar to the taking of Iwo Jima and seats will be defended like the soil of the fatherland. If you've gone to buy a ticket you won't get a seat—and you'll be stuck in town another two days. The thought of this should give you the fortitude to shoulder aside that old grandmother. You can buy your ticket on the bus.

You can travel almost anywhere by bus. As a general rule, the more remote the area, the more decrepit the vehicle. The larger cities often have first-class bus lines that travel the major routes. If at all possible ride first class on long trips. Many of the first-class buses have moderately comfortable reclining seats with headrests and sufficient leg room. On a sixteen-hour trip this makes an enormous difference. The Bluebird buses are designed for a population with a maximum height of 5'6" and they have fixed seats. On many of these buses I rode with my knees touching the seat in front of me while it was impossible for Bill to squeeze in at all. (He sat in the aisle seat so his knees could stick out.) Also, first-class lines usually reserve seats whereas second- and third-class lines pack the bus to the walls, with people and animals sitting and standing in the aisles. On a bus trip from Copacabana to La Paz I counted fifty-two people on our very small bus.

On the cheapo lines, large animals are carried on the roof while small ones travel inside. Steve Miller and I rode from Cochabamba to Villa

Tunari, Bolivia, with a lamb next to me and a mother hen and her baby chicks on the rack above my head. The bus had no muffler, no shock absorbers and several missing windows. Every so often the hen hung over the edge and told me what she thought of the whole affair, and twice during the ride the babies bailed out on my head. Fortunately for me and the chickens they did nothing more on my head than land on it. Unfortunately we caught the same bus for the return trip. We absolutely froze coming back over the Andes in this disintegrating wreck. It was a thoroughly miserable experience, which could have been bearable had we taken along our down jackets.

Actually, first-class lines are not that much more expensive than second class. You can ride one to two hundred miles for about a dollar or two, although with worldwide inflation this figure may have been revised upward. Carla and Pauline Swart traveled the length of Peru, from Ecuador to Bolivia, by bus, train and truck. They estimated that they spent ninety hours in vehicles for a total transportation cost of about eighteen dollars.

I'm not a big fan of South American buses, so I try to take other forms of transportation whenever possible.

Collective Taxis

COLOMBIA AND ECUADOR

Fortunately there are other forms of cheap transportation that are much more comfortable than the bus. Collective taxis are one of them. Although they're known by different names in different countries, the concept is the same. In Colombia and Ecuador they're called *colectivos* or *taxis colectivos*. These are regular automobiles, station wagons, vans with seats or microbuses *(busetas* or *micros)* that travel between towns on regular runs. For example, *Taxis Verdes* runs daily between Bogotá and the archaeological park in San Agustín with stops in between. *Colectivos* are less crowded than buses and are more comfortable and enjoyable because riding in one is similar to riding in a private car. They depart from a station/office where tickets are sold. Sometimes *colectivos* have definite schedules; other times they leave when full. It's possible for a group of people to hire a *colectivo* and even to drive it themselves.

PERU

In Peru collective taxis are called *comités* and they have specific runs, usually between adjacent cities or towns. For example, *Comité #10* runs several times a day between Chiclayo and Trujillo. Bill and I traveled in *comités* along the coast of Peru from Ecuador to Lima. We divided our trip into day-long segments and spent the nights in hotels. *Comités* are usually ordinary sedans and carry two passengers in front and three in back. The riders protest vigorously if the driver tries to squeeze in more people. *Comités* make forty-five-minute stops at little cafés for lunch and dinner and these are welcome breaks. It's also another reason why I prefer them to buses.

The *colectivo* concept extends to boat travel in the Amazon, where barges or large passenger canoes with outboard motors are called *colectivos* and function as water taxis.

BOLIVIA

In Bolivia the collective taxis are called *rápidos*. They don't have station/offices but depart from specific corners or from the town's plaza or market. Just ask.

Rápidos are likely to be elongated station wagons or vans and are often stuffed to the doors. I rode in one that was so crowded the ticket collector had to crawl in and out the windows to collect fares (since it was impossible to climb over the people) while the *rápido* roared down the highway. *Rápidos* are used for short runs, as opposed to Peru, where *comités* make long trips. In Bolivia, if your trip's going to run over an hour I recommend a first-class bus line rather than a *rápido*. This is a rare instance in which I prefer the bus (fast, comfortable, new Mercedes buses) to the collective taxis.

On the whole, *colectivos* are somewhat more expensive than buses, but well worth it, and by North American or European standards still ridiculously cheap—perhaps one or two cents a mile.

City Buses

City buses are always interesting to ride and, better yet, they're very, very cheap—usually from one to five cents. When I check into a hotel I watch the street to see the number of the bus going by and then I take that bus to and from the downtown area *(el centro)* or the market *(el mercado)*. You can always ask the hotel clerk for directions.

On South American city buses people board both at the front and rear doors and the fare is collected by a conductor, usually a boy about ten, who struggles through the crowd and gives out a receipt when he takes a fare. Try to have small change for him. Although there are buzzers or bells to pull when you want to get off, these are mainly for show and rarely work. More often you position yourself beside one of the doors and yell *"¡Baja!"* ("Down!") or *"¡Esquina!"* ("Corner!"). Remember these two words. Don't say, *"¡Pare!"* ("Stop!") because the driver won't. He'll think you're having an encounter with thieves or getting pinched, rather than talking to him. Try to stay in a position where you can see where you're going—either sitting down or standing near the door or front windshield.

Bus stops are usually marked *"Parada,"* and generally there are other people waiting at them since urban transportation systems are heavily used. If you're alone at a stop and want to flag down a bus, don't wave your arms. Instead, face the approaching bus and stick your right arm straight out. This is the signal for the driver to stop. You may observe local variations on this theme—do what the residents do.

GETTING LOST

What about getting lost? It's a terrible feeling to be on a bus that twists and turns and suddenly takes off in the opposite direction from the one you wanted. I usually keep telling myself the bus will turn around momentarily, all the while getting farther and farther from where I want to be. At this point you have three alternatives. One is to get off and then get right back on another bus headed downtown or back to where you got on. Forget your original destination—just get back to where you started or go to the center of town and start over. The buses are so cheap that it's no great financial loss, although it can be dismal if you're rushing to catch a train. Your second alternative is to get off, catch a taxi and have the driver take you to your destination. This is obviously the best solution if you're rushed. The third alternative is to stay on the bus and ride to the end of the line, pay a second fare and ride the bus all the way back to where you got on. This is a good plan if you're faced with getting off in what looks like a bad neighborhood or if you're alone at night. You could be in for a long ride if the ultimate destination is the outlying suburbs, but this is often the best alternative. And if you're not rushed for time, riding a bus to the end of the line and back is a nice way to explore the city, whether you're lost or not.

City Taxis

All cities and towns have taxi systems and some have several. Many of the fleets resemble the line-up of a demolition derby after the first round. Amazingly, I've never been in a taxi that's broken down, although many were in their death throes. They do get you there.

Taxis are much cheaper than they are in the United States, although they're not as cheap as South American city buses. Taxis that park in front of major hotels are invariably the most expensive. If you walk just a block away, flag down a passing cab and bargain on a fare, you'll get the same ride at a considerable savings.

Lima and La Paz have several different kinds of taxis. Most familiar is the ordinary kind, where one passenger (or perhaps several) flags down a cab and obtains a ride. Some of these are metered while some aren't. In Lima you'll also find taxis similar to *comités,* and these have specific runs—for example, from the suburb of Miraflores to the Plaza san Martín. The driver holds his left hand out the window, indicating with his fingers the number of passengers he can hold. There is a set price for each run.

In La Paz the ordinary taxi's route is determined by the first passenger who's picked up. Subsequent riders tell the driver where they want to go and he accepts them if their route is the same. You may have to stop three or four taxis before you get a ride, but I've never waited longer than ten minutes before finding one. These taxis have set prices and are very cheap (about fifteen cents).

La Paz also has taxis with specific runs; they're called *trufis.* A flag attached to the fender of a *trufi* signifies its route. *Trufis* run from the Prado in downtown La Paz to the suburbs and also have set fares.

Try to have exact change or plenty of small change for taxis. The drivers have two games which they especially like to play with foreigners. One is called "No change." You hand the driver a five-peso note for a three-peso ride and he says, "No change." The other game is that he pretends that five pesos is really the cost of the ride. To avoid these difficulties I ascertain the true cost of the ride *before* I get in, which is easy in places where the prices are fixed. Ask about fares at your hotel or on the street; then have the exact change when you get in the cab. If you only have large bills, forget it. Get change somewhere before you look for a ride.

For taxis without meters or set fares, always agree on the fare before you get in. This is the first travel rule and it's important—unless you like to be cheated. At such places as the airport and train station, ask a driver what he charges for a ride downtown. Tell him no if the price sounds too high, then ask someone else. If the taxi is metered, the driver will say so and he'll turn the meter on. In many cities taxi drivers are entitled to charge a little more after sunset.

To catch any taxi, the ability to emit a shrill whistle does wonders. Drivers' ears are attuned to this. If you can't whistle, holler "Taxi!"

Trains

I like to ride the train *(el tren)* for several reasons. Trains always have bathrooms; they go off the rails less frequently than buses go off the roads;

you can get up, walk around and stretch your legs; and they often serve food. On the whole, trains aren't any more expensive than buses. Since trains actually leave on schedule, make sure you're at the station on time.

COLOMBIA

In Colombia trains are somewhat slower than first-class buses and *colectivos*, but I opt for them anyway. It's best to get tickets for the fast train *(el tren rápido)* since passenger cars are sometimes attached to freight trains or locals which stop constantly and seem to take forever. On Colombian trains especially you should keep an eye on your belongings. After a conductor warned us very explicitly about thieves, Bill and I ate in shifts so that one of us was always in our car watching the luggage.

Colombia has a fairly extensive railway system that links Bogotá with other major cities (including Santa Marta on the Caribbean) and major cities with each other (for example, Cali with Popayán). Colombia also has instituted a faster passenger service called the *autoferro*, which is basically a passenger car with its own diesel engine. Take the *autoferro* whenever possible; it's faster and more comfortable than the regular train. (In Colombia the regular train is called *el tren*, while *autoferro* refers to the special passenger service.)

ECUADOR

In my first encounter with the train in Ecuador we had to be at Quito's huge, imposing railroad station at some horrid hour in the morning when it was still dark and we were barely coherent and shivering with cold. We stepped out onto the platform as a mighty whistle blast came out of the dawn. There it was: a school bus mounted on the railroad tracks. I was stunned. This was the train?

This bizarre hybrid is also called the *autoferro*. It runs from Quito to Guayaquil (with a line to Cuenca) and is the major passenger route through the Andes. It has a small, putrid toilet and no food. The *autoferro* makes a couple of short stops for coffee and rolls, but you'll starve on the day-long ride unless you pack something to eat. When you buy your ticket be sure to ask for a seat near the front. The toilet is in the rear of the car and it smells like the open sewer it is.

The *autoferro* goes through some of the most beautiful country in the Andes. If you want a better view of this paradise you can ride on the roof with the luggage; just climb up when the *autoferro* stops. Since you're neither hampered (nor protected) by insurance or legislation designed to safeguard the public, no one cares much what you do and it's your tough luck if you fall off. It's exhilarating to ride up there and the opportunities for photography are unparalleled.

There are two railroads (*ferrocarriles*) in Ecuador: *Ferrocarril del Sur* (Quito to Cuenca and Guayaquil) and *Ferrocarril del Norte* (Quito to Ibarra). These lines also run agonizingly slow freight trains with passenger cars attached, so be sure to buy tickets for the *autoferro*, not the *tren*.

PERU

Peru has several railway systems with conventional trains. These railroads were built by foreign companies interested in exploiting Peruvian resources, which means they run from the Andes (usually from mining towns) straight to the coast to connect with international shipping. Because these railroads were not designed to facilitate passenger and freight transportation within Peru, the lines don't connect. Most travelers ride at least one of the lines sooner or later. On all Peruvian trains you should watch your belongings, especially during stops at stations.

The *Ferrocarril del Centro* runs from the port of Callao through Lima to Huancayo in the Andes, with connections to Cerro de Pasco and Huancavelica. It's the first stretch of the five-day, overland trip to Cuzco, which must be completed by truck or bus. This railroad was built to haul the rich ores out of the Cerro de Pasco region and is the highest standard-gauge railway in the world, reaching 15,688 feet. The conductor comes around with oxygen for those affected by the altitude. (I had no problems but some people did.) Most travelers take this train to the Sunday market at Huancayo; it leaves on Saturday and the ride takes a full day. If you take this trip, I suggest that you buy your ticket at least a day ahead of time and go first class since second class is outrageously overcrowded.

On this line, the seats aren't reserved in any of the coaches, so you should be at the station about an hour before the train leaves to join in the mad scramble for seats. The first-class coaches have non-movable seats which face each other with little tables in between. This poses a problem if you don't want to ride backwards. Since the engine isn't attached until the last minute and the train gets switched around when it leaves the yard, it's hard to figure out which end is the front. There are so many switchbacks on this ride that you'll end up riding backwards half the time anyway.

Although food is served on the train, along with coffee, tea and pop, you'd be wise to take your own lunch. (We packed juice, cookies, bread, cheese, candy and dried and fresh fruit.) I don't recall exactly what was served, but I know it was something I didn't want to eat.

The other main railroad, *Ferrocarril del Sur*, is located in southern Peru and runs from Mollendo through Arequipa to Puno and Cuzco. Some trains go directly to Cuzco while others stop at Juliaca and then go on to Puno on Lake Titicaca. Many travelers stay in Puno and then continue by train to Cuzco, while others take the steamer to Bolivia. (Inquire at the train station in Arequipa for schedules and connections.) Again, buy your ticket at least a day ahead of your departure, if not earlier, and be at the station an hour before the train leaves to claim your seat, which isn't reserved. First class is much more comfortable and less crowded than second class, but it costs more.

The first-class coaches on the Arequipa train are like those on the *Ferrocarril del Centro,* with seats facing each other over little tables. Food is served but it's neither good nor substantial and it's expensive. Take your own! The trains are also similar in that the windows are often broken and refuse to stay open or closed. That is, they persist in doing the opposite of what you want. My father produced a piece of rope and tied our window shut, which was definitely necessary since we went through a couple of snowstorms on the *puna.* You can usually buy coffee, tea, pop and sometimes beer. Coffee and tea aren't always available because the cook uses a wood-burning stove and has to take something off in order to mutilate the lunch.

You can always fly to Puno, Cuzco and Huancayo, and you can torture yourself by taking the bus, but the train rides are really too interesting to miss—particularly the trip from Puno to Cuzco. Besides spectacular scenery and the stunning sight of herds of llamas and white alpacas, the ride is a veritable crafts tour. And when the train arrives at the Urcos station near Cuzco you're in for a real treat. The people of Urcos bake a delicious bread called *chuta,* which is timed to come out of the oven just as the train pulls in. You can buy one loaf or a dozen when the children come through your car with their baskets. The loaves are fresh, hot and tasty beyond words. The Peruvian couple who sat across from us bought some *chuta* and passed it around the car in a gesture of friendship. They treated the entire coach, including a Brazilian and a Chilean who were entertaining us with guitar music.

For information on the trains from Cuzco to Macchu Picchu, see Chapter 15, "Archaeology and Pre-Columbian Civilizations."

Warning: theft is extremely common in the Arequipa and Cuzco train stations. (I've already mentioned the loss of my father's camera.) During the rush for seats in the second-class coaches in the Cuzco station, Carla and Pauline Swart saw a thief lift a wallet from the purse of a petite French traveler. She saw him, too, so she turned around and hit him hard in the face. He dropped her wallet, they both reached for it and she won. By the time the train was under way two travelers from the first-class coaches reported that their purses, passports, etc., were missing, so at least two thieves had a successful morning.

BOLIVIA

Bolivia has a passenger service with new cars that are similar to Ecuador's *autoferro*. These passenger-only cars are called *ferrobuses* or *ferroviarios*, and they're in much better shape than their counterparts in Ecuador. In fact, the *ferrobus* was the best train I rode in South America. It was fast, clean, comfortable, inexpensive and served some edible food. I rode the *ferrobus* during the winter (June) and it was bitterly cold, so dress warmly. (This applies to any trip on the *altiplano.*) Bolivia also has older, slower trains that haul both freight and passengers. Ride the *ferrobus* if possible.

Unfortunately, the tracks are often washed out in Bolivia. If the line is in repair you can take the train or *ferrobus* from La Paz to Oruro and Cochabamba; to Lake Titicaca, with steamer connections to Peru; to Arica, Chile; and to Argentina, with connections to Potosí and Sucre. There's also a train from Santa Cruz into Brazil and Argentina.

Trucks

In Peru and Bolivia you can go just about anywhere by truck *(camión)*. You can also take trucks in Colombia and Ecuador, but these countries rely more on buses. Trucks travel to remote areas where buses don't run and also compete on regular bus routes. These trucks are usually large, four-ton vehicles with wooden slat sides. They hold a lot of cargo, people, or both, and are the cheapest form of transportation in the Andes— as well as the most uncomfortable. Since trucks are open, they can be absolutely miserable in wet or cold weather, and in the Andes it's always either wet or cold. Long truck rides can turn into endurance marathons, so be prepared.

My friend Ann Houston, though, prefers trucks to buses: "I found trucks to be more comfortable than bad buses, especially if the cargo under me was something soft like grain. They're also warmer as you are squeezed in so tight with your neighbor that body heat helps. Trucks have much better visibility, and the opportunities for social interaction are also greater."

On my one long truck ride, we left at five in the morning and there was ice on the *altiplano*. Although I was wearing my hooded down jacket, I'd left my gloves at the hotel in a fit of stupidity, so I had a hard time holding on. It was inhumanly cold. At least the company was good— lots of *campesinos* on their way to market in a holiday mood, all of us huddled together with the animals and cargo for warmth.

On that trip I decided the ideal truck ride would be atop a load of mattresses (with an electric blanket), and one morning in La Paz I saw a truck go by with a group of grinning Indians riding on a pile of mattresses about twelve feet high.

In La Paz, trucks heading for all parts of Bolivia load up very early each morning (4 or 5 A.M.) on Calles Tumusla, Buenos Aires and Max Paredes in the Indian quarter. This is a market area and, as a rule, you can always find truck rides around the markets. (Trucks for the Yungas, however, leave from Plaza Villa Fatima above La Paz. You can take a bus or taxi up there.) Be sure to ask the cost of the ride in advance and don't pay more than the other passengers.

Hitchhiking

Because trucks pick up paying passengers and because there are few good roads and even fewer family cars in South America, hitchhiking isn't as easy as it is most other places. For long distances in the country I simply wouldn't count on it. People may stop for you but you'll be expected to contribute something. This is especially true of the drivers of any kind of truck. Hitchhiking is a bit easier when you're traveling short distances in and around big cities.

Hitching is called going *a dedo* (literally, "by finger"). To hitch a ride, hold your thumb out and jerk your hand in the direction you want to go. (Don't just hold your hand stationary.) I only hitched for short distances around Cochabamba, Bolivia's second largest city, and I never hitched alone.

If you do decide to hitch, be prepared to pay for a truck ride if you don't want to spend several days in one spot. Most people hitch both to meet new people and to save money. Since you can meet plenty of natives on trucks and buses and the trucks are really dirt cheap, it's just as easy to pay for a ride.

Renting a Car

Bill and I had two experiences renting a car, both of them bad. But we learned a lot, so I'll pass along what we found out.

In the first instance we were invited to travel with two other *gringos*, Bob and Mary Martin. Our initial handicap was the fact that Peru had instituted gasoline rationing. Every car in the country had a sticker placed on its windshield signifying the two days of the week the car couldn't be driven. (This system was discontinued in May 1975.) We wanted to rent a jeep from Budget, but they didn't have one with a suitable sticker and we didn't want to get stuck halfway to our destination on a no-driving day. The car with the best sticker was a Hillman sedan.

Bob told the Budget people where we planned to go (the Callejón de Huaylas) and asked if the car could handle the trip. They answered *"Claro"* ("Of course"). Before we even got off the Pan American Highway the fan belt broke. Bill and Bob hitchhiked back to the nearest town to find a new belt, which was no easy task. It took hours.

The next obstacle was provided by the Peruvian Road Department or whoever it is that handles such things (the answer is probably nobody). We couldn't find our turn-off into the mountains. Although the turn-off wasn't marked, we knew it was the only route into the mountains, so we expected to see other traffic. We asked directions, followed dead ends, turned left, turned right, went in circles, got out and hiked, used bad language and asked more directions. As the sun began to sink (along with our spirits), we found the road: 130 miles of unpaved, one-lane ruts that climbed to over 13,000 feet to cross the Cordillera Negra. I had my first glimpse of the Southern Cross that night. It was the most beautiful night sky and the worst road I have ever experienced. The combination of feelings was something like ecstatic terror. I couldn't decide whether to be glad or worried that we couldn't see what was above or below us in the mountains except for oncoming headlights.

At about midnight a tire went flat, and then we found out that the jack didn't work. It wouldn't go high enough to get the tire off the ground. We were on a steep, uphill stretch and the road fell away into the cosmic void. We braced the wheels with rocks and balanced the jack on stones, while I reviewed first-aid procedures in my head.

Once we got rolling again we came upon a stopped line of traffic, with two trucks stuck nose to nose. *Machismo* was at stake and neither driver wanted to back up. Besides, it was dangerous. As the vehicles scraped by each other, sending rocks over the edge, I completely forgot about first aid and began writing my obituary and wondering how my parents would take the news.

Then the accelerator pedal fell off. For the rest of the night it alternated between getting stuck, which was exciting even though we weren't going too fast, and falling off. By 2 A.M. we were lost again, and we had violated Travel Rule Two by not having taken along enough food.

There was an inordinate amount of traffic on the road because it had been closed during the day while engineers dynamited to repair the damage done some years earlier by the 1970 earthquake. (This quake killed 100,000 Peruvians; it completely buried the town of Yunguy and its 35,000 inhabitants, besides wiping out a railroad and shaking up the roads in the area.) There were trucks, buses and *comités* on the road, but no other private cars, which goes to show that any Peruvian who owned a car had more sense than we did. When we finally found our destination and a hotel that would admit us, it was 4 A.M.

While we were sleeping at the hotel our second night out, someone hit the car. It didn't look very good the next morning and it wouldn't start. When we finally got it running, the band holding the tail pipe and muffler broke, and these parts then fell down and dragged in the road. Mary tried tying them back up with a piece of rope, but the rope eventually burned through, so we wired them in place with one of my rubber-covered coat hangers. Ultimately, the exhaust pipe and muffler fell off altogether and we put them in the trunk. The door handle also fell off— why I don't know—and the battery fell out of its moorings several times, bringing the self-destructo to a dead halt.

On our return trip to Lima we had to pass Recuay before 7 A.M., at which time the blasting resumed and the road closed until sunset. Just past Recuay we hit an unusually nasty rut. Bob got out to look: the rear axle casing was broken and oil was dripping out onto the dirt. There were no garages for the next hundred miles, but the blasting had already begun and there was no turning back. Partway down the Cordillera Negra Bob noticed there were no brakes. (This was almost as exciting as the accelerator pedal's sticking.)

Many hours later we arrived at a garage in a town on the Pan American Highway. We nearly plowed through its adobe wall before we could stop the car with the hand brake. We wanted the brakes fixed so we could drive the wreck back to Lima, but the men at the garage refused. They said we couldn't take the car back on the highway or our blood would be on their hands.

Bob made a long distance call to the Budget office in Lima and we abandoned the Hillman and took *comités* back to the city. The next day the Budget people pointed out that the fine print in the contract (in Spanish) made Bob responsible for all damages to the car except those caused by the person who hit it at the hotel, since that was covered by collision insurance. Bob threatened to sue them for renting us a car that was dangerously unfit for the road. Besides, we had the whole trip on film and just might sell it to their competitors. Bob got off by forfeiting his deposit and paying an extra seventy-five dollars or so for the damage; then he went over to Avis to rent another car so that he and Mary could return to the Callejón de Huaylas to go backpacking.

Later Bob told me that he wouldn't rent a car again: "There's too much public transportation. It's much easier and cheaper to get a ride in a *comité* or truck or to hire a car and driver." (Then when it falls apart, it's the owner's problem.)

Several months later Bill and I decided to rent a car in La Paz and drive to Lake Titicaca. We thought we'd learned something and checked the car carefully. One tire was bald but the manager assured us it was good. It wasn't. When it went flat on the *altiplano* we discovered a gaping hole in the spare that was hidden when the tire had been bolted in place in the trunk. We had no choice but to return to La Paz.

Obviously, if you're going to rent a car you can do better than we did. Check the car carefully and make sure that the tires and spare are in excellent condition, that the jack functions, that the motor is in decent shape and that there are tools in the trunk. Also have a gas can with some extra gas. There aren't any garages or gas stations in out-of-the-way places, which is just about everywhere outside the cities. In some places, people sell gas (*gasolina*) out of filthy, unlikely-looking barrels, so when you begin to run low, no matter how tiny the hamlet, ask "*¿Dónde se vende gasolina?*" ("Where do they sell gasoline?") and then stop at the indicated hut. Oil is *aceite*.

Remember, too, that there are no highway patrol cars or tow trucks to help you if your car breaks down, although a passing trucker might lend a hand. Furthermore, the roads aren't marked. If you're used to freeways, you'll be tempted to drive past a dirt trail, thinking, "That can't possibly be the highway to Santa Ana." It is. Be prepared to ask directions, to be misled completely, to get hopelessly lost and to ask more directions—if the locals speak Spanish at all. Allow double the amount of time you think you'll need for the trip. Naturally, take plenty of food, water and warm clothing.

Although car rental costs vary, they aren't cheap, and any rental is more expensive than a comparable one in the United States. A good way to rent a car is to get a group of people together who are willing to share the expenses. You may need a credit card for the rental, but you don't need an International Driver's License—just a valid license from your home state. If you leave a cash deposit, be sure you get a receipt.

You can rent cars in all major cities in Colombia, Ecuador and Peru, and you can leave a car rented in one city at the agency's office in another city, although you might have to bribe a clerk to do so. (Remember that when some South Americans say "*No*" or "*Imposible*," they may be looking for a little cash to help them change their mind.) In Bolivia, however, the only car rental agencies are in La Paz, which is somewhat limiting.

Transit Control

Travel in South America is more strictly controlled than it is in North America and Europe. When driving in Peru and Bolivia, you must stop periodically at transit control (*control del tránsito*) stations, where you're asked for your car papers, driver's license, passport, tourist card and something impossible, such as your baptismal certificate, if the guard wants a bribe. Never go through these checkpoints without stopping, and never drive off if an army officer or policeman flags you down. (They'd probably love to try out their American-made weapons on an American-made car.)

Every so often the army conducts searches for guerrillas, subversives and *banditos*, or you might see them out on general maneuvers, terrorizing the local population (which seems to be their main function in these countries anyway, since they don't fight many foreign wars). They conduct their maneuvers with real guns and live ammunition, and I don't trust the military as far as I can spit. They run the show, so do what they tell you.

In Bolivia, you must stop at the first *control del tránsito* station outside the town you're leaving, show your papers and tell the guard your destination. This immediately presented problems for us because we weren't exactly sure where we'd end up. Don't threaten the guard's grip on sanity by saying, "Oh, we're just out driving around." The pleasure drive is another alien concept to South Americans, and if you drive down there you'll soon learn why. Give as your destination (if you don't have one in mind) some town that is the farthest you're thinking of driving. Do this just to be on the safe side, since it's written on a paper called an *hoja de ruta*. It's no legal problem if you don't get there, but your *hoja de ruta* must be stamped at every *control del tránsito* station along the way and turned in when you return. All Bolivian roads are toll roads, so you also pay your tolls at these stations.

Bill and I started out all right, but when we reached our destination we were nabbed by a policeman who said Bill hadn't gotten the paper stamped in all the villages we passed through. I hadn't realized that these places were villages; I thought they were uninhabited ruins. Nevertheless, somewhere among the crumbling adobe huts were *control del tránsito* stations we had missed. Bill and the policeman bargained over the fine, and when the price was set (about five dollars) the policeman took our paper and told Bill he'd fix it so that no one could tell we'd missed any stops. He then stamped the paper into total illegibility so no one could tell we had stopped at the right places either. However, it looked very impressive all stamped to hell and no one questioned it on the way back when we stopped at all the required checkpoints.

Airplanes

There are several things to keep in mind about flying in South America. First, don't read *Alive: The Story of the Andes Survivors* at the airport (*aeropuerto*) before your flight over the Andes. Second, it's much cheaper to fly within a country than between countries because the airlines aren't bound by international tariff agreements on domestic flights. If you take a plane (avión or aeroplano) from Colombia to Ecuador, for example, it costs more per mile because you're crossing an international border. Bill and I flew from Popayán to Pasto, Colombia, for about eight dollars each. It took us twenty minutes and we avoided one of the worst stretches of the Pan American Highway, a fourteen-hour bus ride under good conditions (rare). We then took colectivos to the Ecuadorian border.

We also flew from Guayaquil to Machala, Ecuador, in a single-engine Piper. This also cost about eight dollars each, and it saved us a day-long bus trip. We had a couple of false starts as the engine-compartment door flew open when we taxied down the runway. Bill attempted to fix the lock with his Swiss army knife since no one had the right tools, which raised some questions in my mind about maintenance. After the mechanics finally fixed the door, we wobbled down the runway and headed south—uneventfully.

These short hops are really a blessing. You can save tremendous amounts of time—and more important, energy—by avoiding the worst bus rides. To quote my friend Steve Rogers: "Next time I think I'll fly to La Paz and start from there as I was so burnt out by bus riding by the time I got to La Paz that it was hard to get enthused about seeing much of Bolivia." Steve went overland from Lima to La Paz and wore himself out in the process. There's one stretch of this route in particular where a plane ride can really make a difference—this is the stretch between Ayacucho and Cuzco, where several bridges are perennially washed out, making the bus trip an all-time loser.

Don't worry if you find yourself flying on an airline you've never heard of. In fact, that's a good sign, as it means one of their planes hasn't made the headlines by going down in the mountains. If for some reason an obscure airline's name sticks in your mind, it's probably bad—unless it's been recommended recently by another traveler.

Don't overlook military or non-passenger airlines. In Colombia and Peru, especially in the jungle regions, you can often get rides in air force planes. These are usually cheaper than regular passenger flights. Sometimes you can hook rides to Ecuador's Galapagos Islands in Ecuadorian air force planes, although travel to the Galapagos is highly restricted and this may not be possible any longer. Also check out rides in cargo planes—simply inquire at any airport. For example, you can fly into Ecuador's Oriente and back in a cargo plane, sometimes returning with a planeload of beef destined for the market in Quito. However, don't count on these flights and don't head to out-of-the-way places if you're on a tight schedule. You could get hung up for weeks.

In La Paz, Lloyd Aéreo Boliviano provides a free bus to the airport that leaves from the L.A.B. office on Avenida Camacho and saves you at least two dollars cab fare. The bus departs on time (in fact, it's more punctual than the planes), so be at the office when you're told to.

On my first South American trip, only one fifth of my flights were on time and the rest were anywhere from one to four hours late. Pay attention to the travel rules and be prepared for long waits. It never hurts to have a book along.

AIRLINE TERMINOLOGY

airport ‖ *aeropuerto*

flight ‖ *vuelo*

arrivals ‖ *llegadas*

departures ‖ *salidas*

reservation ‖ *reservación*

ticket ‖ *boleto*

round-trip ticket ‖ *boleto de ida y vuelta*

ticket window ‖ *caja* or *boletería*

station ‖ *estación* or *terminal*

first class ‖ *primera clase*

second class ‖ *segunda clase*

third class ‖ *tercera clase*

When does the ____ leave for ____? ‖ ¿*A qué hora sale* ____ *a* ____?

Where do they sell tickets? ‖ ¿*Dónde se vende boletos?*

How much is a ticket to ____? ‖ ¿*Cuánto cuesta un boleto a* ____?

Boats

Boats (*barcos* or *lanchas*) and your own two feet are the only form of transportation along the Amazon and its tributaries. Of course, you can always fly over the jungle, but you're limited to traveling by boat or by foot if you want to see this area closely.

You'll find several kinds of boats along the tributaries of the Amazon, including large canoes (often with outboard motors) called *colectivos* and two-story houseboat/barge combinations known as *lanchas*.

If you're taking a boat trip there are several mandatory items: insect repellent, mosquito net, a few long-sleeved shirts, sleeping bag and hammock. Don't forget your medical kit, which should include anti-dysentery and antimalaria medicines, since you'll be cooking and drinking river water and it's going to be open season on *you* for the mosquitoes.

You can hang your hammock on the porches of homes along the river. People in isolated areas welcome the company. Although you don't pay for the lodging, you should pay for the food you eat. You should also carry your own food along (preferably canned or packed so it's impervious to moisture). I recommend stocking up on powdered milk as well as canned meat, tuna and fruit. Don't forget cigarettes and liquor to offer as gifts, even if you don't use them yourself.

Carry all your gear in waterproof bags. Before your trip pick up a couple of large pieces of plastic to use as tarps to keep the rain off everything. Tennis shoes or canvas shoes make the best foot gear. You'll be

getting your feet wet constantly and leather shoes or boots will get waterlogged and rot.

You can also buy a *piroga* (dugout) and take off on your own, but I don't recommend this unless you're an experienced jungle and river traveler.

Horseback

Gail Sumner and a party of eleven (including three children and her infant daughter) bought horses in Ecuador, including extra horses for luggage, and plodded along the Pan American Highway. However, feed for the horses was scarce and in two months they covered only sixty miles, so they gave the animals to friends and went back to taking buses. Bill and I took only short trips. Once we rode horseback to the Pre-Columbian ruins at Alto de los Ídolos in San Agustín, Colombia, a trip that frightened me more than any bus, truck or plane trip. One slip and it was straight into the Magdalena River. It was a beautiful way to see the countryside (when I dared to look around) and the cost for the entire day was $2.50 per horse, including the guide. A pretty cheap way to be scared out of your wits.

In areas where you see horses, ask if you can rent one to ride; many farmers appreciate the extra income. However, don't expect old Chico to be Secretariat—go easy. The average saddle you find in the country is a pretty crude affair. If you're a serious rider, carry a saddle from the States or have a local leatherworker make one to your specifications.

A friend who settled in Peru's Urubamba Valley bought a horse for $60 and rode it over the old Inca road to Macchu Picchu, a three-day trip. When he left Peru he sold the horse for what he paid for it. No depreciation.

Llamas carry heavy loads, but not humans, so don't expect to ride one.

Backpacking

> After a long rest the clouds broke up and we moved up
> about 200 meters. I had taken off my boots to fix my socks,
> sitting right on the edge of the ridge. Ken said, "Look
> up!" A huge condor had soared up the other side of the
> ridge and popped up not 20 feet from me! There wasn't
> time to take a picture but for an instant I could almost touch
> him. [All quotes in this section are from a journal kept by
> Bob and Mary Martin while backpacking in the Callejón
> de Huaylas, Peru.]

You aren't likely to have this experience on a bus or train. To really get in touch with the countryside (campo) and the people there's nothing like traveling by foot. This has been the traditional means of travel in the Andes, since the Indians had neither animals they could ride nor the wheel before the Spanish arrived. The Incas constructed thousands of miles of roadways, reaching from Colombia in the north to Chile in the south, with connecting links between the coastal and mountain routes. Most of the Inca roads are still usable, although I haven't found detailed maps of them except for the Cuzco area. Still, all you have to do is get out into the countryside and ask, since the local people know and use the Inca roads and foot trails in the mountains.

> Cries of "Inti! Inti!" awoke us early as travelers passed
> by the campsite to the pass. Curious to know what caused
> the excitement, we poked our heads out of our tents to
> witness what must be the most spectacular sunrise ever.

Any book that shows Inca highways is useful for hiking. Hiram Bingham's papers are housed at Yale University and there's some information available at the National Geographic Society, but you should contact these institutions well in advance of any anticipated visit to obtain permission to see these maps and papers.

Many shops in Cuzco sell maps of the city and its surrounding archaeological sites, and it's well worth buying one. The tourist office in Cuzco has maps, too, including a map of the Macchu Picchu trail. Macchu Picchu is actually last in a chain of Inca fortresses, beginning with Q'ente and continuing with Llacta Pata, Wayllabamba, Qollpa, Sayajmarka, Phuyupatamarka, Wiñay Wayna, Choqesuysuy, Chochabamba and Intipata. Hiking along this trail from Cuzco to Macchu Picchu takes about a week, and you can sleep in a different ruin each night. The map also tells you where drinking water is available. You can borrow this trail map and Xerox it at one of Cuzco's two Xerox centers; ask at the tourist office for directions. The tourist office also has a notebook which contains about a hundred accounts of the Macchu Picchu hike, including suggestions and tips. You can begin the hike from Cuzco or start from Kilometer 88, which is located outside Ollantaytambo and can be reached by train.

In addition to the Macchu Picchu trail, almost anywhere you hike within a hundred-mile radius of Cuzco you'll come across Inca ruins. This entire area is good hiking because the extensive Inca roadways all lead somewhere, so it's hard to get hopelessly lost. One problem with hiking in the Andes, though, is that most of the Indians don't speak Spanish, just Quechua or Aymara, so asking directions can be difficult. (See Chapter Six, "Language," for some useful Quechua phrases.)

Distance in the mountains is measured in leagues *(ligas)* and a league is about 3 miles or 4.8 kilometers. However, as Mary Martin wrote, "a league is a very personal thing."

> One suggestion about asking the locals for directions:
> everyone knows everything, or shall I say, doesn't
> wish to admit he doesn't know. If you say, "Where is such
> and such" in Spanish he may not know what you're
> talking about, for he only knows it by its Quechua name.
> Regardless, he will give you some sort of answer. The
> same applies to distances. We would ask people we met,
> "How far is it to the next town?" They would always give
> us an answer, which was quite different from the answer
> someone else gave us five minutes earlier. If someone said
> "Three leagues" it was often closer to four or five. (Perhaps
> it's because they're used to walking it.) We took the average
> of three answers or if two matched, we relied on that.
> At any rate, you won't get lost; it'll just take you longer
> than they told you it would.

There are also two indispensable guidebooks available which contain maps and descriptions of numerous hikes: *Backpacking in Venezuela, Colombia and Ecuador* ($7.95) and *Backpacking in Peru and Bolivia* ($8.95). To order send a check or money order to:

> Bradt Enterprises,
> 95 Harvey Street, Apt. M
> Cambridge, Mass. 02140.

The Bradts publish two books on South American river rafting and carry an extensive selection of maps, including a very detailed one of South America (in two sections, $9.95 each). For a more complete listing of their titles and maps send 50 cents for a catalog to the above address.

SEVERAL THINGS TO REMEMBER

§ Be in good physical shape and be prepared for the high altitudes and rough terrain of the mountains. There aren't any park rangers to rescue you if you get into trouble.

> The trail was one that'd been obviously used for years and years . . . It was often no more than worn boulders—a pretty rough trail for heavy packs and high altitudes. We all agreed that the trail had originally been cut as steeply as a pack animal could handle, which was nearly more than we could. [This from the Martins, who were experienced backpackers.]

§ In the Andes you can expect rain and quite often snow. Always have along your rain poncho, down jacket and a tarp or tent for shelter. For more on what to take, see the list supplied by the Martins (page 157).

§ Be careful of the environment. Don't relieve yourself on the trail. Go off a ways and bury your shit. There's nothing like coming upon a nice ruin where you'd like to spend the night only to discover that the previous hikers used it for a latrine. This is a problem along the Macchu Picchu trail.

§ Always close gates behind you. Just about every nook and cranny of the Andes is inhabited, even if you see no obvious signs of life. Don't cause trouble for local people by leaving gates open and letting their livestock loose.

§ In the same vein, don't count on living off the land (which usually means some Indian's garden) and don't count on local people to supply you with food. Take plenty of freeze-dried food from home. The Martins supplemented their freeze-dried meals with fish they caught. They also managed to buy some food in villages, but you can't count on this.

VENTURING INTO REMOTE AREAS

When you venture into remote areas people are startled to see you and are invariably curious, sometimes suspicious. What on earth do you want? You could be taken for a missionary, doctor or the CIA. (People aren't sure what the CIA is, but they know it's something nefarious.) You also could be taken for a drug dealer, government spy or sorcerer and be blamed for all the recent local misfortunes from hailstorms to the miscarriage of Aunt Rosa's llama, in which case you could be stoned or run out of town.

To most South Americans tourism involves good times in the city, not trips to inaccessible, primitive towns like their own. And the concept of camping for pleasure is sometimes hard for countrypeople to grasp, since their whole life is spent camping (and not in Winnebagos with televisions and hot water). Don't expect your explanation to be taken at face value initially, although you can always try *"Somos viajeros"* or *"Somos turistas"* ("We're travelers" or "We're tourists") and *"Estamos paseando,"* which means "We're passing through." (Backpackers are called *mochileros,* from the word *"mochila"* meaning "knapsack" or "backpack.")

I'm not implying that people are usually hostile. Often they're shy but curious, and if you have something to give away, such as American cigarettes, or something to share, you can break the ice quickly, as Mary Martin relates:

> We dropped our packs on a carpet of golf-green grass
> and Ken, Rosa and Bob went off in search of beer while I
> waited and rested with the packs. No sooner had they
> gotten out of sight than a woman brought me a bowl
> of fresh, hot milk with *ocas* floating in it; then three other
> women came up and sat down for conversation and knowl-
> edge of the *extranjeros.* We had all become friends when
> the trio returned with the beer, which we shared with
> the numerous people standing around. Finally we began
> to set up camp (amid much watchfulness and curiosity)
> and we were showered with gifts and welcome—a liter
> of fresh cow's milk, 15 potatoes, 9 eggs, onions, lemons
> and smiles. Beautiful, beautiful people!

You also might be stopped and questioned by the police. Don't worry or act hostile; they're simply unbearably curious, like everyone else. Just imagine what it would be like if a couple of Quechua Indians in traditional dress wandered into your hometown. Invite the policeman to have a beer and be prepared to tell him your life story and to demonstrate all your equipment. He'll probably end up letting you camp in the town's plaza or finding you a place to stay. Good manners and the simple courtesy of asking permission are always in order:

> All of our muscles and Rosa's knee were screaming for a
> stop after 8 miles at a very small *pueblo.* We ate a late lunch
> there and decided it was nuts to push ourselves and went
> to set up camp in the town square . . . Once on the
> *pampa* we went to ask permission of a man nearby and
> he would not hear of it! Instead he invited us to his house.

GEAR

Although I've already mentioned some of the following items in Chapter Two, I'm printing verbatim the Martins' list of what they took backpacking. (The Martins traveled overland through Colombia and Ecuador and had much of their gear air-freighted to Lima. You could, of course, carry everything with you and backpack into the mountains along the way.)

Backpacking equipment
1 Alp pack
1 Kelty pack
1 extra Kelty waist belt
3 sleeping bag straps
3 Pungi cords

Tents
1 backpacking tent
2 large tent stakes
12 regular tent stakes
1 ground cloth

Sleeping equipment
2 mummy sleeping bags
2 sleeping-bag stuff sacks
2 sleeping pads (vinyl-covered foam pads)
2 Ensolite pads

Rope
2 20-foot lengths, ½-inch
1 50-foot length, ⅜-inch

Miscellaneous
1 small towel
1 roll Mystic tape
1 compass
1 bottle matches (waterproof bottle, wooden matches)
1 sheath knife (Buck)
1 pocketknife (Swiss army)
1 ice ax
4 candles
1 flashlight
4 flashlight batteries
2 flashlight bulbs

Kitchen equipment
1 Svea stove plus extra wick and valves. (This stove runs on Coleman fuel, which you can't get there. Ken, our friend who drove, brought it with him.)
1 Optimus stove. (Runs on kerosene, plenty available. Indians often have the same stove. We could never get it to work right. Gave it away to some Indians who said they could fix it.)
1 Coleman funnel
3 1-pint fuel containers
2 food stuff sacks (waterproof)
3 large food bottles
3 medium food bottles
1 small food bottle
2 extra food bottles
3 Gerry (brand) food bottles. (These food bottles are for condiments, coffee, creamer, sugar, etc. Can't get white sugar there.)
1 set nested cooking pots
2 Sierra cups
2 sets eating utensils
1 spatula

First aid
4 tins aspirin
4 bottles Cutter's insect repellent
1 large square Moleskin
1 Ace bandage
1 triangular cloth bandage
1 roll adhesive tape
10 gauge squares
1 fingernail clippers
20–30 Band-aids
1 bottle Lomotil (really needed)
1 tube zinc oxide (protection against sunburn)

Fishing equipment
Up to individual. Ken and Bob had collapsible poles and flies; all fishing equipment was brought from the States. No fishing equipment available in Lima. The fishing was good and we supplemented our freeze-dried food with it. Also, as the Indians fish, we made gifts of dry flies, lines and hooks. Wish we'd taken more than we did.

Clothes: what we actually took hiking (per person)
1 down jacket and hood
1 wool shirt
1 pair mittens (ski)
1 wool balaclava
1 pair heavy underwear (like hunters wear)
1 pair thermal underwear
2 fishnet T-shirts
2 pairs Levis
1 cotton shirt
3 pairs wool boot socks
1 pair hiking boots
1 pair moccasins
1 change underwear
2 extra boot laces
1 rain poncho

In addition to their regular gear, Mary and Bob wished they had brought more gifts:

> Each place we stopped we were surrounded first by children, then by adults. There was no hunger, but poverty by our standards was the rule. A length of rope, a bit of coffee—anything—is appreciated. Of course to them we are very wealthy and may be resented if we have nothing to share with them. Luckily we always found something from our personal gear to give to our new-found friends, but how much easier it would have been to have something for that purpose. I'm not saying that it's necessary to give something to everyone you meet in order to be accepted, rather it's nice to be able to repay these people's kindness and hospitality with something other than words or smiles.

For suggestions on small gifts to carry with you, see Chapter Two, "What to Take."

All I can add to the Martins' recommendations is that they shipped lots of freeze-dried food from the United States (you can't get it in South America), and I strongly suggest that you carry tincture of iodine for purifying the water (see Chapter Thirteen, "Health").

Lodging

nce you find a place to stay and have something to eat, you can begin to explore the town and have some fun. So let's consider getting settled.

In general, you can find first-class hotels in all large South American cities, if that's your preference and price range. Otherwise, every town and city has accommodations ranging from moderately priced ($1 to $3 a night) to dirt cheap (thirty cents a night). South America *doesn't* have youth hostels or other facilities which cater especially to students or young travelers, although sometimes the cheap hotels become de facto youth hostels because of all the young people who stay in them.

Any place that calls itself a *hotel* provides the basic room or bed for the night. These basics range in quality from luxurious to absolutely appalling. An establishment with the name *pensión, casa familial* or *casa residencial, residencia* (boarding house), *alojamiento* (lodging) or *casa de huéspedes* (guest house) is more like a boarding house. These places are aimed at guests who plan on staying at least several days and they often include meals in the price of a room. When they aren't full, they usually welcome over-night guests, so be sure to inquire.

Hotels and Boarding Houses

FINDING A HOTEL

How do you find a hotel? First, decide which part of town you want to stay in—downtown, farther out, by the market, near the bus or train station, wherever—and look in that neighborhood.

The *South American Handbook* includes listings for hotels in just about every city and town in South America, from the very cheapest to first-class accommodations. You can also ask people if they know of a good, clean, cheap hotel. The problem with this is that local people invariably steer you to a place that's much too expensive. Other *gringo* travelers are probably more reliable sources of information. If you do ask residents about hotels, stress the "cheap" and insist that you don't want to stay at the fanciest local establishment. Another good method (if you're traveling with someone) is for one person to stay in the plaza with all the gear while the other makes the rounds unencumbered, comparing prices and accommodations. There's really no way to tell what you're in for from the outside; you have to check out the rooms.

The cheap hotels are usually located near the market since they cater to poor *campesinos* who come into town on business. Other cheapos are located near the bus, truck and train stations or other arrival and departure points. If you stay in a cheapo you're guaranteed to see a lot of local color, from local bedbugs to local whores. Some of these hotels are amazingly clean and pleasant, though, so you should always check them out. Don't be put off by the facades; go inside and see what the rooms are like.

Remember, too, that if you stay near the market you'll get lots of noise when the big diesel trucks gun their motors at 4 A.M. and disgorge a load of Indians, pigs and cattle, some or all of which may bed down for the few remaining hours of darkness on the sidewalk beneath your window or in the courtyard of your hotel. (Try going back to sleep to oinks, grunts, squeals and transistor radios playing Aymara love songs.)

Wherever you stay, if you learn just three words, you'll sleep a lot better. These words are *un cuarto interior,* meaning "an inside room," one that's off the street. If the street is at all busy (which equals noisy) or is located anywhere near the market, request *un cuarto interior.* You may still need earplugs to shut out the noise coming from inside the hotel, but at least you'll miss the worst of the street activity.

If the town is tiny or is located in the middle of nowhere there may be no obvious hotel—or no hotel at all. To find accommodations, ask any official—for example, the mayor *(alcalde)* or the police—or anyone who speaks Spanish rather than Quechua or Aymara. You may be sent to the home of a family who takes in boarders or stashed in the jail, church, rectory or bus station. You'll undoubtedly be the most interesting event in town since the mayor's niece ran off to La Paz with the bus driver, so prepare to be entertained—and to be entertaining. (See the "Backpacking" section in Chapter Ten for advice on venturing into remote areas.)

CHOOSING A ROOM

Once you've found a place where you'd consider staying there are several things to check before actually settling on a room (*cuarto* or *habitación*). (Of course, all of this is academic when you're presented with a straw pallet on the floor of the only *pensión* in town.) If you want a double bed ask for a *cama matrimonial*. These are the exception, not the rule, in South American hotels. Heating is also the exception in the Andes, but some hotels provide small space heaters (*estufas*) if you request them. You may also be able to get a fan (*abanico* or *ventilador*).

Always insist on seeing the room before you commit yourself—not just any room, but the room you'll be staying in. Also check out the bathroom (see page 163). Toilet is *baño* or *servicio sanitorio* and shower or bath is *ducha*. A private bathroom is *baño privado*. Rooms with private baths are more expensive than those without.

If there are two of you, be sure to find out if the price quoted is per person or for the room. Some places actually charge for the bed, not the room, and unless you want to share your room with strangers you'll have to pay for all the beds. Most countries require that hotels post their prices to prevent gouging of tourists, but like other legalities in South America, this regulation can be ignored if the police are paid off.

Find out what the price of the room includes ("*¿Qué está incluido?*"), since breakfast or all three meals may be encompassed in the basic cost of the room. The price is often so low that many travelers don't realize meals are included and miss out on what they've paid for. If all three meals are included but you want to eat elsewhere, you can probably make arrangements for this with a consequent reduction in your bill. Work this out with the proprietor (*dueño*) or desk clerk before you check in, not later. You can also bargain for a lower rate if you're staying a week or longer. It's always worth trying to bargain on the cost of any room. Just be sure to agree on a price before you check in.

CHECKING IN

When you check in at a hotel you're asked to fill out a form that asks much the same questions as the tourist card. If you're an unmarried couple, say that you're married. (This should be agreed upon before entering the country so both your tourist cards say "married.") In some countries it's illegal for hotels to rent rooms to unmarried couples, although how strictly this is enforced is anyone's guess. Say "married" and be safe. As

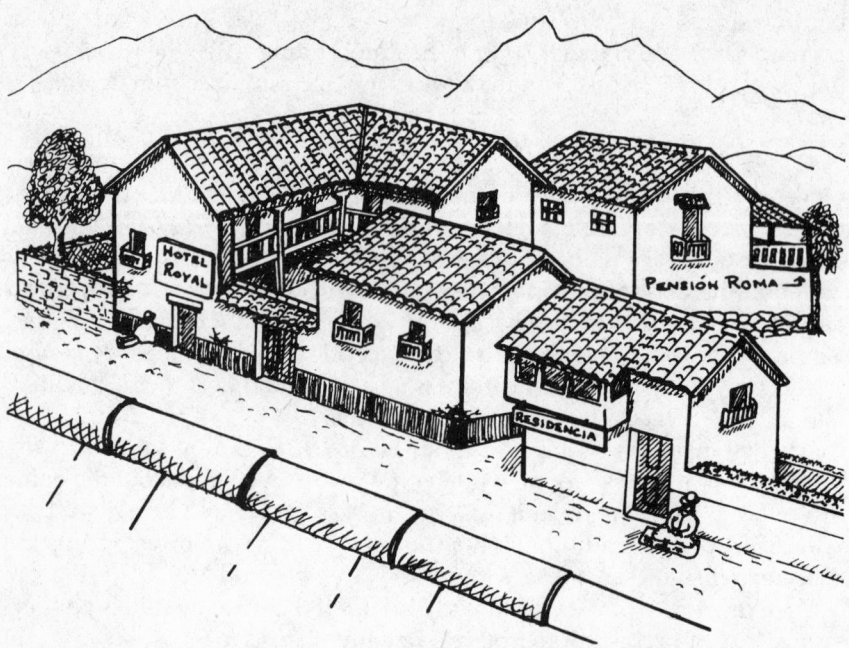

a foreigner you also must present your passport. Do this automatically and don't worry if the desk clerk keeps the passport for a while. The Andean countries usually require hotel managers to present a list of guests to the police, so the clerk may have to copy some information from your passport.

Occasionally the police raid the hotels. This happens fairly often in Cuzco, where the police make periodic drug checks at the cheap hotels where young people hang out. It happened to me in Bolivia during an attempted military coup, and it happens regularly in Colombia because of the crackdown on marijuana use and cocaine smuggling. Two travelers told me that during their stay in five different Colombian cities, the police came to their hotel rooms to search for drugs at 8:30 every morning. The police were more or less polite and very insistent. The point of all this is to alert you to the fact that when you check in at a hotel, your name and place of residence are turned over to the local police as required by law. In eleven months of travel the police never visited my room, although once I was confronted by them in the lobby of my Bolivian hotel during the uprising mentioned earlier. (This was just a passport check.) Also, I traveled through Colombia before its stepped-up antidrug campaign. At any rate, you never know when and for what reason the police might turn up, so be forewarned but not alarmed.

MEALS

I enjoy eating breakfast in the dining room (*comedor*) at the *residencia* because I'm usually too sleepy and disorganized to hunt for a restaurant early in the morning. Sometimes *residencia* cooking is really tasty and it's as close to home cooking as you'll find on your trip. Eating breakfast there is also a good way to meet people, both South Americans and other *gringo* travelers. For lunch and dinner I like to try out places in town and I sometimes go with people I've met earlier at the *residencia*.

KITCHENS

Some hotels, particularly the cheapos, *pensiones* and *residencias,* allow you to use the kitchen (*cocina*) to prepare your own meals or mix up a batch of granola. They usually don't care if you cook in your room since the Indians do it no matter what. (A balcony is a good place for this— there's good ventilation and less of a fire hazard.)

BATHROOM FACILITIES

You've just checked into your room. A twenty-five-watt light bulb flickers and goes out since the town is rationing electricity, but you get a glimpse of the pink and purple wallpaper, a three-legged chair, a picture of the Blessed Virgin smiling across the room at a calendar showing lots of tits and ass, and two sagging, iron constructions purporting to be beds. *"¿Está bien?"* asks the ten-year-old girl who checked you in.

"¿Baño?" you ask. She lights a candle and leads you outside, down two flights of stairs, across the patio, through the kitchen (you make a mental note to eat elsewhere) and into the backyard, where the chickens, pigs and guinea pigs compete for the available space. She shows you a wooden shack with swinging barroom doors and a hole in the concrete floor. No mistaking what it is. You could find it in the dark with your nose.

"¿Ducha?" She proudly shows you to another wooden shack with a hole in the concrete floor, but this one has a pipe at head level with a faucet and a number of wicked-looking wires and switches. There's even *hot* water—when there's electricity, which isn't often.

The chickens and guinea pigs have visited both the *baño* and the *ducha* and left unmistakable evidence. These facilities are also shared by all eleven members of the family and the other thirty-seven guests, but what do you want for thirty cents a night?

If you're willing to stay at a moderately priced hotel, you move up into the middle class and the facilities improve accordingly. There is, for example, a real toilet. It may not work and the cracked and broken plastic seat may fall off or pinch your ass, but it's better than a hole in the floor. There's also a sink with hot *(caliente)* and cold *(frío)* water faucets. (The "C" stands for *caliente,* not cold, although cold is sometimes closer to the truth.) Hot water may come out of the cold water tap and cold out of the hot, or cold water may come out of both faucets, or nothing may come out at all. (I've never, never had hot water come out of both faucets.) It all depends on the plumber's training, the hotel's policy and the town's water supply.

Hot water *(agua caliente)* is a rare commodity in the Andes, and it's usually on the traveler's mind, especially after a sixteen-hour bus ride or a night or two spent at a cheap hotel. The crucial question is not just *if* the establishment has hot water, but *when*. Many places have hot water only at certain, often unpredictable hours. Some hotels have their own water heater which is only turned on for several hours in the morning or evening. This is your one and only chance to get hot water. I stayed at one hotel that charged guests an extra twenty-five cents for hot water and required you to make your request several hours in advance. The management then heated up just enough water for a quick shower.

Hotels in the Andes have come up with amazing devices to provide hot water for guests. A common solution is to connect two electrical wires to the shower pipe. The current is activated by throwing a huge switch, the kind you see in old gangster movies when someone dies in the electric chair. Every time I use one of these electric showers I have the distinct feeling I'm throwing the switch at my own execution, and this isn't wide of the mark. If you stand barefoot in a puddle of water on the shower floor or if you happen to touch the shower pipe, that shower could be your last. I've gotten some whopperoo shocks, although it probably doesn't compare to being struck by lightning.

Here's what to do when faced with one of these switches. First, throw it before you get into the shower, preferably when you still have your shoes on and aren't standing in a puddle. (This may require some contortions.) Once you're in the shower don't touch the shower pipe, shower nozzle or any of the wires or switches. Just enjoy the hot water and don't make any unnecessary connections. You can safely turn the water on and off (famous last words). Only when you're out of the shower and again standing on dry ground should you return the switch to the "off" position.

PUBLIC BATHS

Wherever you're staying, it's possible to get a hot shower or bath even if there isn't one at your lodging. There are public baths *(baños públicos)* in just about every town. These are usually located near the market and a hot shower costs about twenty-five cents. Besides showers (*duchas* or *regaderas*), there are also sauna baths, which are called *baños de vapor*, *baños saunas* or *baños turcos*. A towel and soap are sometimes supplied, but just to be safe, come with your own.

The Andes have many hot springs, some of which are ancient Inca baths. Any town with *aguas calientes* (hot water) as part of its name probably has hot springs nearby. Hot springs are also called *baños termales*, *agua termal* or *termas*, and a visit to one is amazingly restorative. If the springs are public you have to wear a bathing suit, so take one along. In some cases, though, there are rooms at the springs where you can bathe in private. Charges are nominal, about twenty-five to fifty cents.

LOCKING YOUR ROOM

Can you put your hand through the wall? If so, forget about locking your room. The cheapest hotel I ever visited had walls between rooms consisting of fabric nailed to the laths. This made it very easy to drop in on your neighbor and I didn't feel too secure.

Even with solid walls, the locks on hotel-room doors aren't always adequate. In one hotel I was given a skeleton key, and any key looked like it would open any door. This turned out to be true, as I found out the night I caught a thief in my room. Most hotels, though, have better locks than this and I've never had anything stolen from my room. As a general rule, the better the hotel, the safer your possessions.

You usually turn in your key (*llave*) at the main desk whenever you leave the hotel's premises rather than carry it around. If you're concerned about thievery you can check valuables at the desk (get a receipt!) or you can buy a hasp before you leave home. A hasp is an inexpensive lock which can be installed quickly over existing locks. You can also take along an ordinary padlock and hope there's something to lock it over. This makes it difficult for the maid to clean your room, but if she can't get in, neither can anyone else. As a matter of course, your passport and money should be in your money belt or the money checked at the desk along with other valuables.

COMFORT

On reading this chapter, my publisher asked, "What about the decent places?" I told him that for the most part I was describing the decent places, since I avoided the cheapest hotels. Actually, I was fairly comfortable and fairly lucky in my search for moderately priced, clean hotels with hot water—and you will be too, without spending a fortune. Central heating is the exception, even in some of the first-class hotels on the *altiplano*, but you can always request extra blankets *(cobijas* and *frazadas)* and pillows *(almojados)*.

LAUNDRY

I saw only one coin-operated laundromat during my travels, and that was in a rich suburb of Lima. However, just about anyone is happy to take in laundry for the extra income, so all you have to do is ask around.

When you send out laundry or dry-cleaning, you are given a list to check or are asked to make out a list—in Spanish, of course. The following are the most common clothing items:

bathing suit ‖ *traje de baño*

blouse ‖ *blusa*

brassiere ‖ *sostén*

coat ‖ *saco*

dress ‖ *vestido*

dressing gown or robe ‖ *bata*

handkerchief ‖ *pañuelo*

jacket ‖ *chaqueta*

pajamas ‖ *pijamas*

pants or trousers ‖ *pantalones*

panties ‖ *braguitas, medias*

shirt ‖ *camisa*

slip ‖ *combinación, enagua*

stockings ‖ *medias, calcetines*

suit ‖ *terno*

sweater ‖ *chompa*

tie ‖ *corbata*

T-shirt or undershirt ‖ *camiseta*

towel ‖ *toalla*

washcloth ‖ *trapo, estropajo*

a pair, two pairs ‖ *un par, dos pares*

dirty clothes ‖ *ropa sucia*

to dry-clean ‖ *limpiar en seco*

to iron ‖ *planchar*

to wash or to launder ‖ *lavar*

washable ‖ *lavable*

laundry (the place) ‖ *lavandería*

Living with a Family

It's always possible to rent a room from a family and to eat with them, too. You do, of course, have to adapt to their lifestyle. This is a much greater problem for North American or European women than it is for men, since women are so restricted in South America. The arrangement doesn't have to be permanent, though; you could live with a family for several months and then move on to your own place.

Renting a House in a Village

It sounds romantic, doesn't it, renting a house in an Indian village, moving in and making new friends? It can be done and it's very cheap—ten dollars a month would be high. You'd better think twice about your reception, however. Historically, the presence of *blancos* has meant trouble for the Indians—whether it's been tax collectors, missionaries or people out to take their land or recruit them for unpaid labor. The local people can't imagine why anyone would want to move into an adobe hut in their village, when all they want to do is get out or away from the poverty the village represents. Even if they like their village, they can't understand why rich *blancos* would rent a cruddy, adobe hut when they obviously can afford something better. There must be more to this than meets the eye: you're spies for the CIA or national police; you're involved in illicit drugs; or maybe you want to kidnap all the children in the village and grind them up for oil, which everyone knows is in short supply in the United States. A friend of mine was asked by the people of a remote Bolivian town if he knew Charles Manson and if he was "one of them." Such are the pictures of America that precede us. Any outsider is suspect. In his diary Che Guevara reported how Bolivian peasants thought he was in the area for cocaine and wanted to be cut in on the deal.

If local people can't figure out why you're there, neither can the authorities. Their thoughts focus on drugs and Communism and you should be prepared for The Raid. In the case of Tina and Clement, two *gringo* travelers who were living outside a small Bolivian village, this took place at about five o'clock one morning. Their adobe farmhouse was surrounded by a squad of Bolivian soldiers armed with machine guns, and the house was searched for drugs, Communist propaganda and God knows what else. When the commander didn't find anything sinister he confiscated their passports, and they had to ask the British consul for help in getting them back. Sometime after the raid they learned that a neighbor had reported them to the authorities because they had refused to show him their papers. This outraged the neighbor, so he reported them as suspicious. After the raid they were left in peace for the rest of their stay in the area.

Tina and Clement found their farmhouse simply by taking a bus out to the village and then asking around. In the countryside available houses aren't likely to have a *"Se alquila"* ("For rent") sign on them, especially since most of the villagers are illiterate; but because everyone in the village knows everyone else and what's going on, places for rent are advertised by word of mouth. It took Tina and Clement only a couple of days to find their place. They paid five dollars a month for it (which was considered high) in 1974, but an adobe house would probably cost (horrors) double that today. If people are suspicious of you they might not tell you about rentals right away. In that case, try to find a *pensión* in town or board with a family. Behave circumspectly, get to know people and a rental will eventually come up.

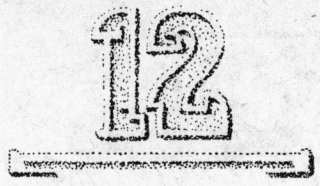

Food

est assured that you'll eat well in the Andean countries, at least in the large cities, and for about half what it costs to eat out in the States. However, most travelers run into two problems when it comes to ordering food. First, they can't read the menus or speak Spanish well enough to order what they want: how do you say "Scrambled eggs, toast and coffee"? So they end up sticking to restaurants located in the large hotels, where the menus are in English and the prices are higher. The second problem is that most travelers don't know very much about typical local foods and specialties and consequently miss out on some real treats. I'm a picky eater and I hate food surprises, so I fall into this category.

I'm always amazed at how much people worry about getting sick from the food. Don't waste your energy worrying. Follow a few basic precautions. First, make sure you have your inoculations to ward off typhoid and hepatitis. Then use common sense and don't buy food from street vendors if it looks or smells like it's been left standing unheated or unrefrigerated for a long period of time. Food spoils quickly when kept at air temperature while both heat and cold retard the growth of toxic bacteria. This means that a ham sandwich left out on a stand can go bad, but food kept hot over a fire is okay. I've had wonderful hot food (sausages and potatoes) from sidewalk stands. Remember, too, that since most

Indians don't have refrigerators in their huts they're experts at keeping food from spoiling. In many instances the women cook up food just in time for train and bus arrivals and keep it hot on stoves or grills. They're good cooks, too.

Appearances are just that—appearances. The fancy tourist restaurant may have spent so much money decorating the dining room that there was nothing left over to fix the plumbing in the restrooms. If a place is crowded with local people, that's a good sign—never mind the greasy tablecloths. A restaurant can't poison its customers regularly and keep them coming back for more.

The markets (*mercados*) are good, cheap places to eat, for both fresh and cooked foods. Cooked-food stands are called *fondas* and are well worth checking out. Be sure to ask the price before you buy something and bargain if you think the price is too high.

In addition to markets, there are supermarkets (*supermercados*) in Bogotá, Quito, Cuzco and Lima. This is an enormous boon to the non-Spanish-speaker because in a supermarket you can stroll down the aisles and pick things out for yourself. In all the Andean countries there are grocery stores called *tiendas* or *almacenes*, where you might find the item you want on a shelf. If you don't see what you want, then you'll have to ask for it. Prices are higher than they are in the local open market, but *tiendas* and *supermercados* carry imported, canned and packaged foods that are often unavailable anywhere else. If you just can't stand it any longer, you can buy a box of good old Kellogg's corn flakes for $2.50 or a package of Betty Crocker brownie mix for about the same price.

Eating Places and Food-sellers

bakery ‖ *Panadería* or *pastelería*. Many bakeries also operate coffee shops so you can pick out a goodie and then sit down for coffee or tea.

bar ‖ *Bar, salón* or *cantina*. Many bars are local, male-only hang-outs, and an unescorted woman entering a *cantina* is taken for a whore and treated as such. If you're a couple, then be sure other couples frequent the place. If you're a woman traveling alone and want a cocktail or beer, your best bet is the bar in the local, first-class hotel. These hotels cater to foreign travelers and a lone woman is not harassed.

café ‖ *Café*. In Bolivia, *confitería*.

candy store ‖ *Bombonería*. Candies are called *dulces* or *bombones*.

chicha tavern ‖ *Chichería*. (See "Beverages.")

Chinese restaurant ‖ *Chifa*. You'll find *chifas* all over South America, and the food is generally very good. I frequently feasted on cashew chicken at a *chifa* in La Paz.

grill (where meat is charcoal-grilled) ‖ *Parrillada*. Another one of my favorite places to eat. Try one!

grocery store ‖ *Almacén* or *tienda*, meaning "store." Groceries are called *abarrotes*, so watch for this sign.

ice-cream parlor ‖ *heladería*

market ‖ *Mercado*. All food, no matter where it's served, is bought in the market, so you might as well go there yourself and eliminate the middle man. In Bolivia the permanent market is called *la cancha*, which is Quechua for "enclosure." The weekly market is known as *la feria* throughout South America.

market stall (where food is cooked and served) ‖ *Fonda*. In Bolivia, *kiosko*. Good, cheap eating.

open-air restaurant ‖ *Quinta*. Besides food, a *quinta*'s attractions include open-air dining and sometimes a beautiful garden.

Peruvian Creole restaurant ‖ *Picantería*. The name comes from their typically peppery hot *(picante)* food.

restaurant ‖ *restaurante*

soda fountain ‖ *fuente de soda*

supermarket ‖ *supermercado*

Restaurants

One evening Irma, Wally, Al and I decided to go out for catfish, which is called *zurubí*. We were told that the best catfish cooking could be found at a small neighborhood tavern and restaurant. By this time we had learned not to judge a restaurant by its facade. If we had, we wouldn't have put a foot in the door. Inside were rowdy, lurching drunks and no women.

The host seated us at a table with a tablecloth that looked as if it were left over from an orgy, with a hog butchering to boot. Irma and I looked at each other and shuddered. I knew I wouldn't put my elbows on the table because if I did I would contract some terrible skin disease. The waiter appeared and cleared off some dirty dishes; then he whisked off the tablecloth with a flourish. Irma and I smiled at each other in obvious relief. The waiter shook the cloth out, turned it over grandly and put it back on the table, with evident pride in this display of cleanliness for the *gringos*. Irma and I looked at each other with an unspoken, "Do we order or do we leave?"

Before we had time to say anything drinks appeared, and so did the other patrons, half of whom told us with great pleasure how much they disliked *yanquis* while the other half apologized for their friends with drunken eloquence. Several men sobbed in the background (not over international relations but over unrequited love) and raucous, maudlin music played at brain-damaging volume. As we were pondering the best way to make a quick, inconspicuous exit, the waiter arrived with four huge, steaming plates of *zurubí*, which he placed in front of us, covering up most of the wretched tablecloth. It was one of the best meals of the trip.

Eating in any South American restaurant is an adventure. Often you're presented with a menu *(el menú)* that's completely misleading because it represents the owner's fantasy of what he'd like to serve under ideal conditions, not what's available. Any restaurant with pretensions to class lists a "Waldorf salad," and every time I ordered one the response was *"No hay"* ("There isn't any"). It's a good idea to have second and third choices. In fact, you can save yourself a lot of trouble if you simply ignore the menu and ask, *"¿Qué hay?"* ("What is there?" "What do you have?").

If prices aren't listed on the menu, be sure to ask and agree on a price before you order or you may be presented with a whopping check—like three dollars for rice and beans.

In order to get a waiter's attention in Bolivian restaurants, clap your hands sharply several times. While this seems strange at first, it isn't considered rude in the least, and you get results fast.

The following lists provide a basic vocabulary for eating in South American restaurants.

MEALS *(Comidas)*

breakfast ‖ *Desayuno. Desayuno americano* is the typical American breakfast of eggs, toast, coffee and juice, while *desayuno continental* is the continental breakfast of roll and coffee.

lunch ‖ *Almuerzo* or *merienda*. In many places there's a businessmen's special or meal of the day served at noon. This is called the *especial* or *el menú del día*. Don't confuse this with *el menú*, which is the menu, or list of dishes. If you order the *especial*, you get rolls, salad, soup, beverage, main meat course, vegetables and dessert for about a dollar. Many restaurants advertise the *especial* in the window or clip it to the menu cover. Watch for these bargains.

tea (served about 5 P.M.) ‖ *té, lonche, las onces*

supper ‖ *Cena*. This term usually refers to a light evening meal, although it can also refer to dinner.

dinner ‖ *Comida* or *cena*. Most South Americans dine late, around 9 P.M. Restaurants are usually open from about noon to 3 P.M. for lunch and then close until 7 P.M., when they reopen for dinner. I could never get used to this and was always starved by 5 P.M. (tea time). You just have to adapt.

STAFF *(Empleados)*

manager or owner ‖ *dueño*

waiter ‖ *mesero, camarero*

waitress ‖ *mesera, camarera*

THE MENU *(El Menú)*

appetizer ‖ *aperitivo*

beverage ‖ *bebida*

bread ‖ *pan*

casserole ‖ *cacerola*

dessert ‖ *postre*

entrée ‖ *entrada*

hors d'oeuvres ‖ *entremeses*

salad ‖ *ensalada*

salad dressing ‖ *salsa*

sandwich ‖ *torta, sandwich*

soup ‖ *Sopa, caldo, caldillo, chupe* or *crema*. In Quechua, *kashki*. (*Sopa seca*—literally, "dry soup"— isn't soup at all; it's a rice dish.)

stew ‖ *guisado, estofado*. A cooked dish in general is called *guiso*.

UTENSILS *(Utensilios)*

bowl ‖ *bola*

cup ‖ *taza, copa*

fork ‖ *tenedor*

glass ‖ *vaso*

knife ‖ *cuchillo, cuchilla*

napkin ‖ *Servilleta*. These are usually totally useless, tiny pieces of waxed paper that smear the food around even more.

plate ‖ *plato*

saucer ‖ *platillo*

spoon ‖ *cuchara*

HOW FOOD IS PREPARED

baked ‖ *Al horno. Horno* actually means "oven," and the large beehive-shaped, adobe ovens you see in the countryside are called *hornos de barro*.

barbecued ‖ *churrasco*

boiled ‖ *hervido, cocido*

charcoal-grilled ‖ *a la parrilla*

chopped, cut up in pieces ‖ *picado*

cold ‖ *frío, helado*

fried ‖ *frito*

hot (peppery, spicy, hot) ‖ *picante*

hot (temperature) ‖ *caliente*

mashed ‖ *puré*

medium ‖ *mediano*

pickled, marinated ‖ *escabeche*

rare ‖ *raro*

raw ‖ *crudo*

roasted ‖ *asado*

sour ‖ *agria*

stuffed ‖ *relleno*

sweet ‖ *dulce*

TIPS

Like everything else, the tipping situation seems designed to confuse you. Many restaurants add a local tax to your bill plus a charge of ten to fifteen percent called the *servicio,* which most people assume is the waiter's tip *(propina)*. However, the *servicio* actually pays for the wages of the waiter, bus boy and cook. These people receive no other wage for their work except for a share of the *servicio*. If you want to tip your waiter, leave a few coins at the table. It needn't be ten or fifteen percent; anything is appreciated. Some restaurants do pay wages but they're terrible—perhaps thirty dollars a month for a fifty-hour week, four weeks a month. If you eat at a café regularly, the *propina* assures you of extra good service.

Restaurant staff are less restricted than their counterparts in the United States. If the place isn't busy it's perfectly all right to invite your waiter or waitress to join you for a beer. I always shared my chocolate-covered peanuts with the waitress at one of my favorite restaurants in Cocha-bamba. She enjoyed both the treat and the chance to chat.

Remember the phrase *"¿Algo más?"* since you'll hear it in restaurants frequently. It means "Something more?" If you've especially enjoyed your meal it never hurts to compliment the chef. You can say, *"Era sabrosa"* ("It was delicious") or *"Me ha gustado"* ("It pleased me" or "I enjoyed it").

Besides the *servicio*, Peru has another surprise in store for you. This is the *cubierto*, which is a cover charge for the knife, fork, spoon, napkin and bread. I consider this larceny, but it's something you have to accept.

A final word: no matter where you eat, *always* check the addition on the bill. I find errors (in the restaurant's favor) about fifty percent of the time. Either the population is utterly retarded in its arithmetic skills and happens to make errors in the establishment's favor or they're actively trying to bilk travelers. Choose whatever explanation seems reasonable and be sure to add up the check yourself.

Traditional Agriculture

Half the food crops grown in the world today were domesticated in the Americas before the arrival of the Spanish. Most significant are corn (maize) and potatoes, which were the economic foundation of the Inca Empire.

Because of the scarcity of level land for farming in the Andes, the Incas constructed extensive agricultural terraces called *andenes* (or *patakuna* in Quechua), many of which are still in use today. The Incas irrigated these terraces and used them primarily for the planting of corn. There are mag-nificent stone-walled *andenes* throughout the Andes. You'll see them at Macchu Picchu and in the towns of Chincheros, Ollantaytambo and Pisac, Peru, and it's especially exciting to see them still being cultivated. Because the Indians had no draft animals before the Spanish arrived, all plowing was done by men using a wooden foot plow known as a *chaqui taccla*. Women followed along behind the men, breaking up clumps of earth with a short hoe called a *lampa*. This method of cultivation is still employed in many parts of the Andes. I watched Indians working with a *chaqui taccla* in fields (*chacras*) outside Chincheros. Otherwise, you'll see plowing done with a yoke of oxen. I never saw a tractor anywhere in the Andean highlands.

In Inca society, corn was grown primarily for beer-making as well as for holiday and ritual use. Traditionally, a *Sara Mama* (Corn Mother) made of corn cobs and wrapped in fine textiles was kept in a shrine in each home. She represented the strength of the corn crop. During the year she was asked if she was "strong." If so, she remained, but if she was "weak" she was destroyed and another *Sara Mama* was made in her place. After each yearly harvest a new *Sara Mama* was made from ears of corn taken from the most fruitful corn plant. Like so many other traditions, this ritual is still observed in parts of the Andes today.

The first corn-planting each year took place in August or September and was ceremonially performed by the Inca (emperor) himself. Life-size replicas of corn plants, coca bushes, llamas, alpacas and other plants and animals were fashioned from gold and placed in the Inca's sacred garden located in the *Coricancha*. These images were among the treasures taken from Cuzco by the Spanish and melted down into gold ingots.

While corn was a higher status crop, the potato was (and is) the Indians' staple food. Potatoes grow at higher altitudes and in colder climates than corn and can be planted on just about any kind of terrain. Even today, the first potato-planting each year is a ceremonial occasion. Among the Bolivian Aymara, a group of flute-players assembles and pours *chicha* (corn beer) on the ground as an offering to *Pacha Mama* (Mother Earth). *Chicha* is also offered to several potatoes, which are then cut open and stuffed with sheep's fat and coca leaves. These potatoes are the first to be planted. Everyone present at the ceremony then chews some coca leaves, drinks a little *chicha* and begins planting in earnest. In some areas, a llama is sacrificed to ensure the success of the new crop, another custom dating back to Inca times, if not earlier.

Indian life in the Andes has always been organized around the agricultural cycle. After the introduction of Christianity, many of the ancient agricultural fiestas came to be celebrated ostensibly as Catholic feasts and saints' days, but the basic cycle of celebrations has remained unchanged. For more on this subject, see Chapter Seventeen, "Fiestas, Music and Dance."

Sara Mama

Today, the typical highland diet includes some kind of tuber, usually potatoes, plus corn and beans. Occasionally the Indians eat guinea pigs and many communities make cheese from cow, sheep and goat milk. Rice was introduced by the Spanish and is now a common food in the Sierra. Overall, this diet is high in carbohydrates and low in protein.

There are local variations in diet, however. Generally, the lower the elevation, the more variety there is in the diet. Many seasonal varieties of fruits and vegetables are grown, and, if you have money in the highlands, you can buy citrus fruits, which are transported from semitropical areas. However, you should expect a basic diet of rice, beans, corn and potatoes any time you wander off the beaten path.

Fruits

Fruit is *fruta* in Spanish, *ruru* in Quechua and *achu* in Aymara. Trying to list and describe all the fruits found in South America is nearly impossible because there are so many of them and because many fruits have more than one name in Spanish and English, depending on the locale. It's the same as calling a peanut a goober. When more than one name is used, I list the most common one first.

All of the fruits listed are available in the markets, although you can't buy all fruits in all markets. The best places to buy fruit are along the coast and in the Yungas, the subtropical valleys on the eastern slope of the Andes. The higher you go, the fewer fruits are grown. Some fruit is trucked up to the *altiplano*, and I saw oranges and grapefruits for sale around Lake Titicaca.

You can buy fruit individually or by the kilo, half kilo *(libra)* and quarter kilo *(media libra)*. Be sure to bargain. You're allowed to touch the fruits in the market, although this isn't much help if you don't know what they're supposed to feel like when ripe. Occasionally a vendor will offer you a sample. If you want to learn what something is, ask, "*¿Qué es?*" ("What is it?") or "*¿Cómo se llama?*" ("What is it called?"). You'll probably get a quick answer in Spanish (or maybe even Quechua or Aymara) and if you remember the word you might find it in the list that follows. To ask "Is it ripe?" try "*¿Está maduro?*" or "*¿Está listo para comer?*" Don't buy too much fruit at once since food spoils quickly in the tropics. For health precautions and instructions for washing fruit, see Chapter Thirteen, "Health."

What we commonly call fruits and vegetables aren't always botanically fruits and vegetables. For example, tomatoes, peppers and squash are members of the fruit family. Each food in the following list is a true fruit, meaning it's the matured ovary of a seed-bearing plant. In most fruits the seeds are surrounded by flesh or pulp which nourishes and protects the seeds. Sometimes we eat just the pulp (oranges), sometimes we eat just the seeds (pomegranates) and sometimes we eat both (pumpkins).

I've included sketches and descriptions of some of the less familiar fruits, since it's a shame to miss out on these treats just because you don't know what they are or how to eat them. (Do I eat the whole thing, or throw away the skin, or eat the pulp and not the seeds, or eat the seeds and not the pulp? Or are all the people laughing at me because it's only fed to livestock?)

In this list and all subsequent food listings, a star (*) means that the food is native to the Americas.

achocha* || A member of the squash family found in Peru. It's usually pickled rather than cooked.

apple || *Manzana;* also spelled *mansana.*

apricot || *Damasco.* In Bolivia, *amarillo.*

assai* || A small, blue fruit about the size of a cherry. It's mashed in water and eaten with manioc.

avocado* || *Palta.* Named after the tribe in southern Ecuador which apparently introduced the fruit to the Andes. (Our word for avocado is taken from the Mexican Nahuatl term for the fruit, *ahuacatl.*)

aya-tasco or *tacsonia** || A plum-like fruit which comes from a member of the passionflower *Passiflora)* genus. It has a pale yellow skin, black seeds and a red-orange pulp. Eat both the pulp and the seeds. This fruit has a number of names: *purupuru* in Ecuador, *curuba* in Colombia, *tumbo* in Peru and Bolivia and *tintin* in Quechua. There are at least twenty species of *Passiflora* in Peru alone, many with edible fruit.

banana || *Plátano.* In Aymara, *pokota.* There are many, many varieties. The familiar yellow banana is eaten raw while other kinds are better when boiled, baked or fried. If you aren't sure, ask the vendor, *"¿Necesito cocerlo?"* ("Must I cook it?"). The small finger bananas make delicious traveling food. In Ecuador, the world's largest exporter of bananas, regular bananas are called *guineos,* finger bananas are called *oritas,* and the short, fat, red bananas are called *maqueños.*

berries || *Bayas* or *fresas.* Berries are called *cerezas* in Bolivia. This is going to confuse you, since *fresas* and *cerezas* usually mean "strawberries" and "cherries" respectively. Try *bayas* first, and if you get a blank look try the other terms.

blackberries || *Moras.* Mulberries are also called *moras.*

borojoa* || Common in Colombia, it's usually made into juice.

breadfruit ‖ *Fruta de pan*. A round fruit, about six to eight inches in diameter, that has a thick, tan, warty skin. It's usually roasted and is very starchy.

cactus pear ‖ *Tuna*, the fruit of the prickly pear cactus. When ripe it's reddish outside, with a deep red pulp. It tastes like melon and is surprisingly good.

cantaloupe ‖ *melón*

carob ‖ *Algarroba*. In Quechua, *cunuri*. The carob tree is a small evergreen that's actually a member of the pea family. The flat, dark brown pods are used for cattle fodder. In the United States, carob is used as a substitute for chocolate.

casábana★ ‖ A fragrant member of the melon and squash family, common in Peru and Brazil. It's sometimes made into jams and jellies rather than eaten cooked.

chayote★ ‖ A member of the squash and melon family. It's greenish, hairy, contains only one seed, and looks like a small, hairy squash. It's cooked like squash

(baked or boiled), not eaten raw. The seed is the best part of all.

cherries ‖ *Cerezas* or *guindas*. In Bolivia, *fresas*.

cocona★ ‖ An orange-colored fruit common in Colombia.

coconut ‖ *Coco*. Good for both its meat and milk.

cucumber ‖ *Pepino*. In South America cucumbers come in an astonishing array of shapes and colors. They can be round, oval or oblong. They can be green, purple and white striped or purple and yellow striped.

currants ‖ *corintos*

custard apple ‖ *Chirimoya*; also spelled *cherimoya*. "Custard apple" is the name given to a number of fruits of the Anonaceae family. These fruits grow on small trees and have a custard-like taste, hence the name. The most common are the *chirimoya*, soursop and sweetsop. *Chirimoyas* are common throughout the Andes. They're about four to six inches long with a green skin somewhat like that of a pineapple. The white pulp can be served chilled and is eaten out of the skin with a spoon.

dates ‖ *dátiles*

egg fruit★ ‖ *Lucuma*. A yellow, egg-shaped fruit. Like the custard apple, the egg fruit is a member of a family of fruits which are related, but have extremely different physical characteristics. They're

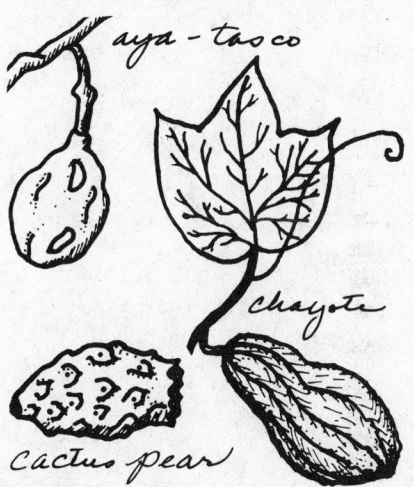

aya - tasco

chayote

cactus pear

members of the *sapotacae* species and are the fruit of the *lúcomo* (or *sapodilla* or *chicle*) tree, whose latex gives us chewing gum—hence the name "Chiclets." Other common fruits of this group include the star apple, *sapodilla* and *mamey*. Eat the pulp, but not the skin and seeds.

eggplant ‖ *berenjena*

fig ‖ *higo*

grapes ‖ *uvas*

grapefruit* ‖ *Toronja*. In Bolivia, *pomelo*.

guava* ‖ *Guayaba;* also called *pacai*. In Quechua, *sahuinto*. In Colombia, *guama*. A very common fruit that looks something like a cross between a pear and a crab apple. It's light yellow when ripe and has a juicy pulp and many seeds. Some varieties are a bit tart. Guavas are often made into jams and jellies, especially in Colombia. Some varieties are reddish, rather than yellow, when ripe. Guavas have a very high vitamin c content, higher than most other fruits.

lemon ‖ *Lima*. Don't confuse this with the lime, which is *limón* in Spanish. Both fruits may be yellow in color and both are served with tea, depending on what's available.

lime ‖ *Limón*. Especially good on papayas. Green or yellow in color.

lulo ‖ Found in Colombia, *lulo* is an orange-colored fruit, the size of a plum, with a pomegranate-like inside.

mamey or *sapote** ‖ Another fruit from the *chicle* tree species. It's a round, orange-to-coconut-sized fruit with a sweet, somewhat spicy, red pulp.

mamoncillo ‖ A relative of the litchi nut, it's a small, green, plum-like fruit.

mango ‖ A very common fruit that's been imported into the United States, so you may be familiar with it. It's oval-shaped and can fit in the palm of your hand. When ripe, the color varies from green, to green and yellow, to yellow and red. Discard the skin and pit and eat the orange pulp, which is nice and sweet. Mangoes are impossible to eat without getting very sticky, which is when your Wash 'n Dri towelettes come in handy.

medlar ‖ *Níspero*. A small, round fruit with a skin that forms a bell with five pointed lobes around its bottom rim. Each lobe contains one seed. Some varieties aren't good until they're very soft and brown. Although they look over-ripe, they're just ready to eat.

melon ‖ *Melón*. This word is used for all melons except watermelon.

mulberries ‖ *moras*

musk melon ‖ *melón almizclero*

*naranjilla** ‖ A small fruit that looks like a fuzzy, orange-to-green-colored crab apple. It's found mainly in Ecuador, where you're served *naranjilla* juice rather than orange juice in the morning. The juice has a weird, green color but is delicious.

orange ‖ *Naranja*. Oranges are plentiful. Because they're not dyed, they're often green when ripe—ask the vendor.

palm heart ‖ *Palmito*. This fruit reminds me of an artichoke heart and is often served as an appetizer or salad.

paterna ‖ A green, cucumber-like fruit.

papaya★ ‖ Since the *papaya* is becoming increasingly common in the United States, you may be familiar with it. It's usually yellow or orange when ripe. The pulp is high in sugar and contains an enzyme called papain, which breaks down protein and is used as a meat tenderizer. *Papaya* is best with lime juice squeezed on the pulp. In Ecuador, the *chamburo* and *chilguacan* are varieties of *papaya*.

passion fruit or granadilla★ ‖ *Granadilla*. In Quechua, *apincoya*. This is an egg-sized fruit that has a hard, orange-brown skin when ripe, with dark, slimy (but good) seeds. Split it lengthwise and use a spoon to eat both the pulp and the seeds. The name came from the Jesuits' belief that the flower parts represented the hammer and nails used to crucify Christ; also, St. Francis of Assisi

was said to have seen the passion-flower growing on the cross in his visions.

passion fruit or purple granadilla★ ‖ *Maracuya* or *granadilla morada*. This is an egg-sized fruit that has a purple, wrinkled skin when ripe. Eat it the same way as the granadilla.

peach ‖ *Durazno*. In Bolivia dried peaches are called *quissas*.

peach palm★ ‖ *Pejibaya*. This is an egg-sized, orange-colored fruit that grows in clusters, like grapes. It's usually boiled in water, has a nut-like flavor and is high in protein and fat.

pear ‖ *pera*

pepper (green)★ ‖ *Pimentón verde* or *chile verde*. Peppers were domesticated in the Americas and are used as a spice in many dishes. They're an excellent source of vitamin c in the Indians' diet. They range from not very hot (for example, the bell pepper) to mouth-destroying. Generally, the redder the pepper, the hotter it is; but watch out for the yellow ones, too.

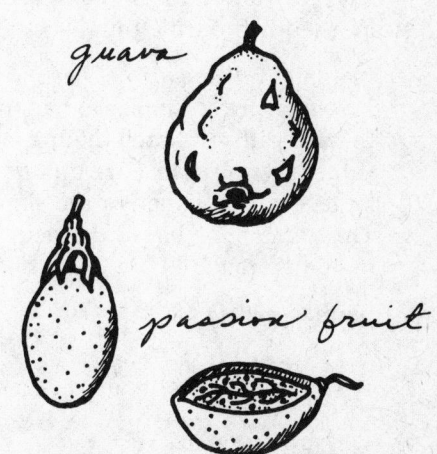

guava

passion fruit

pepper (red and yellow)★ ‖ *Chile* or *aji*. In Quechua, *uchu;* in Aymara, *waika*. In Bolivia, a very hot red pepper is called a *locoto* or *rocoto*. In Peru, however, *rocoto* and *mirasol* refer to a very hot yellow pepper. There are many Quechua and Aymara names for the different peppers, which are all members of the *capsicum* species and include red and green peppers, cayenne pepper and peppers which give us tabasco sauce, chili powder and paprika. *Picante* is the Spanish word for "peppery hot." If you don't want your food hot, ask for it *sin salsa picante* (without hot sauce) or *sin ajis* (without red peppers).

persimmon ‖ *Fruto del dióspiro*. A persimmon tastes somewhat like a pear. When ripe, its smooth, shiny skin is bright orange and the fruit feels soft.

piña de Trujillo ‖ A round, green, speckled fruit found in Peru.

pineapple★ ‖ *Piña* or *anana*. In Quechua, *achupalla*.

pitaya or *pitahaya*★ ‖ This is the fruit of a cactus. It's a red, oval-shaped fruit and has lots of seeds in a reddish purple pulp.

plantain ‖ *Plantaina* or *chapo*. Plantains are so similar to bananas that it's difficult to tell them apart. Generally, plantains are quite large and have green or red skins. They're usually boiled or fried, not eaten raw.

plum ‖ *ciruela*

pomegranate ‖ *Granada*. One of my all-time favorites. It's red when ripe and has tart, crunchy seeds.

pomelo or shaddock★ ‖ *Pumelo* or *pomelo*. This fruit is probably the ancestor of the grapefruit and is almost identical to it.

prune ‖ *ciruela pasa*

pumpkin★ ‖ *Zapallo*. In Quechua, *shapash*. A pumpkin may also be called a *calabaza*, which is a general term referring to squash or gourds.

quince ‖ *Membrillo*. The quince looks like a cross between an apple and a pear and is greenish yellow in color. It's somewhat acidic and is often made into jam or jelly.

raisins ‖ *pasas* or *uvas secas*

raspberries ‖ *frambuesas*

sapodilla or naseberry★ ‖ *Sapota;* also spelled *zapote*. This fruit is round and brown and resembles a hairless coconut. You don't eat the skin and seeds, but the orange-colored pulp is excellent. It comes from the *chicle* tree, a member of the *sapotacae* species.

soursop★ ‖ *Guanábana*. Another one of the custard apples. The soursop is not as sweet as the others and is much larger. It's green in color and can grow as large as a watermelon.

squash★ ‖ *Zapallo;* also *calabaza*. All squash are eaten cooked, not raw.

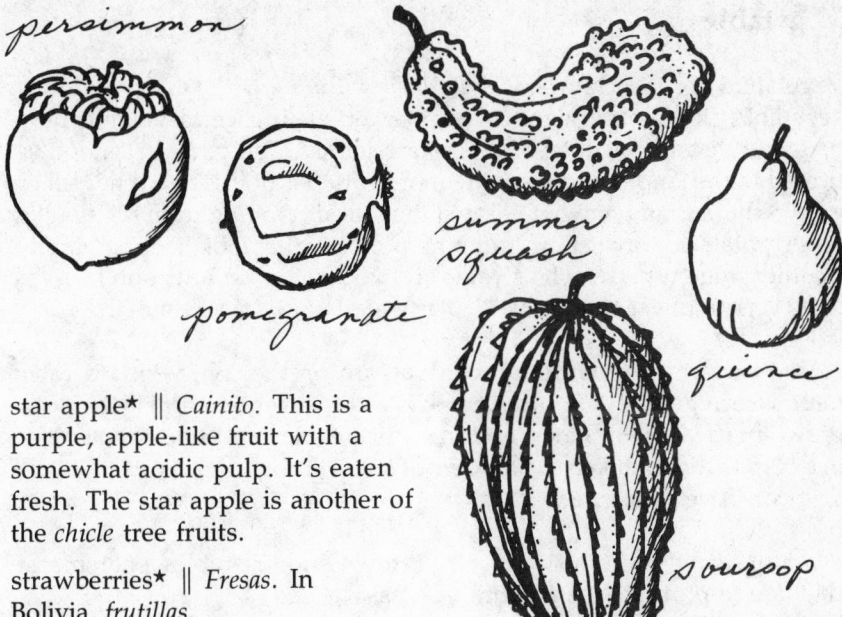

persimmon

pomegranate

summer squash

quince

soursop

star apple★ || *Cainito*. This is a purple, apple-like fruit with a somewhat acidic pulp. It's eaten fresh. The star apple is another of the *chicle* tree fruits.

strawberries★ || *Fresas*. In Bolivia, *frutillas*.

summer squash★ || *Cidrachayote de verano* or *zapallito de verano*. Bright yellow or orange with warts. Delicious!

sweetsop★ || *Anona*. Another custard apple.

tamarind || *Tamarindo*. A legume—that is, a member of the same group of plants as peas and beans, which are pod-bearing plants. The tamarind looks like a big, brown bean pod. Eat the pulp but not the seeds.

tangerine || *Mandarina*. This is one of my favorite traveling foods because the juice is a good thirst-quencher and you can peel and eat the fruit without getting hopelessly sticky. Tangerines keep for a long time.

tomato★ || *tomate*

tree tomato★ || *Tomate de árbol*. Most common in Peru, this is a small, juicy, egg-shaped fruit that belongs to the same family as the tomato. Just picture a red egg growing on a tree. It can be eaten raw but is usually stewed.

tumbo★ || One of the passion fruits common to Peru. It's small, smooth-skinned and green or yellow when ripe.

uvilla (Ecuador) or *uchuba* (Colombia) || This plant is a member of the nightshade family and has distinctive green lanterns, each of which contains one edible berry.

watermelon || *sandia*

zucchini squash || *zapallo italiano*

Vegetables

Vegetables are called *verduras* or *legumbres*. Probably the most unfamiliar vegetables you'll come across in the markets are the weird-looking members and distant relations of the potato family. The potato was domesticated in the Andes and there are more varieties of this and other tubers grown there than anywhere else in the world, ranging from the familiar white potato to tiny yellow and pink potatoes that look like rock candy, to other huge tubers such as yams and yucca. Restaurants don't serve a wide variety of vegetables, particularly on the *altiplano*, where the potato is king.

Don't miss an opportunity to have corn on the cob, which is called *choclo*. Corn grown in South America has much larger kernels than corn grown in the United States, and the ears are juicy and sweet. I ate *choclo* in Ecuador that had kernels the size of small grapes and it was by far the best corn I've ever eaten.

achira or *canna*★ ‖ A fleshy rhizome (a root-like plant stem) that was domesticated in the Amazon Basin and is now commonly found in the Apurimac Valley in Peru. It is light-colored and sweet inside and is usually baked. Traditionally, baked *achira* is sold in Cuzco on the Feast of Corpus Christi.

añu★ ‖ *Añu* or *mashua* in Quechua; *isañu* (also spelled *ysañu*) in Aymara. In Colombia, *cubio*. A small tuber similar to *oca* and potato (actually a relative of the nasturtium). It's very colorful —either yellow or green with purple spots. Because *añu* is somewhat bitter, it's boiled and then frozen or dried before it's eaten. *Añu* is seen in almost all Andean markets.

arracacha★ ‖ Also called *racacha* or *rakkacha*. Another tuber commonly found in the Andes. It's

brown and resembles a parsnip or cassava.

artichoke ‖ *alcachofa*

beans★ ‖ *Habas, frijoles* or *frejoles*. In Quechua, *porotos*. All beans (except French beans) belong to the *Phaseolus* genus and were domesticated in the Americas, and archaeologists have found beans in Peruvian graves dating from 3800 B.C. Beans contain about twenty-five percent

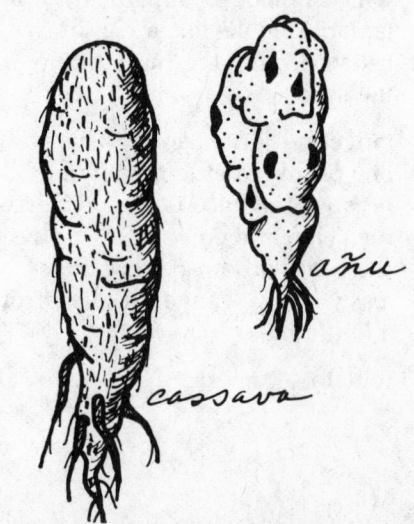

añu

cassava

protein, so they're an important source of protein in the Indians' diet.

kidney, green, snap or wax bean★ ‖ *Frijol* or *frejol*. In Quechua, kidney bean is *pushpu*.

lima bean★ ‖ *Haba grande*. In Quechua, *pallar* or *atun awash*.

string bean★ ‖ *vainita*

wax bean★ ‖ *vainita amarilla*

beet ‖ *remolacha, betarraga*

broccoli ‖ *brécol*

brussels sprouts ‖ *bruselitas*

cabbage ‖ *repollo*

carrot ‖ *zanahoria*

cassava or manioc★ ‖ *Cazabe*; also spelled *casabe*. A dry, starchy tuber with a low-protein content that was domesticated in the Amazon Basin in about 2000 B.C. It's white inside with a brown skin and can grow up to two feet long. There are both bitter and sweet varieties. The bitter ones contain prussic acid and are poisonous if eaten raw; they must be boiled, fermented or squeezed before they're cooked and eaten. Generally, the sweet varieties grow along both coasts while the bitter varieties flourish in the Amazon jungle. Cassava is made into a flour meal which is called *farinha* in Brazil and is also processed to make tapioca.

cauliflower ‖ *coliflor*

celery ‖ *apio*

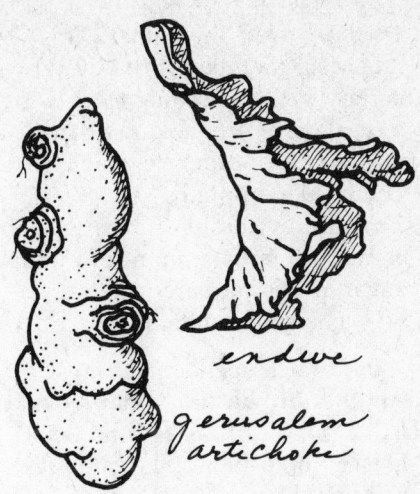

endive

jerusalem artichoke

chick pea ‖ *garbanzo*

chuño★ (also spelled *chuñu*) ‖ *Chuño* refers generally to freeze-dried potatoes or other tubers which are usually eaten in thick soups or stews. Freeze-drying actually was invented in the Andes. To make *chuño*, tubers are alternately frozen and thawed and the water squeezed out for three or four days in a row. The resulting pebble-like morsels keep for years. The Incas stored *chuño* in state warehouses as protection against famine. Most *chuño* sold in the markets is brown in color; white *chuño* is called *tunta*.

corn ‖ *Maíz*. In Quechua, corn in general is *sara*; in Aymara, *tonko*. *Choclo* refers to corn on the cob as well as corn kernels. (For more information, see "Grains.")

endive ‖ *escarola*

Jerusalem artichoke★ ‖ *Cotufa, pataca* or *aguaturma*. "Jerusalem artichoke" is a misnomer. This tuber is a member of the daisy family and has nothing to do with Jerusalem or artichokes. I hate to describe another vegetable that "looks like a potato," so let's say it's a lumpy, brown tuber. It contains a large amount of inulin sugar and is prepared the same way as a sweet potato.

jícama★ (also spelled *jíquima*) ‖ Another brown tuber that looks like a potato. It tastes somewhat like an apple and can be eaten raw or cooked.

kaya★ (also spelled *caya*) ‖ freeze-dried *oca*

leek ‖ *puerro, porro*

lentil ‖ *lenteja*

lettuce ‖ *lechuga*

llullucha ‖ seaweed

luki★ ‖ A bitter, potato-like tuber that grows only *above* 8000 feet. There are many varieties.

lupine ‖ *Chocho.* In Quechua, *tawri.* A legume with bitter beans which must be soaked for several days before being cooked.

maca★ ‖ In Quechua, *tatu.* This root is grown at very high elevations in the Andes. It resembles a purple radish and is very starchy. It can be cooked or dried into *chuño* and made into a mush.

malanga or *yautia*★ ‖ In Quechua, *uncucha.* Another edible, lumpy, brown tuber.

mushroom ‖ *Hongo.* When cooked in a dish mushrooms are called *champiñones.* For example, *crema de champiñones* means "cream of mushroom soup."

oca★ ‖ In Aymara, *apilla.* An Andean root crop second in importance only to the potato. It looks like a small, skinny, lumpy potato.

onion ‖ *cebolla*

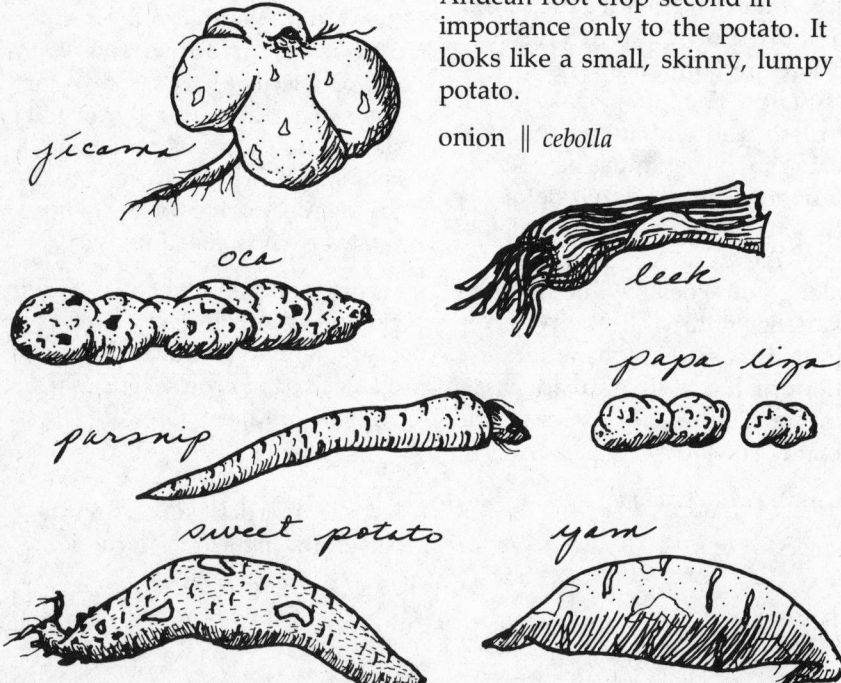

jícama

oca

leek

papa liza

parsnip

sweet potato

yam

papa liza★ ‖ *Ullucu* in Quechua and Aymara. A tuber similar to *oca* that looks like candy or a tiny, brightly colored, pink or yellow potato. It's sure to catch your eye in the markets.

parsnip ‖ *chirivia, berraza*

pea ‖ *Guisante.* In Bolivia, *arveja.*

potato★ ‖ *Papa.* In Quechua, *pusasuaylla;* in Aymara, *tata.* The potato was domesticated by the Aymara Indians of the Colla region of Bolivia. There is an astonishing number of varieties— 220 different kinds in the Colla alone. Some potatoes, such as the *luki,* won't grow at altitudes lower than 8000 feet. Many of these high-altitude varieties are bitter and are always freeze-dried into *chuño.* There are many different names for potatoes in Quechua, such as *yunge, cawka, markus, shapash, kunchu kanu* and *lasapa.* In Aymara there are at least 200 different words for the various potatoes, including *papa koya, saya* (white potatoes in general), *papa sani, papa isla, papa kjati, papa phala* and more. You'll see and eat so many potatoes that you may be potatoed out for life.

baked potatoes ‖ *papas al horno*

fried potatoes ‖ *papas fritas*

frozen (but not dried) potatoes ‖ *kachochuño*

mashed potatoes ‖ *puré de papas*

radish ‖ *rábano*

rhubarb ‖ *ruibarbo*

spinach ‖ *espinaca*

sweet potato★ ‖ *Camote.* In Quechua, *apichu* or *cumara;* in Aymara, *apichu.* Although sweet potatoes and yams look a lot alike, they're different tubers. The sweet potato is more nutritious than the white potato, and has yellow insides. It was domesticated in the Amazon Basin.

Swiss chard ‖ *acelga*

tonka bean★ ‖ The *tonka* seed (it's mistakenly called a bean) is rich in coumarin, which is some-times used as a substitute for vanilla.

tunta★ ‖ White, freeze-dried potatoes or tubers. (See "*chuño.*")

turnip ‖ *Nabo.* In Quechua, *yuyupapa.*

watercress ‖ *berro*

yam ‖ *Cara* or *ñame.* A yam is not the same as a sweet potato, although they look a lot alike. There are many varieties of yams, which vary in size from tiny up to a hundred pounds. A yam has a red skin and yellow insides and looks like a sweet potato.

yam bean or manioc bean★ ‖ The yam bean is usually grown for its root, which is brown and lumpy and looks like a turnip. The tubers are eaten more often than the pods because the pods can be poisonous when ripe.

yucca or manioc★ ‖ *Yuca*. In Quechua, *rumu*. Yucca is a member of the genus *Manihot*, to which the cassava also belongs. Food crops of this genus are some of the most efficient food crops known; their yield is very high in calories per acre, although these calories are mainly carbohydrates. As I discussed with cassava, some members of the genus are poisonous since they contain prussic acid. While the term *manioc* is applied to both sweet and poisonous varieties, as far as I know, what is called *yuca* is *not* poisonous and can be served without any special preparation. Yucca looks like cassava, with a rather hairy brown skin, and has an inside that's pure white, hard and dry. It's usually fried, and I love it. Most of the time you encounter these tubers already prepared, and the cooks know what they're doing. If you buy unprepared tubers and aren't sure if you have to leach out the prussic acid, ask *"¿Cómo se prepara esto?"* ("How do you prepare this?"). In my experience, anything sold in the market as *"yuca"* has been nonpoisonous, so I wouldn't worry.

Grains

The most important native grains (*granos*) are corn, *quínoa* and *cañihua*. The Spanish introduced wheat, alfalfa, rice and oats. Brown rice and sprouts are difficult, if not impossible, to find. Soybeans (*frijoles de soya*) are available only in Colombia. If you plan on staying any length of time and these foods are an integral part of your diet, take some along with you—or adapt, which is much easier than dragging around fifty pounds of brown rice.

alfalfa ‖ *Alfalfa* makes good fodder. The Spanish brought it to the Americas for their horses. The green hay can be seen in markets throughout the Andes.

amaranth★ ‖ *Amaranto, jataco* or *achita*. A food seed grown and used like *quínoa*.

barley ‖ *Cebeda*. This grain can adapt to high altitudes and cold weather. Barley hay is frequently seen in Andean markets.

cañihua★ (also spelled *kañua*) ‖ A close relative of *quínoa*, but can be grown at even higher elevations because it has a shorter growing season. Like *quínoa*, its stalks are burned to form *lejia*, a stick chewed with coca leaves (see page 235). The calcium in the ashes releases the active alkaloid in the coca leaf.

corn★ ‖ *Maíz*. In Quechua, *sara*; in Aymara, *tonko*. There are many different Quechua and Aymara names for the different colors and varieties of corn. It is believed that corn was domesticated in Mexico and that it spread from there to all parts of the Americas. Corn was the single most important crop in the Mayan and Aztec civilizations, while it was third in importance in the Inca world. (Potatoes and *quínoa* were more valuable since they adapted better to the cold weather and higher elevations found throughout the Inca Empire.) There are at least twenty varieties of corn grown in the Andes.

choclo ‖ corn on the cob or corn kernels

kamcha or *kamka* ‖ roasted corn

mote or *muti* ‖ stewed corn

sarapata ‖ cooked and cracked corn

sémola ‖ grits

oats ‖ *Avena*. Oatmeal is also called *avena* and is a common hot cereal in the Andes.

quínoa★ (also spelled *quinua*) ‖ In Aymara, *jupa*. A food grain that's very high in protein (fifteen percent), it also contains fifty-five percent carbohydrates and four percent fat. It was probably domesticated near Lake Titicaca and is still grown there in quantity. The Incas regarded *quínoa* as sacred and it was their second most important food crop. The seeds are small, round and light-colored and can be toasted, boiled, ground into flour or made into *chicha*. The stems and leaves are used for salad greens and the seeds are also fed to livestock and poultry.

rice ‖ *Arroz*. An important part of the *altiplano* diet, rice is trucked in from lower, wetter areas.

wheat ‖ *trigo*

FLOUR

Flour is called *harina* in Spanish and *hakku* in Quechua and Aymara. When buying flour you have to specify the kind you want: *harina de maíz* (corn), *de trigo* (wheat), *de quínoa*, etc. Whole wheat flour is called *harina integral*. Flour made from toasted ground cassava or yucca is called *fariña*. In the Andes, barley flour is called *machicha* or *mashca*.

BREAD

Bread is *pan* in Spanish and *tanta* in Quechua and Aymara.

dark bread ‖ *pan negro*

French bread ‖ *pan francés*

manioc or yucca bread ‖ *cazabe*

muffin ‖ *panecillo*

quínoa bread || *kkispiña* (Bolivia)

roll || *panecito, panecillo, rollo* or *rosca* (Bolivia)

rye bread || *pan de centeno*

white bread || *pan blanco*

whole wheat bread || *pan integral*

TYPICAL BREADS (Panes Típicos)

allulla || Sounds like "azhuzha." A small roll sold in central Ecuador in and around Latacunga.

almohabana || A corn muffin with cottage cheese made in Colombia.

chimas || A yellow cornbread roll that's common in the eastern part of Bolivia.

chuta || A round, yeast bread sold at the Urcos train station in Peru. Absolutely delicious.

horneado || A round, wheat bread made in Santa Cruz, Bolivia.

mogolla || A whole wheat muffin with raisins in the center that's made in Colombia.

Seeds and Nuts

In Spanish, seeds are called *semillas* or *pepas (pepitas)* and nuts are called *nueces*.

almonds || *almendras*

Brazil nuts★ || There are probably many local names for these nuts, but in Bolivia, they're called *almendras de Beni*. Brazil nuts are the seeds of a large, round, brown fruit, within which they're arranged like the segments of an orange. Because the fruit is so hard, it usually must be hacked open across the top and is sometimes called a "monkey pot" because a monkey will stick its

baking in the horno de barro

paw in a fruit that's been gnawed open by rodents, grab some nuts and then find that its fist has gotten stuck. The fruit trees grow in the upper Amazon, and the nuts can be found in Andean markets that have access to this area. Brazil nuts contain fourteen percent protein and sixty-six percent fat.

cashews★ ‖ *Anacardos*. These nuts are very nutritious (they contain twenty percent protein and forty-five percent fat) and grow on a tropical tree native to Brazil. Cashews are actually the seeds of a fruit and the way they grow is quite strange. From each large fleshy fruit on the tree hangs a tiny pod containing one cashew.

chestnuts ‖ *castañas*

filberts or hazelnuts ‖ *avellanas*

peanuts★ ‖ *Manis*. In Quechua, *inchis*. Peanuts are very high in protein (thirty percent) and oil and are rich in vitamins B and E. They were domesticated in the lowlands of northwestern Argentina.

pecans★ ‖ *pacanas*

pine nuts★ ‖ *piñones*

popcorn★ ‖ *Palomitas*. South American popcorn looks like enormous kernels of puffed wheat and is delicious. It's sold in enormous baskets in the markets and on the streets.

pumpkin seeds★ (also squash and melon seeds in general) ‖ *Pepitas*. In Aymara, *chiras*. Often sold freshly roasted in the markets.

sesame seeds ‖ *ajonjolíes*

sunflower seeds★ ‖ *Pepitas de girasol, mirasol* or *helianto*. The giant sunflower was venerated by the Incas as a symbol of the sun god; the maidens of the sun *(las ñustas)* wore sunflower disks of pure gold on their breasts.

walnuts (black)★ ‖ *Nogales*. Black-walnut shells are made into one of the few natural dyes still in use in the Andes; they give a rich brown color.

Herbs and Spices

Herbs *(hierbas* or *yerbas)* and spices *(especias)* can be bought in *tiendas* or in the markets. They're sold by the pinch and by the handful.

allspice ‖ *pimienta de Jamaica*

anise ‖ *anís*

basil ‖ *albahaca*

Bolivian herbs ‖ *huakataya* or

quirquiña (used in Indian cooking)

caraway seeds ‖ *alcaraveas*

cardamom ‖ *cardamomo*

celery seeds || *semillas de apio*

chives || *cebollina, cebolleta*

cinnamon || *canela*

cloves || *clavos de olor*

coriander || *culantro*

cumin || *comino*

dill || *eneldo*

garlic || *ajo*

ginger || *jengibre*

mace || *macis*

marjoram || *mejorana*

mint || *minta, menta* or *hierba buena*

nutmeg || *nuez moscada*

oregano || *orégano*

paprika || *paprika*

parsley || *perejil*

poppy seeds || *semillas de amapola*

rosemary || *romero*

saffron || *azafrán*

sage || *salvia*

savory || *ajedrea*

tarragon || *estragón*

thyme || *tomillo*

vanilla* || *Vainilla*. The plant is a climbing orchid native to Central America; the flavoring comes from the long, dark pods.

Eggs and Dairy Products

Eggs (*huevos*) are available everywhere—the chicken is ubiquitous. Dairy products are harder to come by. The large cities have milk-pasteurization plants, and milk, butter and cream are available in *tiendas* and *supermercados*. When you get into the countryside it's another story. If you buy milk that's unpasteurized, boil it before you use it (see Chapter Thirteen, "Health"). Pasteurization was invented to destroy the many disease-producing microorganisms transmitted in raw milk; so use common sense. Unrefrigerated dairy products spoil quickly, so watch out for them, too.

Sour cream and cottage cheese generally aren't available. However, yogurt (*yogu*) is sold in the larger cities of all four Andean countries. If you plan to live in a remote area and want yogurt, take a starter along with you.

butter || *Mantequilla*. While South America has some of the best bread and rolls I've ever had, it's not customary to serve butter along with them. You're served butter only in the fanciest restaurants, if it's available at all.

cheese || *Queso*. Various unpasteurized cheeses are sold in the market, and they're safe if used in cooking. I didn't eat any uncooked cheese during my trip.

cream || *crema*

custard ‖ *Flan*. This vanilla custard is the national dessert of many Latin American countries, and I love it. *Flan* mix is sold in *tiendas*. Because toxic bacteria multiply rapidly in unrefrigerated custard, do not buy *flan* from sidewalk vendors.

egg ‖ *Huevo*. In Quechua, *runtu;* in Aymara, *kkauna*.

egg white ‖ *clara*

egg yolk ‖ *yema*

fried eggs ‖ *huevos fritos*

hard-boiled eggs ‖ *huevos duros*

omelet ‖ *tortilla de huevos*

scrambled eggs ‖ *huevos revueltos*

soft-boiled eggs ‖ *huevos pasados por agua*. The Latin American idea of a soft-boiled egg is a lukewarm, raw egg. It's very difficult to get your usual four-minute egg. We asked for *huevos pasados, pero medio duro* (soft-boiled eggs, but medium hard) and usually got satisfactory eggs.

ice cream ‖ *Helado*. In South America, *helado* has three meanings: "ice cream," "ice" and "cold." If you ask for a drink *sin helado,* it means "without ice." If you ask for *cerveza helada,* it means "cold beer." The context determines the meaning. A sign on a wall advertising *"Helados"* means "Ice Cream." You can debate whether or not the ice cream is safe since it's made with water. I like ice cream too much to worry, and I've never gotten sick from it.

milk ‖ *Leche*. Cow's milk is *leche de vaca*. Like butter, milk is rarely found on the *altiplano*. There may be a few altitude-sick cows, but the *campesinos* usually save the milk for their own families. At lower altitudes and in the cities you usually can get good, safe milk. If it's delivered or sold in a bucket, you probably should boil it yourself.

partridge egg ‖ *Huevo de perdiz*. Partridge eggs are the only eggs I've seen for sale in the markets other than chicken eggs. They're small, gray and speckled.

sherbet ‖ *sorbete*

spumoni ice cream ‖ *Cassata*. Watch for this on menus—it's good.

Seafood and Freshwater Fish

The Atlantic and Pacific coasts have fantastic seafood *(mariscos)* at reasonable prices, so get ready for a seafood feast. It's a wonderful change from the mountain diet! While fish is available primarily along the coasts, the Andean lakes have excellent trout and Lake Titicaca has a delicious pink trout that looks and tastes like salmon.

Besides the usual ways of serving seafood, there are two popular Latin American dishes you may not be familiar with. *Ceviche* (also spelled *cebiche* or *seviche*) is raw or cooked seafood that's served cold with lemon, onions and peppers. *Ceviche de camarones,* for example, is shrimp *ceviche.* The other dish is *escabeche,* which is pickled seafood served with various combinations of onions, peppers, hard-boiled eggs, olives and spices. Both dishes are delicious but are best bought in decent restaurants. Bad seafood can really knock you for a loop, and there's no way of knowing how long seafood sold by street vendors has been unrefrigerated. Use your nose. If seafood sold *anywhere* smells bad, don't eat it.

abalone ‖ *abulón*

anchovy ‖ *Anchoa* or *anchova.* Historically, the waters off Peru contained millions of anchovies, which were prized by the Pre-Columbian Indian cultures. Anchovies have been overfished, however, and schools are now dangerously depleted. Most anchovies have gone into cattle meal to feed the beef-hungry citizens of the United States rather than the protein-starved Peruvians.

bass from Lake Titicaca ‖ *boga*

catfish ‖ *Zurubí;* also spelled *surubí.*

clam ‖ *almeja*

codfish ‖ *bacalao*

crab ‖ *Congrejo.* In Quechua, *apangoray.*

crab claw ‖ *muela de congrejo*

eel ‖ *anguila*

fish (in general) ‖ *Pescado.* In Quechua, *challwa;* in Aymara, *chaulla.*

flounder ‖ *lenguado*

frog ‖ *Rana.* In Quechua, *kaira.*

hake ‖ *brotola*

herring ‖ *arenque*

lobster ‖ *langosta*

mackerel ‖ *caballa*

mussel ‖ *Mejillón* or *almeja.* A *choro* is also a variety of mussel.

octopus ‖ *pulpo, pólipo*

oyster ‖ *Ostra* in Colombia; *ostión* elsewhere.

redfish ‖ *Pirarucú.* In Peru, *paiche.* An enormous freshwater fish (average weight of fifty to sixty pounds) caught in Amazon Basin rivers. It is delicious fresh and is also sold dried.

red snapper ‖ *huachinango*

salmon ‖ *salmón*

sardine ‖ *sardina*

scallop ‖ *venera, pechina*

sea bass ‖ *Corvina.* This was new to me, and when Bill and I discovered a restaurant in Guayaquil that served *corvina a la plancha* (corvina fillet), we found ourselves going there for lunch and dinner every day.

shark ‖ *tiburón*

shrimp ‖ *Camarón*. In Quechua, *yujra*.

shrimp (jumbo) ‖ *Langostino*. This term is also used for crayfish in many places.

silverside (a variety of mackerel) ‖ *pejerrey*

snail ‖ *Caracol*. It's known as *quipa* (also spelled *kipa*) in the Ecuadorian Andes.

squid ‖ *calamare*

sturgeon ‖ *marión, marón*

swordfish ‖ *pez espeda*

trout ‖ *trucha*

tuna ‖ *atún*

turtle ‖ *Tortuga*. In Quechua, *quirquinchu.*

Meat

It's hard for me to be as enthusiastic about meat (*carne* in Spanish; *aicha* in Quechua and Aymara) as I am about seafood. One reason is that South American meat usually isn't aged and consequently is tough. On the *altiplano* you're served a leathery, dry piece of something that could be anything from leg of llama to a chicken run over by a truck, and it's impossible to tell the difference—or to eat it. Fortunately there are exceptions. Colombia and Argentina have excellent beef; people there raise cattle for slaughter rather than merely killing an animal when it's no longer good for anything and calling the carcass "beef." You can also find some tasty meat in the large cities of other countries. Bill had excellent pepper steak in La Paz, somewhat to our astonishment.

The method of cooking also makes a difference. There are restaurants called *parrilladas* which specialize in charcoal-grilled meat. Sometimes the food is cooked right at your table on a little hibachi. My experience with *parrilladas* has always been positive, and I recommend them if you're a confirmed carnivore.

Peru has beef-rationing, which means no beef is to be sold (or presumably consumed) during the first fifteen days of each month. This renders useless most of the normally misleading menus in the country. You are handed a menu that has no relation to what is available—a good half of the items are unobtainable. As I mentioned earlier, you can save yourself a lot of trouble by first asking what the restaurant actually has that day.

Anyone with a taste for the gory will have a good time in the meat section of the market. Dogs run off with intestines, children blow up lungs like balloons and *cargadores* almost knock you off your feet with fifty-pound loads of cow's heads. At least you know that the meat's fresh. Although there isn't any refrigeration, the animals are so freshly slaughtered that you really don't have to worry about the meat being spoiled. Cooked meat, on the other hand, can be dubious, particularly if it isn't refrigerated or kept hot. In any case, I've never gotten sick from the meat, but then I don't eat much of it to begin with.

The meat you find in the jungle is whatever the hunters bring in and includes monkeys, anteaters, *capybaras, pakas* and various birds.

MEAT OF . . . (*Carne de . . .*)

calf (veal) ‖ *ternera*

cow (beef) ‖ *Vaca* or *res*. In Aymara, *waka*.

goat ‖ *Cabra, cabrón* or *cabrito*. In Peru, goat is frequently served the first fifteen days of each month, when beef is unavailable due to rationing.

guinea pig★ ‖ *Cui;* also spelled *cuy*. In Quechua, *aka*. It's also called *conejo de las Indias* (rabbit of the Indies) in Spanish. The guinea pig was domesticated in the Andes, and it was, and still is, an important source of protein for the Indians. The only way *cui* seems to be served is roasted whole. In many markets the cooked animals are stacked up like cordwood with their little paws sticking out and their eyes and teeth showing. At the fiestas following the baptism of my god-children in Ecuador I was served whole roast *cui* and came to love the meat. Try it.

lamb ‖ *cordero*

pig ‖ *Cerdo* or *chancho*. In Quechua and Aymara, *kuchi*. Whole roast pig is another common sight, especially in Ecuadorian markets, but the sight of the dripping, greasy carcass usually ruins my appetite.

pork ‖ *puerco*

sheep (mutton) ‖ *carnero*

viscacha ‖ A small rodent which is a member of the chinchilla family. It looks like a rabbit with a squirrel's tail and is hunted by the Indians.

CUTS AND GUTS

bacon ‖ *tocino*

blood ‖ *Sangre*. In Quechua, *yaguar*.

bones ‖ *huesos*

brains ‖ *sesos*

chop ‖ *chuleta*

dried meat (usually llama, sheep or pig) ‖ *Charqui* in Quechua. We get our word "jerky," as in "beef jerky," from the Quechua.

filet ‖ *filete*

ground meat ‖ *carne molida*

ham ‖ *jamón*

hamburger ‖ *hamburguesa*

head ‖ *cabeza*

heart ‖ *corazón*

hot dog ‖ *perro caliente*

intestines ‖ *Menudo*. Miscellaneous innards are also called *mondongo* or *entrañas*.

kidney ‖ *riñón*

leg ‖ *pierna*

liver ‖ *Hígado*. In Quechua, *kukupin.*

loin ‖ *vacio*

neck ‖ *cogote*

oxtail ‖ *cola de novillo*

pig's feet ‖ *patitas de cerdo*

pork sausage ‖ *chorizo*

pork skin (fried crispy) ‖ *chicharrón*

rib ‖ *Costilla*. In Quechua, *waqtan.*

roast ‖ *Asada* or *carne asada*. In Aymara, *kanka.*

salted and dried lamb or mutton ‖ *chalona*

sausage (in general) ‖ *salchicha*

shoulder ‖ *paleta*

steak ‖ *Filete, lomo* or *bistec* (also spelled *bifstec* or *biftec*, meaning "beefsteak." However, *bistec* is sometimes applied to any steak, such as *bistec de llama*).

sweetbreads ‖ *mollejas*

tail ‖ *rabo*

tenderloin ‖ *Lomo*. Like *bistec, lomo* often refers to steak in general.

tongue ‖ *Lengua*. In Quechua, *kallu.*

tripe ‖ *Tripas*. In Ecuador, *longanisa.*

Poultry

South American poultry (*aves de corral*) is good. Most chickens are allowed to run free and scratch around. Because they aren't cooped up in cages and fed methedrine-laced food, they have a little flavor.

chicken ‖ *Pollo*. In Aymara, *chiwchi.*

dove ‖ *Paloma*. In Quechua and Aymara, *urpi.*

duck ‖ *Pato*. In Quechua, *ñuñuma. Choka* (Quechua) refers to a duck with black feathers.

goose ‖ *ganso*

hen ‖ *Gallina*. In Aymara, *wallpa.*

partridge ‖ *Perdiz*. In Quechua, *yutu;* in Aymara, *phisakka.*

pigeon ‖ *pichón*

rooster ‖ *Gallo*. In Aymara, *kkankka.*

turkey ‖ *pavo*

The terms for various cuts of poultry are the same as those for meat, with the addition of breast (*pechuga* or *pecho;* in Aymara, *ñuñu*) and wing (*ala*).

Typical Dishes

Listed below are typical dishes (*platos típicos*) that you're likely to run across during your travels. The name of a country in parentheses following the name of a dish means the dish is a specialty of that country, although you may find it served elsewhere.

acu (Bolivia) ‖ An Aymara barley-meal mush.

ajiaco ‖ A spicy stew with peppers, vegetables and meat. *Pollo ajiaco* is excellent.

ajoqueso ‖ rarebit

a la chorrillana ‖ Food cooked with onions, tomatoes and vegetables in wine. For example, *corvina* (sea bass) or *bistec* (beefsteak) *a la chorrillana.*

anticuchos (Peru) ‖ Shish kebab made with beef heart or chicken liver, garlic and peppers, dipped in a spicy sauce. This is a real treat, but buy it in a restaurant rather than on the street since sidewalk vendors sometimes have spoiled meat.

arapas (Colombia) ‖ corn pancakes

arroz graneado (Peru) ‖ Rice boiled with oil, cloves, garlic and lemon juice.

carnitas ‖ Pieces of fried pork combined with *chiles* and cumin.

cau-cau (Peru) ‖ Tripe, potatoes, peppers, spices and rice. It's better than you might think.

causa ‖ A potato dish with eggs, olives, corn, lemons and onion sauce.

causa a la chiclayana (Peru) ‖ *Causa* with fish.

cazuela de frutas del mar (Colombia) ‖ A coastal dish—seafood bouillabaisse with squid, clams, oysters, etc.

cazuelado (Peru) ‖ In Quechua, *aka picchu.* A fiesta dish comprised of roast guinea pig and boiled potatoes.

chaca (Bolivia) ‖ corn mush

chacho or *ch'ajchu* (Bolivia) ‖ A dish containing meat, potatoes, cheese, eggs and peppers.

chairo (*paceño*) (Bolivia) ‖ A soup made with beef, lamb or *chalona* (salted or dried lamb), along with peas, beans, carrots, *chuño,* wheat hominy, peppers and spices.

chauchas ‖ Green beans and potatoes.

chiflimote (Ecuador) ‖ Somewhat like succotash, made with corn and broad beans (*habas*).

chiriuchu (Peru) ‖ Guinea pig, rabbit, chicken, peppers, corn meal, fish, cheese and eggs. Traditionally served in Cuzco on the Feast of Corpus Christi.

choros con choclo (Peru) ‖ Mussels with corn.

chumale (Ecuador) ‖ Steamed cornmeal wrapped in corn leaves, sometimes with a little meat or vegetables added. Similar to a Mexican *tamale*.

coli (Colombia) ‖ banana soup

conchitas a la criolla (Peru) ‖ Grilled scallops served in their shells with a sauce made from cheese and *chile* peppers.

cuchuco (Colombia) ‖ Soup made with pork or lamb.

empanada, empanadilla or *empanadita* ‖ A baked pastry with a meat or (more often) cheese filling. Fantastic when hot from the oven.

estofado de carne (Peru) ‖ A meat stew.

fiche (Colombia) ‖ Blood, sheep tripe and vegetables. It's probably better than it sounds.

fruta en sartén (Bolivia) ‖ An Aymara dish in which lard, eggs, sugar, milk, salt, wine, cinnamon, cloves, anis and flour are beaten together and then fried.

fruta seca (Bolivia) ‖ Very similar to *fruta en sartén*, but baked rather than fried.

garapacho ‖ Meat cooked in clam or oyster shells.

huachinango asado ‖ Baked red snapper with onions, green peppers, *chile* peppers, olives and spices.

huevos péricos (Colombia) ‖ Eggs scrambled with tomatoes and onions. Similar to Mexican *huevos rancheros*.

humita ‖ A corn tamale that has many local variations.

kamka (Peru) ‖ parched corn

langosta criolla ‖ Lobster with tomato sauce.

lechón al horno (Bolivia) ‖ Roast suckling pig. It's called *lechona* in Colombia.

llajua (Quechua) or *jallpjahuayca* (Aymara) ‖ A hot sauce made with super-hot *locoto* peppers, tomatoes, salt and *quirquiña*.

llapingacho (Ecuador) ‖ A fried mashed-potato and cheese patty that reminds me of a potato pancake.

llaucha (Bolivia) ‖ A baked yeast pastry with a red pepper and cheese filling.

lluchuskha (Bolivia) ‖ A cereal made from ground corn that's

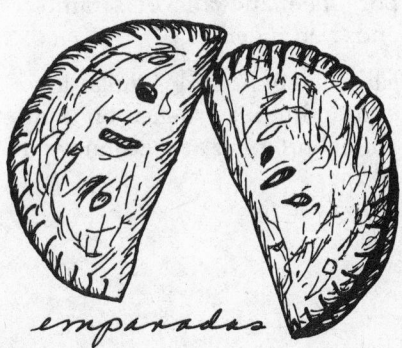

empanadas

sold in Cochabamba Valley markets. The hot, cooked cereal is called *pataskha*.

locro (Colombia and Ecuador) ‖ A thick soup or stew primarily consisting of potatoes and corn.

lomo montado (Bolivia) ‖ A fried steak topped with fried eggs and banana.

maejuana (Colombia) ‖ A dish made from beans, bananas and coconut.

mazamorra ‖ A thick soup with a corn base that also contains potatoes, cabbage, onions and spices.

mocoto ‖ calf's-foot stew

mote de maíz cocido (often simply called *mote)* ‖ Hominy, a stewed corn.

ocopa (Bolivia) ‖ A dish made with shrimp, nuts, garlic, tomatoes, yellow peppers and oil. It's served on potatoes and lettuce leaves.

ocopa arequipeña (Peru) ‖ Boiled potatoes on lettuce, garnished with hard-boiled eggs, olives and hot sauce.

paella ‖ A rice dish made with tomatoes, onions and spices, along with meat, chicken or fish.

papas a la huancaina (Peru and Bolivia) ‖ Potatoes covered with *locoto* sauce, which is made from peppers, milk, oil and ground, roasted peanuts.

papas al lamparín (Peru) ‖ Cold, boiled potatoes with hard-boiled eggs and a slightly *picante* (hot) sauce. A dish somewhat similar to potato salad.

papas chorriadas (Colombia) ‖ Potatoes topped with onions, tomatoes and cheese.

pataskha (Bolivia) ‖ A hot, cooked cereal sold in Cochabamba Valley markets. It's made of ground corn and is dark, yellow or white, depending on the kind of corn that's used. It's always served with *quesillo de leche,* a milk sauce.

patitas (Peru) ‖ Fried pig's feet served with *picante* sauce.

picana (Bolivia) ‖ Lamb chops, pork, beef and chicken cooked together and served with potatoes and corn and a sauce made from beer, wine, carrots, turnips, onions, peppers and spices.

piquete (Colombia) ‖ A dish combining chicken, pork and various vegetables (including corn, sweet and white potatoes) that's served with a sauce made from bread, milk and cheese.

potaje de guisantes ‖ pea soup

puchero (Colombia) ‖ Vegetables, pork, beef and chicken scrambled and fried together.

pukacapa (Bolivia) ‖ Similar to a *llaucha,* but it's brushed on top with shortening and ground red pepper.

pusandao (Colombia) ‖ A stew comprised of bananas, fish, beef, potatoes and onions.

run dawn (Colombian islands of San Andrés and Providencia) ‖ Fish and yams cooked in coconut milk.

saice (Bolivia) ‖ A complicated dish. It's a stew made with meat, peas, corn, tomatoes, onions, parsley, peppers and spices that's served over rice and boiled potatoes. A salad of tomatoes, onions, parsley and *locoto* peppers is added on top.

sajta de pollo ‖ A spicy chicken dish.

salpicón de pollo ‖ Cold chicken salad.

salteña (Bolivia) ‖ A baked pastry stuffed with onions, peppers, meat, potatoes, eggs, peas, spices and black olives (watch out for the pits). *Salteñas* originated in Sucre and are a kind of national snack. They're served in restaurants at about 10 or 11 A.M. for the midmorning coffee break and are usually completely sold out by noon. We were introduced to *salteñas* in La Paz and really grew to like them. They're also rather *picante*.

sancocho (Colombia) ‖ A soup or stew made with root vegetables

(potatoes, yams, yuccas, etc.), beef, chicken and fish.

sango (Colombia) ‖ A soup made from ground corn.

sangresita (Peru) ‖ chicken-blood pudding

selele (Colombia) ‖ A stew that contains *menudo* and vegetables.

shakwi (Peru) ‖ *haba*-bean soup

sopa a la criolla (Peru) ‖ A soup made with noodles, beef hearts, eggs, vegetables and spices.

sopa de maíz ‖ Not a soup at all, but rather a corn pudding that contains onions, tomatoes, cheese and milk.

soufflé de calabaza (Peru) ‖ Squash soufflé with seafood.

tostada de maíz (Ecuador) ‖ A small round corn pancake that's sold in the markets. Really good!

tostado (Ecuador) ‖ parched corn

vitivite (Colombia) ‖ A corn, coconut, sugar and rice dish.

viudo de pescado (Colombia) ‖ Fish stew that's baked in a hole in the ground.

yacu chupe (Peru) ‖ A thick, chowdery soup made with potatoes, cheese, parsley, onions, eggs, mint, peppers and spices.

Desserts and Treats

baklava ‖ *árabe*

brownie ‖ *cholito*

buñuelos (Bolivia) ‖ Fritters. A Christmas dish.

cacho (Ecuador) ‖ A roll somewhat like a croissant.

cake ‖ *queque, torta*

canasta de coco (Colombia) ‖ A coconut custard and meringue pastry.

candy ‖ *dulces, bombones, confitados*

canned fruit ‖ *compota*

cassata ‖ spumoni ice cream

cocada al horno (Peru) ‖ A baked dessert made with coconut, egg yolks, wine, butter and sesame seeds.

cookie or cracker ‖ *galleta*

dessert (in general) ‖ *postre*

dulce de leche ‖ Condensed milk boiled in the can until it becomes caramel-like. It's sometimes served on bread.

dulce de membrillo ‖ A square pastry filled with *membrillo* paste.

flan ‖ The Latin American vanilla custard.

gasnate (Peru and Bolivia) ‖ A thin, crispy pastry rolled up with a honey or *dulce de leche* filling.

hinchare ‖ A deep-fried cream puff filled with whipped cream.

ice cream ‖ *helado*

macaroon ‖ *Merengue* (a word that also refers to meringue).

mazamorra morada (Peru) ‖ A pudding made from purple cornmeal, lemons, dried fruit, cinnamon and cloves.

natilla (Colombia) ‖ A dessert made from green corn, coconut and sugar.

pancake ‖ *panqueque*

pan dulce ‖ A sweet yeast bread.

pastellillo (Peru) ‖ A fritter made from sweet potato and yucca flour, sugar and anise that's fried and then dipped in powdered sugar.

pastry ‖ *pastel*

picarón (Peru) ‖ A doughnut made from manioc or sweet potato or pumpkin flour and served with honey.

pie ‖ *Pie, pay* or *pastel*. "*Una pieza de pie*" means "a piece of pie."

pudding ‖ *pudín, budín*

quesadilla ‖ A baked pastry made from sugar, butter, eggs and cornstarch.

roscón (Colombia) ‖ A roll filled with guava jelly and sprinkled with sugar.

tungo (Colombia) ‖ A bun made from cornmeal, milk and honey.

vienesa ‖ A coffee float—cold coffee with a scoop of vanilla ice cream and whipped cream topping. One of my favorites.

zango de pasas (Peru) ‖ A dessert made from raisins, corn syrup and sugar.

Beverages

Since you shouldn't drink (unboiled) water anywhere in South America, it's a good idea to become acquainted with local beverages *(bebidas)*.

aqua de panela (Colombia) ‖ A typical drink that's made of raw sugar boiled in water.

aguardiente (also called *trago comiteco, cuervo, viuda* and *herradura* ‖ A local distilled sugar cane liquor. A bottle of *aguardiente* makes a nice present for people you visit in the jungle.

algarrobina (Peru) ‖ *Pisco* with *algarrobina* syrup.

api (Bolivia) ‖ A very thick, high-calorie, starchy drink made from corn. It's served hot on the streets in Bolivia, especially at night. There are two varieties: white *(blanco)* and purple *(morado)*. Try a *combinado* (mixed white and purple).

beer ‖ *Cerveza*. South America has superb beer. I learned to like beer in Bolivia, where it was the only safe drink available other than pop, which I refuse to drink. Beer is sold in one-liter *(un litro)* bottles. In Bolivia, a liter is called *una botella*.

brandy ‖ *coñac*

canelazo (also spelled *canelaso*) ‖ An Ecuadorian and Colombian drink that's actually *aguardiente* spiced with cinnamon, sugar and lime.

capitán (Peru) ‖ *Pisco* and vermouth.

chaguarmishqui (Ecuador) ‖ A drink similar to Mexican *pulque* that's made from the fermented sap of the *agave* cactus, which is called *cabuya* cactus in the Andes. It's sometimes made unfermented.

changua (Colombia) ‖ Another common drink made with water, salt, milk and onions.

chicha ‖ In Quechua, *akha*; in Aymara, *kusa*. A very ancient drink that predates the Incas. *Chicha* is fermented corn beer made from sprouted corn *(jora)*. It's sometimes made from *quínoa* when corn isn't available. There are also other varieties: *chicha de uvas* (grapes), *chicha de plátanos* (bananas), etc. Corn beer is called *chicha de jora* in Peru. *Chicha* is a very popular Indian drink in the Andes, and there's usually a *chichería* near every market. Your nose will lead you to it; the beer gives off a strong, yeasty smell. Small homemade flags, usually red or white, flying from houses indicate that *chicha* is for sale. Before drinking, the Indians spill a little *chicha* on the ground as an offering to *Pacha Mama*.

chicha morada ‖ A non-alcoholic drink made from purple corn. It reminds me of Kool-Aid.

drinking chicha at the Calca market

chilcano (Peru) ‖ *Pisco* and ginger ale.

chinchibi (Bolivia and the Yungas) ‖ A drink made with pineapple juice, cinnamon, honey and water.

chufliy (Bolivia) ‖ Bolivia's national drink. It's made with *Singani,* ginger ale and lemon.

cocoa (or hot chocolate) ‖ *Chocolate caliente.* Cocoa *(cacao)* is native to the Americas. Cocoa beans grow in huge pods on trees and contain about fifty percent fat. When the beans inside the pod are fermented, they turn a deep red color. Chocolate is sold

in candy bars and in huge hunks in the markets and is also made into a hot chocolate drink.

coffee ‖ *Café.* If you're a coffee lover, you're in for a disappointment. While Colombia has delicious coffee, when you reach Ecuador things aren't quite the same. Instead of freshly brewed coffee, there are little jars on restaurant tables containing a liquid that looks like raw petroleum. This is *esencia* of coffee, which is called *tintura* in Bolivia. *Esencia* is coffee that has been boiled and boiled until only a sludge is left. When you want hot coffee, *esencia* is poured into your cup and then hot water or hot milk is added. I found this drink so nasty that I gave up coffee altogether when not in Colombia. However, this is a personal prejudice and some travelers like *esencia*.

> black ‖ *Tinto* in Colombia, *café cortado* in Bolivia and *café negro* elsewhere.
>
> with sugar ‖ *café con azúcar*
>
> with cream ‖ *café con crema*
>
> with milk ‖ *café con leche*

cognac ‖ *Coñac*. This word also refers to brandy in general.

cojosa ‖ Sour milk

draque (Ecuador) ‖ Water that's boiled with sugar, lemon and cinnamon, with a little *aguardiente* thrown in.

fresco (Ecuador) ‖ A cold drink made from wine or fruit juice and sugar.

guarapo ‖ A hard liquor made from fermented molasses or raw sugar that's served in Colombia, Bolivia and Ecuador (especially in the Amazon Basin).

guarrúz (Colombia) ‖ A drink made from fermented rice and honey.

guinda (Peru) ‖ Cherry brandy

juice ‖ *Jugo*. In Aymara, *uma*. The "Fruits" section earlier in this chapter should give you an idea of the tremendous variety of delicious juices available. Juices are usually served pure—that is, without water. In Bolivia, however, *jugo* refers to juice made with water or milk, while pure juice is called *zumo* (also spelled *sumo*).

mate ‖ *Hierba* (or *yerba*) *mate* is a tea made from the leaves of a small tree which is grown chiefly in Brazil and Paraguay. The drink is sold all over South America. It contains some caffeine and is mildly stimulating. In Argentina and Paraguay, *mate* is sipped through silver straws (*bombillas*) out of small gourds, many of which are embellished with silver. Perhaps because of this practice, gourds are called *mates* in many parts of the Andes. Try *mate* if you come across it in your travels.

> cold, iced ‖ *mate tetre*
>
> hot ‖ *mate cocida*
>
> with sugar ‖ *mate dulce*
>
> without sugar ‖ *mate amargo*

mate de coca ‖ A tea made from coca leaves. Since coca leaves are legal in the Andes, *mate de coca* is a common drink. I find it about as stimulating as a good cup of coffee. It's also recommended for altitude sickness (*soroche*).

mazato (also spelled *masato*) ‖ A typical drink in the Amazon that's made from rice, corn or yucca. In the jungle the method of fermenting *mazato* made from yucca is to chew it and spit it back into the pot, since the enzymes in saliva are necessary to start the fermentation. *Mazato* made from corn and rice is fermented by adding sugar, a more appetizing method.

milk ǁ *Leche*. In Quechua, *ñuñu*.

milk shake or malted milk ǁ *Malteada*. True malts are rare, but milk shakes are good.

mineral water ǁ *Agua mineral*. This is an excellent, safe substitute for regular water. In Ecuador it may be listed on the menu as *Guitig*, which is a good, local brand.

monconchinchin (Bolivia) ǁ A drink sold in Cochabamba Valley markets. It looks like apple juice but is made from dried peaches boiled in water. A little cinnamon is added to the drink and a peach pit is put in the bottom of the glass. It's safe to drink since the water's been boiled.

naranjilla colada (Ecuador) ǁ *Naranjilla* juice and sugar, thickened with cornstarch or tapioca.

paico (Ecuador) ǁ A drink made with fresh lemon and *aguardiente*.

Pisco (Peru) ǁ A famous Peruvian grape brandy used in *Pisco* sours.

rum ǁ *ron*

sherry ǁ *jerez*

Singani (Bolivia) ǁ A Bolivian whiskey made from white grapes grown in Tarija.

soft drink, pop ǁ *Gaseosa* in Colombia; *refresco* elsewhere. There are many local brands of soft drinks, such as *Inca Cola*, if you get tired of imported American Coca-Cola, Pepsi or 7-Up. Orange Crush is commonly called *Crush*, pronounced "kroosh."

tea ǁ *Té*. There are two commonly sold brands of tea bags—Lipton's and Horniman's. You also can order chamomile (*manzanilla*), balm (*toronjil*) and various herb teas, such as *hierba mate, hierba luisa* and *mate de coca*. In the southern Ecuadorian highlands, the most common tea is *guayusa*, which is made from a mountain plant that grows around Sucúa, on the eastern slopes of the Andes.

water ǁ *Agua*. In Quechua, *unu* or *yaku*. *Agua potable* means "potable (drinkable) water." However, in many places *agua potable* refers to water distributed by pipes, conduits and plumbing (as opposed to water from a well). It does *not* mean the water is safe to drink.

wine ǁ *Vino*. Red wine is *vino tinto* and white wine is *vino blanco*. Dry wine is called *vino seco*. Chilean wines are especially good.

Condiments

baking powder || *polvo de hornear*

baking soda || *bicarbonato*

cake mix || *harina preparada para tortas*

candied fruit || *fruta abrillantada*

capers || *alcaparras*

caramel or butterscotch || *caramelo*

catsup || *salsa de tomate*

cereal (breakfast) || *Cereal*. Usually sold by u.s. brand names—very expensive.

chili sauce || *salsa picante*

chocolate chips || *trocitos de chocolate*

cornstarch || *Maizena* (brand name)

corn syrup || *Miel de maíz*. Karo is a common brand.

cream of tartar || *cremor tártaro*

evaporated milk || *leche evaporada*

food coloring || *color vegetal*

honey || *Miel de abeja*. In Aymara, *miskki*.

jam || *mermelada*

jello || *gelatina*

jelly || *jalea*

lard || *lardo*

margarine || *margarina*

marmalade || *mermelada*

mayonnaise || *mayonesa*

mocha || *moka*

molasses || *melaza, miel de caña*

mustard || *mostaza*

noodles || *tallarines, pasta*

oil (vegetable) || *aceite*

olives || *aceitunas*

peanut butter || *Mantequilla de manis*. Hard to find. You may have to buy imported American brands.

pepper (ground, black) || *Pimienta negra*. In Quechua, *uchu*.

pickles || *Pepinos* or *pepinillos en escabeche*; also *encurtidos*.

powdered milk || *Leche en polvo*. *Nido* or *KLIM* are good brands.

preserves || *conservas*

salt || *Sal*. In Quechua, *cachi*; in Aymara, *jayu*. You can buy regular table salt in *tiendas* or big hunks of rock salt in markets.

soy sauce || *salsa soya*

spaghetti || *tallarines*

sugar (white) || *azúcar, azúcar granulada*

    brown || *azúcar morena*

    crude brown (Bolivia) || *chancaca*

    powdered || *azúcar molida*

    raw || *Panela*. Sold in markets

in plate-sized discs wrapped
in husks or in basket containers.
It's also sold in hunks. Looks
like hard-packed brown sugar.

sugar cane ‖ *caña*

vermicelli ‖ *fideos*

vinegar ‖ *vinagre*

Worcestershire sauce ‖ *salsa
inglesa*

yeast ‖ *levadura, espuma, fermento*

Health

ou don't have to get sick on your trip. If you get the recommended inoculations before leaving home and observe a few simple precautions while traveling, chances are you'll stay healthy and have a good time.

Please read this chapter carefully. The list of required and recommended inoculations was compiled with the help of doctors working for American clinics and the Peace Corps in South America and with the extensive advice of Herb Sigmond, M.D., who studied at London University's School of Tropical Medicine.

There are a few things to remember when preparing for your trip. First, it's a good idea to be feeling completely well when you leave. If you're just getting over a bug, delay your trip for a couple of weeks. If you're planning to be gone a long time, be sure to have things like your dental work and eyeglass situation under control. Don't expect to replace any medicine or medical necessities in South America. Although you might be able to do this, you can't count on it; so carry along a sufficient supply of whatever medications you normally take.

Staying well anywhere has a good deal to do with staying centered, rested and well fed. Don't subject yourself to too many strains at once. There's nothing like several frantic weeks of running around followed by a couple of sleepless nights before you leave to set yourself up for a good cold or upset stomach. Also, be sure to start your shots early so that you aren't packing with a sore arm. Then, when you arrive in South America, slow down. Take a nap—and don't get upset, even if your luggage gets lost at the airport. Throughout your trip, eat a balanced diet, including sufficient protein. Enjoy yourself and observe some minimal health precautions, but don't worry constantly about getting sick.

If you plan to live in South America for quite a while or plan to venture off the beaten path, you also should have a working knowledge of first aid. You may want to take the following books along with you, although I suggest that you read and learn what you can from them before you leave.

Emergency Medical Guide, 2nd ed., by John Henderson, M.D. (New York: McGraw-Hill, 1969). This is a good reference book to own. It tells you what to do in case of auto accident, snake bite, poisoning, unattended childbirth, burns and other medical emergencies. If you're driving, take it along; otherwise it's quite heavy to carry.

The Merck Manual of Diagnosis and Therapy, edited by Charles E. Lyght (West Point, Pa.: Merck, Sharpe and Dhome Research Laboratories, 1966). *The Merck Manual* can be found in the office of just about every physician in the United States. It's highly technical and extremely comprehensive. Merck discourages the sale of this manual to the general public because it's so technical, but you can find it in the bookstores of many colleges and all medical schools. It's an excellent reference for the treatment of tropical diseases and is necessary only if you're going off to live in a remote village for a year or more.

Where There Is No Doctor, by David Werner (The Hesperian Foundation, Box 1692, Palo Alto, California 94302). This medically sound and culturally sensitive book was written for health-care workers in Mexico and is also published in Spanish. It includes treatment plans for almost everything you're likely to encounter. Travelers are often asked to treat people in the back country, and this book could save a life. Take along a Spanish copy and leave it in South America.

How to Use This Chapter

Read the following material from beginning to end and then make an appointment for your inoculations. It's your responsibility to tell the doctor where you're going to travel and inform him of any special medical problems you may have, such as pregnancy or allergies, and to see that your health card is stamped after each immunization. If you get your shots at more than one place, be sure that you provide all this information for each doctor you visit.

Use common sense regarding the medications recommended in this chapter. It's a good idea to make a list of any prescription drugs you think you'll need to buy before your trip, so that your doctor can write the prescriptions and counsel you on their use. This is especially important if you don't think you'll have the opportunity to buy the drugs in South America.

When you go to visit your doctor you might want to take this book along. Dr. Sigmond and I didn't write this chapter to replace your doctor, but to aid him or her, since most physicians in the United States don't have the opportunity to treat tropical diseases and probably have no idea what health conditions are like in South America or what medicines or medical facilities are available there. You can show your physician our recommendations of drugs that you buy here and in South America and obtain his opinion. If you're allergic to a certain medication, your doctor can prescribe a substitute, which you should make sure to buy before you leave. Remember, too, that if you get all your inoculations and observe basic health precautions during your trip, the need for any kind of medication is significantly reduced.

Inoculations

Inoculations are vitally important. Most of the worst tropical diseases can be prevented through inoculation, so make sure your immunizations are up-to-date before you leave. The following list of recommended inoculations should not be taken lightly; don't let a friend or your family physician talk you out of these shots without good medical reasons.

According to the Federal Public Health Service there have been no known cases of smallpox anywhere in the world since 1978; the disease has been eradicated. (Do you believe this? I don't. I'm convinced that smallpox is still lurking out there among a remote tribe in a far corner of the planet and we'll all be sorry we let our vaccinations lapse.) A smallpox vaccination is no longer required for admission to the Andean countries. Colombia, Ecuador and Peru no longer require any inoculations, although all three countries recommend a yellow fever shot if you are visiting the jungle. Bolivia *does* require a *yellow fever inoculation* within the past ten years.

Yellow fever shots are given free at federal public health facilities. Look in the white pages of your telephone directory under "United States Government Offices, Health and Human Services Department." Or check in the front of the directory for the number of the "Federal Information Center." Yellow fever shots are not valid until ten days after inoculation, so don't plan to arrive in South America before then.

You should have all inoculations entered on your health card. This card, otherwise known as the International Certificates of Vaccination, has been approved for travelers by the World Health Organization. An entry on the card must have the name of the vaccinator followed by the official seal or stamp, or you could be refused entry into a country. Carry the card in your money belt with your passport so you don't lose it.

Many inoculations, including yellow fever, are not recommended for pregnant women. If you're pregnant, or have other medical or religious reasons for not obtaining certain shots, contact the consulates of the countries you plan to visit. In lieu of inoculations you're usually required to get a letter from your doctor or minister which must be certified by your local health department, or you might be able to present an itinerary to the consulate showing you will not be traveling in a region where a disease exists.

Although the following inoculations aren't required by law, they're *absolutely mandatory* for a safe and healthy trip:

Typhoid-paratyphoid immunization. This involves two injections given at least four weeks apart, with one booster shot every three years. The shot may cause a fever and sore arm and make you irritable for a few days, so don't have one at the last minute. If you're pushed for time you can get the second shot as early as two weeks after the first, although protection might be lessened. It's possible to contract a mild case of typhoid despite the shots.

Diphtheria-tetanus (D-T), combined adult toxoid. Most people are given the initial immunization as a child. You should have a booster every ten years beginning at age six, so it's probably time for one now. If you have no idea what immunizations you had as a child, check with your parents or childhood doctor.

Polio vaccine (oral). If you received the series of three oral doses as a child, you only need a booster before you leave. The booster is also oral. It's not recommended for pregnant women.

Gamma globulin. This is one of the most important shots you can get. It's given to prevent infectious hepatitis, which is rampant in South America. While I was there, four people I knew contracted hepatitis while traveling, and none of them had had a preventive shot of gamma globulin. The American Embassy in La Paz insists that embassy personnel in Bolivia each receive a 2-ml dose of gamma globulin every four months. Under this regimen not a single person has come down with hepatitis. Dr. Sigmond recommends a 4- or 5-ml dose for adults.

It's really impossible to overemphasize the importance of getting a gamma globulin shot. Since the vaccine *must* be kept refrigerated, it's best to get the shot before you leave or at a good clinic in South America.

Although I had one shot that provided protection for nine months, the shot usually is given every four to six months when you're abroad. This shot should be given at least three weeks *after* the last of the live-virus vaccines, which include those for polio, influenza, yellow fever, rubella, measles, mumps and smallpox.

It's best to plan ahead for these shots. Since some vaccines can't be given together and others are given in a series, begin immunizations at least six weeks before you leave. Dr. Sigmond suggests the following immunization schedule for adults:

Day one. Smallpox, polio booster, diphtheria-tetanus booster (if needed), first typhoid, yellow fever. (Note that smallpox and yellow fever shots can be given at the same time *on different arms* and their effectiveness isn't impaired.)

Day thirty-six. Second typhoid, gamma globulin. (If you're pressed for time, the second series can be given on day twenty-one.)

Vaccinations against typhus, cholera and plague are not necessary unless there's a current outbreak of these diseases in South America. How do you know if you need preventive shots? Call the United States Public Health Service and check with the appropriate consulates. Newspapers and magazines such as *Time* and *Newsweek* usually report epidemics, also.

If you're taking children to the Andean countries, it's vital that their shots be up-to-date, including measles/rubella/mumps and diphtheria/pertussis/tetanus. Check with your pediatrician about other inoculations, health precautions and pediatric dosages of medicine.

Drug Allergies and Special Medical Problems

If you're allergic to any medication (penicillin, for example) or have a special medical problem, you should wear a bracelet or necktag stating this. For seven dollars, the non-profit Medic Alert Foundation will keep a record of the medical history of any United States resident and issue that person a stainless-steel bracelet with the essential information and Medic Alert's telephone number engraved on it. For further information, write to the following:

> Medic Alert Foundation
> Turlock, California 95380

Medical Kit

Besides your health card, eyeglass prescription, Chapstick and such, you should travel with a small medical kit. Exactly what to take depends on the kind of trip you're planning. If you're flying to Bogotá or Quito for a three-week vacation, you need much less than if you're planning a year-long backpacking trip.

The following list begins with general items that are useful for traveling anywhere and moves on to more specialized items. In this list—and in general—be aware that drugs have *generic* and *brand* names. When a drug patent expires, that drug can be marketed by many different companies under their own brand names. For example, tetracycline (generic name) is sold by the brand names Vibramycin, Terramycin, Minocin, etc. Both at home and in South America, it's cheaper to buy a drug by its generic name rather than asking for a specific brand.

You should buy the following before you leave:

§ Aspirin (5-grain tablets) for pain and fever. You can also buy aspirin in South America.

§ Aspergum or children's aspirin for those times (such as bus rides) when there's no water available.

§ A few Band-Aids for blisters or minor cuts.

§ Two-percent tincture of iodine for water purification. One ounce per month of travel should be more than enough. Buy one 2-oz bottle with an eyedropper or several smaller bottles. If you're allergic to iodine, or can't use it for some other reason, your best alternative is Clorox or any household chlorine bleach. Carry a small amount in a plastic bottle. Halazone tablets are *not* recommended because they have a short shelf-life and lose potency quickly. You can buy iodine here or in South America, where it's called *yodo*. (See "Precautions to Take While Traveling" for instructions on use.)

§ Sunscreen lotion, not just suntan lotion, to prevent sunburn. You can get badly sunburned high in the Andes, where the atmosphere is thin, as well as at the beach.

§ A good insect repellent, such as Cutter's, Off or Jungle Juice, which was developed by the United States Army for use in Vietnam.

§ Contraceptives, if applicable. Women should carry enough birth-control pills to last the entire trip. Although pills are available in South America, you might not find your particular kind. Women who use a

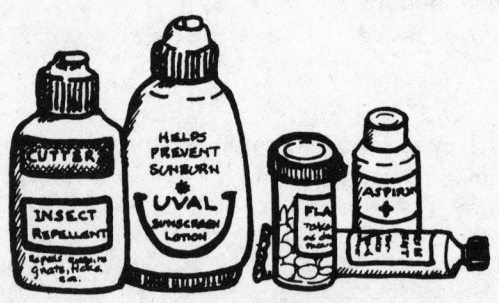

diaphragm should take along sufficient spermatocidal jelly or cream. Men should take enough condoms to last the trip.

§ Multiple vitamins containing vitamin B complex and vitamin C. (Women might consider a type that includes iron.) There are many brands available. Stuartnatal 1 + 1 and Beminal–500 are good brands. (Stuartnatal 1 + 1 contains iron and was originally designed for pregnant women; it's also expensive.)

§ Dramamine or Marezine for motion sickness. Unfortunately, I'm all too familiar with these drugs. If you get motion-sick under normal circumstances, you're really in for it in the Andes. Start out with a supply of either of these drugs, although both kinds are available in South America.

§ A small tube of antibiotic ointment, such as Bacitracin, Neosporin or Polysporin, for wounds.

§ A small-size antifungal cream or lotion, such as MicaTin (a prescription drug in the United States) or Tinactin, for athlete's foot, ringworm and other fungus infections.

§ Lomotil (2.5-mg tablets) for diarrhea. This is a prescription drug in the United States. You should start out with some, but it's also available in South America. (See "Precautions to Take While Traveling" for instructions on use.)

§ Antibiotic tablets for diarrhea, food poisoning and infections. Tetracycline is available by such trade names as Minocin, Vibramycin and Terramycin in 250-mg tablets. Women who are susceptible to monilial (yeast) infections should try Terrastatin or Mysteclin-F, both of which are tetracyclines with an antimonilial drug added. For people who are allergic to tetracyclines, for women who are pregnant or breast-feeding and for children under eight, substitute Ampicillin (a synthetic penicillin) in 250-mg tablets. A third alternative is Furoxone (in 100-mg tablets), which is available in South America under the name Furoxona. Dr. Sigmond says this is a weaker antibiotic and recommends the others unless you're allergic to them. All of these antibiotics are prescription drugs in the United States. However, except for Mysteclin-F, they're available in South America without a prescription.

Whether you need the following drugs depends on the type of trip you're taking. (See "Precautions to Take While Traveling" for instructions on use.)

§ Antimalarials. Aralen (chloroquine phosphate), which comes in

500-mg tablets, is the first choice. The alternative drug is Daraprim (Pyrimethamine), which comes in 25-mg tablets. Both are prescription drugs in the United States but are available in South America without a prescription. You won't need antimalarials if you're only visiting major cities or are staying above 4000 feet where malaria-carrying mosquitoes are rarely found.

§ Flagyl for amoebic dysentery. This is a prescription drug in the United States; it's available in South America without a prescription.

§ Kwell shampoo or lotion for lice and scabies. This is a prescription medication in the United States. I don't know if it's available in South America, so take some along with you.

§ Vermox (mebendazole), in 100-mg tablets, for worms. This is an expensive prescription drug in the United States, but it's highly recommended because it's effective against ninety percent of the different kinds of worms you might be exposed to. I don't know if it can be found in South America, so take it with you if you think you're going to need it.

§ Antihistamine. Use either Chlortrimeton (4-mg tablets) or Vistaril (50-mg capsules) for hay fever, stuffy nose, itching or swelling. One tablet should be taken every four hours as needed; a side effect is drowsiness.

Buying Medicine in South America

It's best to buy the first thirteen items on the medical-kit list before you leave home. Otherwise, buy Lomotil and the antibiotics as soon as you arrive in South America, since inevitably you'll get sick at some inconvenient time, such as on a long bus trip, when you can't get to a pharmacy. If you're not sure how to pronounce the name of a drug, print its name very clearly in capital letters and show this to the pharmacist to avoid inadvertently buying the wrong one. When buying drugs in South America, be sure to note the expiration date on all packages so that you don't buy or use outdated medicine.

Pills are called *comprimidos;* capsules are *cápsulas;* a liquid (that is, a suspension) is *suspensión* and suppositories are *supositorios.* Cream is *crema* and lotion is *loción.*

MEDICATIONS TO AVOID

There are several medications available abroad which can be harmful. Beware of cough and cold remedies containing chloramphenicol. This antibiotic can cause a fatal form of anemia and it should be taken only under a doctor's supervision. Entero-Vioform (iodochlorhydroxyquin) has long been a traditional remedy for *turista*, but it was recently outlawed in Japan and several other countries because of eye and nerve damage associated with its use. Substitute one of the antidiarrhea drugs for Entero-Vioform.

HERBAL MEDICINE

If an Indian should offer you an herbal medicine to remedy a discomfort, should you take it? The jungle tribes in particular have a wide knowledge of medicinal plants, and various modern drugs (*e.g.*, curare, cocaine, quinine) were introduced to us by the Indians. What you're given quite possibly may help you, so if you feel a little adventuresome, you might try an herbal medicine if you're sick. Dr. Sigmond recommends that you first find out what you're taking—muscle relaxant, tranquilizer, narcotic, hallucinogen, etc.

Finding a Doctor Abroad

How do you find a good doctor in South America? Several organizations have compiled directories of recommended physicians outside the United States. The International Association for Medical Assistance to Travelers (IAMAT) publishes a free directory of English-speaking doctors throughout the world. These doctors provide twenty-four-hour service to travelers at reasonable, preset rates. Membership in IAMAT is free, although the organization appreciates a donation for their directory. Intermedic and the World Medical Association also publish listings of English-speaking physicians abroad. Write to these organizations at the following addresses:

>   International Association for Medical Assistance to Travelers
>   350 Fifth Avenue, Suite 5620
>   New York, New York 10001
>
>   Intermedic
>   777 Third Avenue
>   New York, New York 10001
>
>   World Medical Association
>   10 Columbus Circle
>   New York, New York 10015

Once you're in South America, you can consult American embassies or consulates, Cooks International, major hotels, religious missions, tourist bureaus or the Peace Corps for recommended physicians and hospitals. The following medical facilities are also recommended:

Colombia. In Bogotá, try the *Clínica Samper,* Calle 75, No. 7–81. Telephone 48-34-28. English is spoken, and an American dentist is also on staff.

Ecuador. In Quito, the *Hospital Vozandes,* Villalengua 267, is run by missionaries and has several nurses who speak English.

Peru. In Lima, contact the *Clínica Anglo-American,* located at Alfredo Salazar 300, in the neighboring suburb of San Isidro. Telephone 40-35-70.

Bolivia. In the suburb of Calacoto, near La Paz, Methodists run the *Hospital Metodisto.* This hospital has American personnel and an excellent reputation. The *Hospital de Clínicas,* located on Avenida Saavedra in downtown La Paz, is also recommended. In Cochabamba, try the Roman Catholic *Hospital Elizabeth Seton,* which is located outside the city.

Precautions to Take While Traveling

WATER

By getting all the recommended shots, you go a long way toward avoiding the most serious tropical diseases. Once you're in the Andean countries, you should take a few more precautions. The first is *not* to drink the water anywhere. Many diseases, from typhoid to infectious hepatitis, are transmitted by sewage-contaminated water. Even if a city has a water-treatment plant, water still can be contaminated due to leaking pipes or faulty plumbing, so don't drink water or brush your teeth with it unless you treat it first.

There are three ways you can purify water. If you have a stove, simply boil the water for twenty minutes. Otherwise, add five drops of two-percent tincture of iodine per quart of water (ten drops if the water is cloudy) and wait for thirty minutes. You can also use this solution to disinfect fruits and vegetables. When you buy iodine (*yodo*), be sure to ask for *yodo para lavar legumbres* (iodine for washing vegetables), so that you get the right kind. The third method of purifying water is to use two drops of six-percent liquid chlorine bleach (such as Clorox) per quart of water and wait for thirty minutes. Besides tasting bad, chlorine isn't as effective as iodine against infectious hepatitis and is probably better for washing fruits and vegetables than it is for purifying drinking water.

Naturally, you should also avoid having ice cubes in your drinks. Ask for your drinks *sin hielo* (without ice).

MEAT

You can't spend all your time worrying about the food, and I certainly didn't! However, one rule to follow anywhere is to avoid unrefrigerated meat, poultry and seafood that's been left sitting out for some time—sandwiches are a good example. As Dr. Sigmond suggests, the rule for meat is freshly cooked and hot—or not at all. (Extreme heat and cold retard the growth of toxic bacteria that can cause food poisoning. This way you avoid the kind of situation you occasionally hear about in the United States when 500 people at a church picnic become extremely ill because the food sat out too long.) As always, be sure that all pork has been well cooked before you eat it. Also be wary of rancid grease, especially in street-vended food. It wreaks havoc with your stomach.

DAIRY PRODUCTS

Many diseases, including typhoid, tuberculosis and brucellosis, are transmitted by unpasteurized and unrefrigerated dairy products, so avoid these. Don't buy custard on the street or eat uncooked, unpasteurized cheese sold in the markets. If you buy milk from a farmer in the country and are unsure that it's fresh, pasteurize it yourself. Simply bring the milk to a boil, let it cool down for about ten minutes and then bring it to a boil a second time. Generally you can find pasteurized milk in such large cities as Bogotá, Quito, Lima and La Paz.

FRUITS AND VEGETABLES

The basic rule is never to eat unwashed, uncooked or unpeeled fruits and vegetables. When you shop in the market, you can follow this advice easily enough by choosing peelable produce. Many of the foods which travel best, such as bananas and tangerines, are easily peelable, although if your hands are dirty you're probably contaminating the fruit anyway. After a while this becomes a moot point. You went to the bathroom and there was no place to wash your hands. What then? What about that nice salad served at the restaurant? What good does it do to have the food washed if the water is contaminated? Should you avoid lettuce altogether? The reason for avoiding lettuce and other ground plants is that they may have been contaminated by impure water. But what about peaches?

You can waste a lot of energy worrying about these things. There are times when you may not have a quart of purified water handy, such as when you're traveling on the bus, so be sensible. If you carry moistened towelettes in your pocket or purse, you can at least wash your hands after going to the bathroom or wipe off your pocketknife. Then disinfect or peel whatever you can. The idea is to do the best you can to prevent yourself from contracting a number of serious diseases which are all caused by fecal contamination of food through irrigation water, washing water, careless handling, flies, etc. The diseases transmitted in this way range from diarrhea to amoebic dysentery to hepatitis.

Common Maladies and What to Do About Them

TRAVELER'S DIARRHEA (Turista)

All right, it finally happens. You have *turista*, traveler's diarrhea, and you're suffering from abdominal pains, aches, a fever and chills. Recent studies implicate *Escherichia coli*, a type of bacteria which is normally present in our intestines. There are many varieties of this bacteria throughout the world, and they're probably responsible for the discomfort we experience whenever we travel until our body finally adapts to its new surroundings.

Diarrhea actually can be a healing mechanism, flushing irritants from your intestines, so it's generally a good idea to just stay in your hotel room and wait a couple of days for *turista* to run its course. However, if you're in the middle of a bus ride or are in some other situation where you can't trot off to the bathroom or bushes every fifteen minutes, there are drugs you can take to stop the diarrhea and cramps. Lomotil (2.5-mg tablets) stops the *symptoms only*. Take two pills three or four times a day. Lomotil should *not* be given to children under three. For small children, use Kaopectate; the dosage is one tablespoon after each loose bowel movement.

Dr. Sigmond emphasizes how important it is to drink plenty of fluids—purified water, tea, pop, whatever—to avoid getting dehydrated. There's a tendency to avoid liquids when you're feeling ill or have diarrhea. In tropical climates becoming dehydrated only makes you feel worse.

If you have what seems to be *turista* for four days without a sign of its letting up, or if you're really sick after a day or two with diarrhea, blood in your stool, constant severe abdominal pain and vomiting, you've probably got something more serious, such as food poisoning, amoebiasis or typhoid.

FOOD POISONING

Food poisoning in most cases is a bacterial (*Salmonella, Shigella* or *Staphylococcus*) infection. Take tetracycline, which comes in either 250-mg or 500-mg tablets or capsules. If you have the 250-mg size, take four capsules to start and then two capsules four times daily for two days. Then take one capsule four times daily for another three days.

If you use Ampicillin (recommended for people who are allergic to tetracycline, for women who are pregnant or breast-feeding and for children under eight), take 250-mg tablets or capsules in the same dosages as tetracycline. Both of these drugs are broad-spectrum antibiotics, which means they're effective against a wide range of bacterial (not viral) infections, including pneumonia, infected wounds and gonorrhea. In addition, Ampicillin is prescribed for typhoid, which is resistant to most tetracyclines.

If you're allergic to both of the above antibiotics, then try Furoxone. Take one 100-mg tablet four times daily for three to five days. No matter which drug you choose, don't stop taking it before the five days are up!

Being this sick can really bring you down. However, if you rest, take the prescribed medication and drink plenty of fluids, you should start to feel better in a few days. In the meantime, remind yourself of the exciting things you plan to do as soon as you're on your feet and curse the café that sold you the contaminated food.

AMOEBIASIS

Amoebiasis is caused by amoebas *(Entamoeba histolytica)*, which create discomfort in the large intestine, where they live on red blood cells and cell juices. Amoebas are passed in feces, and the cysts, if kept moist and cool, can live for many weeks outside the body. These cysts can then be ingested by another host (you?) through contaminated food and water.

Amoebiasis diagnosis is tricky in that there may be either no symptoms of dysentery at all or very severe symptoms, including stomach cramps and evidence of blood and mucous in the feces. Fever may or may not be present. In severe and chronic cases, abscesses can form in the lung and liver, and the disease can be fatal.

How do you know if you have amoebiasis? Have a specimen of your stool examined by a lab. South American labs seem to be better at this than those in the United States since the South Americans are more used to looking for amoebas. If you have cramps, on-and-off diarrhea or blood or mucous in your stool, there's a good reason to suspect amoebas. I always seem to pick up amoebas and usually can tell when I have—first by the feeling that I've eaten ground glass and later by blood and mucous.

The antibiotics mentioned earlier are good for curing amoebas of the large intestine. Take the dosages recommended under "Food Poisoning," but continue it for a total of ten days. An alternative drug is Flagyl. Take three 250-mg tablets three times daily for ten days. Children between four and eight should be given one tablet twice daily for ten days, and children over eight should be given one tablet three times daily for ten days. Don't drink alcohol while using Flagyl since the combination can nauseate you. If you develop a yeast infection from either of these medications, see the recommended treatments discussed later in this chapter.

TYPHOID

Typhoid is a severe disease caused by *Salmonella typhosa* bacteria, which are transmitted in the feces and urine of infected people and carriers through food, liquids, unpasteurized milk, etc. The best protection is your inoculation. Conceivably, you could get a mild case of typhoid in spite of your shot, but you're risking a severe, possibly fatal case without it.

Typhoid's symptoms are also similar to *turista*'s, but can include fever, severe abdominal pain and constipation rather than diarrhea. If you get progressively sicker and sicker, and it lasts over five days, you may have contracted typhoid. This illness is successfully treated with Ampicillin or with the antibiotic chloramphenicol. The latter drug can cause severe anemia and should be taken only under a doctor's supervision. If you have any reason to think you've contracted typhoid, get to a doctor immediately.

INFECTIOUS HEPATITIS

Infectious hepatitis is caused by a virus which attacks the liver. It's transmitted in feces, urine and contaminated food and water; you can even contract it by shaking hands with someone who has the virus on his hands and then touching your mouth with your hand. Hepatitis is common in South America, and the best protection possible is a gamma globulin shot. The symptoms of hepatitis are fatigue, jaundiced (yellow) eyes and skin, dark brown urine and a sore liver. It's a serious disease— you have only one liver and you can't live without it. If you think you have hepatitis, see a doctor right away.

The treatment for hepatitis is plenty of rest, vitamins, adequate fluids and a diet high in protein and fruits. Recovery takes four to six weeks, during which time all physical activity should be limited to walking to and from the bathroom. You absolutely must not smoke, take drugs or drink alcohol; your liver needs to rest so that it can heal properly. Since the disease is infectious, you must be careful not to infect others. Wash your hands after going to the toilet and don't share eating utensils. All people in contact with you should get a gamma globulin shot immediately.

YEAST INFECTIONS

All antibiotics are capable of upsetting the normal bacterial organisms living in your mouth, intestines and vagina. The drugs kill so many bacteria in these areas that there's room for other bacteria and certain fungi to take up residence. The biggest problem is the *Candida* fungus. In women, it usually causes a yeast (monilial) infection of the vagina. In both men and women it may cause yeast infections of the mouth, resulting in a red mouth and tongue. Infants usually get monilia in the mouth or in the diaper area.

The drug to take for yeast infections is Mycostatin, which is available without a prescription in South America. It comes in both suppositories and pills. The vaginal suppositories should be inserted every morning and evening for ten days. My personal physician says you can also use the suppositories in your mouth. They taste chalky, but they're safe and much less expensive than the pills. If you do buy the pills, take one three times daily for ten days and the infection should clear up. There's an oral suspension available for infants whose mouths are infected. The dosage is five to ten drops in the mouth three or four times daily; treatment should continue until two days after the symptoms disappear. For the diaper-area rash, use a Mycostatin cream. This rash can be distinguished from ordinary diaper rash by its prominent bright red spots.

ALTITUDE SICKNESS (Soroche)

Soroche is caused by the transition from sea level to higher elevations (including places such as Bogotá, Quito, Cuzco or La Paz). If you travel by bus or train, your body has more time to become accustomed to the lesser amount of oxygen than if you fly, although you may still feel tired and out of breath at first. Whenever you make an abrupt change to a higher elevation, take it easy for the first few days. Don't overeat or over-drink and don't walk too fast. You'll soon adapt.

All kinds of remedies have been suggested for *soroche*. South Americans recommend a tea called *mate de coca*. Since *mate de coca* is a mild stimulant, it probably will perk you up. One traveler suggested sucking on lemons. Sucking on hard candy also gives you a needed energy boost.

HEAT EXHAUSTION AND SUN STROKE

Both heat exhaustion and sun stroke (also called heat stroke) are caused by exposure to sun and high temperatures, although their symptoms are different.

Heat exhaustion is much less serious than sun stroke and is characterized by fainting, perspiring and skin that is cold, clammy and pale. The victim should be placed in a cool, comfortable spot. Heat exhaustion is often accompanied by a depletion of the body's salts through sweating, so salt tablets or a salt water solution can be given. Keep the person cool and rested and he or she will recover. One good way to avoid heat exhaustion is to salt your food!

In sun stroke the body's heat-regulating mechanism goes haywire, and there's usually a sudden loss of consciousness. The most obvious symptom of sun stroke is an extremely high body temperature, which is a medical emergency. After exposure to sun and heat, the victim collapses and appears hot, flushed and dry. His or her body temperature can rise to 106°F, and even as high as 112°F, which is damaging to the brain, liver and kidneys.

The most important step in treating sun stroke is to cool the victim immediately in order to bring his or her temperature down. Place the person in a cold bath or cool him or her down by whatever means possible—wrapping in cold, wet sheets, fanning, etc. Sun stroke is a true emergency, so a doctor should be called. If this isn't possible, do everything you can to cool the victim's body and keep it cool, and make sure the person gets plenty of rest.

Heat exhaustion and sun stroke can be prevented if you take it easy in hot weather and wear a hat. The Indians know what they're doing when they wear hats in the mountains. In the Andes, near the equator, the amount of solar rays that filter through the atmosphere is easily double or triple the amount received on a sunny day in Chicago. You therefore tan (or burn) a lot faster and also become overheated much more quickly. The same condition exists in coastal and jungle regions near the equator, where high humidity compounds the effects of extreme heat.

LICE AND SCABIES

Pediculus capitis is the head louse. When you have these visitors, your head itches and you can feel them crawling around. The adults lay eggs called nits, which attach themselves to your hair. If you contract lice, apply Kwell (benzene hexachloride) shampoo and rub it into your scalp for five minutes. Then rinse your hair and comb out the nits with a fine-toothed comb. Wait twenty-four hours and repeat the process. All sheets should be washed and, if possible (unlikely in the Andes), dried in a hot-air dryer. To avoid re-infection, don't sleep in your sleeping bag for four days. This way you make sure the adult lice perish since they can't live away from your body for more than two days.

There are other types of lice which live on different parts of the body. *Pediculus corporis*, the body louse or "cootie," can rarely be seen on the skin, while *Pediculus pubis*, the pubic louse or "crab," is about the size of the head of a pin and can be seen and felt crawling about the pubic area. Both kinds itch like hell. To kill them, apply a thin film of Kwell lotion from neck to toes and leave it on for twenty-four hours. Then shower and reapply the lotion for another twenty-four hours. Each day, be sure to change all your clothes, sheets and pillow cases to avoid being re-infected. Everything should be washed in hot water, since the lice may try to hide in your clothes and bedding while the Kwell is on your body. Since adult lice can't live away from your body for more than two days, put your sleeping bag, down jacket, etc., aside for about four days to be sure all the lice are dead.

Scabies are a type of mite, and they crawl around on and then burrow into your skin. They make a permanent home in the superficial layer of skin on the webs between your fingers and on your wrists, belly button, penis and armpits. (In adults, the face, palms and soles of the feet are never infected.) The affected areas of skin become red and itchy. Eventually scratch marks and sores develop, and you look like you fell into a bale of barbed wire. The treatment is the same as for body lice. Apply Kwell lotion as noted above and wash all your clothes and bedding. It often takes two weeks for the itching to stop, even though the mites are dead.

SNAKE AND INSECT BITES

There are a number of poisonous snakes in South American jungles, including two with bites that are exceedingly venomous and for which there's no known antidote: the bushmaster *(shushupe* or *verdugo)* and the fer-de-lance *(taya).* (Don't you just love to read things like this?) Fortunately, most snakes are shy and retiring and aren't likely to give you any trouble unless you tromp on them. Nevertheless, if you're going into the jungle, you should always carry a snake-bite kit and know how to use it. To treat a snake bite, first place a tourniquet around the limb just above the bite, but don't make it so tight that it blocks the flow of arterial blood. (This means that if you put a tourniquet around the upper arm, you should be able to feel the victim's pulse at the wrist.) The idea is to prevent the venous blood flow from carrying the poison toward the heart. Leave the tourniquet on for three-quarters of an hour, release for ten minutes and then reapply for thirty minutes. Meanwhile, make a small incision over the bite (one-quarter to one-half inch deep and one-quarter to one-half inch long), suck out the venom and spit it out.

Like snakes, spiders and scorpions are shy and retiring. The best way to avoid getting bitten is to observe a few simple precautions. Don't go barefoot and always watch where you walk. Never reach up onto a ledge without looking first. Don't flip logs over with your hands; use a stick instead. Get into the habit of shaking out your shoes and clothing before putting them on in the morning in case something interesting has nestled in during the night. Also check your bedding or sleeping bag before you hop in.

Spider bites (tarantula or black widow) and scorpion stings should receive medical attention if possible because there are antivenins which can be given. The "if possible" is the crux of the matter in South America. First aid is the same as for snake bites—make a small incision over the bite and suck out the venom.

Jungle insects, including mosquitoes, piums, gnats and flies, are far more aggressive than reptiles and even attack in swarms. Be sure to wear long pants and a long-sleeved cotton shirt and to apply an insect repellent. At night, use a mosquito net. When you do get bitten (and everyone does), try not to scratch the bites since they become infected quite easily. Short of putting a bullet through your skull, it's impossible to stop the itching completely, but try baking soda baths and antihistamine tablets such as Chlortrimeton or Vistaril.

Bee and wasp stings should be treated with an application of Epsom salts, which draws out the poison and reduces the swelling and pain. An antihistamine tablet can help relieve the itching.

RABIES

Stay away from animals that behave strangely since rabies is common in South America. If you're bitten by an animal, try to capture it so that it can be tested for rabies and see a doctor immediately. A domestic animal, such as a dog or cat, should be quarantined for ten days. If it dies, you can assume that it had rabies. If you can't capture the animal, it's safest to assume that it had rabies and to get treatment, since untreated rabies is *always* fatal. The symptoms of rabies appear in three to six weeks, earlier if you're bitten around the face. This gives you time to reach a good medical center, even if it means flying home. While rabies treatment is painful (a series of shots), it will save your life!

WORMS

You can acquire worms through the skin (usually on your feet, so never go barefoot) and through contaminated food and water. Washing your fruits and vegetables in treated water greatly lessens your chances of contracting worms. If you do get worms while traveling, take one 100-mg Vermox (mebendazole) tablet twice a day for three days or go to a doctor or clinic for treatment.

YELLOW FEVER AND MALARIA

The organisms causing both of these diseases are transmitted by the bite of a mosquito. Mosquito control has helped reduce the incidence of these diseases. The best prevention for yellow fever is your inoculation. For malarial regions (such as the Amazon Basin), it's vital that you take anti-malarials. Aralen (chloroquine phosphate), which comes in 500-mg tablets, should be started before you even get into the jungle. Take one tablet a week on exactly the same day of the week for two weeks *before* entering the area and continue until six weeks *after* leaving. (This schedule catches the organisms in all stages of reproduction wherever they reside in your body.) You may experience side effects from Aralen, including mild headache, itching, blurred vision and hives, but these are nothing compared to malaria! The alternative drug is Daraprim (pyrimethamine), which comes in 25-mg tablets. (Daraprim isn't considered as effective as Aralen, but it has fewer side effects.) Adults should take one tablet weekly (two in heavily infected areas). See your physician for children's dosages of both medications. You can also avoid getting malaria by keeping mosquitoes away from you—sleep with mosquito netting, use a good insect repellent and wear long-sleeved shirts.

Recently, a strain of malaria has developed which is resistant to both chloroquine and Pyrimethamine. This strain exists in the jungle along the Colombia–Ecuador border and may be spreading. If you plan to travel in this region, you should take chloroquine as directed above, *plus* another medication called Fansidar. Fansidar isn't available in the United States, but is sold in Colombia (and perhaps by now in Ecuador). Take one Fansidar tablet every two weeks while you are in a malarial region, continuing for six weeks after leaving the area.

If you are planning a trip to the Amazon Basin you might want to check with the federal public health service in your city, or call the Centers for Disease Control in Atlanta, Georgia, to find out which kinds of malaria are prevalent in the areas you plan to visit, and which medications they recommend you take.

VERRUGA

Verruga, also known as human bartonellosis or Carrion's disease, is caused by a bacteria-like organism which is transmitted by the bite of a tiny sandfly, the *Phlebotomus verrucarum*. The disease occurs only in certain mountainous regions of Colombia, Ecuador and Peru between about 2500 and 9500 feet. The fly has been controlled for the most part by DDT, and verruga remains a problem primarily in central Peru. There are two forms of the disease—one causes anemia and the other results in rashy bumps all over the body which resemble tiny, fatty tumors. Tetracyclines usually are effective against verruga, which can be serious if left untreated.

CHAGAS' DISEASE

Chagas' disease is found in eastern Bolivia (the Cochabamba Valley and the jungle), Chile, Argentina, Brazil, Uruguay, Paraguay, French Guiana and Venezuela. It's primarily a hazard for travelers living under primitive conditions. Travelers staying in hotels won't encounter the disease, which is caused by the bite of a blood-sucking insect that lives in thatch-roofed houses and shelters. The insect, known locally as the *venchuga* (kissing bug), defecates when it bites and passes a parasite in its feces. If the bite is scratched the parasite can get into the bloodstream.

The *venchuga* comes out at night and usually bites around the eyes, nose or mouth, so if you wake up with a bite in these areas, don't scratch it. Instead, carefully wash the area, being careful not to get the water in your eyes or mouth. Symptoms include swelling and inflamed lymph glands around the bite as well as an enlarged liver and spleen. The disease involves progressive degeneration of the smooth muscles, including the heart muscle, and can be fatal in several weeks or several years. While there's no known cure, experimental drugs are now being tested, so seek medical help if you think you've contracted the disease. Your best protection is to use a mosquito net at night if you're sleeping in thatch-roofed buildings in areas where the disease is prevalent.

Medical Terminology

Where can I find a good _____. || ¿Dónde puedo encontrar una buen____?

    doctor || *doctor, médico*

    dentist || *dentista*

    clinic || *clínica*

    hospital || *hospital*

    pharmacy, drugstore || *farmacia, botica*

I have____. || *Tengo____.*

    a cold || *un resfriado*

    a cough || *tos*

    diarrhea || *diarrea*

    stomach ache || *dolor de estómago*

    sunburn || *quemadura del sol*

    toothache || *dolor de muelas*

    sore throat || *dolor de garganta*

    fever || *fiebre*

    the flu || *la influenza, la gripe*

    motion sickness || *mareo*

My _____ hurts. || *Me duele _____.*

    head || *la cabeza*

    stomach || *el estómago*

    eye || *el ojo*

    ear || *el oído*

Drugs and Hallucinogens

If you plan to go to South America in search of cheap and easy highs, forget it. Stay home if you want to stay stoned. Bored, stoned, culturally insensitive hippies are probably the worst travelers around, mainly because they're oblivious to local mores. What makes it worse is that drug-culture refugees make it impossible for more centered young travelers to move about freely or to settle in small villages without undue police harassment. A few indiscreet, insensitive people can create such bad feelings among local residents that other travelers may not be welcome in an area for years. The Colombian town of San Agustín, site of a magnificent archaeological park, is a case in point. In late 1973, all young foreigners were forced to leave the area because of the behavior of a few who didn't seem to realize that a small, Catholic, Colombian town was not the place to attempt a life-style based on ecstatic visions.

Besides the disruption of local life and the creation of obstacles for other travelers, drug use in South America is extremely dangerous—primarily to your freedom and finances. It's much easier and safer to buy and use drugs in the United States than it is in the Andean countries.

While long hair and hippie dress isn't synonymous with drug use in the United States, it still has that connotation in South America. Anyone who looks like a hippie might just as well wear a sign saying, "Arrest me. I use drugs." Because of this association, the cheap, so-called "hippie" hotels in Cuzco and La Paz are frequently raided, and in Colombia young people are subjected to innumerable drug searches everywhere. So far, though, I haven't come across any evidence that the police are planting drugs on innocent travelers. They have their hands full with the actual users.

You should be aware that guilt by association is common in South America. Suppose you have no drugs on you, or you don't even use them, but you're rounded up with everyone in a hotel-room party. Forget protesting your innocence—they've heard it all before. You are guilty by association and, along with the rest of the party-goers, will probably be jailed and deported, at the same time receiving a little red stamp on your passport that says you can't come back. (However, so far, the United States embassies and Immigration officials aren't keeping a list of the people who've been thrown out. So if you get a new passport you can probably re-enter the country after a decent length of time has elapsed.)

Also be forewarned that American embassies and consulates abroad are most *un*helpful to anyone arrested on a drug charge. Their attitude seems to be that anyone arrested for drugs deserves whatever happens to him. The charge could be excessive and it wouldn't matter to the State Department. This attitude has contributed to the widespread abuses in the Mexican judicial system, and it looks like the same thing is starting to happen in South America.

Marijuana

The possession or use of marijuana (*Cannabis sativa*) and hashish is illegal in all the South American countries. What happens if you're caught? It depends. The law is interpreted erratically and is often enforced just to squeeze money out of young foreigners. Some South American officials have no particular moral objection to marijuana use, but they do have moral objections to the behavior of hippies—that is, cohabitation, nudity, not working. Other officials do harbor a strong moral objection to drug use and are fearful of its influence on their youth. "It's bad for our country," they tell you as they escort you to jail.

I can't emphasize enough the dangers of marijuana use. The same goes for dealing or smuggling. The penalty for possessing a few joints can include a ruined vacation, a persona-non-grata stamp on your passport, a fine of several hundred dollars and an indeterminate stay in a disgusting jail. Possession of several kilos or more usually is interpreted to mean the person is a dealer (*traficante*). Because of current drug crackdowns, *traficantes* (real or imagined) are really in for trouble. Unless the person is a big-time dealer and can pay off high-level officials, he's usually arrested, beaten up and locked away. The local newspapers have a field day, greatly exaggerating the amount of drugs found on the person, and the South American nation uses the arrest to prove to the United States that its antidrug money is producing results (while the large-scale smugglers carry on business as usual).

Colombia is the only Andean nation in which marijuana is commonly available, and officials there have been carrying out such an intensive antidrug campaign that I wouldn't even mention the word "drug" in the country. Travel in Colombia can sometimes be unpleasant because of the numerous and unpredictable hotel, airport and body searches. Colombian law dictates the same penalties for all drug convictions—whether it's marijuana, barbiturates, cocaine or heroin. In each case, the penalty for trafficking is three to twelve years, plus a fine of up to $16,500. The police quite often fail to distinguish between possession and trafficking charges.

A word of warning about Colombians who offer to sell you drugs in their country—the same people who offer to sell you a few joints are likely to turn you over to the police. They may even *be* the police. A common set-up: you're enticed into an alley, sold a couple of joints and then arrested on the spot by the police (or people who say they are—you never know), who suddenly appear out of nowhere. It's a hundred dollars a joint—or jail. Most people pay. The same goes if you're caught with marijuana you've brought from home, and you always run the risk of going straight to jail as an example to other travelers. If you're ever caught with grass, try bribing your way out immediately. The more people who become involved, the more expensive it gets, and if you actually end up in jail it's more costly yet.

As of April 1976 there were at least a hundred Americans in Colombian jails on drug charges. Reports indicate that living conditions are often squalid, while efforts to help free these people or shorten their sentences have met with very little success.

My friend Laney, who's lived in Colombia for the past four years, wrote to me with this advice in January 1976: "Colombian officials often are not bribable like they used to be, even for minor grass infractions. This is not a good country to get in trouble in (never was, but it's far worse now). People shouldn't come here hoping to pull something off because their chances are very poor. The embassy cannot be counted on for any type of help."

Ecuador, Peru and Bolivia also frown on marijuana smoking and arrest users. In fact, marijuana is taken much more seriously than cocaine in Bolivia. This is because Bolivians are familiar with cocaine while marijuana is alien and consequently evil and threatening. A friend of mine who lives in Bolivia said that bribes just aren't working there anymore, for either marijuana or cocaine arrests, because officials are determined to halt drug use by travelers.

For those of you who absolutely can't live without marijuana, your only hope (and it's a slim one) is to look so straight when traveling that your parents and friends think you've either converted to a fundamentalist religion or joined the FBI. I mean early-1960s Midwestern fraternity or sorority clothes and hair style. And carry suitcases, not backpacks. The only place to conceal marijuana is in your crotch, since you can count on having your luggage searched and quite possibly your hotel room as well. Your best bet is to look so respectable that officials will hesitate to strip-search you—and they may not hesitate in the least. Frankly, I wouldn't carry or use marijuana at all.

Cocaine

In the minds of confirmed drug-users, South America is synonymous with cocaine (benzoylmethyl ecgonine). Everything I've said about the dangers of marijuana use goes for cocaine—only more so.

Cocaine (*cocaina* in Spanish) is an alkaloid extracted from the leaves of the coca shrub (see page 234 for historical notes as well as a comparison of cocaine use with coca-leaf chewing). The possession and use of coca leaves is legal in Peru and Bolivia. The shrub is also grown and used by many Colombian Indians, although coca leaves are technically illegal in both Colombia and Ecuador. However, in all the Andean countries, the refined extraction called cocaine—a hydrochloride salt that's known to most users as fine, white, crystal rocks or powder—is highly illegal. The refining of coca leaves occurs in hundreds of clandestine laboratories throughout South America, and every so often local newspapers carry lurid stories about the discovery of a lab and the arrest of the operators.

As with marijuana, there's a flourishing business (especially in Colombia) in the sale of cocaine—or what is purported to be cocaine—to young travelers, followed by their immediate arrest. Generally, cocaine possession is a far more serious offense than marijuana possession. Getting caught with a few grams of coke for personal use can result in all the unpleasantness of a marijuana arrest—magnified. Anyone found with a large amount of cocaine is assumed to be a *traficante*, and it's hello, prison. In Bolivia, the sentence is supposed to be the same no matter how much cocaine you're caught with—a flat twenty years. In practice, however, people caught with only a few grams go to jail for a couple of weeks and are then expelled from the country while those caught with more are sentenced to prison.

Because cocaine smuggling is extremely lucrative, the big-time operators undoubtedly are paying off officials. I strongly suspect that many highly placed government officials in South America are actively engaged in trafficking. This means they have the police busily searching young travelers at airports while their own couriers breeze on through, perhaps on diplomatic passports. Invariably it's the amateur who gets caught.

You're just plain dumb if you plan to finance your trip by bringing home a little cocaine to sell. Your chances of being robbed, arrested or sold worthless white powder (or all three at once) are high. You'd be lucky to get your contraband out of South America and even luckier to get it into the United States. Customs officials in all countries are on to the trick of having women carry drugs. I was strip-searched at the La Paz airport before my flight to Lima.

There are presently at least four hundred American men and women in Mexican jails on drug charges, many of whom were arrested while carrying cocaine through Mexico City's international airport. The State Department has concurred with the reports (originally published in *Rolling Stone*) of people being beaten, tortured and forced to sign confessions. Persons accompanying (or suspected of accompanying) a person who's caught with drugs are arrested and prosecuted, too. Panama City's international airport is another nemesis of drug smugglers.

If Worse Comes to Worst

If you're arrested on a drug charge you can count on being virtually abandoned by the American consulate. They'll give you a list of attorneys to choose from, but the lists are notoriously bad. The attorneys on them are unreliable and often dishonest, so you're better off asking a South American to recommend a good lawyer—one with *palanca*. The consulate will also inform your family and/or friends and will see that you're treated the same as a citizen of the country in which you were arrested, but because South American citizens (especially poor ones) aren't treated well by their legal systems, this is no consolation.

You are subject to the laws of the country in which you were arrested and are *not* protected by American laws. (That's why it's safer to be caught smoking marijuana in California or Oregon than in South America.) These countries operate under the Napoleonic Code, which means you're guilty until proven innocent.

If you are arrested it's very important to be respectful and polite. Don't freak out and don't demand your "rights as an American." (You don't have any "rights as an American" in South America.) You *don't* have the right to a phone call or to immediate counsel. Furthermore, don't believe anything you hear; the guards and police may try to frighten you to get you to confess or talk. *Don't* confess to anything, *don't* talk about your case to anyone and *don't* make any deals or inform on anyone else. A deal will not be honored and getting more people in trouble *won't* get you off.

For example, in Bolivia there are two stages to a case following an arrest. The first is an investigative stage during which your case is studied. The law states that this must be done in a reasonable amount of time, whatever that is. In the meantime, don't contact a lawyer or believe what anyone tells you, since no formal charge has been filed. After the investigation has been completed (which could take several days to a month), either a written charge is filed with the court and shown to you or the case is dropped entirely. Once you see the written charge, the time has come to hire a lawyer and fight the case.

You're going to need help on the outside—someone to raise money and find a good attorney (see Chapter Seven, "How Things Work"). A friend or family member must work actively on your behalf to raise funds for the lawyer's fee as well as any bribes he may have to pay. You need money and connections. It's a lawyer's personal connections, above all, that win his cases.

There are various classes of prisons in South America. Depending on your finances, you can be incarcerated first class, second class or economy. Economy prisoners are so poor they have to accept what little the state provides, which is just enough to keep them alive, while those doing time first class can rent complete apartments in prison, order food from the best local restaurants and have tape decks, televisions and conjugal visits. If you end up going to jail, I hope you're rich.

Coca Leaves *(Hojas de Coca)*

While cocaine is illegal in the Andes, coca leaves are legal in Peru and Bolivia. The use of the leaves *(hojas)* has a long and venerable history. Coca was domesticated in the upper Amazon Basin, and coca leaves have been found in Peruvian graves dating from 2000 B.C. Archaeologists have found Mochica pottery dating from about 500 A.D. which is molded in the shape of Indian heads whose cheeks bulge with quids of coca leaves. The Pre-Columbian civilizations of Colombia were also familiar with coca, and the Gold Museum in Bogotá has a collection of magnificent gold *poporos*, the containers used to carry the lime chewed with the leaves.

The coca shrub (*Erythroxylon coca*) grows at altitudes ranging from 3000 to 8000 feet on the subtropical, eastern Andean slopes known as the Yungas in Peru and Bolivia. The Incas cultivated the shrub, and on many coca plantations crops are still grown on the original Inca terraces. These coca fields are called *cocales*.

The coca leaf contains a number of alkaloids, of which cocaine is the most potent. The cocaine alkaloid serves as a central nervous system stimulant, a local anesthetic and an appetite depressant. In other words, it gives you a subtle energy rush and masks the sensations of hunger and pain. An Indian who chews an ounce of the leaves a day consumes about 0.14 grain of cocaine, which is a very tiny amount. The mild, stimulating effect of coca-leaf-chewing is similar to the effect felt from drinking coffee.

For the alkaloids to be released, coca leaves must be chewed with something alkaline. This can be in the form of lime (*cal*) or sticks made from the ashes of *quínoa* or *cañihua* mixed with water. These sticks are called *lejia, llictha* or *lluqllu* in Bolivia and *llipta* in Peru. *Lejia*, which translates literally as "lye," looks like gray rocks or thick sticks and is usually kept in a basket alongside the bales of coca leaves in the market. Either *cal* or *lejia* is included in the coca-leaf sale. When the Indians chew the leaves, they only swallow the juice, and the streets and sidewalks of Andean towns are littered with small, green, spit-out quids (*acullicu* or *jach'u*).

MYTHS AND HISTORY

There are many legends concerning the origin of coca. According to one Peruvian legend dating from at least as early as the sixteenth century, a beautiful but loose woman was killed by the Indians because of her sexual indiscretions and from her body grew the coca plant.

A more recent Bolivian legend says that the god of snow and storms became angered by the smoke created when the Indians burned the forested eastern slopes of the Andes for farming, and so he sent a storm which flooded the Yungas, destroyed the roads and isolated the Indians. When the Indians came out of the caves in which they'd hidden from the storm they found their land devastated—the myth of the Deluge with an Indian twist. Then someone discovered a mysterious shrub and, after eating its leaves, the Indians found themselves feeling happy and strong, with their hunger abated. They brought the plant back to the highlands and introduced it to the wise men (*amautas*) and healers (*yatiris*).

According to a contemporary Bolivian Quechua legend, coca is the daughter of *Pacha Mama* (Mother Earth), born as a sacred plant with the power to drive away evil. Because of this belief in the protective power of *Mama Coca*, coca leaves are burned by the Indians whenever someone moves into a new house and on other special occasions. An offering of twelve perfect coca leaves, a bit of red wool and some llama fat are placed on a fire. The smoke of *Mama Coca* penetrates the house, drives away the evil spirits and then rises into the sky in the shape of a human body.

Coca was a divine plant to the Incas, and it was frequently used as an offering in religious rituals. Pure gold replicas of coca shrubs were among the gold plants included in the Inca's garden in the *Coricancha*. Only the Inca nobility were allowed to chew the leaf and this right was one of the highest awards the Inca could confer. Coca leaves also were buried with dead nobility to sustain them in the afterlife.

It was the Spanish who spread the coca habit to the rest of the Indian population when they discovered that the Indians would work harder, longer and on less food when allowed to chew the leaf. And, of course, there were fortunes to be made in selling the leaf.

Coca leaves were especially important to the silver-mining industry in Potosí, Bolivia, during the sixteenth century. The Indians of the area were forced into labor in the mines and they simply didn't work without the leaves. I was told that La Paz was founded because it was a convenient stopping point en route between the coca plantations in the Yungas and the silver mines to the south.

Along with the Spanish *conquistadores*, various other visitors to the land of the Incas noticed the pleasant effects of chewing coca leaves. While chewing the leaves never became popular in the United States and Europe, various drinks made from coca leaves did. In the nineteenth century, a Corsican named Angelo Mariani introduced a red wine made from coca leaves which he called *Vin Mariani, a la Coca du Perou.* Among the users of Mariani's product was Pope Leo XIII. In 1885, an American named John Styth Pemberton introduced French Wine Coca and the next year came up with Coca-Cola, which also was made from coca leaves.

Cocaine was first isolated from the coca leaf in 1844, but not much use was made of it until the 1880s, when it was issued to Bavarian soldiers during autumn maneuvers one year. Sigmund Freud read an account of this experiment and subsequently became an active user and proponent of the drug. He prescribed it for patients and friends and even sent some to his fiancée, Martha. In the 1880s cocaine was added to various tonics, catarrh remedies and other patent medicines. The catarrh remedies were sniffed, which gave people the idea of sniffing cocaine, leading to the first known dependency on the drug.

By the 1890s medical literature was beginning to accumulate concerning the potential addicting and psychosis-producing nature of cocaine.

In fact, the classic drug fiend, the one who thought he saw spiders or had ants under his skin, was likely to be a heavy cocaine-user. In 1906 Congress passed the Pure Food and Drug Act, which took the coca out of Coca-Cola and the cocaine out of patent medicines, as well as regulating the use and sale of opiates.

A word should be said about the use of the term "addicting" with reference to cocaine. Cocaine is not a central nervous system depressant like alcohol, barbiturates and heroin, and a regular user does not go into a dramatic physical withdrawal when he stops using the drug. Cocaine is a central nervous system stimulant like amphetamines, coffee and tobacco. Cocaine withdrawal is characterized by severe depression, for which more cocaine seems to be the only answer. Regular users also seem to develop some tolerance of the drug (the need to increase their dose) and end up not being able to function without it. If it isn't addicting, it certainly is habit-forming, and a strong dependency can develop. A cocaine-user can easily consume up to forty times the daily amount ingested by an Indian who chews coca leaves. In terms of dependency, there's really no comparison between using cocaine and chewing coca leaves, and there's no medical evidence to indicate that leaf-chewing is addicting. In terms of the dangers—legal, physiological and psychological—it makes sense to enjoy the leaves, not the powder, in South America.

CONTEMPORARY USE

The use of coca leaves pervades just about every aspect of Indian life in the Andes of Peru and Bolivia. Coca leaves aren't used in the Ecuadorian Andes (they're illegal), although coca was used during Inca

coca vendors

and Colonial times and is still grown in Ecuador's Oriente. However, the use of coca leaves isn't limited to the Peruvian and Bolivian highlands. Although it's technically illegal, Colombian Indians in the Sierra Nevada de Santa Marta use coca, as do Indians of the Cauca Valley. These Colombian coca-users are called *coqueros*. Various tribes in the Amazon Basin chew the leaves, and several northwest Amazonian tribes use the leaves to make a powder which is then dissolved in the mouth.

Both the Aymara and Quechua make use of coca leaves in magic and religious rituals. They sacrifice the leaves to *Pacha Mama* during sowing and at other times to protect the crops. In formal offerings *(aitas)* among the Peruvian Aymara, the leaves are lined up end to end during the ceremony. Quechua and Aymara curers and diviners *(yatiri)* also use coca leaves in their rituals and are often paid for their services with the leaves. The Aymara also use the leaves to divine the sex of an unborn child—round leaves signify a girl and longer ones signify a boy. The list of ritual uses is endless.

Coca leaves also serve very practical purposes. The Indians in the Andes often measure distance in a unit called the *cocada*, which is the distance that can be walked in the time it takes to chew one wad of leaves. Indians also are frequently paid in coca leaves rather than wages or are given leaves as a supplement to their wages. In many places in the Andes the leaves actually take the place of money as a medium of exchange.

Although coca-leaf-chewing is associated primarily with the Indians, many *mestizos* engage in the habit. However, because of its Indian association, leaf-chewing is looked upon as déclassé by white, upper-class South Americans. It just isn't done. This is probably one reason why a storekeeper in Peru thought our desire to try the leaf was so funny.

Male Indians of the *altiplano* carry their coca leaves in beautiful, handwoven pouches called *chuspas,* while women carry their leaves in small, square, handwoven textiles called *taris.* Both sexes recently have taken to using plastic bags for their leaves and I watched one Indian woman stuff a plastic bag of leaves under her hat.

Coca leaves used to be sold in the markets in twenty-five-pound bales called *arrobas,* but now they've gone metric. The leaves are brought to highland markets in square containers *(cojoros)* that are made from banana leaves. These bales weigh thirty kilos each and are called *tercios.* A *cesto* is a measure of coca leaves weighing about half a *tercio.* The *tercios* are wholesaled to the Indians (who then sell them at their local markets and *tiendas* or take them home for their own consumption) or sold to the local clandestine laboratory.

In many Bolivian towns entire streets near the market are lined with nothing but coca-leaf warehouses. At each market, a large section is set aside for the coca sellers (usually women, as are most market vendors), each with her sack of leaves, *lejia*, scales and plastic bags. The leaves are very cheap. I don't remember exactly what we paid, but it was just a few cents for an ounce.

If you're interested in trying the leaves, you'll find them for sale in every market in the Peruvian and Bolivian Andes, as well as in many small *tiendas*. You don't need to buy much—an ounce will do—and be sure to obtain the *lejia (llipta)* or *cal*. Ask any of the locals what proportions to use and how to chew it.

In a spirit of intense curiosity we decided to try the leaves in Peru and felt vaguely furtive, even though it was perfectly legal. The shopkeeper who sold us the leaves thought it was hilariously funny that the *blancos* wanted to chew coca leaves, but good-naturedly gave us instructions, which we totally ignored since we wanted to be sure that we really noticed the effect. In this particular store powdered lime was given out with the leaves, and we all used way too much and burned our gums. Beyond that, my tongue and gums became totally numb and I was suddenly inspired to write pages and pages in my journal. In fact, I could do with some of the leaves right now.

Mate de coca (coca-leaf tea) is a traditional remedy for *soroche* (altitude sickness), but we weren't suffering from altitude sickness when we ordered it at a Peruvian Tourist Hotel. The desire for a nice, warm glow was closer to the truth. The tea is pleasant enough, but it doesn't affect me as much as a good, strong cup of Colombian coffee.

Hallucinogens and Medicinal Plants

South America, particularly the Amazon Basin, is rich in hallucinogenic and medicinal plants. In parts of Colombia there are more known psychotropic plants in use than anywhere else in the world.

Like coca, many of these plants were known to Indian civilizations long predating the Incas. The medicinal plants were used to treat health problems and the hallucinogens were used for religious, divining or healing purposes. These plants were later introduced to the Spanish. Much ethnobotanical and pharmaceutical research on these plants is currently under way and new discoveries (that is, new to us) are regularly being made. Quinine, the antimalaria drug, comes from the bark of cinchona trees, which are called *quinaquina* by the Quechua. Curare, the famous Amazon poison that's rubbed on the tips of arrows and darts, comes from the vine *Chondodendron toxicoferum*, although some curare recipes contain at least thirty different ingredients. Curare produces paralysis of the skeletal muscles so that the victim dies of respiratory failure. It's not at all harmful if taken orally; it must enter the bloodstream to be effective. Today, doctors use curare in surgery as a muscle relaxant.

The Peruvian pepper tree (*Schinus molle*) was another tree held sacred by the Incas. Called *lentisco del Peru* in Spanish, it was one of the most important medicinal plants used by these Indians. The bark was used as a remedy for stomach aches and the crushed leaves as a pain-reliever. An alcoholic beverage was made from the berries and used as a nerve tonic, while the tree's resin was used as a poultice on sores and abscesses.

The most intriguing healers of the Andes are the Callahuayas (also spelled Callawayas), whose name comes from a variant spelling of the word Colla or Kolla, the quarter of the Inca Empire that included Bolivia. The Callahuayas were court physicians to the Incas, and today their descendants speak a distinct Quechua dialect (in addition to Aymara, Quechua, Puquina and Spanish) that's believed to be the esoteric language of the Inca nobility, now lost to all but the Callahuayas themselves. They come from the Bolivian mountains north of Lake Titicaca and are famous throughout the Andes as curers. The plant remedies known to the Callahuayas number in the thousands and include plants from both the highlands and the jungle. In addition, these Indians are sending their sons to Western medical schools.

The Callahuayas are also fine horsemen and their high status and relative wealth (for Indians) is reflected in the silver of their saddles and stirrups. Their horsemanship is unique among the highland Indians; horses are a rare sight on the *altiplano* and a mounted Indian is even rarer.

The Callahuayas wander the length of the Andes, visiting the local *ferias*, healing and selling amulets. They're credited by some historians with introducing quinine and ipecac to the Spanish, a likely possibility since their knowledge of medicinal plants is formidable. During the early part of this century a Callahuaya was called in to cure the daughter of Peruvian President Augusto Leguia and was successful.

YÁKEE OR EPENÁ (Virola theiodora)

The Amazonian Indians in northern South America use a number of hallucinogenic snuffs that are made from the seeds or resins of various trees. The ethnobotanist Richard Evans Schultes identified the snuff *yákee* (made from a blood-red tree resin) as coming from various species of virolas, which are members of the Myrustucacea family, to which the nutmeg also belongs. The active ingredient in *yákee* is myristicine (which also makes nutmeg an hallucinogen), an oil that contains dimethyltryptamine. Schultes noted that even the Indians considered the use of *yákee* dangerous, as fatal overdoses were known to occur. Most of these hallucinogenic snuffs cause intense, sometimes violent intoxication, during which the shaman communes with the spirits and obtains knowledge useful to the community. Schultes tried *yákee* using the traditional V-shaped tube, one end of which goes in the mouth and the other in a nostril. Although he took only a fourth of a shaman's dose, he experienced some pretty intense effects, an indication of the snuff's strength.

VILCA OR *COHOBA* (Probably *Anadenanthera colubrina*)

The *vilca* (also spelled *huilca*) tree was also considered sacred by the Incas. It grows in the *montaña*, the subtropical eastern slopes of the Andes. A hallucinogenic powder or snuff is made from its seeds and usually is inhaled through a two-stemmed tube, with oneself or a helper puffing on one end while the other end is held in a nostril. (There are also fancy Y-shaped inhalers. The stem is puffed by a helper while the top is held to the sniffer's nostrils.) The Inca priests used *vilca* to induce visionary states during which they conversed with the spirits and gods. *Vilca* was also used in healing rituals to discover the cause of illness and was employed medicinally as a laxative and emetic.

Vilca played an interesting role in the rediscovery of Macchu Picchu. In 1911, Hiram Bingham was searching for the last hidden capital of the Incas, variously known as Vitcos or Vilcapampa, meaning "the plain where *vilca* grows." A clue was the fact that the Urubamba River was known to the Incas as the *Vilca Mayu* or Vilca River. (The upper Urubamba is also known today as the Vilcañota.) It made sense, therefore, to follow the *Vilca Mayu* downstream toward the Amazon in hope of finding an area where the *vilca* tree grew. In doing so, Bingham found Vitcos, now called Rosapata, and he also found Macchu Picchu.

Vilca (or *cohoba*) is still used today by Amazonian tribes. Although there's controversy over the exact botanical identification of the *vilca* tree (and there are apparently other trees called *vilca*), it's probably the *Anadenanthera colubrina*.

YOPO OR *COHOBA* (*Anadenanthera peregrina* or *Piptadenia peregrina*)

This tree is closely related to the *vilca*. It's a member of the Leguminosae family (the legumes) and is found in tropical, northern South America. A hallucinogenic snuff is made from its seeds and is widely used by tribes in the Amazon Basin of Colombia, Venezuela and Brazil. *Yopo* is used in much the same way as *vilca*—that is, for religious, divining or healing purposes—and is sometimes called *cohoba*. The Gold Museum in Bogotá has an excellent display of the psychotropic plants and paraphernalia that are still in use among Colombian Indians, including various tubes used to inhale *yopo*.

The active alkaloids in both *vilca* and *yopo* are members of the trypta-
mine group, including mono- and dimethyltryptamine. Since the term
"alkaloid" keeps coming up, a definition of the word may be helpful.
An alkaloid is a plant-derived organic base, typically with a C-C-N-C-C
ring, where the nitrogen (N) is an amino group (the C is carbon). Alkaloids
are physiologically active—that is, they affect your body, especially
your senses. Alkaloidal drugs generally have a bitter taste and include
quinine, nicotine, atropine, morphine, curare, strychnine, belladonna
and cocaine. The chemical formula for morphine is $C_{17}H_{19}NO_3$ while the
formula for cocaine is $C_{17}H_{21}NO_4$. The variation in the number of hydro-
gen and oxygen molecules makes an enormous difference: morphine is
a central nervous system depressant while cocaine is a stimulant. *Pacha
Mama* certainly has an interesting bunch of offspring in the alkaloids.

YAGE (*Banisteriopsis caapi, B. inebrians* and other species)

This jungle vine, also known as *yaje, natéma* or *caapi,* has as many names
as the hundreds of Indian tribes who use it. However, it's commonly
known in literature as *yage* or *ayahuasca,* which is Quechua for "vine of the
dead." The drug is an extremely potent hallucinogen used to induce
brightly colored visions, which appear after episodes of nausea and
vomiting. As you might have guessed, *yage* contains a number of active
alkaloids, specifically harmine, harmaline and d-tetrahydroharmine.

The vine is usually mashed and boiled with careful, ritual preparation, although methods vary from tribe to tribe. Sometimes leaves from
other plants are added to the mixture; some of these have been identified
as coming from the shrubs *Psychotria viridis* and *Haemadictyon amazonica.*

The use of *yage* varies widely in the Amazon. It's used in healing to
discover the cause of illness and possible cures and is also used in
divination, coming-of-age rituals, for obtaining knowledge useful to
the community (such as the whereabouts of tribal enemies), at funerals
and in contacting the gods and the dead. Some of these occasions involve group use of the drug; at other times it is used by the shaman or
curer alone.

The visions produced by *yage* range from beautiful to terrifying and
often involve animals—particularly felines and reptiles. The user
sometimes finds himself transported to distant places or in communication with the gods or the dead. The set—or cultural context—undoubtedly has a lot to do with the content of the visions.

The book *Flesh of the Gods* contains excellent discussions of *yage* use,
although the most interesting account by far can be found in *Wizard of
the Upper Amazon* (see "Suggested Reading" at the end of this chapter).

In Colombia I met two American medical students who had gone into the Amazon and found a *brujo* to guide them through *yage* sessions, as they were interested in Indian healing methods. Their quest took them many days off the road into the jungle. As Andrew Weil noted in his introduction to *Wizard of the Upper Amazon*, it's possible to buy debased *yage* sessions in Amazonian towns. These experiences are extremely disappointing because of the sloppiness of the ritual preparation and conduct. If you wish to try *yage*, you should be exceedingly well prepared mentally and spiritually and should endeavor to find a *brujo* or *bruja* who's serious and who'll help you make sense of the experience. This won't happen if you buy a cheap ceremony in a jungle town. *Yage* is used ritually by the Indians and should not be thought of as a cheap, fun high. *Aguardiente*, the potent cane alcohol, is the jungle's cheap and easy high, if that's what you're after.

DATURAS

The plants and trees of the *Datura* genus are members of the Solanaceae family. This family includes the potato, eggplant and tomato, as well as the deadly nightshades, tobacco, belladonna and henbane. Belladonna and henbane are hallucinogens that were common ingredients in European witches' brews. The daturas contain powerful alkaloids, including atropine, scopolamine and hyoscyamine.

The New World daturas are classified into four subgenera with many different species, and all these American daturas have been used as hallucinogens by various American Indian groups, from the Algonquin and Zuñi Indians in the United States to the Aztecs and modern Mexican Indians. (*Datura inoxia*, or Jimson weed, was one of the hallucinogens given to Carlos Castaneda by Don Juan.)

All the South American daturas are trees. The use of datura varies widely, as does its preparation, but usually its seeds are ground and put in a drink. Datura is extremely potent. The initial stage of intoxication is marked by furious violence, often requiring restraint. This is followed by a deep, hallucinated sleep, and the hallucinations are often frightening.

Daturas have been found around Inca temples, and it is thought that these hallucinogens may have been given to patients to put them in a stupor before operations. The Chibchas of Colombia used datura to stupefy wives and slaves who were to be buried alive with their dead husbands and owners. Among the contemporary Jivaro (Shuara) of Ecuador, datura is given to disobedient children on the grounds that, when intoxicated, children see the spirit world and discover that what their parents tell them is true. The Jivaro also give datura to dogs to help the animals gain supernatural power.

San Pedro cactus in the market

MUSHROOMS (Including *Conocybe* and *Psilocybe*)

As you might expect, there are various mushrooms in South America which are hallucinogenic. I know of no ethnographic data describing South American Indian use of these mushrooms, but I've talked to several travelers who have picked and eaten various *Psilocybe*. I have two warnings for those of you who wish to sample these fungi. First, know your mushrooms. Some hallucinogenic mushrooms closely resemble the poisonous varieties, and no one wants his or her journey into other realms to be permanent. The second warning is to ingest the mushrooms in a private, secluded place so that your ecstasies don't attract the police.

SAN PEDRO CACTUS (*Trichocereus pachanoi*)

There's even an hallucinogenic South American cactus, the San Pedro, which has been used in Peru for thousands of years and is depicted on ancient Mochica and Chavín pottery. Its active alkaloid is mescaline. San Pedro is found in the hot, dry deserts of Peru and Bolivia, where it grows in the form of tall, often spineless, ribbed columns.

The San Pedro cactus is used extensively in Peruvian folk healing. It's taken by the *curandero* (healer), his assistants and the person to be healed. Unlike the peyote cactus, the San Pedro isn't eaten. Slices of the cactus are boiled in water for seven hours, and then the liquid is consumed. A very comprehensive article on the use of the San Pedro cactus in Peruvian healing is found in *Flesh of the Gods* (see following section).

SUGGESTED READING

The following books are all paperback, possible take-along-on-the-trip titles. (If you're interested in further pursuing the subjects of ethnobotany and hallucinogenic and medicinal plants, you'll find a wealth of additional information at your local library.)

Flesh of the Gods: The Ritual Use of Hallucinogens, edited by Peter Furst (New York: Frederick A. Praeger, 1972). This book contains good, scientific writing about various hallucinogens, including the San Pedro cactus and *yage,* by experts in this field. Lots of solid, botanical information and an excellent first chapter, "An Overview of Hallucinogens in the Western Hemisphere," written by Richard Evans Schultes.

The Natural Mind: A New Way of Looking at Drugs and the Higher Consciousness, by Andrew Weil (Boston: Houghton Mifflin Co., 1973). Weil includes a short discussion of drug use in the Amazon. Weil also talks about why people use drugs, discusses alternative methods of attaining higher consciousness and gives some excellent guidelines for drug use taken from the Indians.

History of Coca: "The Divine Plant of the Incas," by W. Golden Mortimer, M.D. (San Francisco: And/Or Press, 1974). This book was originally published in 1901, before cocaine was outlawed in the United States. I have a feeling the publishers are trying to cash in on the contemporary cocaine craze by coming out with this republication. Mortimer carries on at great length about the supposed benefits of cocaine use and makes other dubious assertions. Why did I buy the book? Because it contains information about travel in the Andes in the early 1900s, lots of coca lore and some beautiful old photographs of Inca textiles and Peruvian Indians.

Wizard of the Upper Amazon: The Story of Manuel Cordova-Ríos, by F. Bruce Lamb (Boston: Houghton Mifflin Co., 1975). This is one of my favorite books about South America, an absolutely intriguing story. It's the account of a man's capture by the Amahuaca Indians while he was gathering rubber in the Peruvian jungle in the early 1900s. Cordova-Ríos lived with the tribe for several years and was even trained to be their chief. He participated in many *ayahuasca* ceremonies, including some involving simultaneous group visions. The story is beautiful and, what's more, true.

Witch Doctor's Apprentice, by Nicole Maxwell (New York: Collier Books, 1975). This is a woman's story of her search in the late 1950s for medicinal drugs used by the Indians along the Amazon and Putumayo rivers. Her discoveries are amazing and so is her account of the carelessness with which her priceless plant specimens were treated by the large pharmaceutical companies in the United States. Maxwell is quite an experienced jungle traveler, and her book offers useful bits of information for anyone planning a jungle trip.

Amazonian Cosmos: The Sexual and Religious Symbolism of the Tukano Indians, by Gerardo Reichel-Dolmatoff (Chicago: The University of Chicago Press, 1971). This book isn't strictly about drug use per se, but is good reading in terms of understanding the wholeness of Amazonian Indian cultures, how a shaman *(payé)* functions and community myths. It contains descriptions of the use of coca, as well as *yage* and *yopo* (called *ghapí* and *vihó* respectively by the Desana). If you're interested in mythology and the Amazonian Indian cultures, it's certainly a book to have.

The Jivaro: People of the Sacred Waterfall, by Michael J. Harner (New York: Doubleday/Anchor Books, 1973). I like this book almost as much as *Wizard of the Upper Amazon,* and for an anthropological work that's saying something. The subject is fascinating—the Jivaro (or Shuara, as they prefer to be called), the famous headhunters and shrinkers of Ecuador's Oriente. Like other jungle tribes, the Jivaro make ample use of local plants, including such hallucinogens as datura and *yage.* This account of the Jivaro has an excellent historical perspective.

Visionary Vine: Psychedelic Healing in the Peruvian Amazon, by Marlene Dobkin de Rios (San Francisco: Chandler Publishing Co., 1972). This is the most recent addition to my library. It focuses on the use of *ayahuasca* for healing purposes in Iquitos, Peru, but also contains a great deal of information on other South American psychedelics and their uses. I highly recommend it to anyone interested in this subject.

Archaeology
and Pre-Columbian
Civilizations

hen
up the ladder of earth I climbed
through the barbed jungle's thickets
until I reached you Macchu Picchu.

Tall city of stepped stone,
home at long last of whatever earth
had never hidden in her sleeping clothes.
In you two lineages that had run parallel
met where the cradle both of man and light
rocked in a wind of thorns.

Mother of stone and sperm of condors.

High reef of the human dawn.

Spade buried in primordial sand.

This was the habitation, this is the site:
here the fat grains of maize grew high
to fall again like red hail.

The fleece of the vicuna was carded here
to clothe men's loves in gold, their tombs and mothers,
the king, the prayers, the warriors.

Up here men's feet found rest at night
near eagles' talons in the high
meat-stuffed eyries. And in the dawn
with thunder steps they trod the thinning mists,
touching the earth and stones that they might recognize
that touch come night, come death.

I gaze at clothes and hands,
traces of water in the booming cistern,
a wall burnished by the touch of a face
that witnessed with my eyes the earth's carpet of tapers,
oiled with my hands the vanished wood:
for everything, apparel, skin, pots, words,
wine, loaves, has disappeared
fallen to earth.

And the air came in with lemon blossom fingers
to touch those sleeping faces:
a thousand years of air, months, weeks of air,
blue wind and iron cordilleras —
these came with gentle footstep hurricanes
cleansing the lonely precinct of stone.

PABLO NERUDA
"The Heights of Macchu Picchu," Canto VI

No trip to South America is complete without some kind of contact with the Pre-Columbian civilizations, including visits to museums, ruins and other archaeological sites. In fact, many travelers' primary reason for journeying to South America is to visit Macchu Picchu, one of the most beautiful Inca ruins on the continent.

Because there are so many excellent books available on the Pre-Columbian cultures, I suggest that you buy at least one and take it along on your trip. Since one of the themes of this book is the continuity between the Pre-Columbian and modern Indian cultures, you'll find further discussions of Pre-Columbian cultural traits throughout the book where appropriate, especially in Chapters Twelve, "Food"; Sixteen, "Native Cultures, Folk Art and Markets"; and Seventeen, "Fiestas, Music and Dance."

Note: When discussing South American civilizations, the term "Pre-Columbian" means before the arrival of Columbus (1492) while "Pre-Hispanic" means before the conquest of these peoples by the Spanish. (The Inca Empire fell in 1533.) However, throughout this book I use "Pre-Columbian" loosely to refer to the Indian cultures before their conquest by the Spanish.

Ancient South America

The people Columbus called "Indians" (because he thought he'd reached the East Indies) did not originate in the Americas. Their ancestors, an Asian Mongoloid people, migrated from Asia to Alaska about 40,000 years ago by means of a land bridge across the Bering Straits. As the great glaciers advanced and receded, the bridge was alternately exposed and inundated. During periods when the land bridge was exposed, there were many waves of migrants.

After migrating through North and Central America, these people reached the South American continent by about 12,000 B.C. We know that by 6700 B.C. humans had reached Tierra del Fuego, the southernmost tip of South America. Furthermore, strong similarities between South American Indian and Polynesian–Southeast-Asian cultures suggest trans-Pacific contacts. Voyages across the Pacific were probably made at several different times, although questions of when and in what direction still remain unanswered.

The early Americans were hunters and gatherers who followed the great herds of mammoths, camels and horses. These herds vanished in the Americas by about 9000 B.C., perhaps hunted to extinction. However, what made the great Indian civilizations possible was the development of agriculture—that is, the domestication of plants. When the adults of a group are constantly on the move following game, all their energy is expended obtaining the food necessary for survival. A society that engages in agriculture settles in one area and becomes capable of producing surplus food, thereby freeing some adults for other activities, such as war, the priesthood, arts and handicrafts.

The change from a hunting-and-gathering to a farming-and-fishing society occurred on the coast of what is now Peru by 3000 B.C. The crucial plant in the Americas was corn (maize). It had been domesticated in Mexico and had spread from there to the coast of Peru by 1400 B.C. The great Aztec and Mayan civilizations, as well as the Peruvian ones, were based on the cultivation of corn. (Chapter Twelve, "Food," contains more detailed information about the enormous number of food plants domesticated in the Americas, including the three great staples of the American Indian diet—corn, squash and beans—as well as chili peppers, potatoes, manioc, peanuts and many others.)

The Indians fished as well as farmed in the early Peruvian coastal settlements. This area is one of the driest deserts in the world, broken only by rivers from the Andes which empty into the Pacific. Each river valley was the site of an early settlement, and these sites have been explored extensively by archaeologists, giving us a clearer picture of the development of civilization. Cotton and weaving appeared by 3000 B.C., corn by 1400 B.C. and pottery by 1200 B.C. If you're interested in reading more on this subject, see the list of recommended reading for Peru later in this chapter.

The myriad South American Indian cultures developed from these early settlements in diverse and intriguing ways. Although the books I recommend throughout this chapter describe these Indian civilizations in detail, there are several important cultural characteristics I'd like to mention here. Keep in mind that by the time the Spanish arrived, the great Indian cultures were highly advanced in some areas, including metallurgy (some of the finest gold and silverwork in the world), textiles (also some of the finest known), stonework and ceramics. All of these cultures were theocracies—that is, the church and state were one and the same. The Incas, furthermore, had one of the most extensive and best-organized empires in the history of pre-industrial societies and had developed social-welfare provisions far in advance of anything since.

Then why were the Indians so easily conquered? Partially because they didn't have draft animals, firearms, the wheel or writing. More importantly, at the time of Pizarro's arrival in Peru (1532), the Indians were engaged in a disastrous civil war in which two of the Inca's sons claimed succession to the throne, and the Spanish took advantage of this internecine warfare.

Archaeological Sites and Museums

One of South America's greatest attractions for me is its Pre-Columbian civilizations, or rather, what I can learn about them from the remaining ruins and artifacts. When I visit the ruins of an Inca fortress, walk on an old Inca highway or run my hands over incredible Inca stonework, everything I've heard or read starts to become real.

doll from Chancay

I like to spend a lot of time in ruins and archaeological sites with as few people around as possible so that I can tune in to these places and repopulate them in my mind. If you meditate, try doing it in an old temple. There's something very special about meditating or praying in a sacred spot—any culture's holy place. It's also helpful to do some background reading before your visit or to carry a book about the ruins along with you, so that you know you're meditating in a former temple and not in a corncrib.

A few of the more popular archaeological sites charge a nominal admission fee (usually not more than fifty cents), but most places are free. Transportation to some of these sites is erratic and you may have to hike into others, particularly the more remote Inca ruins. There are often no facilities at the sites, which surprises people from the United States, who are used to national parks complete with rangers and hot dog stands. If you fall off a wall that's your problem, but you also can camp in many of the ruins and explore them to your heart's content without anyone telling you to stay on the walkway. It goes without saying that you should always respect these historical places. Never dig or take anything from a site or deface it in any way, and always clean up after yourself if you camp there.

For some reason, which I don't completely understand, many travelers tend to avoid museums. Yet visits to museums such as Padre Crespi's in Cuenca, Ecuador, were truly memorable and enjoyable for me. Then, too, South American museums aren't merely composed of one gallery of paintings after another, but contain archaeological artifacts ranging from mummies (which never fail to fascinate me) to Pre-Columbian textiles and ceramics, as well as ethnographic displays and the more usual kinds of museum exhibits. You don't have to overdose on museums, but you really are missing out if you don't visit at least one major museum in each country. One thing I learned: don't forget to take your Spanish–English dictionary along since exhibit labels are in Spanish. More than once I've seen a fascinatingly bizarre God-knows-what and been unable to figure out what it was because I didn't have my dictionary with me.

ARCHAEOLOGICAL TERMINOLOGY

agricultural terraces ‖ *andenes*

amphitheater ‖ *anfiteatro*

aqueduct ‖ *acueducto*

archaeological site ‖ *sitio arqueológico*

astronomy observatory ‖ *observatorio astronómico*

barracks ‖ *cuartel*

bridge ‖ *puente*

burial mound ‖ *tola*

cave ‖ *cueva, caverna, covacha, guarida, antro*

cemetery ‖ *cementerio*

ceremonial center ‖ *centro ceremonial*

chamber, hall ‖ *cámara*

door ‖ *puerta*

dungeon, cell ‖ *calabozo*

enclosure ‖ *recinto*

excavation ‖ *excavación*

façade ‖ *fachada*

flight of steps ‖ *escalinta*

fortress ‖ *fortaleza, castillo, cuidadela, alcázar*

foundation of a building ‖ *cimiento*

granary ‖ *granero, alhóndiga*

grave, tomb ‖ *sepultura, sepulcro, hoya, fosa, tumba, cárcava*

grotto, cavern ‖ *gruta*

house ‖ *casa*

inn, roadhouse ‖ *tambo* (Quechua)

jail, prison ‖ *carcel*

lookout, watchtower ‖ *puesto de vigilancia*

monolith ‖ *monolito*

molding ‖ *moldura*

palace ‖ *palacio*

pit, hole in the ground ‖ *foso*

portal ‖ *portada*

pyramid ‖ *pirámide*

reservoir ‖ *estanque, alberca*

room, apartment ‖ *aposento*

round, fortified tower ‖ *torreón*

ruin ‖ *ruina*

sacred place or thing ‖ *huaca* (Quechua)

sculpture, carved work ‖ *escultura*

shrine, temple ‖ *templete*

stone seat, bench ‖ *poyo*

storehouse ‖ *depósito*

temple ‖ *templo, adoratorio*

throne ‖ *trono*

wall ‖ *muro, muralla, pared, tapia*

warehouse ‖ *bodega*

Colombia

At the time of the Spanish Conquest, the Inca Empire reached as far as the southern edge of what is now Colombia. However, other great Indian civilizations flourished in Colombia, and many of these predated the Incas by thousands of years. While the Colombian Indians generally didn't construct massive stoneworks as did the Incas, they were among the finest metalworkers (especially goldworkers) in the Americas. The goldwork of such cultures as the Tairona, Quimbaya, Calima and Chibcha are on display in the *Museo del Oro* (Gold Museum) in Bogotá. This new museum has the largest and finest collection of Pre-Columbian gold-work in the world, and it's one of my all-time favorite museums for many reasons, including its excellent displays, good lighting and wisely-placed benches for those of us with tired feet. And photography is permitted! The Gold Museum is located at the corner of Calle 16 and Carrera 6 on the Parque Santander in downtown Bogotá.

Another fine museum in Bogotá is the *Museo Nacional*, which contains the *Museo Nacional de Antropología*; it's located on Carrera 7, No.

bird statue at San Agustín

28–66, out by the bullring. The *Museo Nacional* is composed of many submuseums, and it's easy to spend a full day in both the Pre-Columbian art and ethnographic exhibits, not to mention the history and fine-arts sections.

The museums have nominal admission fees (usually about a quarter) and it's a shame to get all the way to South America and then miss out on them. Since many travelers start their South American travels in Bogotá, visiting these museums is an excellent way to begin getting acquainted with South American Indian cultures. If you see an exhibit that is absolutely intriguing, you can then visit that area to check it out further.

There are several interesting archaeological sites in Colombia that are well worth your time and energy. These include Tairona Park, located outside Santa Marta on the Atlantic coast; the Tierradentro burial caves near Inzá, in the department of Cauca; and the archaeological park in San Agustín, in the department of Huila.

If you're seriously interested in the Pre-Columbian cultures of Colombia, I recommend buying the paperback *Colombia,* by G. Reichel-Dolmatoff (New York: Frederick A. Praeger, 1965). Reichel-Dolmatoff has also written a book about San Agustín entitled *San Agustín: A Culture of Colombia* (New York: Frederick A. Praeger, 1972), though I don't know if it's available in paperback.

Ecuador

Ecuador was occupied by the Incas for only fifty years prior to the Spanish Conquest, but early Spanish travelers to the region described many awesome Inca ruins. Most of these have been destroyed, although there are some ruins located on private property which aren't open to the public.

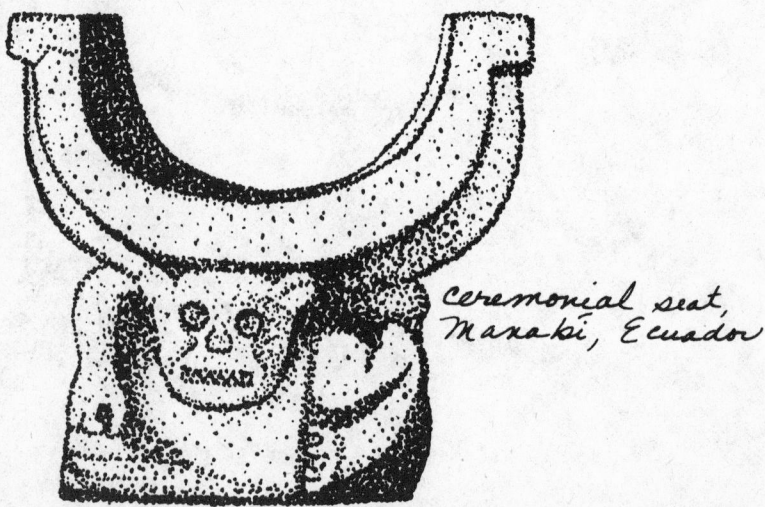

ceremonial seat,
Manabí, Ecuador

The most accessible Inca ruins are in the south. Cuenca was the site of Tomebamba, an important Inca center. There are five perfect Inca stone-work niches in Cuenca on the bank of the Tomebamba River near the Avenida Huayna Capac bridge. Most of the Inca buildings were torn down in Colonial times and a mill was built using the stones. Remains of Inca walls and ashlars line the hillside. Farther downriver major ruins are being excavated by the *Museo del Banco Central*, and you can visit the site.

North of Cuenca near Cañar is the fortress of Ingapirca, the most extensive ruin in Ecuador. Ask at the tourist office on the main plaza in Cuenca for directions. In addition, there are Inca ruins around Paqui-shapa and Saraguro in the far south, but these are difficult to find unless you hire a local resident to guide you.

There are several museums which house substantial collections of Pre-Columbian Ecuadorian art. One is the *Museo del Banco Central del Ecuador*, located on Avenida Diez de Agosto in Quito. This new museum has beautifully displayed Pre-Columbian and Colonial art and is definitely worth visiting.

The famous *Museo de Padre Crespi* in Cuenca no longer exists. The collection, which Padre Crespi accumulated during fifty years in southern Ecuador, was bought by the *Museo del Banco Central*. Since Padre Crespi accepted anything people gave him, archaeologists are busy separating the genuine treasures from the remnants from *Carnaval*. When and where the Crespi collection will be displayed is uncertain, but you can inquire at the tourist information office on the main plaza in Cuenca.

Guayaquil also has several museums with collections of Pre-Columbian art, including the *Casa de Cultura* on the Plaza Centenario and the Guayaquil Municipal Museum on Calle Pedro Carbo.

There are two good paperbacks available on Pre-Columbian Ecuadorian cultures: *Ecuador*, by Betty Jane Meggers (New York: Frederick A. Praeger, 1966), and *Ancient Ecuador: Culture, Clay and Creativity 3000–300 B.C.*, by Donald W. Lathrap (Chicago: Field Museum of Natural History, 1975).

Peru

Although the Incas immediately come to mind when we think of Peru, they were the last of the great Indian civilizations that flourished in this country, beginning in about 1200 A.D. and ending with the Spanish Conquest. There were complex cultures in Peru thousands of years before the Incas, among them the Chavín, Paracas, Nazca, Moche, Huari-Tiahuanaco, Chancay and others, up to the Chimú, who were conquered by the Incas. Traces of all these civilizations still remain, mostly in the form of artifacts. Fortunately for us, the dry desert of coastal Peru, the site of many of these civilizations, is the ideal climate for the preservation of textiles and the natural mummification of corpses. Grave finds have provided archaeologists with a wealth of information.

The Incas literally erased the history of the people they conquered and reinterpreted their history on an Inca model. They also imposed Quechua on these tribes, as well as sun worship, which was the official Inca religion. In fact, the Incas carried out such a rigorous campaign of cultural indoctrination that the languages and cultures of many tribes were extinct by the time the Spanish arrived. (The Spanish in turn did what they could to obliterate Inca culture and religion, which they regarded as heathen and the work of the devil.)

There are extensive ruins of pre-Inca civilizations all along the coast of Peru, as well as interesting sites in the Andes. If you're coming to Peru from Ecuador, try to familiarize yourself with the location of these ruins so that you can stop at some of them. Among the major ruins on the coast between the Ecuadorian border and Lima are Huaca Prieta, near Chicama; Chan Chan, outside Trujillo; Sechin near Casma; Paramonga, north of Pativilca; and Chancay, near the town of the same name. Our visit to Chancan (the ruins of a Chimú city which cover about fourteen square miles) was the highlight of our journey down the coast.

There are ruins as you travel inland, too, including Cajamarca, where Atahualpa was captured and killed by Pizarro, and Chavín de Huantar, which is located across the Cordillera Blanca from Huaráz. There are also ruins in the vicinity of Lima, including Pachacámac. Once you reach Lima you can buy *hojas de ruta* (see page 24) which show the hundreds of archaeological sites and ruins throughout Peru, including such well-known sites in the south as the giant markings in the Nazca Desert.

LIMA

Lima has two especially fine Pre-Columbian art museums. The *Museo de Antropología y Arqueología*, often simply called the *Museo Antropológico*, is located on Avenida General Vivanco in Pueblo Libre, a district of Lima. This museum is enormous and nearly overwhelming, but then so is Peru's cultural heritage.

Even if you're a confirmed museum-hater you'll enjoy the *Museo de Rafael Larco Herrera* because of its extensive collection of Mochica erotic art. These treasures are tucked away in a basement building separate from the main collection, which includes pottery, jewelry, mummies and textiles from the Nazca, Paracas, Chimú, Inca and other cultures. If you limit yourself to just one museum in Lima, this is the one to see. It's also located in Pueblo Libre, at Avenida Bolívar 1515.

adobe reliefs at Chan Chan

CUZCO

Cuzco was the capital of the *Tahuantinsuyo*, the Four Quarters of the Inca Empire. The word *"cuzco"* means "navel," and Cuzco was considered the center of the world. It's the oldest continually inhabited city in the Americas.

Today, everywhere you turn there are the remains of Inca stone walls, which often have Colonial buildings resting on them. One day, as I was eating with my parents in a restaurant on the Plaza de Armas, my father told me to turn around. The entire side wall of the restaurant was original Inca stonework, complete with trapezoidal niches. It was so eerie and beautiful that it made me shiver.

Many shops and bookstores in Cuzco sell maps of the city and the surrounding countryside which give you the locations of museums as well as archaeological monuments. We bought one and found it invaluable.

Almost every traveler to Cuzco visits the fortress of Sacsahuaman, the baths at Tambo Machay and the ruins of Puca Pucará and Kenko in the hills just outside the city. You can buy a tour, hire a cab, ride in a truck or bus, or hike, which is a nice way to get in shape if you plan to hike the Macchu Picchu trail (see the "Backpacking" section of Chapter Ten).

The *Museo Arqueológico* houses a good collection of Inca art. The museum is located in a handsome Colonial house at Tigre 115, two blocks from the Plaza de Armas.

Cuzco was laid out to form a puma, with the fortress of Sacsahuaman as its head and the buildings and streets in the city below as the body, legs and tail. Much of the city was destroyed during the Spanish Conquest and subsequent uprisings, but enough Inca stonework remains to give you a sense of what Inca Cuzco was like.

MACCHU PICCHU

Even people traveling on those ten-countries-in-twenty-days tours make it to Macchu Picchu. It's a major tourist attraction and for good reason—it's beautiful beyond words, an absolutely magical place.

If you have no other opportunity to take a train in South America, you're certain to ride the train to Macchu Picchu. Actually there are several trains. Various tours have private cars, which are rather like *autoferros,* and you pay through the nose for the privilege of riding in them. There's also a first-class tourist train, and this is the train to take, if possible. Buy your ticket several days ahead of time at the Santa Ana station in Cuzco. (This is the Macchu Picchu train station, not the Cuzco–Puno–Arequipa station; it's located behind the main market in Cuzco.)

The first-class train leaves early—about 6 A.M. Its main advantage is that it also arrives early at Macchu Picchu, giving you plenty of time to see the ruins if you aren't planning to spend the night. Insist on buying tickets for this earlier, faster train.

Although I had specified the first-class tourist train, I was sold tickets for the local. This slow, slow train leaves later (about 7 A.M.) and stops everywhere along the way. (We were even shunted off on a siding while a fast train came through.) It was an older train, as well, and didn't serve food. We arrived at Macchu Picchu about one o'clock in the afternoon and therefore didn't have much time to see the ruins. Obviously you should pack food and wear something warm for the ride. Take your rain poncho, too. Although there's a restaurant at Macchu Picchu the food is expensive, and it's actually a lot more fun to picnic in the ruins.

There's also a Tourist Hotel at Macchu Picchu, but it's expensive and is booked months in advance. Usually someone doesn't show, however, so if you check around 2 P.M. you can probably get a room for the night. There used to be a shelter where travelers with sleeping bags could camp for the night, but this has been closed permanently. You *can't* camp in the ruins—it's prohibited and the area is patrolled. If you want to spend the night cheaply, take the bus back down the mountain to the railway station and then walk a mile back toward Cuzco to the Aguas Calientes station. Here you'll find hotels and hostels where you can stay very cheaply, although you have to provide your own bedding. The stop is aptly named in that there are wonderful hot springs in the vicinity. Be sure to wear a bathing suit at the springs if you don't want to get arrested.

If you plan to take advantage of these alternative hotels, ask other travelers in Cuzco for the latest information about them. Perhaps the shelter at Macchu Picchu has reopened (although I doubt it) or maybe a hotel with bedding has opened at Aguas Calientes.

If you spend the night at Aguas Calientes and want to return to the ruins, just hike back up the railroad tracks and catch a bus to the top.

Do it early. Most of the fun in staying over is having the ruins to yourself before the tourist trains arrive at about 11 A.M. I felt bothered by the hundreds of other tourists, who were shrieking, hollering and taking pictures of each other, because my visit was a pilgrimage to a sacred place. I didn't mind their presence—after all, I was a tourist, too—but I disliked their noise and lack of respect for the site. Fortunately it began to pour and the less hardy retired to the Tourist Hotel and restaurant. I crawled into a cave on the path to Huayna Picchu, lit some incense and read Pablo Neruda's *The Heights of Macchu Picchu*, feeling the centuries slip away behind me. There's definitely an air about Macchu Picchu—it's a powerful place.

RECOMMENDED READING

Your visit to Peru, and especially to Cuzco and Macchu Picchu, is going to mean a lot more if you know something about the Incas. I'd like to be able to suggest a television special for you to see before your trip, but there haven't been any on the Incas. In fact, except for the usual news reports on earthquake disasters and political coups, South America is barely acknowledged by the broadcast media; so your best source of information is still books. If you want to pursue this subject further, I suggest obtaining the following paperbacks:

The Ancient Civilizations of Peru, rev. ed., by J. Alden Mason (Harmondsworth, England: Penguin Books, 1969). This book is amazingly comprehensive, with good photographs. It includes the history of early man in the Americas and culminates with the Inca civilization. If you limit yourself to just one book on ancient Peru, this is the one to buy. Incidentally, this book and most of the paperbacks listed below are available (in English) in bookstores and tourist shops in Lima and Cuzco; so you can buy them down there instead of carrying them from home.

Peru, rev. ed., by G.H.S. Bushnell (New York: Frederick A. Praeger, 1963). This book covers the civilizations up to and including the Incas. Technical and somewhat dry reading, but lots of information.

Peru Before the Incas, by Edward P. Lanning (Englewood Cliffs, N. J.: Prentice–Hall, 1967). Another good history of the pre-Inca civilizations.

If you want to read something about the Incas that's not too technical or too dry, I suggest:

Lost City of the Incas: The Story of Machu Picchu and Its Builders, by Hiram Bingham (New York: Atheneum, 1972). Bingham rediscovered Machu Picchu in 1911. We read his account of his explorations and of Inca civilization before we visited Macchu Picchu, and I suggest that you do the same. Even though it deals more with Bingham's adventures than it does with the Incas, it's a great book to read while traveling.

The following three paperbacks offer introductions to Inca civilization:

The History of the Incas, by Alfred Métraux, translated by George Ordish (New York: Schocken Books, 1970). This is amazingly readable and one of my favorite books about the Incas.

Realm of the Incas, by Victor W. Von Hagen (New York: New American Library, 1961). I enjoyed having this book along because of its excellent diagrams and explanations of the Peruvian Inca ruins. Lots of good information on Inca civilization. Von Hagen's style is smooth, chatty and interesting, so you'll find that the book is good, light reading.

The Incas, by Garcilaso de la Vega, edited by Alain Gheerbrant (New York: Avon Books, 1964). Garcilaso Inca de la Vega was the son of a Spanish conquistador and an Inca princess. He wrote these commentaries in 1609, and they are among the only descriptions of Inca civilization by someone who was an Inca and who had access to the stories of the Inca nobility. Heavy going at times, however. It's not what you'd call light reading.

The next two books are classic accounts of the conquest of the Incas and contain an enormous amount of information about Inca civilization:

The Conquest of Peru, by William H. Prescott (New York: New American Library, 1961).

The Conquest of the Incas, by John Hemming (New York: Harcourt Brace Jovanovich, 1970).

Bolivia

Bolivia, too, was once part of the Inca Empire, but within this country are the remains of only a few Inca structures, most notably those on the Island of the Sun in Lake Titicaca, accessible by boat from Copacabana and at Incallacta and Inca Rakay, which are located outside Cochabamba. Cochabamba also has a surprisingly good *Museo Arqueológico* at the *Universidad Mayor de San Simón,* the local university. The museum is directed by Dr. Geraldine de Caballero, an Englishwoman who's married to a Bolivian (she also serves as the British consul for Cochabamba). Her knowledge of local archaeology and ethnology is extensive, and it's a treat to be able to ask questions in English.

Bolivia was also the site of the Tiahuanaco culture, a great pre-Inca civilization which influenced other cultures throughout ancient Bolivia and Peru. The ruins of Tiahuanaco are located at the southern end of Lake Titicaca, near Desaguadero and the Peruvian border. Buses traveling from Peru to Bolivia via Desaguadero stop at the ruins for about thirty minutes, which really isn't enough time for you to see everything. It's better to take a bus back to Tiahuanaco from La Paz and enjoy a more leisurely visit.

The Colla and Lupaca were Aymara peoples who were conquered by the Incas in about 1450. These spunky Indians frequently revolted until they finally were subdued somewhere around 1485. The most interesting, visible Colla remains are *chullpas* (tombs). *Chullpas* are tall (thirty feet), round, burial towers. Some are made of adobe and others are built of mortarless stonework. The stonework rivals anything the Incas constructed. The most accessible *chullpas* are located in Sillustani, Peru, near Puno. My parents and I hired a cab to get there and found the ruins impressive.

Two museums in La Paz exhibit Pre-Columbian art. The first is the *Museo Arqueológico Tiwanaku*, located just off the Prado on Calle Tiwanaku. The other one is the *Museo Abierto*, also called the *Templete Arqueológico Semisubterráneo*, located in a plaza on Avenida Saavedra. This outdoor site includes monoliths from Tiahuanaco and is a good place to visit if you don't happen to get to Tiahuanaco itself.

As for books, there just aren't very many that are written in English. Most of the recommended reading for Peru contains something about Bolivian civilizations, especially Tiahuanaco.

Colonial Art

I'm not enthusiastic about Colonial art, primarily because I'm not a big fan of the Spanish Conquest and the resulting devastation of native

chullpa

South American cultures. I've always felt that if you've seen one antique painting of a conquistador you've seen them all, and the same goes for Baroque churches. Yet the Spanish architectural style is an integral part of South American architecture, and some Colonial cities are beautiful indeed. I love walking around these cities and towns and feeling myself go backward in time. In Colombia, the cities of Tunja, Cartagena and Popayán are Colonial gems, and Bogotá has some Colonial churches. In Ecuador, Quito and Cuenca have a Colonial flavor, particularly the old street of La Ronda (now known as Calle Morales) in Quito. Although there are many small Peruvian towns that have a Colonial feeling, you're most likely to come across Colonial buildings in Lima and Cuzco. For the most part Lima is very modern, but Colonial architecture survives in and around the Plaza de Armas. Cuzco is a treat because many Colonial buildings are built on Inca walls. In Bolivia, La Paz is a modern city while Sucre is almost completely Colonial. Potosí, the former silver-mining center, has many Colonial monuments.

All the capitals and many of the smaller cities have museums that specialize in Colonial art. Just ask at your hotel or at the local tourist office. Anyone interested in reading more about this subject should consider buying the paperback *A History of Latin American Art and Architecture: From Pre-Columbian Times to the Present,* by Leopoldo Castedo, translated and edited by Phyllis Freeman (New York: Frederick A. Praeger, 1969).

Buying Pre-Columbian Art and Antiques

All the Andean countries have laws on the books prohibiting the export of Pre-Columbian art. In actual practice, however, Colombia and Ecuador allow certain pieces to leave the country. (At least they make no effort to prevent it.) This doesn't mean priceless goldwork—just the more common kinds of Pre-Columbian pottery and beads that are well represented in museum collections. You also can take home potsherds and broken pieces of ceramics and statues, such as little Tumaco heads.

There are stores that sell Pre-Columbian art in both Bogotá and Quito, as well as in smaller towns. Reputable shops vouch in writing for the authenticity of their goods and should be able to furnish you with the dates and cultures of the pieces you buy. Colombia has begun to post regulations in these shops which tell you what is permitted to leave the country; pay attention to these notices.

What about fakes? Tairona beads and Carchi, Cara and Nariño pots are fairly common, and there doesn't seem to be much interest in faking them—especially when *huaqueros* (grave robbers) can dig them up so easily. However, there are fakes of Tairona whistles, so look out for these.

The Indians often come into the markets with potsherds and ceramic pieces; these are authentic and are usually quite cheap. In some places the Pan American Highway has been put through ancient Indian burial grounds, and the sides of the road are littered with pieces of Pre-Columbian pottery and statuary. You're permitted to take these fragments out of all the Andean countries; the officials don't seem to mind.

In practice, if not in theory, Colombia and Ecuador also permit you to take Colonial antiques out of the country, including gold and silver coins. Again, this doesn't apply to national treasures and rare works, but then the average tourist isn't about to trundle off with a seventeenth-century, gold-leaf altar. Incidentally, antiques are allowed into the United States duty free. (An antique is defined as any item 100 years old or older at the time of entry.)

Beware of any piece that's described as *retocado*, which means "retouched," or *tinajo*, which means "replica." These words are euphemisms for outright fakes. A fast talker may tell you that something is a *"tinajo auténtico,"* with the emphasis on the *auténtico*. What this means, of course, is that the piece is an authentic replica!

Peru is another story altogether. The export of any Pre-Columbian artifacts, Colonial antiques and official documents for the period prior to 1920 is prohibited. This law is enforced for the most part, although small pieces of Pre-Columbian textiles and Pre-Columbian beads are sold openly in tourist shops and seem to be allowed out of the country.

Pre-Columbian pottery and goldwork are definitely *not* allowed out of the country, and since these are truly national treasures and because Peru has been pillaged for centuries, I would respect their wishes. Besides, there's a thriving business in the manufacture of fake Pre-Columbian pottery, and you're very likely to be sold a phony piece. This illegitimate industry centers around Trujillo, where contemporary potters use Pre-Columbian clay beds as well as Pre-Columbian molds. The pottery is astonishingly good and amazingly authentic in appearance, but it's *not* the real thing; so don't fall for it. If you do buy such pottery, buy it as a reproduction and pay the price of a reproduction. Get a signed paper from the vendor saying the piece is a reproduction and declare the piece when you leave Peru so that you won't be accused of smuggling should it be discovered in your belongings. In 1981 the United States and Peru signed an agreement for the recovery and return of Peruvian documents and archaeological and Colonial pieces. United States Customs is enforcing this law, so don't try to smuggle.

Antiques from the time of Peruvian independence (1826) onward are permitted to leave Peru, as are gold and silver coins from any era. The export of Colonial antiques is forbidden.

Bolivia also forbids the export of Pre-Columbian art. However, there really isn't much available for sale and there doesn't seem to be a thriving business in fakes like there is in Peru. The export of Bolivian antiques was prohibited in December 1975.

When I recently visited the Bolivian consul in San Francisco, he took a look at my earrings, which I had made from old (1809) Bolivian silver coins, and called me a *contrabandista* (smuggler). This was meant as a joke because these coins, with holes indicating they've been used previously in jewelry, are sold openly on the street in La Paz and are utterly worthless to collectors because of their holes. While taking these coins out of the country is technically illegal (although I didn't know it at the time), no one objects because they're worthless as art objects and are quite common. Use common sense and good judgment in these situations and refrain from taking home pieces which you know good and well should remain in South America.

Unless you're an expert in antiques or in Pre-Columbian art, don't buy a piece as an investment and expect to sell it at a profit when you return home. The market is simply too tricky for amateurs and, once again, it's illegal to take the really fine pieces out of their country of origin. You'll be happiest if you buy only those pieces that you truly like, appreciate and can live with. You can always attempt to sell them later, but if you don't find buyers (or you find out that you bought fakes) you'll still have something you enjoy.

There are a number of magnificent, outrageously expensive hardcover books on Pre-Columbian art, books you'd just love to own if you had a spare forty or fifty dollars. Fortunately for us *pobrecitos* there are good paperbacks on the market:

Ancient Arts of the Americas, by G.H.S. Bushnell (New York: Frederick A. Praeger, 1967). This book is excellent, with plenty of color and black-and-white photographs. It's a good take-along book.

Medieval American Art: Masterpieces of the New World Before Columbus, 3rd rev. ed. in 2 vols., by Pál Kelemen (New York: Dover Publications, 1969). These two volumes are also good references, but they're too large and heavy to carry along. They're well worth buying, however.

The Andean Heritage: Masterpieces of Peruvian Art from the Collections of the Peabody Museum, by Garth Bawden and Geoffrey W. Conrad (Cambridge, Mass.: Harvard University Press, 1982). An exhibition catalog with good photographs, capsule summaries of Peru's Pre-Columbian cultures (incorporating latest archaeological findings) and a good discussion of the different art styles.

Native Cultures,
Folk Art
and Markets

he purpose of this book is to give you enough background information so that you can explore and discover the Andean countries for yourself, as well as to minimize your impact on the native cultures of this area. In this chapter I'm not giving you a country-by-country listing of "what to buy"; I'm discussing crafts in general—various techniques, a few of the folk art specialties of each country and some background information on the artisans. I've also tried to indicate which crafts are unique to a country, region or town, so that you won't mistakenly assume that you'll see more and better examples of a craft later on, when in fact the market you just attended or the city you just visited is the best place to find that particular craft. During my travels I was surprised at how different the handicrafts and folk art of the Andean countries are from each other. The history and customs of the native cultures have played a part in this, as I'll point out throughout the chapter.

Folk Art and Handicrafts

I'm always attracted to handmade things, primarily because I make things myself—I spin, weave, sew and make baskets. Whenever I see a beautiful item I invariably want to know who made it, where it came from, how it's used, if it has a special meaning in the culture and if it's a traditional item. This knowledge adds to my delight and appreciation.

Many people who write about traditional textiles, including Dr. Junius Bird, Grace Goodell, Marjorie Cason and Adele Cahlander, scrupulously avoid naming villages because they're afraid that the Indian artisans will be exploited and the very crafts they're describing will be destroyed. As soon as someone writes that a certain village has the most beautifully woven, intricate belts in the country, travelers begin pouring in. Some are genuinely interested in the weavings and buy a belt or two. Others buy up every belt in the village—not out of their love for textiles, but to sell in the United States. These entrepreneurs then urge the weavers to make more belts, only not as intricate as usual, so that the belts can be finished faster. They also suggest the use of red, white and blue, instead of the traditional yellow and brown colors, so the belts can be sold in a Philadelphia gift shop. Thus begins the destruction of an art and the disruption of a village's ecology and economy. This is the last thing I want to be guilty of, and I find it a difficult problem to deal with when writing about folk art and handicrafts.

Remember that what follows is *not* an itemized listing of everything you can buy. Also keep in mind your own responsibility, which is to offer the artisans a fair price for their crafts (although bargaining is always in order and is a way of participating in their culture) and to be aware of your impact on an area.

Now, what are handicrafts (*artesanías*) and what is folk art (*arte popular* or *artesanía folklórica*)? Generally speaking, handicrafts are items that are made by hand. They can be made for the craftsperson's own use or they can be made to sell. Folk art, on the other hand, is usually defined as something (invariably handmade) that's produced by the common people for their own use and is recognized and valued by members of their own community. It also has an unmistakably personal touch. Because folk art originates and is handed down among the common people, it's part of a community's tradition.

All folk arts are handicrafts although the reverse isn't true. The dividing line between folk art and handicrafts is often hazy. If a man weaves a belt for his wife, is the belt folk art? The belt could be considered folk art if it is traditional and is used in the weaver's community, even though the weaver may make a few extra to sell. However, if the weaver were to give up all other activities and weave belts and purses for the tourist trade, then these items would fall into the category of handicrafts or commercialized folk art. If folk art is produced for the commercial market, it's important that it remain as faithful as possible to traditional designs and materials.

One problem that arises when artisans shift their focus from folk art to tourist handicrafts is a tendency to produce lesser-quality work. Beauty may be in the eye of the beholder, but the craftsmanship is right there in the piece. It's unlikely that an artisan would make a slipshod piece for himself—he has his pride. However, he might turn out sloppy work for tourists who don't know or care about the difference. This is always the danger when tourists and buyers invade remote areas and create a demand for local crafts.

I'm not necessarily prejudiced against tourist handicrafts in favor of folk art. Indeed, most handicrafts have their roots in folk art and traditional techniques. If a belt-weaver produces a non-traditional purse using traditional colors, motifs and techniques, or even if he's completely innovative and weaves a unique, stunning purse which he wants to sell to make some extra cash, I'm delighted to buy it. On the other hand, if he produces a sloppily-made traditional belt, I don't want it, no matter how traditional or how inexpensive it is. Promoting good workmanship and high standards by refusing to buy shoddy crafts helps the artisans in the long run, especially if they can obtain prices consistent with the effort necessary to do high-quality work.

Various government agencies, the Peace Corps and the United Nations all have been involved in the promotion and, in some instances, the re-introduction of traditional handicrafts and folk art in the Andean countries and in seeing that the artisans are fairly paid. I like to support these efforts, and one way of doing this is to help educate foreign travelers and potential handicrafts-buyers. In the process I'm educating myself.

Some people object to programs instituted by the Peace Corps and other agencies to help communities produce items for the commercial market, especially when new designs and techniques are introduced. I feel that this purist attitude doesn't take into account the high unemployment rate in South America, especially among the uneducated. If someone suggests that a community make hats for the tourist trade in addition to (not instead of) their own traditional hats, who are we to criticize? We can only hope that a balance is preserved between the demands of the commercial market and the folk art tradition.

Please note: it is my policy *not* to recommend stores, *except for* craft cooperatives or government-sponsored outlets. I find several problems involved in recommending stores. The first is that tastes vary, and I hesitate to inflict mine on anyone else. Also, a sudden influx of travelers and customers can destroy the ambience of a store and cause prices to rise precipitously. Besides, once you know that certain crafts exist, you can track them down yourself if you're interested. Another reason I don't recommend stores is to avoid being offered a bribe to list a store in my book. I don't like getting into these situations, and they're best avoided by not recommending any craft stores (or hotels, restaurants, etc.). While most handicrafts and folk art find their way into stores in the larger Andean cities, I most enjoy looking for them in the markets.

Markets

ANCIENT MARKETS

In the Andes, markets held for trade purposes and socializing are more ancient than we can calculate. Some markets, such as the one at Otavalo, Ecuador, were thriving long before the Incas arrived in the area.

The Inca Pachacuti, who ruled from 1438 to 1471, is credited with having established three official market days (*catus*) each month, during which the Indians heard official decrees and exchanged surplus goods. The Peruvian Quechua still call markets *catus* and women market vendors *cateras*. Under Inca rule, the population did not pay taxes in the form of money, but instead contributed labor (*mita*) to the state. An Indian's *mita* service included serving in the army and working on state projects, such as the construction of roads, terraces and fortresses. If an Indian had to leave home in order to complete a *mita* project, his family was cared for by the government while he was away.

Under the Incas, each community's land was divided into thirds: a third was devoted to crops for the state, a third for the sun and a third for the community's own use. The crops for the state were stored in granaries throughout the empire; they were used to feed the army and laborers working on state projects and were distributed to the people in times of famine. Civil servants and artisans also were supported from the state granaries. The sun's share was used to support Inca noblemen and priests.

Because there was no property tax and no official money, the Indians were free to barter whatever surplus crops they grew on their plots and whatever extra goods they made—food, weavings, carved gourds, etc. This type of trade was purely local.

General commerce was a state monopoly, and there was a thriving trade among the communities of the coasts, mountains and jungle, with luxury goods reserved for the use of the Inca and the nobility. Travel was restricted throughout the Inca Empire in order to keep the roads free for the army and to keep the peasants on their land.

When the Spanish arrived, they were greatly impressed by the bustling markets they found in Cuzco and other cities. After the Conquest the Spanish attempted (in many cases successfully) to change local market days to Sunday, to lure the Indians in to mass. On the whole,

market days haven't changed since this time, and many Andean markets take place on Sunday, especially in Peru.

CONTEMPORARY MARKETS

The local market day is called *la feria* (the fair) while the permanent marketplace (if there is one) is called *el mercado* or, in Bolivia, *la cancha*, which is Quechua for "the enclosure." To find out a town's market day, ask, *"¿Qué día es la feria?"* ("What day is the fair?") or *"¿Cuándo es la feria?"* ("When is the fair?"). If you've just come into town and want to locate the marketplace, ask, *"¿Dónde está el mercado?"* ("Where is the market?"). The *feria* or *feria franca* is the "free fair," to which anyone can bring something to trade or sell. Vendors who sell at the permanent market must rent space there, and they sometimes join unions which regulate their affairs and handle booth assignments.

Larger cities and towns usually have a permanent marketplace or market building where there's some activity every day. Then, on the weekly market day, thousands of *campesinos* pour in from the surrounding countryside. In large cities and at some of the larger Indian markets, including Riobamba and Ambato, Ecuador, and Cochabamba, Bolivia, there are separate buildings or areas devoted to various kinds of activities. If you don't see what you're looking for in one place, ask until you find it.

In smaller markets, there are generally separate sections for food, hardware, livestock and handicrafts, although sometimes everything is jumbled together, which means you find yourself bargaining for a poncho over the squeals of a hundred hogs. Small villages usually have no permanent market and some have no market day either, in which case the villagers attend the market at the nearest larger town.

While some markets are strictly local, others cater to tourists and travelers and are famous for their handicrafts or pageantry; still others carry goods for the national and international trade. When a big fiesta coincides with market day, things get especially interesting.

What goes on at the market? Eating, drinking, bartering, buying and selling, socializing, feuding and more. What can you buy? It varies enormously, depending on the size and location of the town. You'll see food, textiles, handicrafts, clothing, sandals, plastic shoes, kerosene lanterns, baby animals, big animals, herbal remedies, old tools, baskets, rope, used clothing, plows and rusty nails—sort of like a thrift store, supermarket, department store and dime store rolled into one and spread out over many city blocks. Most of the food discussed in Chapter Twelve is available in the markets, which are always good places to eat or to stock up on food for traveling.

In many Andean Indian markets, merchandise is still bartered silently—potatoes for corn or onions for sandals—although vendors are happy to accept cash for anything you may want to purchase. Be sure to have small change with you since vendors often have no change at all.

How much should you pay for an item? For a general discussion of bargaining, see Chapter Seven, "How Things Work." You also can ask other travelers what they paid for an item and use that price as a guide. If someone paid $12, expect to pay between $10 and $15. No matter what you spend, you'll invariably run into someone who says, "Oh, I bought that for $3 less." However, maybe your vendor had to pay more for his or her raw materials, or maybe your piece is made better, or maybe the price has gone up in general—don't worry about it.

It's a good idea to record your purchases in a notebook. That way you can offer price guidelines to other travelers. You'll also have a list of exactly what you spent on crafts to show to United States Customs when you return home, since market vendors don't give receipts (see "United States Customs and Duty" at the end of this book).

Colombia

Native Cultures

The Guambiano (or Moguez) and Páez, located in the Department of Cauca, are the only two surviving Andean Indian cultures in Colombia. The Spanish first entered southwestern Colombia in 1535–36 and by 1538 had crossed the territory of the Pijao and Páez, where they encountered Indian resistance as they traveled to Bogotá to investigate stories of *El Dorado*, the Gilded Man. The Spanish wanted to secure the area in order to maintain contact between Quito and Bogotá and to appropriate the rich farmlands of the Cauca Valley. By 1608 they had squelched most Indian resistance. A number of Indian tribes, including the Pijao, fought to extermination; others became acculturated and still others moved. The Guambiano and Páez survived because they retreated to rugged, mountainous territory where the Spanish found it difficult to pursue them, and today these Indians are still defending their lands against white and *mestizo* encroachment.

The Guambiano and Páez cultures are so similar that I'm discussing them here as one group. They still speak various dialects of the ancient Chibcha language, as well as Spanish. While their original territory was located just north of the northernmost limits of the Inca Empire, they've incorporated a few Quechua words into their language.

You'll encounter the Guambiano and Páez at the markets in Silvia, Inzá, San Andrés and Belalcázar. It's easy to recognize them among *campesinos* wearing conventional dress. A man wears a cotton shirt with a traditional, handwoven, blue skirt or light-colored wool trousers. He usually wears two handwoven ponchos (a white one covered by one that's either dark blue, gray, brown or black), high-topped shoes, tennis shoes or sandals (*alpargatas*) and a *fique* (sisal) or felt hat. He also carries a plain or patterned bag (*mochila*) made from *fique* fiber.

A woman wears the same shoes and hat as a man, one or more hand-woven gray or black wool skirts, a cotton blouse and one or more dark gray, black or blue wool shawls (*mantas*). She also carries a beautifully patterned *mochila*. Some women wear earrings and necklaces made of European glass trade beads which sometimes have silver crosses.

Most of the handicrafts made by these Indians are for their own use, but you might be able to purchase a few of these crafts in the market. The men make hats by coiling *fique* fiber, and some are so tightly coiled that they actually can hold water. Early Spanish settlers named these hats *tacillas de Páez*, meaning "Páez bowls," and the name stuck. Women make plain *mochilas* from *fique* fiber by a knotless netting process, using a needle. They also make fine, patterned *mochilas* from wool or *fique* with triangular, stepped and zigzag designs which are much more elaborate than the simple, horizontal stripes usually found on Colombian *mochilas*.

Guambiano and Páez women spin wool with the drop spindle as do other Andean Indians. Only the women weave, and their weavings include blankets, ponchos, shawls (*mantas*), belts (*fajas*) and the wool material used in pants and skirts. The women also make coiled ceramic pots for preparing and storing *chicha* and *guarapo*, as well as simple serving trays.

The most famous Guambiano craft is the distinctive woman's necklace which is composed of European glass trade beads, including simulated coral, and a silver cross with three pendants. The silver cross traditionally has been made by Guambiano silversmiths in Silvia, and many of the finest pieces date back to Colonial times.

Folk Art and Handicrafts

Colombia has a vital folk culture, and beautiful handicrafts are produced in many parts of the country. You don't have to venture into remote areas to find these crafts, however, since many fine pieces can be found in Bogotá and other large cities. *Artesanías de Colombia*, a government agency which encourages the production of traditional crafts, operates stores in every major Colombian city, and these stores carry a wide variety of crafts from every part of the country. The store personnel usually can tell you where an item comes from and what tribe or group made it.

If you're seriously interested in Colombian handicrafts, the *Museo de Arte y Tradiciones Populares* (Museum of Popular Arts and Traditions) is an excellent place to begin learning about them. The museum is located on Carrera 8a, No. 7–21, near the Presidential Palace in downtown Bogotá. While just about every shop and business in Bogotá closes from noon to 2 P.M., the museum stays open, so it's the perfect place to visit at lunchtime. On the first floor of the museum you'll find the *Salón Indígena*, which includes an exhibit of the household items and hut of an Amazonian tribe, as well as a shop that sells Colombian crafts, many of which are unavailable elsewhere. The handicrafts exhibits on the second floor include woodwork, metalwork, basketry, textiles, ceramics and dolls. There are maps, photos and drawings of artisans at work on these crafts as well as beautiful examples of the crafts themselves.

Guambiano Cross

In Chapter Fifteen ("Archaeology and Pre-Columbian Civilizations") I mentioned the National Museum complex, which has two galleries with Pre-Columbian artifacts along with photos and handicrafts of contemporary Indians. Since I'm also interested in the continuities between ancient and surviving Indian cultures, this is one of my favorite museums.

TEXTILES

Before the arrival of the Spanish, the Indians wove with cotton *(algodón)*, sisal *(fique)* and other wild-plant fibers. Llamas, alpacas and vicuñas aren't found in Colombia because they don't thrive in the climate. Sheep, which were introduced by the Spanish, are suited to the country's cold, damp highlands and consequently Colombia has a thriving wool *(lana)* industry.

Because of the prevailing dampness, only a few remnants of Pre-Columbian textiles *(tejidos)* have survived—those that had been buried in graves. Chibcha textiles include cotton ponchos with stamped designs, purses, *fique* sandals and rope. Cotton was obtained from the Amazon and the hot Pacific coastal lowlands and was spun on simple spindles identical to ones used today. The Indians used a variety of natural vegetable and mineral dyes, including moss, cochineal, indigo, asphodel, holm oak, wild fuschia and mulberry. Aniline dyes were introduced from Germany shortly after World War I, and these dyes predominate today, although a few natural dyes, such as mulberry, indigo, moss, alder bark, mugwort and cochineal, are still in use. Natural dyeing is the exception, not the rule, however.

Today, the department of Boyacá is one of Colombia's leading textile centers. In some places the artisans are weavers exclusively and usually work with floor looms, while many others are farmers who weave for themselves and for the national and tourist markets when farm chores are done. Although there are many flocks of sheep in Boyacá, artisans sometimes have to buy fleece trucked in from the vicinity of Bogotá and Medellín. The artisans of Boyacá weave fine wool *ruanas,* blankets and rugs, and many *campesinas* carry small, woven, crocheted or knitted bags *(bolsas)* that occasionally turn up for sale in the markets and shops.

Fine cotton spinning and weaving, especially sashes, belts and large bags, are done by the Guajira Indians of the Guajira Peninsula.

Looms. Before the Spanish Conquest, the Indians living in what is now Colombia wove on several different looms *(telares)*, including the vertical frame loom and a v-shaped loom made from the branch of a tree or from sticks lashed together. For some reason, these weavers didn't (and don't) use the backstrap loom which is so common in other parts of Central and South America.

warping the vertical frame loom, Boyacá

Pre-Columbian-style looms are still in use today, along with the floor loom, which was introduced by the Spanish and traditionally is used only by men in Latin America. Floor looms are easier to use and more efficient than Pre-Columbian-style looms because the feet are used to treadle and raise the harnesses, leaving the hands free to pass the shuttle. In Colombia the floor loom is called a *telar de suelo, telar de pedal* (pedal loom) or *telar criollo* (Creole loom). The vertical frame or v-shaped loom is called a *telar manual* (manual or hand loom) or *telar de cintura* (waist loom) because it's sometimes held in the weaver's lap with one end propped against her waist and the other end leaned against a wall. The backstrap loom is used in only a few areas near the Ecuadorian border and appears to have been introduced from Ecuador.

Today, floor looms (usually two- or four-harness) are used to weave blankets *(cobijas)*, shawls *(paños)*, rugs *(tepetes)* and Colombian ponchos *(ruanas)* as well as yardage. Most, but not all, large items woven for the tourist trade are made on floor looms. Floor looms usually have a maximum weaving width of sixty centimeters, about two feet. If a piece is to be wider than sixty centimeters, it's woven in two pieces which are later sewn together.

The four-harness floor loom allows for a greater variety of patterns than does the two-harness loom. Vertical frame looms almost always have what amounts to two harnesses, a heddle stick and a shed stick. However, there's some overlap as far as what's woven on floor and frame looms, since floor looms are expensive. Frame looms range in size from about a foot square (for small purses) to three feet wide and seven or eight feet tall (for *ruanas*, rugs, etc.).

Spinning and Weaving. To begin the spinning, the fleece (*vellón*) is washed thoroughly to remove any grease and dirt and is then dried. It's carded with the fingers, spun, washed again with soap to cut the remaining grease, dried and then dyed. In Colombia, salt or lemon juice is used as a mordant for aniline dyes. (A mordant is a substance that fixes the dye to the fiber by combining chemically with the dye to form an insoluble compound.)

Today, spinners are usually women, and they use a simple spindle (*huso*) consisting of a shaft of wood (*palo*) and a whorl of clay, stone or wood (*tortero*). In many parts of the Andes you'll see spinners who spin as they walk, with their spindle dangling in the air.

After spinning and dyeing, the loom is warped. Warping for a floor loom is done on eight or nine pegs stuck in the ground in a straight line. Frame looms are usually warped directly.

After they're woven, woolen textiles are taken off the loom and brushed to give them a soft, fuzzy nap. The brush used for this purpose is called a *cardencha* and is made from the heads of teasel plants which have been lashed together. You'll see this brush used throughout South America. (For a complete discussion of the weaving process, see page 316.)

The Museum of Popular Arts and Traditions in Bogotá has an excellent display of typical looms and textiles if you want to pursue this subject further.

RUANAS

Ponchos are called *ruanas* in Colombia, and these beautiful, handwoven, wool garments are Colombia's national coat. Each time I arrive in Bogotá I enjoy seeing Colombian businessmen dressed in their gray flannel

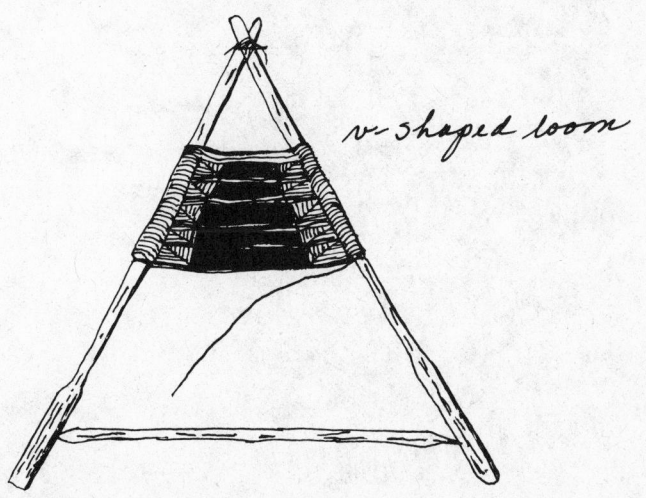

v-shaped loom

suits and bright *ruanas*. Unlike Peru and Bolivia, ponchos are worn by the upper and middle classes in this country. *Ruanas* come in several styles, including a woman's style that has a collar and buttons and opens down the front. They're made in a multitude of colors in stripes, plaids and plain weaves.

Ruanas are handwoven on floor looms and are made in several departments, including Boyacá, Santander, Cundinamarca, Caldas and Nariño. The rectangular, wool *ruana* was introduced into Colombia by Quechua Indians in the seventeenth century, although cotton varieties were worn by Colombian Indians before the arrival of the Spanish. The traditional, classic *ruana* was made of virgin wool in a natural white, gray or brown color without designs.

PAÑOLONES

Pañolones (fringed shawls from Nemocón, Cundinamarca) are rectangular, handwoven, wool shawls with about four feet of thick, flowing, macraméd, rayon fringe. These elegant shawls are of Spanish, not Indian, origin. They're unique to Colombia and can't be found in any of the other Andean countries. My gold *pañolon* with gold fringe is one of my favorite Colombian textiles. I feel like the sun when I wear it.

DIVISORIOS

The *divisorios* of San Jacinto (Bolívar) are a relatively recent addition to Colombian textile art. The Peace Corps apparently introduced the idea and it's caught on—especially for the export market. These cotton wall hangings are double-woven in two or three colors and usually have brocading and pile fringe. They come in a variety of rectangular sizes and also are made in the shape of Christmas trees. While some of the

divisorio,
San Jacinto,
Bolívar

color combinations are jarring, others are lovely. *Divisorios* have been such a hit with travelers that the Otavalo Indians of Ecuador have also started making them.

MOLAS

Molas are the reverse-appliqué panels of the blouses worn by Cuna (also spelled Kuna) Indian women of the San Blas Islands, which are located off the Atlantic coast of Panama and Colombia. *Mola*-making is about a hundred years old and is believed to have developed from traditional Cuna body-painting. The ability to make a beautiful *mola* is prized by the Cuna, and there's a *mola*-makers' cooperative on the islands that works to maintain quality, even on *molas* made specifically for the tourist trade.

Mola designs range from religious symbols and scenes from daily life to abstract, geometric patterns. These patterns may represent ancient tribal motifs whose meaning has been lost to the Cuna. All sorts of motifs are worked into *mola* designs, including letters of the alphabet, which are used in whatever way is aesthetically pleasing, including backwards and upside-down.

To make a *mola* panel, three or four pieces of cotton cloth (obtained from traders) are laid one on top of the other, usually with red on the top, black on the bottom and yellow or orange in between. The pieces are basted together and the design is sketched out and cut. Then the cut edges of each piece of cloth are turned under and sewn to the layer underneath, with fine, almost invisible stitching. Some *molas* are decorated with commercial and homemade rick-rack (often used to represent teeth) and embroidery. A woman usually makes two identical *mola* panels for a blouse, one for the front and one for the back, and each panel can take up to six weeks to complete. A well-made *mola* is a true work of art.

As is the case with many Indian textiles, *molas* are made to be worn by the artisans themselves and are sold when the women are tired of them, with the exception of a few that are made specifically for the tourist trade. For this reason, the finest *molas*—the ones with the most intricate designs and most careful needlework—are often dirty and spotted. These lovely, traditional *molas* can be found in Cartagena and Bogotá, where the blouses are cut up and only the *mola* panels are saved. I managed to stop a shopkeeper in the midst of this destruction and was able to buy two complete blouses, one of which is illustrated on the following page.

Because of the increasing tourist demand for *molas*, some simple, slipshod ones are now being made. These lesser-quality *molas* usually consist

mola blouse

of only two layers of cloth with large, simple designs. However, according to anthropologist Mari Lyn Salvador, who recently researched *mola*-making in the San Blas Islands, high-quality traditional *molas* are still being made.

Artesanías de Colombia often carries reverse-appliqué, *mola*-type panels with imaginative themes made by Colombian school children.

QUILLACINGA BELTS AND "CROWNS"

The Quillacinga, also called the Sibundoy, live in the department of Putumayo, near the Ecuadorian border. The Quechua word *"quillacinga"* means "moon in the nose," and the name was given to these Indians by the Incas because of their gold, half-moon-shaped, nose ornaments. While most travelers aren't likely to visit their territory, I mention them here because their fine cotton and wool belts (called *chumbis* or *chumpis* in Quechua) can be found in tourist shops and *Artesanías de Colombia* stores in Popayán. Another distinctive Quillacinga craft you're likely to see is the *corona*, which is worn by both sexes on festive occasions. The *corona* is a woolen crown from which beautifully woven wool streamers trail; it's a lovely piece of folk art.

FIQUE

Fique (sisal) fiber comes from the century plant (*Agave americana*) and is used extensively in South America for a variety of items. The cactus itself is known by a number of names, including *fique* (the most common term in Colombia), *pita*, *motua*, *henequén*, *cocuy*, *cabuya* (Ecuador), *penca*

(Quechua) and *maguey*. It is often planted as a hedge or as a divider between fields and is also grown commercially on plantations. We know that *fique* has been used since ancient times, as fine ropes and bags made from the fiber have been found in Pre-Columbian graves.

To obtain the fiber, the pulp and spines of the leaves are removed by means of a mechanical stripper or by pulling the leaves through a wooden clamp with metal teeth that's usually attached to a tree for stability. The leaves are washed repeatedly and are sometimes beaten to remove the last traces of pulp. Finally they're dried in the sun.

For some articles, such as sandals *(alpargatas)*, place mats *(individuales)*, rope, *(cuerda)*, rugs *(tapetes)* and decorative animals *(animales decorativas)*, the fiber is simply twisted or braided *(fique trenza* or *fique clineja)*, coiled into shape and sewn together. The animals and place mats are often made on simple molds that consist of nails pounded into a wooden board to the item's shape. *Alpargatas*, which are worn by *campesinos* throughout Colombia as well as in and around Otavalo, Ecuador, have a heel strap and toe piece *(capellada)* made of cotton; the toe piece is woven on a v-shaped loom.

Fique fiber also is spun *(fique hilada)*. The artisans use a small spindle (the same as for cotton and wool) or a special bow-spindle *(carrumba)* which takes two people to work—one guides the fiber and the other pumps the bow and turns the spindle. Items made from spun *fique* include round bags *(mochilas)*, large rectangular carrying and storage bags *(costales)*, square bags *(bolsas)*, horse cinches *(cinchas)* and some rugs. Large bags and purses made from *fique* are woven on the vertical or semivertical frame looms used for weaving woolen items.

The department of Boyacá is a center for *fique* crafts.

MOCHILAS

Mochilas are round carrying bags made by knotless netting from *fique*, wool or cotton. The fiber is sometimes dyed bright colors with aniline dyes. Many tribes and groups make *mochilas*, including the Cágaba and Ica of the Sierra Nevada de Santa Marta (who use them to carry coca leaves, lime-filled gourds and other items) and the Páez and Guambiano Indians of Cauca. *Mochilas* are similar to Ecuadorian *shigras* and are excellent for carrying food while traveling.

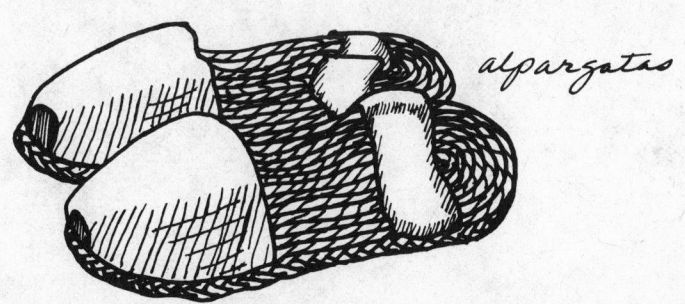

alpargatas

BASKETS

Colombia is a basket-lover's heaven. Although all the Andean countries have fine basketry, Colombia is somewhat unusual in that baskets from such inaccessible regions as the Amazon are available in the large cities, mainly through *Artesanías de Colombia*.

Baskets in general are called *cestas*, and baskets without carrying handles are called *canastas*. Throughout Colombia you'll see the traditional *cesto*, a handbasket or carrying basket with one large handle that's often used in marketing.

Many different plant fibers are used in basketry, including *fique*, which is wrapped around either *esparto* grass or *paja toquilla*, and bamboo, most frequently called *chin* but also called *caña común* or *bambú*. Bamboo grows wild throughout Colombia and often is used to make large baskets. A species of bamboo called *chusque* is also used.

Esparto grass grows wild on the high, cold *páramos* and is used extensively in basketry. The strands are thin, round, flexible and very strong, and are sometimes dyed red, green or purple with aniline dyes. *Esparto* was used by the Chibcha in their basketry; today it's woven into both baskets and hats.

Bejuco (bind weed) is a plant whose dark, woody stem is used to make the large, shallow, two-handled baskets used to hold fruits and vegetables in the market. In Boyacá, very compact and tightly woven baskets that look like hanging birds' nests are made from *bejuco* to hold gourds containing *chicha* or *guarapo*. *Campesinos* have made these baskets for centuries.

Woven palm baskets from the Amazon with finely worked geometric designs are also available, as are interesting coiled baskets made in the department of Vaupes.

esparto grass basket, Boyacá

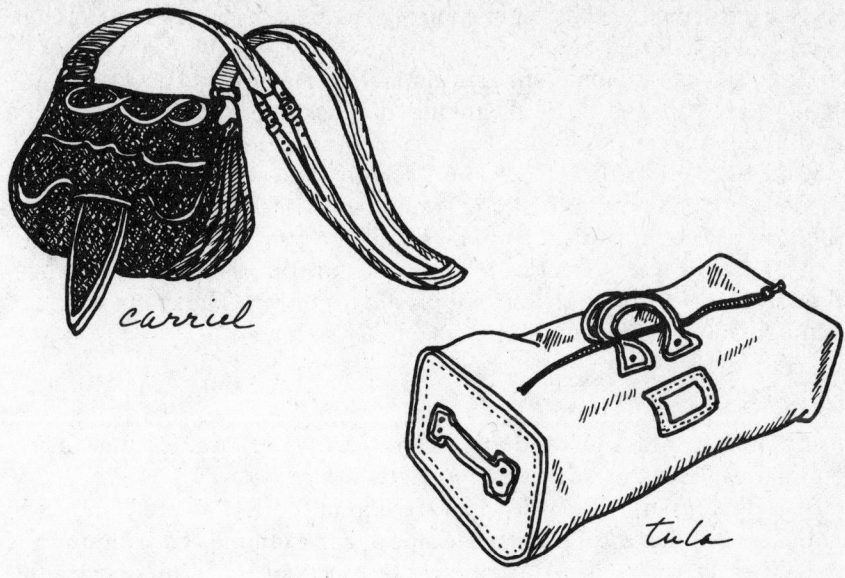

carriel

tula

STRAW HATS

Every fiber used in basketry also is used in making brimmed hats. Anyone who has visited Cartagena will be familiar with the black-and-yellow *costeño* "straw" hat, which is actually made from a palm fiber. The most common material used in making plaited (or woven) hats is *paja toquilla*, a variety of palm. *Paja* hats *(sombreros de paja)* are made on the coast as well as in Aguadas (Caldas) and Sandoná (Nariño). These *paja* hats have been misnamed "Panama" hats (see page 295).

LEATHER

Colombia ranks third in the production of cattle in South America. Consequently, you'll come across many handicrafts that are made from cowhide *(cuero)*. Of the four Andean countries, Colombia is by far the best place to buy leather goods. You can usually spot travelers who've been to Colombia because most of them carry a yellow-tan leather duffle bag *(tula)* or shoulder bag *(bolsa)*. Most of these bags come from Nariño and Cauca, near the Ecuadorian border. Leather goods of all kinds, including suitcases, boots, belts, vests and suede *(gamuza)* clothes in a range of prices and quality, are available in Popayán, Bogotá and other cities.

When buying the less expensive (usually yellow-tan) leather goods, make sure that the stitching is secure and the zipper works. The seams may need to be resewn somewhere along your route, since the original thread often breaks. The higher-quality (usually higher-priced) leatherwork holds together better.

Antioquia is the home of a traditional handbag called the *carriel antioqueño*. This purse is made of untanned calfskin *(piel de ternera)*, with a multitude of accordion pleats and secret compartments. *Carrieles* are still carried by men on horseback, and one of the secret compartments is made specifically to hold a gun. Traditionally, *carrieles* were made from the skin of otters, jaguars or pumas (called *tigres,* the general name for large cats in South America). These calfskin purses are attractive, although some of them have tacky plastic trimming. The craftspeople of Antioquia also make cowhide rugs *(tapetes de cuero).*

CERAMICS

In Colombia, both men and women are potters; the production of ceramics *(cerámicas)* isn't limited to just one sex.

The department of Boyacá is a traditional pottery center, and individual towns have different specialties. For example, Chiquinquirá is noted for its green-glazed earthenware *(vidriado),* including such utilitarian objects as cups, plates and bowls, as well as decorative pieces, such as nativity sets. Because the green glaze is oxidized lead obtained from automobile batteries, you shouldn't use these glazed dishes with acidic foods or fruit juices, which can leach the lead out and cause lead poisoning. Originally, there were nine family pottery workshops in Chiquinquirá, but in 1976 there were just three—and only one family was making the traditional green-glazed ware.

The people in the vicinity of the towns of Raquirá and Tuaté are known for their unglazed kitchenware and cooking pots *(ollas).* Dinnerware *(vajillas)* and pots are thrown on a foot-powered wheel. The potter's wheel was introduced by Europeans; the Pre-Columbian cultures did not have the wheel. However, long before the introduction of the potter's wheel, the Chibcha living around Raquirá made fine ceramics.

Clay *(arcilla)* is dug from the hills surrounding Raquirá and Tuaté and is ground by hand with a wooden mallet and stone mortar. The pots are fired with wood fires in stone and adobe kilns, although some country artisans simply cover the pieces with brush and wood and then set fire to the pile. The pots are generally transported by mule to the markets in Chiquinquirá, Tunja and Villa de Leyva.

Raquirá is also a center for decorative, moldmade, mass-produced pieces, such as nativity scenes, statues of the Three Kings, turtle banks and little horses *(caballitos).* The horses have been made since about 1910. Some of these pieces have a green, yellow or black glaze. A number of artisans are making ceramic churches *(iglesias),* inspired by the small pottery churches made in Ayacucho, Peru (see page 333)—a good example of cultural diffusion.

Fine pottery, including piggy banks and red and black dinnerware, also is available in La Chamba (Tolima).

Replicas of Pre-Columbian pottery are made in Colombia and are usually (but not always) sold as replicas.

TAGUA

The town of Chiquinquirá is a center for Colombian *tagua* crafts. These white, ivory-like items include miniature tea sets, tiny musicians, animals, etc., that are carved from the nut of a palm. For more information on *tagua*-carving, see page 304.

GOLDWORK

Before the Spanish Conquest, Antioquia was the home of the Quimbaya Indians, the finest goldsmiths in South America. Every goldworking technique known today was practiced by them, including *ciré perdu* (lost-wax casting), *mise en couleur* (metal coloring), cold hammering over a mold, soldering and the making of a gold–copper alloy known as *tumbaga*. The Quimbaya washed gold from streams and mined it in the Cauca Valley. Although these goldworking techniques probably originated in Peru (there are gold artifacts from Peru's Chavín culture dating back to 500 B.C.), goldwork reached its height in Colombia. The Tairona, Chibcha, Sinú, Calima and other cultures all worked in gold, and the Chibcha custom of gilding their chief at his coronation gave rise to the legend of *El Dorado*, the Gilded Man. The Gold Museum in Bogotá has a fabulous collection of ancient goldwork, including jewelry, tweezers and fishhooks.

Colombia also produces elegant modern goldwork, so it's a good place to buy gold jewelry. In some areas, such as Barbacoas (Nariño), blacks have taken over the ancient Indian techniques. Working out of their homes, these craftsmen heat the gold in charcoal furnaces while

unglazed vasijas from Raquirá and Tuaté

their wives and children spin the gold into thread and then twist or braid the thread into necklaces and bracelets. Gold thread also is coiled into filagree. A small curl or piece of filagree is called a *churo*, a Quechua word meaning "curled" or "rolled up." Filagree earrings and necklaces from Barbacoas are sold in Bogotá. Modern filagree goldwork is also done in Mompos (Bolívar). Contemporary goldsmiths also make fine replicas of Pre-Columbian pieces.

Gold content is measured in karats. Pure gold is 24 karats, so 12 karats is fifty percent gold, while 18 karats is seventy-five percent gold. The remaining material is some other metal, often copper (see page 303 for a listing of jewelry terminology).

EMERALDS

Colombia is the world's primary producer of high-quality emeralds (*esmeraldas*). When the Spanish arrived, they found emeralds through-out the Americas, even as far north as Florida; all these gems were brought by trade from the Muzo region of Colombia, which was then under the control of the Chibcha.

Emeralds were crystalized during times of great geological heat and are composed of chromium and beryllium. Chromium gives emeralds their bright green color—the more chromium, the deeper the green and the higher the value, assuming the crystal isn't flawed.

The Chibcha traded emeralds for gold and buried their chiefs with emeralds placed on their eyes, ears, nose, mouth and navel. The gems were highly valued by the Incas, Aztecs and other tribes, as well as by the Spanish, who were stunned to see emeralds the size of eggs and tortured the Indians to discover their source.

In 1905 the Colombian government nationalized the emerald indus-try, and today the mines in the Muzo area are still under the control of the Colombian government. The only private mine in existence is Chivor, which was recognized as a private enterprise before 1905 and had paid state taxes in perpetuity.

You can buy emeralds in jewelry stores in Bogotá; many of them are beautifully set in gold or silver. There's also a thriving black market in emeralds, and one whole street in Bogotá is devoted to this trade. I strongly advise you to buy emeralds in a reputable shop, however, unless you're knowledgeable about gemstones—you could easily get stuck with a piece of green glass cut from the bottom of a 7-Up bottle.

When I was in Bogotá, a man followed me down the street with what appeared to be a huge emerald, which he urged me to buy. I told him I didn't believe that his stone was an emerald, and that it was probably glass. He insisted it was an emerald and, to prove it, ran the stone down a plate-glass storefront window, leaving a six-foot gash. I still didn't buy the stone and we both left the vicinity of the store—fast.

HORN-CARVING

Throughout Latin America, it's customary for people in jail to engage in crafts: horn-carving in Colombia (all those cattle), weaving in Ecuador, leatherwork and weaving in Peru and hammock-making in Mexico. Although Colombian horn *(cuerno)* crafts are marketed through *Artesanías de Colombia,* you can also ask in any town if handicrafts are made in the local jail and then buy the crafts directly from the prisoners, who are allowed to keep the money they make. Prisoners carve such things as shoehorns *(calzadores),* flowerholders *(floreros),* cups *(copas)* and hair barrettes *(hebillas).*

PASTO VARNISH

The Spanish were intrigued to learn that the Indians of the Pasto area made a varnish *(barniz)* which they applied to wood, gourds and metal. This varnish was permanent and retained a lovely luster. While the exact ingredients of the varnish have been kept secret, we know that it's made from the resin of a fruit called the *mopa mopa (Elaeagia utilis),* which grows in the Mocoa area of the department of Putumayo. The artisans chew the seeds of the fruit, mix them with different colors and then paint the varnish on an object. The resulting surface is impervious even to hot water. Today, this varnish is used mainly on low, wooden stools which are sold in and around Pasto and Popayán.

WOOD CRAFTS

The departments of Nariño and Boyacá are noted especially for their woodcarving *(tallados de madera).* The woodcarving from Ipiales and Pasto (Nariño) is so similar to the work done in the Ecuadorian town of San Antonio de Ibarra that it wouldn't surprise me if the Colombian carvers learned the craft there (see page 303).

Several of my favorite Colombian handicrafts come from Boyacá, including hand-carved, dark brown, wooden plates *(platos)* and bowls *(escudillas* or *tazas)* which have designs burned around the edges. These and less sophisticated, traditional spoons *(cucharas),* chocolate-beaters *(mollinos),* trays *(bandejas)* and troughs for kneading dough *(artesas)* are hand-carved from various local woods, including alder, soaptree, willow, cedar, oak, walnut and others.

The Duitama area is known for its reproductions of Colonial furniture *(muebles coloniales),* especially the heavy wood and leather pieces of the mid-sixteenth century. This industry started about twenty years ago at the time when genuine antiques became a fad in Bogotá and other cities. Cedar, pine and *amarillo* are the woods most often used for this work.

MUSICAL INSTRUMENTS

The town of Chiquinquirá is a center for handmade musical instruments, an industry which started in the early nineteenth century. Today there are ten workshops, each of which employs one or two artisans who make the traditional guitar, *tiple* (five-stringed guitar), mandolin *(bandola)* and *requinto* (small guitar). The artisans do shell-inlay work and use such local woods as cedar, walnut, *chuguacá* and *comino* in addition to imported Canadian pine.

DON'T BUY . . .

Stuffed baby crocodiles and caimans (a relative of the crocodile) are sold in tourist shops on the Caribbean coast. Don't buy them or you'll encourage the depredation of these animals. Also refuse to buy anything made of snakeskin—shoes, belts, handbags, etc. If no one buys these products, the senseless killing will stop.

Remember, too, that any products made from animals on the endangered species list can't be taken into the United States and will be confiscated by United States Customs (see page 413).

RECOMMENDED READING

Artesanías de Colombia recently has published a paperback book (in Spanish) about the handicrafts of Boyacá, which includes many photographs of the artisans at work. As far as I know, the book—*Artesanía Boyacense*, by Pablo Solano (Bogotá: Artesanías de Colombia s.a., 1974)—is available only in Colombia.

Markets

Just about every Colombian town has a special weekly market day, and most of the larger cities have a permanent market area where activity occurs every day. Sunday markets are held in many towns in the department of Boyacá; to find out more about them, check with local tourist offices. Since most Boyacá craft centers are only a few hours' ride from Bogotá, a visit to one of these markets makes a nice Sunday outing.

You may find many small-town markets to be somewhat disappointing when it comes to crafts, as they primarily carry manufactured goods—shoes, clothing, tools, etc. Still, attending any market is an adventure and it's always an opportunity for you to stock up on food. The fact that a market is listed here doesn't guarantee that it's a good market— I've simply listed every market day I know. Ask about market days wherever you go. The travelers' grapevine is an excellent source of up-to-date information on interesting markets and crafts.

MARKET DAYS IN COLOMBIA

Barranquilla (Atlántico dept.) ‖ every day

Cartagena (Bolívar) ‖ every day

Medellín (Antioquia) ‖ every day

Chocontá (Cundinamarca) ‖ Monday

Bogotá (Bogotá), Siete de Agosto Market, Carrera 24 between calles 66 and 67 ‖ every day

Girardot (Cundinamarca) ‖ Monday

Duitama (Boyacá) ‖ Tuesday

Raquirá (Boyacá) ‖ Sunday

Arauca (Caldas) ‖ Sunday

Cali (Valle) ‖ every day

San Agustín (Huila) ‖ Monday

Silvia (Cauca) ‖ Tuesday

Inzá (Cauca) ‖ Saturday

San Andrés (Cauca) ‖ Wednesday

Belalcázar (Cauca) ‖ Saturday

Pasto (Nariño) ‖ every day

Ipiales (Nariño) ‖ Saturday

Ecuador

Native Cultures

Unlike Colombia, Ecuador still has a large Indian population, comprised of a number of distinct ethnic groups.

OTAVALO

The Otavalo Indians of Otavalo (Imbabura) originally were known as the Cara. The Cara language was related to that of the Pre-Columbian Chibcha of Colombia and also was similar to the language spoken today by the Cayapa and Colorado Indians of the western province of Pichincha. The Cara probably came to Ecuador from Colombia by sea about a thousand years ago.

In 1455 the Inca army moved north from Peru. They conquered the Ecuadorian Palta, Cañari, Puruhá, Panzaleo and, after seventeen years of fighting, the Cara. Near Otavalo is Yaguar Cocha (Bloody Lake), so named because the Incas threw the bodies of defeated Cara warriors into it. According to legend, a Cara princess was married to the Inca Huayna Capac, and the Inca Atahualpa was the son of this union. (While historically questionable, it's a good story.) Under Inca rule, the Quechua language replaced Cara except for a few place names. Until 1798 the remains of the Inca sun temple and *accla wasi* (house of the chosen women) were visible at Caranqui, near Ibarra.

Serfdom existed legally in Ecuador until 1964, the year that an agrarian-reform law outlawed the practice of *huasipungo*. In Quechua, the word *"huasi"* (or *"wasi"*) means "house" and *"pungo"* means "door." *Huasi-pungos* (including many *Otavaleños* and most of the Indians of the Ecua-dorian Sierra) were serfs who lived and worked on large *haciendas*. Each *huasipungo* received a small plot of land in return for unpaid work on the landowner's property, was required to furnish members of his family as unpaid workers in the landowner's house and was forbidden to leave the *hacienda*. Although the Indians are gradually receiving their own parcels of land as the practice of *huasipungo* continues to be phased out in the 1970s, the Indians still have mountainside plots rather than the more fertile, productive land located on the valley floor.

While no Andean Indians have an easy life, the Otavalo area is one of the least depressing places to visit. First of all, the setting is stupen-dous: the mountain Taita Imbabura lies to the east of Otavalo and the snowcapped Cotacachi to the west. Second, because the Otavalo In-dians are among the most prosperous Andean weavers, they've man-aged to purchase back their lovely valley lands from many *haciendas*. The Otavalo sell their goods in every market in Ecuador, and I've seen them in Colombia and Panama. They occasionally travel as far as New York and Europe.

The town of Otavalo is inhabited mainly by *blancos* and *mestizos*, while the approximately 38,000 Otavalo Indians live in the surrounding coun-tryside. The Otavalo have resisted acculturation and have retained pride

Otavalo market

in their clothing and customs. You'll recognize the Otavalo by their distinctive hair style and dress. Each man wears his hair in a long braid down his back and almost always wears a brown or black felt hat. He also wears a white cotton shirt; a reversible dark blue or gray poncho; a pair of white, wool, calf-length pants; and sandals similar to Colombian *alpargatas*, which in Ecuador are called *alpargatas* or *usutas*.

A woman's traditional dress consists of a blue and white cotton head-cloth *(fachalina)*; a white embroidered blouse; a shawl *(macana* or *chal)*; a long black skirt *(anacu)*; and two belts, *a mama chumbi* (also spelled *chumpi*) and a *wawa chumbi* (that is, a "mama" and a "baby" belt). The wider *mama chumbi* is wrapped around the waist first and the narrower *wawa chumbi* is wrapped over it.

Otavalo women wear interesting jewelry, including many strands of gold-colored glass beads that are actually Czechoslovakian Christmas-tree ornaments. They also wear long strands *(sartas)* of coral or plastic beads on both wrists. Women used to wear necklaces made from coral, brass beads, silver crucifixes and tiny silver hands *(manos)* used to protect the wearer against the evil eye. Simulated coral *(veintimilla)*, which was imported from Italy during the administration of Ecuadorian President Veintimilla in the late nineteenth century, is also commonly used in necklaces. The *veintimilla* bead has a white center, which distinguishes it from real coral. Women also wear many silver and copper rings on each hand.

Originally, all weaving was done on the backstrap loom, called a *ruana pusito* (poncho-weaver), but European floor looms were introduced by the Spanish. In Colonial times and even after Ecuador's independence, the Indians were forced to work in weaving factories called *obrajes*. In 1917 the modern weaving industry got off the ground when a weaver from Peguche began making imitation Scottish tweeds and soon developed a booming business. While the market for suit fabrics has declined due to competition from mechanized industry, the tourist market has now taken up the slack.

Today most of the woven goods you see in the market are made on floor looms with up to eight harnesses, but some Indians still weave ponchos (for their own use) and belts on backstrap looms. The best discussion of warping and weaving on a backstrap loom in traditional Otavalo style can be found in *Backstrap Weaving of Northern Ecuador*, by Redwood (Loom Book, 318 Pacheco Street, Santa Cruz, Calif. 95060, 1973, $4.25).

The Otavalo Indians obtain most of their wool from areas farther south in Ecuador, and they spin it on both hand spindles and Spanish spinning wheels. (For a detailed discussion of drop-spindle spinning, dyeing and backstrap-loom weaving, see page 321.) The whole family is involved in the weaving process. Children and adults of both sexes spin and weave, although women predominate as spinners and men as weavers. Most dyeing is done with commercial aniline dyes, which are sold by the pinch in the market. Walnut *(nogal)* shells, which yield a brown color, are one of the few natural dyes still in use. Commercially spun wool, cotton and Orlon threads are also used and are sold at the Saturday market.

The Otavalo market was famous long before the arrival of the Incas; the Amazonian Indians came with cotton, *achiote* (a fruit and dye), monkeys, parrots and plants, which they traded for dogs, salt and woven cotton blankets. The present-day Otavalo market starts early— by 6 A.M. There are two main market areas, with activity on the side streets, too. One plaza includes food, mats and commercially manu- factured goods while the second plaza is the crafts market. Treasures for sale here include ponchos, knitted and woven shawls *(chales)*, blan- kets *(cobijas)*, scarves *(bufandas)*, bags *(bolsas)* and belts *(fajas* or *chumbis)*. Orlon is used in most items. Fortunately, the Orlon used in Ecuador is less obviously a synthetic fiber than the acrylics used elsewhere in the Andes. In fact, it looks and feels like real wool *(lana)*. Since the Indians use the term *lana* loosely, if you want to know which of these fibers was used, ask if an item is *lana de Orlón* or *lana de oveja* (sheep's wool).

The Otavalo Indians have learned to make Colombian wall hangings *(divisorios)* and imitation Salasaca tapestries *(tapices)*. They also make embroidered cotton clothes, rope and sandals from *cabuya* fiber and baskets *(canastas)* and mats *(esteras)* from reeds that grow in nearby Lago San Pablo.

There are now at least 75 Indian-owned stores in Otavalo, a phe- nomenon which began in 1969. Otavaleños also operate shops in Quito where they sell their weavings and crafts, and there's a colony of Ota- valo Indians in Ambato. You'll see Otavalo vendors at every Ecuadorian market and by all the major hotels in Quito and Guayaquil.

If you wish to know more about these people, I recommend *The Awakening Valley*, by John Collier, Jr. and Anibal Buitron (Chicago: The University of Chicago Press, 1949). This photographic study was a pio- neering work in visual anthropology and is sold in bookstores through- out Ecuador.

Also see Frank Salomon's article, "Weavers of Otavalo," in *People and Cultures of Native South America*, edited by Daniel R. Gross (Garden City, N.Y.: Doubleday / The Natural History Press, 1973).

SALASACA

The Salasaca Indians of Salasaca (Tungurahua) originally lived in Bo- livia. In the fifteenth century the Incas transported them to Ecuador as *mitimaes* (laborer/colonists), probably because of some transgression or rebellion. The Incas actually had two distinct categories of *mitimaes*. One category included recalcitrant groups of Indians the Incas believed might rebel. These people were transported far from their homelands, usually into the heart of the Inca Empire, where they were surrounded by loyal, watchful Quechua. There were many *mitimaes* around Cuzco, for example. This policy also accounts for the present-day enclave of Aymara-speakers in Abancay, Peru. The second category of *mitimaes* was composed of loyal Quechua who were moved to the far reaches of the empire to supervise the local people and instruct them in Quechua and sun worship. The Cochabamba and Sucre valleys of Bolivia were populated by loyal Quechua *mitimaes* and are Quechua-speaking to this day.

Today, the 2000 Salasaca Indians speak Quechua, as do all highland Ecuadorian Indians who speak a language other than Spanish. After the Spanish Conquest the Salasaca community remained adamantly closed to outsiders. They resisted acculturation, missionaries, roads— any incursions from the outside—and used to be called *los bravos* (the hostile ones). It wasn't until 1947 that missionaries became established in the community, and today the Laurita nuns run an elementary school there. Several Salasaca women teach at this school and are a source of pride to the community.

Even today, anyone who marries into the community must learn to speak Quechua and adopt Salasaca dress, which consists of the traditional black poncho or *manta* and a flat, white, wide-brimmed hat. Anyone who leaves the community must abandon Salasaca dress, particularly the black poncho. (According to Salasaca legend, the black poncho is worn in mourning for the death of the Inca Atahualpa, who was killed by Pizarro in 1533.)

The Salasaca Indians raise sheep to obtain wool and they weave with the traditional backstrap loom. Wool is handspun on wood spindles and is dyed with aniline dyes. The Indians use the distaff, a tool of Inca origin, to hold the raw wool as they spin. A Salasaca weaver makes his own backstrap loom, called a *chumbi ahuana* (Quechua for "belt-warp-things"), and will never sell this loom since the Indians believe that if a weaver sells his loom he also sells his weaving ability.

Salasaca tapestry

The Salasaca are primarily agricultural, and weaving is a secondary occupation that gives them a much-needed cash income. In the early 1960s the Peace Corps organized a weaving cooperative in the community called *Artesano de Salasaca* and introduced the idea of making tapestries *(tapices)* on floor looms. Basically, tapestry is a weaving technique in which a pattern is made by covering the warp with the weft. In each row of weaving, different-colored weft yarns create the design. Tapestry must be done by hand; there's no way that a mechanized loom can change the weft yarns.

Originally, Salasaca tapestries made use of traditional designs, especially those woven into belts and embroidered on wedding pants and shawls. However, the Peace Corps has introduced Pre-Columbian motifs from various regions of Ecuador, as well as Jivaro de Navajo designs. Tapestries based on M.C. Escher drawings were introduced by John Ortman, a Peace Corps volunteer. In recent years the crafty Otavalo Indians began copying Salasaca tapestries, which they now sell in the Otavalo market.

Besides tapestries and rope made from *cabuya* fiber, the Salasaca have no handicrafts for sale. Because the community has no market day of its own, the Indians attend the markets in Pelileo and Ambato and sell their tapestries through various craft stores, including *Artesano de Salasaca* in Salasaca and *Productos Andinos*, which are former Peace Corps–run cooperative stores located in Quito and Cuenca. Operating on the principle that if you can't beat them, join them, several Salasaca families moved to Otavalo, where they sell their own tapestries in the Saturday market.

El Mundo de los Salasacas, by Ulf Scheller (Guayaquil: Fundación Antropológica Ecuatoriana, 1972), is a book about the Salasaca that has many beautiful black-and-white and color photographs. The text is written in Spanish, but a rather garbled English translation is included in the jacket pocket. It's available in bookstores throughout Ecuador.

INDIANS OF CENTRAL ECUADOR

The Quito (or Panzaleo) Indians occupied what are now the provinces of Pichincha, Cotopaxi and Tungurahua, while the Puruhá lived in Chimborazo and Bolívar. By the time the Spanish arrived, the Incas had been in control of the region for at least fifty years, and the native cultures and languages had been replaced by Inca social and political organization and language. Nevertheless, some Puruhá was spoken in the area as late as 1692.

The Puruhá towns of Riobamba and Latacunga were important administrative centers where the Incas built temples, warehouses, palaces and *accla wasi*. They also constructed highways along which *tambos* and fortresses were placed. By 1560 the Spanish had completely destroyed these and other Inca stoneworks in Ecuador, so that today you'd hardly know the Incas had occupied the country.

The present-day descendants of the Panzaleo and Puruhá are referred to collectively as the Chimborazo Indians, but actually include several different groups of Indians who attend the markets in Ambato, Riobamba and surrounding towns. Each of these groups wears a distinctive hat. For example, the descendants of the Panzaleo wear white hats that look like jungle pith helmets. Colta Indian women can be identified quite easily because they dye the hair around their faces a striking bright red-blonde. The Colta live south of Riobamba, near Laguna de Colta; they come to the Riobamba market to sell baskets (*canastas*) and mats (*esteras*) made from lake reeds.

The Indians live in settlements called *anejos* or *parcialidades*, each of which consists of a thatch-roofed adobe house separated from its neighbors by fields. You'll see these *anejos* if you take the *autoferro* through Ecuador. The countryside surrounding Riobamba and Ambato is lush, rich, farming country and is very densely populated. Since the Ecuadorian Andes receive far more rain than the Peruvian and Bolivian highlands, Ecuador is much greener and gentler. The Inca Huayna Capac's preference for Ecuador contributed to the downfall of the Inca Empire. He spent most of his life in Quito, and when he died he left one son (Atahualpa) in Quito and another son (Huascar) in Cuzco, each of whom claimed to be *the* Inca. The civil war between the two contenders tore the empire apart and was nearing its conclusion, with Huascar the loser, when the Spanish arrived.

Today, the Riobamba area is a major handicrafts center, and the Riobamba and Ambato markets are the largest in Ecuador. There are separate plazas or streets for animals, sheepskins and raw wool (Riobamba), meat, grains, fruits and vegetables, tools and hardware, and clothing and handicrafts.

CAÑARI

The Cañari had a highly developed culture in the Cuenca Basin even before the arrival of the Incas. They produced superb gold jewelry and copper tools, as well as fine textiles and pottery which the Spanish found in their graves.

In the second half of the fifteenth century the Incas entered southern Ecuador and embarked on a conquest of the native tribes, including the Cañari. At one point the Cañari revolted unsuccessfully against the Incas and in revenge the Incas killed thousands of Cañari and removed thousands more to Cuzco as *mitimaes*. The Cañari village of Cojitambo

Cañari (double weave) belt

was then repopulated by loyal *mitimaes* from Cuzco. Once the Cuenca Basin was secure, Topa Inca built the palace of Tomebamba near what is now the city of Cuenca, and his son, Inca Huayna Capac, was born there. Huayna Capac later built the fortress of Ingapirca near Cañar, and today it's the only major Inca ruin in Ecuador that's open to the public and not located on private land.

A group of Cuzco Cañari eventually became the personal bodyguards of Huascar, the son of Huayna Capac. When Huayna Capac died in Quito in 1527, the unfortunate Cañari sided with the losing Huascar in the civil war between him and his half-brother, Atahualpa. In revenge, Atahualpa decimated the Cañari tribe.

After Atahualpa was killed by Pizarro in 1533, the Cañari became willing allies of the Spanish, fighting with them against the Incas and helping to recapture the fortress of Sacsahuaman outside Cuzco in 1536. The Spanish further decimated the Cañari between 1537 and 1592 by forcing them to work in the area's gold mines.

After the Inca and Spanish conquests, all that has survived of the original Cañari language are a few place names, including Deleg (the oldest community in the Cuenca area) and Chordeleg.

Today, the Cañari are famous for their weaving and leatherwork, and they make some of the finest belts in Ecuador. These belts are warp-faced (that is, the warp threads predominate on the surface) and double-woven in two colors (often primaries, such as red and blue), with the top set of warp threads in one color and the bottom set in another. The belts have very fine pick-up designs: red against blue on one side and blue against red on the reverse. The motifs range from traditional people and animals to sewing machines, trains and automobiles. Some fine weaving is also done by Indians serving time in the Cañar jail, and occasionally it's possible to buy belts from these prisoners.

Cañari men weave and wear an interesting garment called a *cushma* (the Quechua word for a poncho-type textile). *Cushmas* are black wool ponchos with red and white stripes down the sides; they're belted in front and hang loose in the back. The men also wear sheepskin chaps.

Other Cañari crafts include handwoven woolen horse blankets and leatherwork, which was introduced by the Spanish. The Cañari make especially fine leather stirrups and belts. These items are made for the Indians' own use and, except for belts, the Cañari are not really producing goods for the tourist trade.

Folk Art and Handicrafts

PANAMA HATS

Cuenca is an important handicrafts center. The famous, but misnamed, Panama hats actually come from Cuenca and the Ecuadorian coast. They were named "Panama" hats because the Forty-niners bought them in Panama on their way to California during the Gold Rush. Although these hats were made as early as the sixteenth century, the modern industry started in the 1880s when Ecuador began to export the hats in quantity, principally to the United States.

The hats are made from the fiber of the *paja toquilla (Carludovica palmata)*, a relative of the palm. This shrubby, palm-like plant grows in the region of Montecristi and Jipijapa on the Ecuadorian coast, and the fiber is brought into Cuenca by truck or train. Because these hats are made on the coast, too, they're sometimes known as *jipijapas* or *sombreros de Montecristi*.

The fiber is obtained from the young leaves of the *paja* plant. The coarse veins are stripped away and the leaves are boiled. The resulting fiber is then brought into the market and sold by a wholesaler. The

purchaser shreds the *paja* into strips, the width depending on how fine a weave the artisan desires. The fiber is sometimes left natural, sometimes bleached in a sulphur solution and occasionally dyed bright colors. Since *paja* must be damp when woven, it's usually worked indoors but may be woven outdoors in the shade or on cloudy days.

In the Cuenca area, hat-making is a true cottage industry. The craftspeople weave the crown of the hat on a mold and leave its brim unfinished and bristly. This stage of the work can take anywhere from several days of continuous work to a month and a half for the finest hats. The legendary hats of extremely fine weave are said to be so fine that they can be passed through a finger ring.

On your way to the Azogues market you'll see *campesinas* coming into town, each with a few unfinished hats to sell to the wholesale buyer. This wholesaler, who attends country markets to buy unfinished hats for an exporter, is called a *perrito* (little dog). In the market plaza you'll see hundreds of unfinished hats piling up as a woman sells her week's work. She then buys a bundle of *paja* straw to make more hats. Styles vary and include intricate openwork *(calado)* and a combination of white and brown *paja* straw, although colored hats are made elsewhere in the region.

The unfinished *paja* hats are finished and blocked in factories, after which they're exported or sold. There are a number of hat-finishing factories in Cuenca.

After World War II, when hat fashions changed in the United States, the bottom dropped out of the *paja*-hat market. Now the hats seem to run in about five-year cycles—in for a year, then out for about four. This has been hard on the local economy. To help remedy this situation, the Peace Corps has organized straw workers into a number of different cooperatives which make and export a wide range of *paja* crafts. These include coasters, napkin rings, place mats, cigarette cases, baskets, imaginatively-made animals such as kangaroos and rabbits and an enormous range of Christmas-tree ornaments and Christmas decorations.

SHIGRAS

"*Shigra*" is the Quechua word for "sack" or "purse." *Shigras* are round bags made from *cabuya* fiber. They're the Ecuadorian Indians' version of the Bolivian and Peruvian carrying cloth and are used to hold everything from a few potatoes to a big, fat pig. *Shigras* are made by a process of knotless netting, using a needle. The fiber is dyed before the netting is done in order to produce the design. At the markets, occasionally you'll see a woman carefully looping one row of netting to the next with a needle as she makes one of these bags.

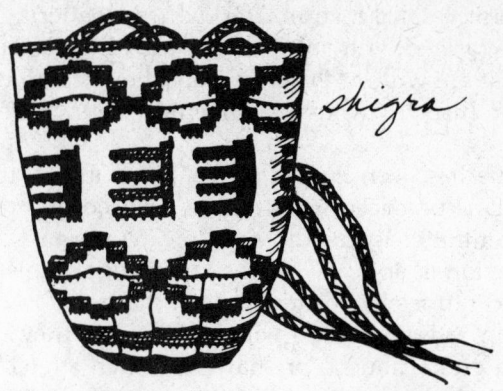

shigra

Shigras vary enormously in size, design and quality of workmanship. Some have wool embroidery on top of the netting. *Shigras* with two straps come from the Riobamba area while those with four straps come from the vicinity of Salcedo.

BASKETS

Baskets *(canastas)* are made throughout Ecuador from a variety of plant fibers, including *cabuya* fiber, *duda* and *paja* straw. The Cayapa, who live in the jungle lowlands to the west of the Andes (Pichincha province), make the finest baskets in Ecuador, using fan-leaf and regular palm fibers in checkerboard, tabby and twill weaves. In the Saquisili area, baskets and mats are made from *totora* reeds, which grow in the lakes of that region. In addition, finely plaited baskets from the Oriente sometimes find their way into the stores in Quito.

PONCHOS

Besides the ponchos worn by the Otavalo, Salasaca and Cañari Indians, you'll see several other varieties in Ecuador. The modern descendants of the Puruhá and Panzaleo wear red wool ponchos that appear to be very tightly woven. These ponchos are made on the traditional backstrap loom and then boiled, so that they shrink and the weave becomes extremely tight. During Colonial times these Indian communities organized weaving workshops *(obrajes)* in which they made cloth to sell to the local population and to pay their tribute tax to the Spanish.

IKAT

Another poncho worn in central and southern Ecuador is made with an *ikat* warp. *Ikat* is a term used to describe tie-dyed thread; in Ecuador *ikat* is called *tejidos amarrados*, tied textiles. To produce a pattern, the thread or yarn is tightly wrapped with string at various intervals and is then dyed. The parts that are wrapped don't absorb the dye and thus retain their original color (usually white), while the exposed areas of the thread pick up the dye.

The *ikat* technique has been known for centuries in South America. The ancient Peruvians practiced warp *ikat*, as evinced by pre-Inca textiles from Peru's central coast, as did the Pre-Columbian Ecuadorians of the Guayaquil region. It appears that the knowledge of this technique persisted over the centuries in isolated parts of these regions.

When Ecuadorian artisans weave with *ikat* thread, they first finish the warping for an entire poncho or shawl and then stretch the warp taut between two vertical poles. Next they carefully tie the threads with hemp fiber to produce a pattern. After the threads have been dyed and dried, the hemp ties are unwrapped. At this point the warp is put on the backstrap loom and the piece is woven. In Ecuador only the warp threads are dyed, which is called warp *ikat*, and the finished pieces are warp-faced—that is, the warp threads predominate on the surface. The most common color combinations for *ikat* thread are white/indigo and white/red. Both cotton thread and wool yarn are used for *ikat* in Ecuador, although never in the same piece. The Riobamba and Cuenca–Gualaceo areas are *ikat* centers.

BELTS

The Indians living around Ambato and Riobamba weave and wear several different kinds of warp-faced belts (*fajas* in Spanish; *chumbis* in Quechua). One type of belt is made of heavy wool (often handspun) in colors of red, black and yellow, in an intermesh weave. Another very similar belt has black, white, red and green in a warp of heavy cotton intermesh weave. Both of these belts are woven on backstrap looms with four sets of heddles. A third type of belt has pick-up patterns. In this case, fine cotton thread is used for the plain weave ground with coarser woolen handspun for the supplementary warp. These belts are woven on backstrap looms with two sets of heddles.

If you're interested in learning the threading drafts for weaving these belts on a four-harness floor loom, read *The Textile Arts*, by Verla Birrell (New York: Schocken Books, 1973).

MACRAMÉ BAGS

Besides doing macramé on the fringes of shawls, women in southern Ecuador also make fine macramé bags (*bolsas*) from *cabuya* fiber. Many of the *bolsas* sold at *Productos Andinos* are fully-lined and thus make excellent purses.

Since Indians in the Loja area speak Quechua, you may hear the word *penko* (rather than *cabuya*) used for the fiber. The finer, bleached *penko*, called *penko blanco*, is used to make these bags.

SWEATERS

Handspun sheep's-wool sweaters *(chompas)* are made in northern Ecuador as well as in southern Ecuador around Cuenca. In the north, handspun wool sweaters originally were made by Indians in the village of Mira, near San Gabriel, for their own use. However, the sweaters caught on commercially and are now being made by a sweater-knitting cooperative called *Chompas de los Andes*. The wool is usually undyed, so the sweaters come in natural colors of brown, tan, white, gray and black. A good three pounds of wool goes into each sweater. The Indians pay at least thirty-five sucres per pound for wool, which is much more expensive than Orlon. Presently there's a greater demand than supply of wool in Ecuador because most land is used for farming rather than sheep-raising.

BAYETA

Bayeta is handwoven (on floor looms), sometimes handspun, wool fabric that's used extensively by the Indians to make their own pants, skirts and shirts. It's sold in the markets by the *vara*, a measure that's equal to eighty-four centimeters. However, the merchants' *vara* measuring

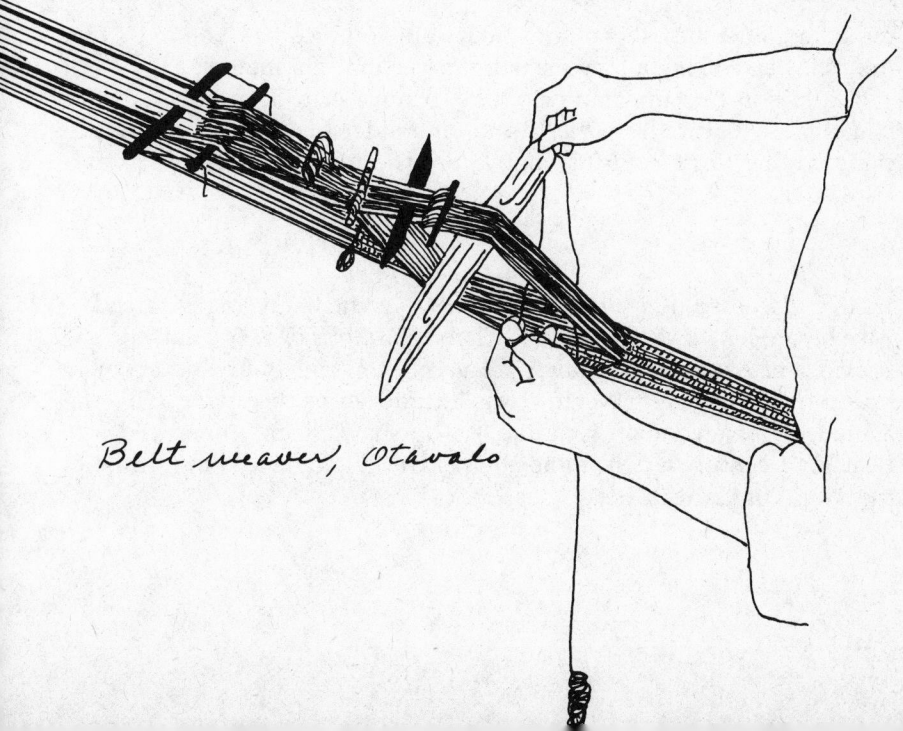

Belt weaver, Otavalo

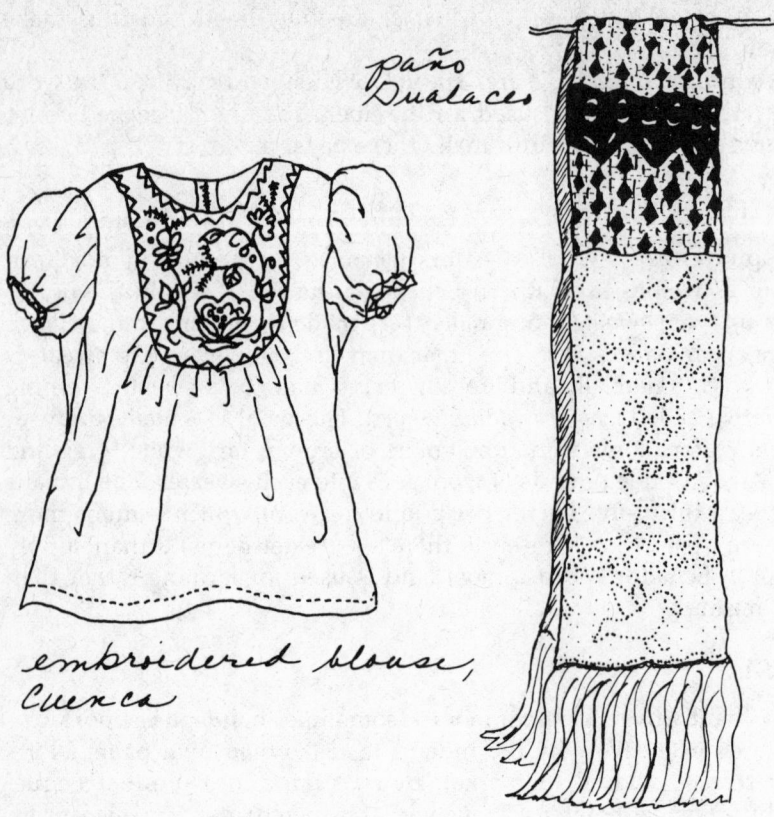

*paño
Gualaces*

*embroidered blouse,
Cuenca*

rods are sometimes short, so if you want to be certain you're buying full *varas*, take along a tape measure marked in centimeters.

In addition to homemade clothing, a number of Riobamba artisans make pillow covers from *bayeta* and embroider traditional Colonial designs on them with colorful wool yarns. These are marketed by *Productos Andinos*.

SHAWLS

As I've discussed, *ikat* (or *tejidos amarrados*) is the tie-dyeing of thread or yarn before it's woven on a loom. Shawls (*macanas* or *paños*) made in the province of Azuay, especially in Gualaceo, combine *ikat* with incredibly fine macramé fringe. (Macramé was introduced by the Spanish; it's not a Pre-Columbian Indian technique). The shawls were introduced into Ecuador a century ago from northern Peru by pilgrims to the shrine of the Virgin of Cisne in Loja, Ecuador.

Azuay shawls are handwoven on backstrap looms. When the weaving is done, the fringe is painstakingly knotted into such designs as birds and flowers. It's the most intricate macramé work I've ever seen. The fringe is then starched so that it becomes very stiff. Traditional color combinations for the shawls are indigo/white or rose/white, although I've seen indigo/black and black/rose shawls also. The macramé fringe is always white.

You'll find these lovely shawls in the market and *Productos Andinos* store in Cuenca, as well as in nearby towns. If you buy one, don't wash it or the dyes will run and make a mess. Dry-cleaning is best.

EMBROIDERED CLOTHING

I was surprised at the availability of embroidered cotton clothes *(ropas bordados)* in Ecuador. Though most Andean textiles are made from wool, in Ecuador you'll find cotton shirts *(camisas)*, blouses *(blusas)*, aprons *(delantales)*, long dresses *(vestidos)* and children's and babies' clothing. Much embroidery is done in the town of La Esperanza, in northern Ecuador, but it's also done throughout Ecuador and sold in tourist shops, handicrafts stores and at *Productos Andinos*.

Because much of this clothing is made specifically for the tourist trade, there are sizes large enough to fit six-footers and hefty people. All clothing from La Esperanza is hand-embroidered, but some machine-embroidered clothing is made in Cuenca. To tell whether an item is hand- or machine-embroidered, look at the inside of the garment. Hand embroidery is always the same color on both sides. Machine embroidery is usually two different colors: the top (outside) thread is colored and the bottom (inside), or bobbin thread is white. Embroidered clothing from La Esperanza is preshrunk and colorfast, and Cuenca embroidery is colorfast also. Since other embroidered clothing may shrink or run, it's worthwhile buying in a shop that guarantees the quality of its textiles.

RUGS

There are rug factories in both Ambato and Guano (north of Riobamba) in which artisans weave pile-knotted wool rugs *(alfombras)*. The Indians also sell handwoven, pile-knotted, scatter-size, wool rugs at the Riobamba market.

LEATHER

Ambato artisans produce the finest leatherwork in Ecuador, including purses *(carteras)*, luggage and belts. However, it's difficult to find these items for sale. Some leatherwork is also produced in Cuenca and may be found at *Productos Andinos*.

BREAD BABIES

Bread babies (*Másapan* or *Guaguas* [*Wawas*] *de Pan*)—little figures made of bread dough—are thought to have originated in Pre-Columbian times as a replacement for humans and animals in sacrifices. Throughout the Andes these bread-dough figures are made for All Souls' Day and probably represent the souls of the dead.

The making of *guaguas de pan* for sale and export is a folk art unique to Ecuador. The bread-dough figures made in the village of Calderón (Pichincha) are especially artistic. The dough is dyed bright colors, shaped in the form of people, animals and Christmas tree ornaments and then varnished. These figures are meant to be used as decorations, not eaten, and preservatives have been added to the dough to retard spoilage.

JEWELRY

The artisans of Chordeleg make fine gold and silver filagree jewelry (*joyas* or *joyería*). Earrings, pins and rings are made from sterling silver and 18-karat gold and generally are designed with Colonial motifs.

Saraguro is also a jewelry center. The ancestors of the present-day Saraguro Indians were *mitimaes,* loyal Quechua-speakers who originally lived near Cuzco but were sent to Ecuador by the Incas as colonists and administrators. The Saraguro Indians dress somewhat like the Salasaca, with black ponchos and white broad-brimmed hats. Saraguro used to be one of Ecuador's major silverworking centers, and the artisans there used melted Peruvian silver *soles* to make jewelry. Since *soles* are now scarce and therefore expensive, Saraguro jewelers are working with nickel instead. Although *tupos* (shawl pins) are now made primarily of nickel, filagree earrings (*sarcillos*) are still made of silver, since nickel can't be worked into the thin, fine strands necessary for filagree work.

The term "sterling silver" means the silver content of a piece is 925 parts per thousand and the remainder is copper or some other metal. Sterling is high-quality silver, but since the Indians usually don't stamp the metal content on their work, you have to either develop your own

bread dough angel

sense of what is high-quality silver or buy only from a shop that guarantees that its pieces are sterling.

Throughout the Andes you'll have a problem determining whether something is nickel or silver. Many items sold as silver actually are completely or mostly made of nickel. How can you tell the difference? Nickel is heavier than silver and doesn't tarnish. Silver is lighter in weight, and old silver pieces often exhibit a dark black tarnish. Also, silver can be drawn into much finer strands than nickel, so almost anything filagreed is silver or gold.

Following is a list of jewelry terminology:

Metals *(Metales)*

copper ‖ *cobre*

gold ‖ *oro*

iron ‖ *hierro*

lead ‖ *plomo*

nickel ‖ *níquel*

silver ‖ *plata*

tin ‖ *estaño, lata*

zinc ‖ *zinc, cinc*

Alloys *(Mezclas)*

brass (copper and zinc) ‖ *latón, bronce*

bronze (copper and tin) ‖ *bronce*

nickel and silver ‖ *alpaca* (Peru, Bolivia)

Pre-Columbian Alloys

82 percent gold / 18 percent copper ‖ *tumbaga* (Colombia)

copper, lead and gold ‖ *llacsa* (Inca, Peru)

Jewelry *(Joyas* or *Joyería)*

beads ‖ *cuentas*

bracelet ‖ *pulsera*

brooch ‖ *broche* (also means "cuff links" in Ecuador)

earrings ‖ *aretes*

necklace ‖ *collar*

pin or brooch ‖ *prendedor*

ring ‖ *anillo*

shawl pin ‖ *tupo*

WOODCARVINGS

San Antonio de Ibarra (Imbabura) is the only Ecuadorian town in which woodcarving is done commercially on any scale. In the 1890s Daniel Reyes, a native of Ibarra, traveled to Quito to learn the art. He returned to Ibarra and accepted apprentices. Today, about a thousand Ibarra residents are involved in woodcarving and a school has been established in honor of Reyes.

Although styles vary, traditional figures include saints, Indians and lots of beggars. Many types of wood are used, including cedar, walnut and occasionally ebony. Because the supply of wood around Ibarra has been depleted, wood must be transported from the Oriente. The retailer pays the artisan about one sucre per centimeter to carve the statue and then has the piece sanded, stained and waxed.

WOODEN UTENSIL SETS

Paute (Azuay) is located on the eastern edge of the Andes, close to the jungle lowlands. The artisans there make kitchen-utensil sets from soft jungle woods. Each set consists of a spatula, knife, beater, fork, ladle and sieve-spoon which are carved with Pre-Columbian motifs. I haven't seen sets like these anywhere else in the Andes.

TAGUA

The *tagua* palm grows in the hot tropical lowlands of Colombia, Ecuador, Venezuela and Brazil. The fruit can be as large as a pumpkin and weigh up to twenty-five pounds. Each fruit contains six to nine seeds or nuts, which look like egg-sized avocado seeds. The white pulp of the nut becomes as hard as ivory (hence the name "vegetable ivory") when carved and exposed to the air. *Tagua* nuts used to be made into buttons which were exported to Europe and the United States, but today they're used mostly for novelty items. Riobamba is Ecuador's *tagua*-crafts center, and you'll find miniature cups, saucers, rings, chess pieces and busts for sale throughout this town.

DON'T BUY . . .

Don't buy *tsantsas* (shrunken heads). The sale of authentic shrunken human heads is illegal, and the Ecuadorian government has been largely successful in preventing the warfare that results in heads being taken. Most shrunken heads offered for sale these days are really the heads of monkeys and other animals.

RECOMMENDED READING

There's only one book available on Ecuadorian crafts in general: *Artesanía Folclórica en el Ecuador,* by Ulf Scheller et. al. (Guayaquil: Cromos Cia., Ltda., 1972). This book discusses only a few handicrafts and includes photographs. The text is in Spanish and English. See also my articles listed in the bibliography.

Markets

The following list of market days is quite complete and includes the major highland markets you'll encounter as you travel from north to south in Ecuador. If a town doesn't have a market day, its residents attend markets in neighboring towns. For example, the people of Ibarra, El Quinche, Zuleta and La Esperanza go into Otavalo on market day, while the Salasaca attend markets in Pelileo and Ambato. If you're not sure whether a town has its own market, ask.

I'm not recommending any markets in particular, since I don't want to send travelers off on long trips on the basis of my tastes alone. Then, too, nothing destroys the ambience of a market faster than a sudden influx of hundreds of tourists. Finally, because I dislike being told exactly where to go and what to do by guidebooks, I'm leaving open the possibility for you to explore and discover these markets on your own.

Bear in mind that most Ecuadorian *campesinos* are farmers first and artisans second, so that the availability of many crafts is seasonal and varies according to the amount of farm work to be done. This is especially true for smaller markets.

Bargaining is in order in all markets, as well as in many shops (unless there's a "Fixed Prices" sign). Don't be afraid to bargain hard, but be fair. If it comes down to a quarter or fifty cents, the Indian undoubtedly could use the money more than you, and if you pass up the item you'll regret it later.

MARKET DAYS IN ECUADOR

The first day listed is the main market day.

Tulcán (Carchi) ‖ Thursday and Sunday

Otavalo (Imbabura) ‖ Saturday and Wednesday

Peguche (Imbabura) ‖ Sunday

Saquisili (Cotopaxi) ‖ Thursday

Latacunga (Cotopaxi) ‖ Saturday and Tuesday

Salcedo (Cotopaxi) ‖ Sunday

Pujili (Cotopaxi) ‖ Sunday

Zumbahua (Cotopaxi) ‖ Saturday

Ambato (Tungurahua ‖ Monday

Pelileo (Tungurahua) ‖ Saturday

Guaranda (Bolívar) ‖ Saturday

Riobamba (Chimborazo) ‖ Saturday

Licto (Chimborazo) ‖ Sunday

Guamote (Chimborazo) ‖ Sunday

Alausí (Chimborazo) ‖ Sunday

Cañar (Cañar) ‖ Sunday

Biblián (Cañar) ‖ Sunday

Quito (Pichincha)
  Clothing and Crafts Market,
  Avenida 24 de Mayo and Calle
  Benalcázar ‖ Tuesday and
  Saturday

  Santa Clara Market, calles
  Versailles and Veintimilla ‖
  Wednesday and Sunday

  Ipiales Black Market, northwest
  corner of Plaza San Francisco ‖
  every day

  La Floresta Market, near Colegio
  Cardinal Spellman ‖
  Wednesday

Sangolquí (Pichincha) ‖ Sunday

Santo Domingo de los Colorados
(Pichincha) ‖ Sunday

Machachi (Pichincha) ‖ Sunday

Azogues (Cañar) ‖ Saturday

Cuenca (Azuay) ‖ Thursday and
Saturday

Sigsig (Azuay) ‖ Sunday

Gualaceo (Azuay) ‖ Sunday

Chordeleg (Azuay) ‖ Sunday

Saraguro (Loja) ‖ Sunday

Loja (Loja) ‖ Monday

Peru

Native Cultures

The modern-day Peruvian Quechua are a conglomeration of peoples, including descendants of the Incas and of conquered Peruvian tribes, and descendants of *mitimaes,* who were brought to Peru from all corners of the *Tahuantinsuyu* and were taught Quechua and Inca ways until they have become, in time, Quechua themselves. The Peruvian Aymara are located around Lake Titicaca, in the department of Puno. Their ancestors were the Colla, the original inhabitants of this territory, whose language was Aymara.

PRE-COLUMBIAN INDIAN DRESS

Pre-Columbian Peruvian clothes were either square or rectangular in shape. Although a few pieces were shaped on the loom, fabric was never cut to fit. Instead, two or more four-selvedge pieces were sewn together edge-to-edge to make a garment.

The costumes I describe below, with local variations in size, color and decoration, were worn from the earliest cultures through Inca times.

Each man wore a breechcloth *(wara)* held up with a tie or belt *(chumpi)*, and some men also wore a wrap skirt. The upper body was covered by a shirt or tunic *(unku;* also spelled *uncu)* which was similar to a modern poncho but had sides that were sewn together except for the arm openings. (Some *unkus* were made with sleeves.) A man's clothing also included a rectangular cloak *(yacolla)*, a small bag *(chuspa)* used to carry coca leaves or personal items, and such jewelry as silver or gold bracelets. Inca noblemen also wore large earplugs, which led the Spanish to call these Indians *orejones* (big ears). Sandals were worn for footwear. Coastal sandals were made from plant fibers while highland varieties were made from untanned llama hide. Finally, each man wore a headdress. When the Incas expanded their empire they insisted that each group retain its individual hair and headdress style, so headdresses varied from class to class and from tribe to tribe. Some tribes wore pile-knotted hats resembling pillbox hats while others wore turbans or looped caps similar to knitted hats worn today. Each Quechua man wore a headband *(llautu)* that wrapped around the head several times. The *llautu* of the Inca himself had gold tubes with red fringe (the royal insignia) over the forehead.

Each woman wore a long, tunic-like dress *(urcu* or *anacu)* that was held at the waist with a belt and fastened over the shoulders with pins. Over this she wore a mantle *(lliclla)* held shut with a long straight pin *(tupo)* made of bone, copper, silver or gold. She wore sandals like those worn by men, and her jewelry was limited to the *tupo* and perhaps a shell or bone necklace. A woman wore a headband which was wrapped around the head only once, and over this she usually wore a headcloth *(chucu)*.

Under Inca rule, a government official periodically was sent to every Indian village to classify all girls who had reached about ten years of age. Those who were beautiful and physically perfect were chosen to be educated and were known as *acclakuna* (chosen women). The others were called *hawa sipaskuna* (left-out girls) and remained in their villages, where they eventually married.

Most *acclakuna* were sent to convents to be educated while a few were set aside to be sacrificed on such important occasions as the inauguration of the Inca. The *acclakuna* were trained in spinning, weaving, *chicha*-making, cooking and various household tasks. When they matured they became *mamakuna* (mamas). Some were given as wives to noblemen and chiefs, while others became royal concubines and wove the Inca's clothing and prepared his food. Still other *mamakuna* became virgin servants of the sun; these women prepared ritual food and *chicha* and tended the shrines. Because the Inca's garments were burned after they had been worn only once, and because textiles were also burned as offerings, the *acclakuna* and *mamakuna* were always busy weaving.

The Quechua distinguished three kinds of woven cloth. *Kosi*, the lowest-grade, coarsest cloth, was made from relatively coarsely spun llama or alpaca hair and was used only for blankets. The middle grade of cloth was made from alpaca hair and was called *awasqa,* which means "woven material." This cloth was used for ordinary clothing and was usually plain and warp-faced, although it sometimes had warp stripes or geometric warp-faced patterns. It is the *awasqa* weaving tradition— the cloth of the common people—that has survived to the present day. The highest grade cloth was called *qompi.* It was woven in a tapestry technique on a vertical frame loom and was finished on both sides. All of the Inca's garments were made of this cloth. *Qompi* was often woven from the finest, softest vicuña, which the Spanish described as comparable to silk. Some of this cloth had feathers, which were inserted during the weaving process, and other *qompi* was decorated with figures made of thinly-hammered gold and silver. The tapestry technique for weaving clothing disappeared in the seventeenth century along with the kind of loom used to make *qompi.*

Ancient Peruvian textiles have been studied extensively. Most of the books recommended in Chapter Fifteen include discussions of textiles should you want to pursue this subject further. In addition, see the books and monographs by D'Harcourt, Fisher, King, Casteñada Léon and Tidball listed in the bibliography.

COLONIAL INDIAN DRESS

The Spanish brought change to almost every facet of Indian life, including dress. They introduced new fibers (sheep's wool and silk) as well as the concept of tailoring. From time to time they also issued edicts forbidding the wearing of Inca-style clothing and headgear. This occurred in the 1570s and 1580s and again following the Indian rebellions at the end of the eighteenth century.

By the 1690s, the higher an Indian man's social status, the more likely he was to dress in European-style clothing, while an Indian noblewoman continued to wear Inca-style clothing. Although ordinary Indians still wore Pre-Columbian dress, they began to adopt European hat styles.

In 1779 the Chayanta revolted in southern Bolivia, and in 1780 the highland Peruvian Indians rebelled under the leadership of José Gabriel Condorcanqui. This wealthy upper-class Indian took the name of Tupac Amaru II, in honor of the Inca Tupac Amaru, who was beheaded by the Spanish in 1571 and from whom he was descended. The revolt soon spread to northern Bolivia, where the Aymara laid siege to La Paz. All three of these rebellions were eventually quelled and the Spanish renewed their efforts to Hispanicize the Indians and crush Indian nationalism. In Peru, this led to the confiscation of portraits of the Incas and to the discovery and execution of all known direct descendants of the Incas. Priests were urged to teach the Indians Spanish and to renew their efforts to stamp out idolatry. The Spanish also forbade the use of the conch shell trumpet (used to call the Indians to battle under the Incas), prohibited the Indians from wearing black in mourning for their murdered Inca and forced the Indians to wear Spanish-style short pants instead of breechcloths and Spanish-style hats instead of *llautus*. Tupac Amaru himself wore an odd mixture of Spanish and Inca clothing, including an *unku* over a velvet Spanish suit and a three-cornered hat over a *llautu*.

It's difficult to date changes in clothing from Colonial to contemporary times, especially since it depended (and still depends) on the degree of contact with whites. By the time of Tupac Amaru's revolt, for example, many Peruvian Indian women had taken to wearing Spanish-style dress, yet the women's *llautu* is still worn today in a remote region of northern Bolivia.

CONTEMPORARY INDIAN MAN'S DRESS

What we think of as traditional Indian dress is actually a mixture of Pre-Columbian and Spanish Colonial peasant dress. The contemporary

Indian man's shirt (*camisa* in Spanish; *kutun* in Quechua) usually is made from white factory-woven cotton or from sheep's wool that's either factory-woven or homespun and handwoven. The pants (*pantalones*) almost invariably are made from white or black *bayeta*. (Solid-color, handwoven wool cloth is called *bayeta*, while patterned wool cloth is called *jerga*.) In the Callejón de Huaylas, pants are called *wara*, after the Inca breechcloth, and are similar to pants worn throughout Peru— they're knee or midcalf length and sometimes have a slit at the bottom of each leg. Shirts and pants are European-style and are sewn by tailors who usually use treadle sewing machines. (In most markets today, you'll find a tailor pumping away on his old machine, so take advantage of the opportunity to have your clothes mended.) In some parts of Peru a *bayeta* vest (*chaleco*) is worn over the shirt.

Sandals (*usutas* or *ujutas*) made from leather or tire rubber are also worn and can be found for sale in the markets.

Hats. The brimmed hats (*monteras*) worn today by Peruvian Indians and *cholos* are derived from Spanish Colonial hats. In their own stubborn fashion, the Indians adopted Spanish-style hats after the Conquest but continued to observe the old Inca law requiring each village or tribal group to wear distinctive headgear. In the Cuzco area especially, you'll find a wide variety of *monteras*. Sometimes an Indian man wears a *montera* over a knitted hat known as a *chullo*. The Indians also have taken to more modern hat fashions. A good example is the English bowler style adopted by the Aymara in about 1900. As you travel throughout Peru, you'll learn to recognize the various local hat styles.

The hand-knitted hat with ear flaps (*chullo* in Quechua; *gorro* in Spanish) originally was worn only by the Aymara but is now worn by babies and men throughout the highlands. My favorite *chullos* come from the Cuzco area and are decorated with buttons.

Paja hats also are made in Peru, especially in Celendin (Cajamarca) and Moyabamba (San Martín).

Ponchos. The poncho was introduced from Chile into Peru during the seventeenth century and is probably of Araucanian Indian origin. Although ponchos are worn today throughout Peru, Inca-style *unkus* are still worn in remote villages such as Queros (Cuzco). As a rule, each adult Indian receives just one poncho, which must last him a lifetime.

Ponchos are invariably made of two pieces of four-selvedge cloth (*khallu*) that have been sewn together, with a hole left for the head. The modern poncho is woven the same way as the *unku* except that it's not sewn together at the sides. Ponchos are warp-faced and usually are made from sheep's wool, although alpaca is sometimes used for the

chullo

weft. While *unkus* were plain weave, the contemporary ponchos of the Cuzco area have elaborate warp-faced pattern bands. The more elaborate weaving patterns developed over the past 400 years. Since Inca belts and *chuspas* had pattern weaves, the Indians simply applied this style of weaving to larger pieces. Each locality (especially in the Cuzco area) has a distinctive poncho with characteristic colors, patterns and motifs. An Indian man sometimes wears a neck scarf with a center design that matches his poncho.

The Spanish introduced such motifs as horses, butterflies and the double-headed bird (the Hapsburg eagle). Representations of men, llamas, birds and felines, as well as geometrics, are found on Inca pieces, while today's pattern bands are usually woven with geometric motifs.

Grace Goodell and Dr. Junius Bird have estimated the amount of time necessary to spin and dye the yarn, warp the loom and weave a traditional, warp-faced, patterned poncho similar to ones sold in the Cuzco and Pisac markets. It takes between 500 and 600 hours—that is, three to six months of on-and-off work. Given the price at which a poncho is sold, the weaver receives about three or four cents an hour for his or her work—and this doesn't include the cost of supplies! If a weaver were to receive the legal American minimum wage, the price of a traditional poncho would range between $1200 and $1500! This makes it easier to understand why we are witnessing the slow death of traditional weaving. Can you blame an Indian for choosing to make a less elaborate piece or for buying a manufactured item rather than investing so much time and energy for so little in return? For this reason I emphasize the importance of paying the Indians a fair price for their work, especially if you buy directly from the artisans themselves. While there's no guarantee that paying a better price will encourage the production of fine textiles, we can hope that it will. The overall impact of tourism on traditional weaving is difficult to assess, but perhaps travelers can be instrumental in the preservation of this traditional folk art.

Another factor mitigates against the continuation of fine weaving. The Indians are at the bottom of the heap, economically and socially, so their traditional costumes aren't generally admired. Middle- and upper-class South Americans are often astonished to learn that travelers treasure "those dirty old Indian things." In the past, Spanish *caballeros* (gentlemen) considered a plain brown, gray or black poncho to be a sign of class and looked down on the brightly colored and patterned varieties. Consequently, in Peru and Bolivia today, many Indians prefer dark-colored, plain or striped ponchos. Entire communities, including Cajamarca, Huaráz, Urcos and Checacupe, now wear this drabber garb, and brown ponchos have become increasingly common throughout the Sierra. Most of the ponchos I saw in Chincheros, a traditional weaving village, were brown.

Belts. Both Indian men and women wear warp-faced, patterned belts (*fajas* in Spanish; *chumpis* in Quechua; *wachukos* in the Callejón de Huaylas). The man's belt is usually wider than the woman's. Today, these belts are more decorative than functional since skirts and trousers are now made with waistbands. As with ponchos, each region and town has its own particular style.

One interesting, contemporary, warp-faced belt can be found in the Huancayo area. The women here were inspired by the railroad built between 1870 and 1893 and began to weave train motifs into their belts. Often the price of the belt and the date it was made are woven in, too. In addition to wool, synthetic yarns have been used in the warp for at least the past thirty years.

Coca Pouches. The small pouches (*chuspas*) worn by Indian men to hold their coca leaves and *cal* date back to early Pre-Columbian times. Although plastic bags seem to have replaced *chuspas* in most places, these pouches are still woven and worn in the Cuzco area. Like ponchos and belts, *chuspas* usually are warp-faced and made from wool and can be identified as to origin by their colors and patterns.

The *chuspa* pictured on the next page has two-ply background yarns and four-ply pattern yarns. The pattern appears slightly raised because of its thicker yarns and its supplementary warp floats. Each design has a

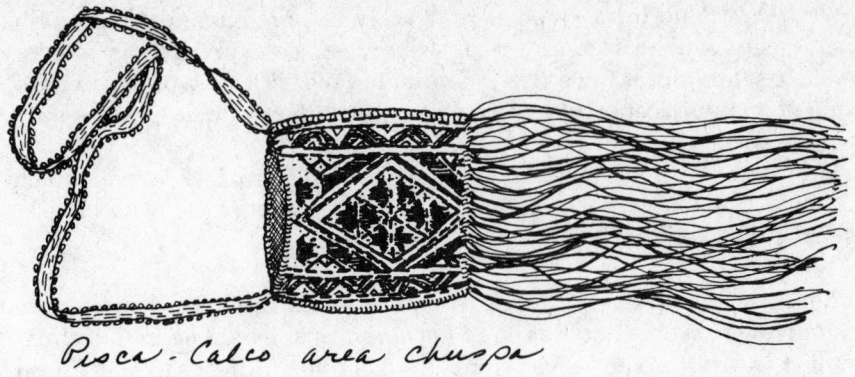

Pisca-Calco area chuspa

name and this one is called a *wacratica* (which means "hornflower" in Quechua). The strap was woven separately and was then sewn to the bag. The glass beads were attached to the edges of the strap by the weft during the weaving process. The colors (primarily red and white) and pattern are typical of the Pisac–Calca area.

Staffs of Office. If you attend the Sunday mass and market at Pisac or Chincheros or visit an Indian community on New Year's Day (see page 377), you'll see a number of men carrying *varas,* or staffs of office. *Varas* are carried by *varayoks,* who are the elected or appointed officials, such as the *alcalde* (mayor), of an Indian community. *Varas* can vary from one foot to four feet in length (usually according to the status of the office) and generally are made from the wood of the *chonta* palm. They have iron tips and beautiful hammered-silver bands with crucifixes and portraits of the saints.

While the titles of the various community leaders are Spanish and political organization in general is a mixture of Spanish and Inca traditions, the *vara* itself is of Inca origin.

CONTEMPORARY INDIAN WOMAN'S DRESS

An Indian woman wears her hair in two braids that are fastened in back with a tie. Like a man, she wears a *montera,* sandals and a blouse *(blusa* in Spanish; *munillu* in the Callejón de Huaylas)* that's usually made from white factory-woven cotton. She also wears a full, gathered, wool skirt *(falda* in Spanish; *millqay* in Quechua; or *pollera,* the term used throughout the Andes). *Polleras* are usually made from *bayeta* and have some sort of decoration around the hem, such as embroidery in Huancayo and handwoven braid *(cinta)* in the Cuzco area. In a number of markets it's possible to buy *bayeta* yardage which has already been embroidered — either by hand or by machine. Although traditional *polleras* are black, skirts also come in navy blue, red, hot pink, orange and yellow. On festive occasions a woman customarily wears as many *polleras* as possible, one on top of the other. The number of *polleras* a woman owns is therefore an indication of her wealth; many Indian women possess only one or two.

In the Cuzco area a woman also wears a short *bayeta* jacket *(saco)* which often is elaborately decorated with buttons and braiding. The blouse, skirt and jacket are all of Spanish peasant origin.

Shoulder Wraps. Every Indian woman wears a rectangular or square, handwoven, wool shoulder wrap *(manta* in Spanish; *lliclla* in Quechua)* which is a direct carry-over from Pre-Columbian dress. In the Cuzco area, a village's *llicllas* and ponchos are woven in similar colors, motifs and patterns. *Llicllas* usually have warp-faced pattern bands separated by bands of plain weave and, like ponchos, are woven in two pieces which are sewn together edge-to-edge.

A woman carries bundles either in her *lliclla* or in a separate carrying cloth *(q'epirina* or *inkuña)*. In general, carrying cloths are less elaborate than *llicllas;* they usually have simple striped patterns.

Shawl Pins. A *tupo* traditionally is used to hold a *lliclla* in place and it, too, is of Pre-Columbian origin. Inca *tupos* were straight pins which usually had a hammered, flat, circular head whose edges were sharp enough to be used as a knife. They were made from copper, silver or gold, depending on a woman's social class. Spanish influences also can be seen in modern *tupos,* including the peacock and hand-holding-a-key motifs. In addition, I suspect that the spoon-shaped *tupo* still worn

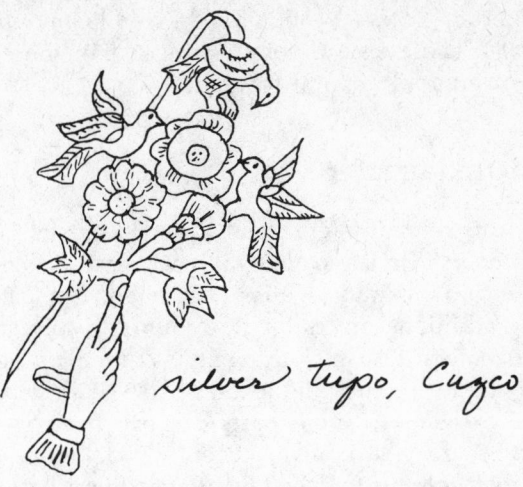

silver tupo, Cuzco

today on festive occasions was either copied from Spanish Colonial silver spoons or is, in fact, an old spoon with the handle filed to a point.

Today, the most common *tupo* is the ordinary safety pin, and fine silver *tupos* are becoming increasingly rare. Most antique *tupos* were made from silver *sol* pieces, which are 900 parts silver (almost sterling). Contemporary reproductions of antique *tupos* have a high nickel content.

On Sundays and feast days, an Indian woman may wear copper or silver rings and earrings in addition to her *tupo*.

Belts. A woman's belt is always warp-faced, with patterns, and measures about two inches wide and about four feet long. Like men's belts, women's belts vary from town to town. The Chincheros woman's belt is woven with its warps "on opposites," as complementary warps, so that the warp-float pattern is the same on both sides, but the colors are reversed. The circle, s-shaped and diamond motifs are commonly used in this town, as are bright shades of red, green, orange, yellow and pink. The warp sometimes contains acrylic yarn as well as sheep's wool.

Headcloths. In the department of Puno, Aymara women in the villages of Ichu and Taraco still wear the Pre-Columbian-style headcloth (*chucu*) made from black *bayeta*. The *chucu* also is worn by Quechua women in the vicinity of Tinta (Cuzco).

CONTEMPORARY INDIAN CHILDREN'S DRESS

Indian girls and boys are dressed like their parents. A baby is swaddled until he's four to six months old. During this time he's carried snug in a *lliclla* on his mother's back. A toddler is dressed in a wraparound skirt called an *inchana*. Thereafter, a child is dressed in the same type of clothing worn by an adult man or woman.

Folk Art and Handicrafts

Peruvian crafts are very different from those found in Colombia and Ecuador for both historical and geographical reasons. For one thing, there are llamas, alpacas and vicuñas (protected, but diminishing) in Peru, providing additional fibers for this country's spinners, weavers, knitters and crocheters. Indian clothing styles differ, too, giving rise to distinctive weaving techniques and textiles. Also, Peru has a long tradition of ceramic excellence. Some parts of Peru have significant clay deposits and these areas have always been major pottery centers.

With such a rich folk art and handicrafts tradition, you'd think that Peru would have a comprehensive folk art museum. It really doesn't. However, there is one museum you should visit, although I found it inadequate—the *Museo Nacional de la Cultura Peruana*, located at Avenida Alfonso Ugarte 650, in downtown Lima. It houses collections of carved gourds, ceramics, Colonial paintings, a few contemporary Indian costumes from the Cuzco area and crafts from the Oriente. Admission is about a dime. Although the museum's exhibits are interesting, all they did was whet my appetite and I wanted to see more. I'll mention additional museums that have exhibits of particular handicrafts as I go along.

Many high-quality handicrafts can be found at *Artesanías del Perú*, which is the official Peruvian handicrafts agency. *Artesanías del Perú* operates stores in Lima, Arequipa, Cuzco and Iquitos.

TEXTILES

Because textiles are a major folk art in the Andes, I've included the following section which gives a detailed description of traditional spinning, dyeing and weaving techniques. While the discussion focuses specifically on Peru, it also applies to most Bolivian textiles. Colombia doesn't have a large Indian population engaged in weaving traditional garments and some European techniques have been adopted by Ecuadorian Indians, but some of the processes described here such as spinning and floor-loom weaving can be observed in those countries as well.

Pre-Columbian Textile Heritage. Peru is a textile-lover's paradise for several reasons. First, the Peruvian Indians have retained their traditional dress and textile techniques far more than the Indians of highland Colombia and Ecuador. Second, Peruvians are fortunate to have had the use of a wide variety of fibers—especially the cameloid fibers, alpaca, llama and vicuña—in addition to sheep's wool and cotton. The ancient Peruvians also made use of viscacha (an *altiplano* rodent), rat and mouse fur, human hair, sisal, kapok, spider webs and various grasses. Third, many of the incredibly fine textiles produced by the ancient Peruvians now reside in museum collections, so it's possible to study the general continuities in Peruvian textile production over a span of about 4200 years. Fortunately for us textile fanatics, the dryness of the coastal desert has helped preserve some of the finest textiles the world has ever known. Due to the lack of moisture, artifacts buried in graves don't decay.

The earliest known Peruvian textiles date from about 2300 B.C. and were excavated from Huaca Prieta on the northern coast by Dr. Junius Bird. Historically, basketry predated weaving in Peru and weaving predated pottery by fully a thousand years, making these two related textile techniques Peru's oldest folk art forms. The Chavín culture, which flourished from 1000 to 600 B.C., marked the origin of fine weaving, while the truly magnificent Paracas textiles date from about 1000 B.C. to 250 A.D. Nazca culture and textiles flourished from 250 A.D., and from about 600 to 1000 A.D. the dominant influence was Huari–Tiahuanaco. From about 1000 to 1500, Chancay was a leading textile center, even after that region had been conquered by the Incas. The Incas, of course, were predominant from about 1200 until the Spanish Conquest, and from that time on, Indians in the Sierra have continued to weave beautiful textiles. The textiles from each of these cultural traditions can be distinguished by their unique colors and motifs, and you'll be surprised at how quickly you can learn to identify the different pieces.

What do I mean when I refer to the excellence of early Peruvian textiles? On backstrap looms, vertical frame looms (some with a variation in which the loom bars were attached to Y- or X-shaped frames) and horizontal ground looms, these Indians produced textiles by every weaving technique known to us today, with the exception of card weaving. These techniques included twining, plain weave, many kinds of tapestry, double and triple cloth, tubular weave, twill, complementary warp and weft, supplementary warp and weft, brocade, gauze, openwork, sprang, scaffold weave, featherwork and more. In addition, they mastered such off-loom techniques as embroidery, braiding, plaiting, network, appliqué, *ikat* and *planghi*.

Overall, Pre-Columbian textiles are unexcelled in sheer quality of workmanship. The cotton, alpaca, vicuña, llama and other fibers used by the ancient Peruvians were all spun by hand and are unsurpassed in evenness, fineness and strength. (Sheep were introduced by the Spanish, so the Pre-Columbians didn't use wool.) Furthermore, the

Indians used vegetable and mineral dyes to produce a complete palette of colors and shades.

Some textile experts believe that the early coastal Peruvians used only three natural dyes: cochineal or a plant related to madder for red, indigo for blue and the Peruvian pepper tree or other unidentified plants for yellow. The astonishing range of shades was achieved by overdyeing as well as by dyeing the natural tan and brown varieties of cotton and the various natural shades of alpaca, llama and vicuña fibers. The coastal Indians may have obtained a purple dye from the *Purpura* mollusk which was similar to the famous Tyrian purple of the Mediterranean.

There were also local variations in dyes. Many natural dyes still in use in the United States and Europe, such as brazilwood, logwood and fustic, come from tropical South American plants and trees. The Indians of the *selva*, who possessed an encyclopedic knowledge of plants, undoubtedly used these dyes and many others. By Inca times the highland Indians had access, through trade, to the dyes of both the jungle and coast. The Incas also used a number of mineral dyes, samples of which are on display in the *Museo Arqueológico* in Cuzco, including copper for green, cobalt for blue and chrome for orange. These minerals, as well as iron, tin and alum, also act as mordants. Although we aren't sure exactly which mordants the Pre-Columbian Indians used, analysis of textiles suggests iron and alum.

Yarn was usually spun before it was dyed. Animal fibers were spun on the traditional drop spindle used today, while cotton was spun on a spindle which rested in a carved gourd or ceramic bowl. Spindles were made from a stick of hardwood, or sometimes from cactus thorns, and generally had wooden, stone or clay whorls, some of which were beautifully carved and painted. In other instances cotton was dyed raw, with the seeds still in it, which led the Spanish to believe that the Indians grew blue cotton. I've tried this method of dyeing cotton, and it works.

On the coast, nearly every grave of a Pre-Columbian female has yielded weaving artifacts such as a weaver's basket with tools, looms with partially woven textiles, spindles, samplers, yarn, tiny models of weavers at their looms and clothed dolls. This suggests that just about every woman knew how to spin and weave. Some of the beautiful *mantas* (shawls or rectangular wraps) found in these graves must have taken the weavers years to make. Because the shawls show no evidence of wear, they probably were made specifically as burial garments. Many of these pieces can be seen in the museums recommended in Chapter Fifteen. Others can be found in the private collection of Mr. Yoshitaro Amano, which can be seen by appointment. The *Museo Amano* is located at Calle Retiro 160, in Miraflores, a suburb of Lima. Telephone 25-00-19 several days in advance for an appointment.

So what were all these early coastal weavers weaving? For the most part clothing, including burial garments, and some temple wall hangings. They may have made blankets, too, although we know very little about their bedding. In general, textiles were made either entirely of cotton or of animal fiber. If these fibers were mixed, the warp was invariably cotton and the weft animal fiber. Twining and netting were used to make bags and nets, and braiding and plaiting to make slings, ropes and cords.

Contemporary Fibers. The most common fibers (*fibras*) you're going to encounter in the highlands are cotton, sheep's wool, llama and alpaca hair and acrylics. It's always a good idea to ask what kind of fiber an item is made from, although you might not always get a truthful answer. Don't merely ask if a textile is made from *lana*, which literally means "wool" in Spanish, since the fabric could be *lana de oveja* (sheep's wool), *lana de alpaca* or maybe even *lana de Orlón*. Instead, ask, "*¿Qué tipo de lana es?*" ("What type of wool is it?"). Technically speaking, only sheep's wool should be called wool. Alpaca, llama and vicuña fibers are actually hairs.

Cotton thread is easy to distinguish. It's handspun or (more often) commercially spun and purchased in the market. Besides using cotton for their own clothing, including shirts and blouses, the Indians sometimes use it as warp in items made for the tourist trade. For example, some blankets are made with a cotton warp and a wool or alpaca weft. Cotton grows in natural colors of white, tan and brown and can be dyed virtually any shade.

Sheep's wool is a fiber familiar to North Americans. It's durable and warm and is used extensively in the Sierra, especially for traditional Indian ponchos, *chullos, chuspas, llicllas* and *bayeta*. Wool comes in natural white, black and black-brown colors and can be dyed every color of the rainbow. The Indians have taken to Day-Glo colors, especially shocking pink, lime green and bilious yellow. Very finely-spun sheep's wool is hard to distinguish from llama and alpaca hair when it's woven in a textile. Wool also is used as warp in such items as rugs and blankets. Many weavers feel that a wool warp and an alpaca weft is a good combination—the finished textile has wool's durability and strength along with alpaca's softness. However, different kinds of fibers are never mixed in the same piece of yarn; that is, they're never spun together.

Acrylic yarns such as Orlon and Acrilan are synthetic, or manmade, fibers, and the acrylics used in the Andes come in all colors and shades. Acrylics are less warm and less durable than animal fibers and are sometimes passed off as sheep's wool, alpaca or even vicuña because of their softness. It's fairly easy to identify acrylic yarns in Peru and Bolivia.

If you look closely, you'll see that the fiber has a distinct shine or glimmer in sunlight. The acrylic yarn used in Ecuador isn't always shiny, which makes it extremely hard to distinguish from wool. Indians throughout the Andes are now using acrylic yarns to make traditional textiles, and I've collected pieces in Ecuador, Peru and Bolivia that contain both acrylic and wool.

Alpaca and the other cameloids are found in Peru and Bolivia. Alpaca hair comes in natural colors ranging from white to gray to black and from tan to brown. Although alpaca can be dyed, it's most often used in its natural colors in textiles made for the tourist market, including blankets, rugs, capes, sweaters, hats, gloves and ponchos. These textiles are brushed so that they have a soft, fuzzy nap. Alpaca hair is longer, softer and silkier than llama hair and sheep's wool, but sometimes it's hard to tell the difference—particularly if you're looking at a woven textile rather than the yarn. Alpaca is frequently used as weft in Indian textiles, and many Indians mistakenly believe that alpaca can't be dyed. The departments of Cuzco, Puno and Hunacavelica, Peru, lead that country in alpaca production.

Llama hair comes in the same range of colors as alpaca. It's coarser and greasier than alpaca, and the Indians also mistakenly believe that it can't be dyed. Llama hair is used most frequently in rope, slings, saddlebags, potato and grain sacks, as the weft or selvedge in ponchos and sometimes in trousers and blankets woven for the Indians' own use.

Vicuñas are extremely rare. These small, deer-like animals have never been domesticated, so they usually must be killed in order to obtain their golden brown and white hair, which is renowned for its luxurious softness and silkiness. Because Andean vicuña herds have been hunted almost to extinction, they're a protected species in Peru and Bolivia, and it's illegal to buy and sell vicuña hides or products made from vicuña hides or yarn. Please respect this law. It's unlikely that you'll encounter any vicuña products; unwary tourists sometimes are sold Orlon textiles which they're told are vicuña.

Just to confuse you, the Aymara crossbreed alpacas, llamas, vicuñas and guanacos, another cameloid. Since vicuñas and guanacos are almost extinct, the most common cross is between llamas and alpacas. The offspring of an alpaca male and llama female is called a *misti* and can reproduce. The cross between a llama male and alpaca female is called a *wariso* and this hybrid is sterile. (*Wariso* is also the name given to llama–guanaco and alpaca–vicuña crosses.) To what extent the fibers of these crossbreeds are used is a mystery.

How can you tell cameloid fibers from sheep's wool? It's impossible to be absolutely sure without a microscope, but sheep's wool is generally crimpy and curly while cameloid fibers are slightly curved. Look closely at one or two fibers. If they're extremely curly you can be quite sure they're sheep's wool.

Many Indians own flocks of sheep, small herds of llamas and alpacas or at least a few animals which provide them with fibers for their own use. Indians who don't own animals buy hides or fleece at the market or receive them from *haciendas* in exchange for working as shepherds.

Sheep are shorn once a year, usually in March, and each animal yields two or three pounds of wool. Llamas are shorn every two years during the rainy season and each animal yields four to six pounds of hair. Like llamas, alpacas are sheared every two or three years during the rainy season and each alpaca yields eleven to fifteen pounds of hair. Occasionally an animal is killed before it's sheared, and the hair is pulled from the hide as needed. Lots of alpaca hides are traded in the market. The meat is usually sold in the market, too, if it isn't kept for food by the animal's owner.

For the most part, Indians in the markets understand the Spanish words for fibers. Diminutive forms are frequently used: *"¿Alpakita es!"* (*"It's alpaca!"*) the ladies tell you. Following is a list of fiber terms:

	Spanish	Quechua	Aymara
alpaca	*alpaca*	*pogocha*	*paku*
acrylic	*Orlón* or	*lana syntética*	——
	lana syntética		
cotton	*algodón*	*utcu*	*kheya*
llama	*llama*	*llama*	*karwa*
sheep	*oveja*	——	*iwisa*
vicuña	*vicuña*	*vicuña*	*wari*
thread, yarn	*hilo*	*kaitu*	*kaitu*
wool	*lana*	*millma*	*taura*
clothing	*ropa*	*pacha*	*isi*

Spinning. "To spin" is *hilar* in Spanish, *puchkay* in Quechua and *k'puña* in Aymara.

For the most part, women predominate as spinners in the Andes, at least in public, and you'll frequently see them spinning as they walk along the road. However, in Peru and Bolivia, Indian and some *cholo* men and women of all ages are involved in spinning. In fact, by the age of six, both boys and girls have learned to spin on small, toy spindles, and some of the finest yarn to be found is spun by girls under ten. Who does what actually varies from community to community. In parts of Peru females and very old men are the only people who spin, while in other areas, such as Cuzco, women spin and men ply the yarn. Overall, I saw more Indian men spinning in Bolivia than in Peru.

In the highlands, some cotton is spun by hand, usually with the spindle *(rueca* in Spanish; *puchka* in Quechua; *puchka* or k'*apu* in Aymara) resting in a gourd or bowl. Sheep's wool and llama, alpaca and (rarely) vicuña hair are spun on the drop spindle.

Generally, before any animal fiber is spun, it's first washed in warm water. The spinner picks out the dirt and burrs and teases the wool with her fingers ("to card" or "to tease" is *carduzar* or *escarmenar* in Spanish; *tisay* in Quechua), arranging the fibers so that they lie roughly parallel to each other. I've never seen wooden, European-style carders with steel teeth used by the Indians, except in Otavalo, Ecuador. However, the Bolivian Quechua living in the northern part of the department of La Paz use a carder called a *karkinchu* which is made from the teasel plant and is similar to the *cardencha* used in Colombia.

In many areas of Peru, including Ayacucho, Huancayo and the Callejón de Huaylas, and in parts of Ecuador, the carded wool is wrapped around a distaff *(kawa)*. Sometimes the distaff is a simple y-shaped stick, but more often it's a carved wooden implement which has a tiny bird carved on each of its two top ends. Although the Incàs introduced *kawas* to the coastal Indians, they aren't used today in the Cuzco and Puno, Peru, areas or anywhere in Bolivia. Instead, the wool is looped around the spinner's forearm and hand.

The spindle usually is held in the right hand and the wool in the left, although I've seen the reverse. A few strands of wool are pulled from

S twist

Z twist

spinning with the drop spindle, Cuzco

the bundle of wool and attached to the spindle, which is then given a spin and dropped. When the yarn (*hilo* in Spanish; *kaitu* in Quechua and Aymara) gets too long, it's wound on the spindle. Yarn spun clockwise has a z twist while yarn spun counterclockwise has an s twist. The z twist is more common. In some areas, s-twist yarn, called *lloq'e* (meaning "left"), is associated with magical practices. For example, only *lloq'e* is used in offerings to Pacha Mama, and a *lloq'e* thread is broken by the Aymara when they want to break an evil spell cast against them. The spun yarn is wound off the spindle into skeins (*madejas*) by looping it over the arm.

I attempted to learn to spin in Cochabamba, Bolivia, and the Indian ladies thought it was hilarious. A woman my age who couldn't spin! Who would ever want me for a wife? There obviously were some serious flaws in my upbringing.

Plying and Overspinning. The Spanish verbs *doblar* (to double) and *torcer* (to twist) are used to describe this process, which is the final step before warping. In plying, two or more threads are twisted together to give the yarn added strength. In most areas of Peru and Bolivia, plying is men's work, and generally only two threads are plyed together. A larger than average spindle (*k'anti* in Quechua and Aymara) and whorl (*piruru* in Quechua and Aymara) are used in plying. The yarn is always doubled in the opposite direction from which it was spun—for example, z-twist yarn is plyed into an s twist—otherwise it would come unspun.

There are several plying techniques used. Sometimes the plier works with each ball of yarn (*ovillo* in Spanish; *kururay* in Quechua; *jaya* in Aymara) attached to his belt, and other times he plies directly from two spindles stuck in the ground.

As the yarn is spun and plied it's overspun—that is, it's given a vigorous spinning until it curls up on itself. Sometimes it's even given a third spinning. Overspinning makes the yarn stronger, tighter, thinner and easier to work with in warp-faced weaves. It also makes the finished piece extremely durable. This explains why you see Indian women spinning what looks like already spun yarn. They're overspinning it.

Dyeing. "To dye" is *teñir* in Spanish.

In Peru, women predominate as dyers. For the most part, aniline dyes (*tintes* or *tinturas anilinas*) are used by the Indians and are purchased at the local market.

Before dyeing begins, the yarn is washed again to remove any remaining grease and dirt. Then it's placed in hot, sometimes boiling, water in a clay or iron pot (*olla*) in which the dye already has been dissolved. The yarn is left to simmer from several hours to a day, depending on the shade desired. The dyed yarn is rinsed in cool water and hung up to dry.

In the Peruvian highlands around Cuzco only a few natural dyes are still in use. The most common are the leaves from walnut trees (*hojas de nogal*), which yield brown, yellow and gold; cochineal (*cochinilla*), which is purchased in powdered form in the market and yields red; and common soot (*carbón de casa*), which is collected from the rafters of houses and yields black and brown. The most common mordants in the Cuzco area are *chicha*, lemon juice (*jugo de limón*) and stale or fermented urine (*orin fermentado*). Walnut is the only natural dye still used in the southern Huancavelica area; it's fixed with alum (*alumbre*), which is mined in the area and sold in the Ayacucho market.

Francisca Meyer, who runs a weaving workshop in Huancayo, Hugo Zumbühl and Barbara Mullins, an English traveler, have been collecting natural dye recipes in Peru and encouraging weavers to use natural dyes. See the bibliography for Mullins' and Zumbühl's books on this subject, which are available in Peru.

Looms. In Peru, men and women weave on backstrap and horizontal ground looms. In the Cuzco area the backstrap loom is called a *baticola*, which translates as "tail beater," an appropriate term because of the strain the loom puts on the weaver's back. In Hualcán (Callejón de Huaylas), the backstrap loom is called a *kallwa*, the same word used for a weaving sword or beater. The horizontal ground loom is called a *qallama* in Aymara.

In the Cuzco area women predominate as weavers, while in Hualcán weaving is a secondary occupation for men, some of whom even own floor looms. In Santiago de Chocorvos (Huancavelica), women weave belts and children's ponchos while men weave adults' clothing. In the latter two places women spin and dye, but men predominate as weavers. Some of these men are full-time weaving specialists whose clients supply them with wool and pay for the woven item with cash, coca leaves, wool or an animal.

The horizontal ground loom and backstrap loom have similar parts with the same names. The only difference is that the bars on the ground loom are lashed to four stakes in the ground rather than being attached to a tree and the weaver. This makes it more difficult to adjust the tension quickly, a task the backstrap-loom weaver can accomplish merely by leaning forward or backward.

In both Peru and Bolivia, most weaving is done outdoors in the sun between July (the last harvest) and October. This is the dry, winter season.

Weaving. "To weave" is *tejer* in Spanish, the same as "to knit," so weaving is sometimes called *tejer con telar* (to weave or knit with a loom) to distinguish it from knitting. "To weave" is *ahuay* in Quechua and *sauña, kausuña* or *kkanaña* in Aymara. There seems to be no exact Quechua or Aymara equivalent for our word "loom," so the Peruvian and Bolivian Indians use the Spanish word *telar*. In Quechua, *awa* (also spelled *ahua*) is the root of the verb *ahuay* (to weave) and is also the word for "warp." The word for "weaver" is *ahuaq*. A loom is sometimes called an *ahuanakuna*, which roughly means "warp-and-things."

The process of arranging all the lengthwise yarn (the warp) on the loom in an orderly fashion is called warping. The warp is the foundation of the fabric. The weft consists of the threads which cross and interlace with the warp.

Before beginning to warp, Peruvian Quechua weavers make a blessing over the tools, ground and yarn or sprinkle some *chicha* to *Pacha Mama*. In Peru warping is a two person operation and a ball of yarn is tossed back and forth between the weaver and a helper, who guide the yarn in the form of a figure eight over two horizontal or vertical poles. This whole process involves a careful thread count and the weaver determines the choice of colors. Warping can take several hours of continuous work, and then the finished warp must be transferred to the loom.

In a plain weave textile, the weft (which is usually wound on a shuttle or bobbin) passes over one warp thread and under the next, across the entire warp. The heddle stick and strings lift one set of warp threads and the shed stick controls the alternates. As each new shed is formed, the sword or beater is inserted and the previous weft is beaten vigorously into place with the beater or a llama-bone pick. This process continues until the piece is woven.

What makes Peruvian (and Bolivian) textiles interesting, both visually and technically, are their unique, warp-patterned bands. Initially, light and dark yarns are warped together in certain sections of the textile; then, as the artisan weaves, he or she picks up the warp in certain ways to create the design. *Pallay*, which is Quechua for "pick up," is the name given to this type of warp-patterned band. The weaver uses his or her fingers, a bone pick or a stick to pick up the warp. I observed and filmed weavers in Cochas Chico (Junín) and Chincheros (Cuzco) who used their fingers when doing pick-up weaving.

Within certain technical limitations, a weaver has tremendous design possibilities. Certain motifs are traditional, however, partly because they're adaptable to this kind of warp-faced weaving. Weavers use no pattern drafts or written instructions and pride themselves on their ability to improvise within the tradition. In the Cuzco area the pattern bands are variations on the diamond, and no two textiles produced by

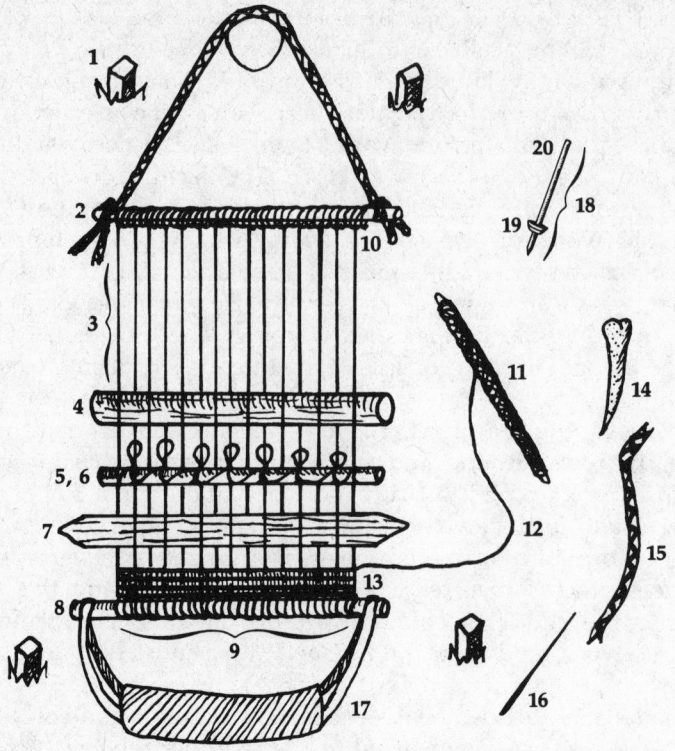

Backstrap and Horizontal Ground Loom. The first Quechua words listed below are those used in the Cuzco area; the words with asterisks (*) are those used in southern Huancavelica. In Ecuador and Bolivia, almost all the Quechua loom terms are different. The Aymara terms listed below are the same for both Peru and Bolivia.

English	Quechua	Aymara
1 stakes	*estacas* (Spanish) or *takarpu*	*chacurus*
2 end or warp beam	*tucukuna hulcha* (pole), *awa kaspi, awa pallqa**	*sawilawa*
3 warp	*awa* (or *ahua*)	*sawu, chanka, asi*
4 shed stick	*tocoro*	*tocoro*
5, 6 heddle stick and strings	*illawa*	*illawa, hakasaya*
7 sword or beater	*kallwa*	*whichcata*
8 end, warp or cloth beam	same as **2** or *kaki**	same as **2**
9 warp lashing	*watcos de hulcha*	*chucurcata*
10 heading cord	*chichin*	——
11 shuttle or bobbin	*kuma, k'espa, kumana**	*ahchi hak'asaya*
12 weft	*mini*	*kepa* (or *qaipa*)
13 woven area	*awasqa*	——
14 llama-bone pick	*wichuña* (long bone), *ruki, chuqchi*	*wichuña*
15 rope	*waskha*	*wiska, soga* (Spanish)
16 pick-up stick	*wichuña, ruki*	——
17 backstrap	*baticola*	——
18 spindle	*puchka*	*puchka, k'apu*
19 shaft (wood)	*tissi*	*tissi*
20 whorl (wood, clay or stone)	*piruru*	*piruru*

a weaver are identical! Ponchos and *llicllas* are woven in two separate pieces which are later sewn together; the weaver uses the first piece as a guide in weaving the second so that the two sides of the poncho or *lliclla* match. Most of these ponchos and *llicllas* have a supplementary warp structure—that is, the background warp yarns form the structure of the fabric, and the pattern (or supplementary) warp yarns float on both sides of the textile, creating the design.

Traditional Peruvian textiles are four selvedge—that is, there are no cut warp ends. This is possible because of the continuous warp, the manner in which the warp is fastened to the loom bars and because the string heddles are easily removed. To produce a four-selvedge textile, the weaver starts weaving at one end of the piece and then weaves from the other end. This technique is called backweaving. When the two woven sections get extremely close to each other, it becomes impossible to insert the shed stick or use the heddles. At this point the weaver continues weaving with a long, wooden, steel or iron needle (*yawri*) and often uses increasingly smaller needles as he or she progresses. Naturally, backweaving takes time. In plain-weave areas, backweaving is relatively easy to do, but in pattern bands it's difficult to pick up the pattern warps, so the backweaving shows as a kind of stippled break in the design. Careful, almost invisible, backweaving is a sure sign of a fine weaver. When the two pieces of a poncho or *lliclla* have been woven and taken off the loom, they're sewn together with the backweaving at opposite ends. *Chuspas* are woven in two pieces in much the same manner as ponchos and *llicllas* except that a fringe is left at the bottom. The two pieces are then sewn together along the bottom and up the sides. Other *chuspas* are woven in one piece.

Fringe (*fleco*) is woven separately and sewn to some ponchos. Like meticulous backweaving, carefully-made, full fringe is the sign of a good weaver. Other ponchos and some *llicllas* have a tubular band (*ribete*) around the outer edges. The warp for this edging is set up with one end attached to a stake in the ground and the other end held in the weaver's hand. The weft is sewn through the edge of the poncho or *lliclla* as part of the weaving process.

Some ponchos sold in the markets are traditional in design, but have no backweaving and aren't four selvedge. Instead, they're cut and hemmed. This saves time and is an example of the commercialization of weaving for the tourist market.

In Chincheros (Cuzco), belts are made on an interesting version of the backstrap loom. There are no end bars on the loom; instead, one heading cord is looped around an iron stake in the ground and the other is looped over the weaver's belt and pinned with a straight pin. A Chincheros woman demonstrated her belt loom for me by looping one end over her big toe and the other over her belt. When using this belt loom, Chincheros weavers have worked out an efficient variation on the weaving process. They use up to five swords, which they insert after picking the design, instead of immediately passing the weft.

For more on traditional Peruvian spinning, dyeing, warping and weaving, see the excellent publications by Dr. Junius Bird, Grace Goodell, Ann Pollard Rowe and I. Neil Stevenson listed in the bibliography. If you're traveling to Peru, you may want to visit the *Museo Histórico Regional de Cusco* in Cuzco, which houses exhibits of Colonial textiles and contemporary looms.

Colors. Indians in the market usually speak and understand enough Spanish to conduct business and should understand the Spanish words for colors. The Quechua and Aymara don't have names for several colors, and in these cases they've adopted the Spanish terms. The rather hideous Day-Glo colors are called *"brilliantes"* and are used and admired by weavers throughout the Andes, perhaps because they add a touch of color to the Indians' lives, which seem to be lived in brown houses amidst brown earth and brown mountains.

The following list should be helpful when you want to indicate a color preference. If you'd like a darker shade of a particular color, ask for one that's *"mas obscuro."* If you want a lighter shade, ask for one that's *"mas claro."*

	Spanish	Quechua	Aymara
black	*negro*	*yana*	*ch'iara*
blue	*azul*	*yana* or *ankas* (indigo)	*larama* or *sajuna*
brown	*cafe, moreno* or *pardo*	*ch'umpi*	*ch'umpi*
gray	*gris*	*chejche*	*ch'eje*
green	*verde*	*k'omer*	*ch'ojña*
orange	*naranja*	*naranjado*	——
pink	*rosado*	*rosado*	——
purple	*morado*	*morado*	——
red	*rojo* or *colorado*	*puca*	*wila, chupika* or *pako*
white	*blanco*	*yuraq*	*hankko*
yellow	*amarillo*	*k'ellu*	*k'ellu*

Cleaning Textiles. The following discussion applies to textiles purchased in all four countries.

Chincheros (complementary warp) belt

Cotton. If you're unsure whether your cotton shirts and blouses will shrink, wash them in lukewarm or cold water and hang them on the line to dry—unless you want to give them to your ten-year-old cousin.

Indian handwoven wool. All handwoven woolen textiles, such as *llicllas*, ponchos and *chuspas*, should be dry-cleaned. If you wash these textiles, the dyes might run and spoil them. When traveling, check out dry cleaners in major cities (and agree on the cost beforehand). Several importers have told me that they prefer to have their Indian textiles cleaned in South America, where the dry cleaners are familiar with the kinds of fibers and dyes used by Indian weavers.

Woven and knitted alpaca. Absolutely *don't* dry-clean alpaca clothing. It takes out all the natural oils and makes the items brittle and dull. Instead, wash your alpaca sweaters, gloves, hats, etc., by hand in cold water with Ivory Snow and lay them flat to dry.

Acrylics. All acrylics must be washed since dry cleaning ruins them. Do them by hand in lukewarm water with mild soap or, if you dare, wash them by machine, using the gentle cycle. When in doubt, wash acrylics by hand.

SAMPLE LOOMS

It's possible to buy small looms *(telares)* which have partially woven textiles still attached to them. These looms are meant to be used as wall hangings since the textiles themselves aren't necessarily complete. You can find small looms, minus the weaving swords, for sale in the Cuzco market. The sticks used in the frames are so thin they'd undoubtedly break under tension, so the textiles were probably lashed to stronger loom bars when they were woven. Because wood is scarce and therefore expensive in the Sierra, weavers can't afford to use heavier wood in these sample looms.

Other interesting loom samplers come from Cajamarca and are woven in lovely brocaded and pick-up patterns. You can buy them in Cajamarca and Lima.

SLINGS

The Inca army fought with slings (*hondas* in Spanish; *warakas* in Quechua), which they used to hurl stones with amazing accuracy. Slings are still used in Peru and Bolivia to herd cattle and for ritual warfare (see page 396). To hurl an object, the ends of the sling are held in one hand with the looped end hooked around the little finger. A rock or clump of earth is placed in the center. The sling is whirled and then one end is released, sending the missile flying. They are made from black, brown and white llama or alpaca hair. The rock-holder is woven while the rest is sixteen-strand plaiting.

RUGS AND BLANKETS

In Peru as in other Latin American countries, including Mexico, Guatemala and Bolivia, only the men use the European treadle or floor loom (*telar de suelo, telar de pedal* or *telar criollo*). This means that men weave *bayeta*, which is almost always woven on floor looms, as well as a number of other items, many of which are made for the tourist trade. In markets and stores throughout Peru you'll encounter handwoven alpaca ponchos, vests, jackets and purses, as well as yardage and even neckties. Several towns are noted for their weaving, especially for fine wool and alpaca rugs (*alfombras*) and blankets (*frazadas colchas* or *cobijas*).

In the city of Ayacucho there are several weaving families, including the Huamans and the Quispes of the Santa Ana barrio, who weave rugs and blankets on rustic two-harness floor looms. Huaman textiles are especially well known and include tapestry rugs made from natural-colored, handspun sheep's wool, as well as brighter, aniline-dyed wool rugs. These rugs range in size from about three feet long by a foot and a half wide, to twelve feet long by about eight feet wide. Sheep's-wool tapestry rugs made by the Quispes and dozens of other lesser known but equally fine craftsmen can be found in the Ayacucho market also. Many of these rugs are small and can be used as throw rugs or wall hangings. They have motifs ranging from butterflies to geometric patterns and come in both dyed and natural colors.

You can also find interesting pile-knotted (*raya* or Ghiordes knot) rugs for sale in the Puno market. These rugs are made from natural-colored alpaca and come from the neighboring town of Pucarcolla.

Hualhuas (Huancayo) is a weaving center known for its rugs, blankets, scarves and curtains. Although the artisans use both sheep's wool and alpaca, most of the weaving is done with natural-colored alpaca. The rugs and blankets often have a sheep's-wool warp and an alpaca weft, which results in a textile that's durable as well as soft. The alpaca tapestry blankets from Hualhuas are among the finest blankets I've ever encountered and can be found for sale in the Huancayo market.

Cajamarca is another rug-making center. The artisans here work in sheep's wool and make seamless rugs up to eight feet square. They do very fine weaving, some of it in muted shades of wine and red.

A weaving cooperative in San Pedro de Cajas (Junín) helps market the textiles produced in that town. There's a two-harness floor loom in practically every home, and the weavers make rugs, blankets, ponchos and tapestry wall hangings (*tapices*) from both cotton and sheep's wool. The *tapices* are of unusually high quality and include both religious and secular motifs.

KNITTING

"To knit" is *tejer* in Spanish, which also means "to weave." Since this causes some confusion, Peruvians usually distinguish knitting by calling it *tejer con palitos*, which means "to weave or knit with little sticks." Knitting with two or more needles was introduced by the Spanish. The Pre-Columbian Indians made netting with a loop stitch that resembles knitting, and the process is sometimes referred to as needle-knitting because of the needle that's used. It's not true knitting, however, and no implements resembling knitting needles or crochet hooks have ever been found in archaeological excavations.

You'll rarely see an Indian woman with idle hands. If a woman isn't spinning she's probably knitting. Some Peruvian knitted items are part of contemporary Indian costume while other pieces are made expressly for the tourist trade. *Mangas* and *chullos* are traditional textiles, although you can find them for sale, too.

Mangas (sleeves) are just that—sleeves that reach from the wrist to the elbow. They're knitted and worn by *campesinos* in the Jauja (Junín) and Huancavelica areas and are the perfect solution to the problem of keeping your lower arms warm when you're wearing a poncho. *Mangas* are made in a variety of bright colors, and some are made with acrylic yarn as well as wool. Indian men also wear handknit knee-high leggings.

Chullos are handknit hats with earflaps that are worn by Indian men and babies throughout the Sierra. In some communities, such as Auzangate (Cuzco), the men knit their own. The hats are made in a variety of colors and designs. You'll see *chullos* made from brightly-dyed (mostly red) sheep's wool and natural-colored alpaca, as well as tiny acrylic *chullos* for babies.

Puno is a major knitting center, and some very fine textiles make their way into the market from the surrounding area, including round or fish-shaped, natural-colored, alpaca coin purses (*killakos* in Aymara). Traditional crafts from the island of Taquili are also sold. Taquili knitting is done with very finely spun sheep's wool, most of which is dyed red or blue. For example, the traditional men's stocking cap has a red base with white designs and a white top and is entirely different from other hats worn in the area. Taquili knitting and weaving are unusually fine.

The knitted items mentioned above are examples of folk art—items made primarily for the Indians' own use rather than for sale. Both Puno and the nearby town of Juliaca have a number of knitted crafts which are made primarily for the tourist market. These include handknit alpaca gloves (*guantes*), vests (*chalecos*), sweaters (*chompas*), hats (*gorros*), scarves (*chalinas*), shawls (*chales*) and women's and children's ponchos, as well as fine knitwear made by a crafts cooperative run by Maryknoll nuns in Juli, near Puno. Brightly colored knitted and stuffed animals called *animalitos*, which are made in Chucuito, Ilave, Ccota and other neighboring towns, also are sold in the Puno market. They can be used as toys, Christmas tree ornaments or whatever you like. *Animalitos* were introduced into the area about ten years ago by the Peace Corps, and production was encouraged by Vivian Burns and Arden Arnautoff, who advised the Peace Corps on crafts development. These whimsical creatures proved to be a great success in the tourist market, and in another fifteen years someone undoubtedly will write about them as "typical folk art."

Fiber Content. When buying knitwear, remember that alpaca naturally comes in white and earth colors and is rarely dyed for knitted clothing. If you're offered a red, brown and white "alpaca" sweater, chances are the red yarn is acrylic. Look closely. If the yarn shines or glimmers in the sunlight, it's synthetic. You still may want to buy the sweater, but you should be aware that it's not one-hundred percent alpaca.

While you sometimes can buy high-quality knitted alpaca in Peru, Bolivian alpaca is generally better in quality although somewhat more expensive. One exception is gloves. It's difficult to find inexpensive knitted alpaca gloves in Bolivia, so buy them in Peru.

Fit. The Indian women who knit textiles don't use standard sizing or Vogue patterns. They make educated guesses as to size, and it's a hit or miss proposition. For the most part, clothing is well proportioned, but once in a while you'll find a sweater with a body designed for a midget and sleeves made for a pituitary giant, or vice versa. Naturally, this will be the sweater you bought in a rush without trying it on. So, no matter how good something looks, try it on before you buy it.

Craftsmanship. Besides fit, check for craftsmanship. The most common flaws in knitwear are slipped stitches and broken yarns, which eventually unravel, leaving gaping holes or detached sleeves. Since alpaca usually is brushed to bring out the nap and make it fuzzy, turn an alpaca garment inside out and check the inside and the seams. If there's a flaw or hole, point this out nicely. Often the vendor will fix it on the spot.

LEATHER

Some (but not many) leather goods are made in Peru, including fine purses and wallets. We purchased beautifully tooled purses, wallets and coin purses in the Huaráz (Ancash) jail.

ALPACA "FUR" ITEMS

The Indians make blankets, bedcovers (*colchas*), rugs and hats from alpaca hide, which is often mistakenly called "fur." A large *colcha* is soft and plush and makes a nice, if heavy, bedspread. Rugs usually are pieced together from several hides and commonly have a design in the middle. They're made expressly for the tourist trade and look as if they come from Woolworth's basement. These rugs are sold in the same places as other alpaca items, including the markets in Huancayo, Puno, Juliaca and Cuzco, as well as the tourist shops in Lima. Be forewarned that the hides used to make these items are often poorly tanned and therefore crack and fall apart after only a couple of years' wear.

CERAMICS

Peru has a venerable ceramic tradition—just take a look at Nazca, Mochica and Inca pottery. Although contemporary pottery can't compare in quality to Pre-Columbian ceramics, Peru still has a lively ceramic folk art industry centered around several cities. In addition to such simple utilitarian items as plates, pots (*ollas*) and bowls, which are made throughout the country, the ceramic pieces and associated craft centers I discuss here are especially interesting.

In Ayacucho and the nearby town of Quinua, you'll see miniature ceramic churches (*iglesias*), between one and two feet tall, cemented to the roofs of houses. These clay (*barro*) churches are believed to protect the house and its inhabitants from evil. They come from Quinua, where they're hand-modeled, fired and then rather crudely painted.

Retablos also are made in the Ayacucho area. The original *retablos* were introduced by the Spanish and basically were small portable altar pieces, similar to triptychs, that illustrated religious themes. The Peruvians adopted the concept and created their own *retablos*, which have both religious and secular themes. A *retablo* is composed of a wooden frame surrounding hand-sculpted and brightly painted ceramic figures. Besides nativity scenes (*pesebres*), there are miniature *tiendas* and *chicherías*, authentic to the last detail. Fortunately for folk art collectors,

retablo

small (about six inches high) ceramic *retablos* and *iglesias* are also made, making it possible to carry them home.

The above folk arts are not produced by anonymous artisans. There are recognized master craftsmen in each specialty, and one of them, a noted *retablo*-maker and ceramicist named Jesus Urbano, has opened a crafts school for children in Ayacucho.

In addition to ceramic churches, the artisans of Quinua make candlesticks *(candeleros)*, crucifixes *(crucifijos)*, small statues *(estatuas)* and *chicha* containers *(músicos* and *animales)*. The *chicha* containers have become quite well known. They're stylistically sculpted in the form of musicians and animals, with an opening cut into the top of the musician's hat or the animal's back, and range in height from about six to eighteen inches. It's fun collecting an entire band, from the drummer to the French horn player.

All Ayacucho and Quinua ceramics are fired in barrel-shaped, brick, wood-fired, updraft kilns *(hornos)*. Because of the problem and expense of obtaining wood in the relatively treeless Sierra, various kinds of kerosene-burning kilns are now coming into use.

If you ride the train from Puno to Cuzco, you'll have an opportunity to buy a famous and authentic piece of Peruvian folk art when the train stops at Pucará. On sale here are pottery bulls *(toros)*, which are actually made in the nearby town of Santiago de Pupuja. Some are made to be used as money banks while others are made to hold *chicha* or flowers. The bulls range in size from a few inches to over a foot and are either multicolored or solid black. They've been sold in Pucará for at least the past fifty years.

During Colonial times Pucará was an important pottery center where dishes, Spanish tiles and wine jugs were made. Roof tiles are still made in the area; the clay is kneaded for an entire day, placed in convex molds and then baked in kilns. Remains of huge old kilns are still standing in Pucará. These kilns were fueled by sheep or llama dung and have an interior that's twenty feet in diameter and fifteen feet high.

Pucará was also an important cattle center, and it was here that the fiesta for marking the herd took place, a ritual similar to ceremonies held today throughout Peru on April 25, the Feast Day of Saint Mark *(San Marcos)*, to give thanks for the fertility of the herd. The finest young bull of the herd was chosen for this ceremony. The bull's feet were tied together, cuts in the shape of a saddle and harness were made on its back, the skin covering its ribs was whitewashed, half moons were cut on its eyelids and cuts were made above its lips and on the fat at the front of its neck. The cuts were treated to stop the bleeding and then the bull was decorated with flowers and fruit. Finally, coca leaves were burned and the ceremony was followed by feasting, music and dancing.

Eventually the Pucará area was overgrazed and land pressures resulted in grazing lands being converted to farming, so that today cattle are no longer raised in the area. However, the traditional cattle-marking ceremony is commemorated in the pottery bull, which has the symbolic saddle and harness markings, cuts on the front of its neck and decorative flower pieces. (The flowers and some of the other ornaments are moldmade, coated with liquid clay slip and pressed onto the bull.)

While I didn't see any wedding cups for sale at the Pucará station, these traditional ceramics also are made in Santiago de Pupuja. Wedding cups are large, round containers, with molded ornaments representing members of the wedding party around the neck, that are used to hold *chicha* for the bride and groom at a wedding. The cups are fired and then the ornaments are painted. Wedding cups probably don't appear at the Pucará station because they're made for the local, not the tourist, market.

Pucará vendors also sell miniature churches, Che Guevara ashtrays and other pottery. They're experts at conducting business during the train's short stop, so if you're interested in their work, hop off and bargain with them.

Cuzco is the third major ceramics center in the Sierra. Several ceramicists work in both clay and gesso and make a variety of figures, including musicians and the ubiquitous religious statues. The gesso work of the Hilario Mendivil family in particular is very carefully modeled and painted and is far less rustic than the work done in Ayacucho, Quinua and Pucará.

In Cuzco and Ayacucho you're more likely to find higher-quality ceramics in folk art stores, rather than markets, since the better craftsmen have developed special outlets for their work.

CONOPAS

Under Inca rule, the highland Indians produced some of the finest stonework in history. The mortarless Inca stone walls are justifiably famous. The Indians also worked such hard stones as carnelian, lapis and crystals for jewelry and carved beautifully proportioned stone bowls and figures. Many of these items are on display in the archaeological museums in Cuzco and Lima.

Conopas (or *illas*) are small fetishes or amulets made of ceramic and date back to Inca times. They're still carved and used today by the Aymara and Quechua in Peru and Bolivia. A *conopa* usually is carved in the form of an animal and often has a small hole in its back to hold an offering. These small animal fetishes (which are also called *carneros*) are thought to bring good luck to a household and are often buried in the fields along with an offering to ensure *Pacha Mama*'s protection of the flocks. Some *conopas* are used to protect entire communities and are hidden among rocks or buried in a secret place. In some instances offerings are made to the *conopa* itself as a representative of the spirit of the animal.

The alpaca *conopa* pictured below was sold to me in Cuzco's Plaza de Armas by a woman from Sicuani. She had several *conopas* in her

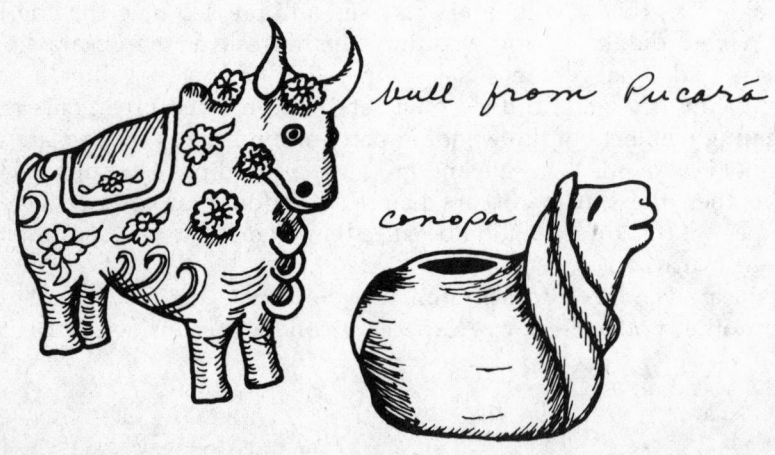

bull from Pucará

conopa

totora-reed boats

carrying cloth, along with all kinds of treasures and junk. Some of her
conopas were very dirty and obviously had been buried. My *conopa* is
virtually identical to Inca pieces on display in the *Museo Arquelógico* in
Cuzco, right down to the number of creases in its neck and the hole
in its back. It differs from the museum *conopas* in color (it's white rather
than black) and in size (it's slightly smaller).

Today, *conopas* are sold at medicine booths *(janpi catu)* in the markets.
In addition to single animals, pairs of animals (one male and one female)
are often carved from a single stone. These stone goats, sheep, llamas
and alpacas are believed to ensure the fertility of the flocks.

TOTORA-REED BOATS

When the Spanish arrived at Lake Titicaca, they found the Aymara and
Uru Indians navigating in small boats made from *totora* reeds, which
grow near the edge of the lake. They called the boats *caballitos de totora*
(little horses of *totora*). These boats are still used today for travel and
fishing and can be seen all around the lake, especially in the Puno area.
They're poled from a standing position in shallow water and from a
kneeling or sitting position in deeper water.

To make one of these boats, green *totora* reeds are cut from the lakeshore and stacked up to dry. When the reeds turn a golden color, they're
lashed together into four long bundles with *ichu,* a tough *altiplano* grass.
The bundles taper at the bow and stern. Some boats have sails made
from split *totora* reeds which have been lashed together. A boat lasts for
about six months, after which it becomes waterlogged and rots—it's
totally biodegradable.

Craftsmen all along the lakeshore make baskets, mats and miniature
boats from *totora* reeds and sell them to tourists in the Puno market.

An interesting—and totally separate—ethnic group called the Uru (or Uro) inhabit manmade, floating, *totora*-reed islands in Lake Titicaca, off the Puno shore. The Uru make excellent *totora*-reed boats and subsist mostly by fishing. They've inhabited the Lake Titicaca region from earliest recorded times and speak a language called Puquina, which is completely unrelated to Aymara or Quechua. Puquina is also spoken by the Chipaya (see page 346) of the Lake Poopó region of Bolivia, and the two groups have retained similar ancient cultural features. However, the Uru are nearly extinct since they've intermarried extensively with the neighboring Aymara, who've persecuted them over the years and despoiled them of their lakeside land. The Aymara use such derogatory nicknames for the Uru as "water-greens eaters" and "big-livered people."

CARVED GOURDS

Gourds are called *mates* or *calabazas* in Spanish and *poros* in Quechua. Gourds with incised designs dating from about 2000 B.C. were excavated in the coastal town of Huaca Prieta, so this tradition is about 4000 years old. Lima's *Museo Nacional de la Cultura Peruana* has a good collection of Pre-Columbian and contemporary carved gourds.

Today, there are two major centers for gourd-carving: Huanta (Ayacucho) and, even more important, the towns of Cochas Chico and Cochas Grande, outside Huancayo (Junín). The Sunday market at Huancayo is the best place to purchase carved gourds, and the especially fine pieces often carry the carver's signature. If you want to have a gourd signed, you can take your purchases to the carver in Cochas Chico or Cochas Grande. Just catch the Monday bus for the fifteen-minute ride to either town and ask to see the carver at any house with a *"Mates Burilados"* ("Carved Gourds") sign. Any carver should be able to identify your gourd by its style and then give you directions to the gourd-carver's home.

Gourds aren't grown in the Huanta or Huancayo areas but are trucked in from the departments of Lambayeque to the north and Ica to the south. There are two basic kinds of carved gourds. One is called *fondo negro* (black background) or *estilo antiguo* (old style). The design, usually a typical scene such as weaving, plowing, a fiesta or going to market, is carved or scratched on the gourd. (I watched an artisan who worked with a sharpened nail set in a block of wood, although most carvers have more sophisticated tools.) Then the background is carefully gouged out. The gourd is completely smeared with oil, sprinkled with powdered charcoal and washed with water. The oil and charcoal are washed off the surface, but remain trapped in the crevices, forming the black background. The gourd is then left in the sun to dry for five minutes.

The second kind of gourd is called *regular* and is basically the reverse of the *fondo negro:* the surface is colored and the background is left natural. The design is scratched onto the surface, which is then burned shades of brown and black by careful use of a eucalyptus brand. The color varies according to how heavily the surface of the gourd is scorched. Finally, the background is gouged out.

In traditional gourd-carving, only round gourds were used since these were most suitable for use as containers or bowls. In the late 1960s, however, the Peace Corps suggested that irregular gourds be carved into purely decorative pieces, such as birds and other animals. Today decorative gourds are dried but aren't cut open and hollowed out, while gourds intended to be used as containers (called *azucareros,* which means "sugar bowls") have removable tops with designs that cleverly conceal the separation. Innovations have been made in design, too. Some gourd-carvers are now traveling to areas outside Huancayo, including the *selva,* and are decorating their gourds with scenes of jungle foliage, monkeys and parrots. Photographs, magazines and calendars also provide inspiration.

Most gourds are still carved with traditional themes, however, and if you don't understand what's depicted, just ask, since some carved gourds tell complete stories. I saw one gourd that illustrated a visit made by the governor of the department to the area and another (carved by Leoncio Veli) which represented a healing session during which a guinea pig was placed on the sick person's body in the hope that the animal would absorb the evil spirit causing the illness. In this case, the person died anyway, and the poor man's funeral was carved into the story, too.

While you can buy carved gourds in Lima, they're naturally less expensive in Huancayo, Cochas Chico and Cochas Grande, where you also have the fun of meeting the carvers, getting the pieces signed and attending the Sunday market. Although you occasionally might spot a carved gourd in Colombia or Bolivia, Peru is really the center for this folk art—so be sure to buy them while you're in Peru.

carved gourds

Markets

As with Colombia and Ecuador, I've listed every market day I know. However, since Peru is the largest of the four countries under consideration and every town and decent-sized village has a market day, it's always best to inquire about a town's market when you arrive there. For a brief history of Inca markets, see the discussion at the beginning of this chapter.

MARKET DAYS IN PERU

Cajamarca (Cajamarca) ‖ every day

Bambamarca (Cajamarca) ‖ Sunday

San Marcos (Cajamarca) ‖ Sunday

Trujillo (La Libertad) ‖ every day

Carhuáz (Ancash) ‖ Sunday

Huaráz (Ancash) ‖ Sunday

Huánuco (Huánuco) ‖ Sunday

Lima (Lima) around Jiron Lima near the Rimac River ‖ every day

Huayucachi (Junín) ‖ Monday

Huancayo (Junín) ‖ Sunday

Perené (Junín) ‖ Saturday and Sunday

Chongos Bajo (Junín) ‖ Friday

Chupaca (Junín) ‖ Saturday

Pucará (Junín) ‖ Thursday

Ayacucho (Ayacucho) ‖ every day

Cuzco (Cuzco) ‖ every day, especially Saturday

Chinchero(s) (Cuzco) ‖ Sunday

Pisac (Cuzco) ‖ Sunday

Calca (Cuzco) ‖ Sunday

Juliaca (Puno) ‖ Sunday and Monday

Puno (Puno) ‖ every day, especially Saturday

Ilave (Puno) ‖ Sunday

Juli (Puno) ‖ Thursday

Tuesday and Friday markets are hardly ever held because Peruvians consider these days unlucky.

Bolivia

Native Cultures

There are about 1,520,000 Quechua in Bolivia, and they live in the departments of Chuquisaca, Cochabamba, Potosí, Oruro and the northern portion of La Paz. Some of these Indians are descendants of *mitimaes* brought in by the Incas and others are descendants of the original inhabitants, who adopted the Quechua tongue. Among Bolivia's Quechua there's tremendous diversity in dress, customs and dialect.

The Aymara make up the second major population group in Bolivia. They number about 900,000 and live in the department of La Paz, their original homeland, as well as in small enclaves in Potosí and Oruro. The Aymara and Quechua form distinct ethnic groups and do not intermarry with each other.

The Bolivian Indians still weave traditional clothing, especially in the more remote parts of the country. As in Peru, there's an increasing tendency for *cholos* (city- and town-dwellers) to wear factory-made clothing; in La Paz, it's considered a sign of status for a woman to be a *de vestido* (literally, "of the dress"), a person who wears commercially-made clothes. However, in the countryside nearly all clothing and household items are homespun and homemade, and traditional weaving customs are still observed in many areas. In some places, a boy weaves a belt for a girl before he proposes to her. If she consents to be married, she weaves a coca pouch for him in return. The Aymara also believe that an amulet in the shape of a human hand prevents fatigue and brings good luck in weaving.

Following are examples of the traditional costumes worn by the Aymara and Quechua. There are many regional variations in dress, especially among the Quechua.

CONTEMPORARY AYMARA WOMAN'S DRESS: LA PAZ

The dress described here is that of an Aymara woman who lives in the city of La Paz. She would probably call herself a *chola* and speak Spanish as well as Aymara. Most of her clothing is factory-made and is typical of Aymara women throughout the department of La Paz, as well as those in the Puno, Peru, region.

The woman's bowler or derby hat was adopted from the English in about 1900 and is either brown, gray or black. I simply can't recall seeing an Aymara woman without one. Her hair is worn in two braids which are tied together in back with a llama or alpaca tie called a *pocacha*, which sometimes has a little colored tuft (*mostacilla*) on each end. She also wears a cotton slip (*mancjancha*) and a blouse (*camisa*) that's factory-made, usually from cotton, although old country women still wear homemade, white *bayeta* blouses. Although the traditional costume includes a short bolero jacket (*chaquetilla*), cardigan sweaters (*chompas*) are now more common and are either homemade or factory-made and bought in the market. The *pollera* skirt is full and gathered and is closed with a tie (*trencilla* in Spanish; *tiznu* in Aymara). It's made of cotton, wool or (for fiestas) crushed velvet and is most commonly red, blue, green or wine-colored. A *pollera* invariably has three or four horizontal tucks *(p'aqui)* about a foot up from the hem, a detail derived from Spanish peasant costume. At fiestas some women may wear two or three *polleras,* one over the other, and I once saw a woman who was wearing thirteen. A *campesina* sometimes wears a handwoven belt *(wak'a)* made from sheep's wool; however, this is less common in La Paz.

Over her skirt and blouse, the woman wears a fringed shawl called a *pfullu.* These are generally brown but, like *polleras,* they're also made in other colors. Although *pfullus* used to be handwoven, today they're usually factory-made. For fiestas and other special occasions the woman wears a machine-embroidered shawl called a *rebozo* instead of her *pfullu.* Shawls used to be held shut with a shawl pin *(tupo),* but safety pins are more common today. Women still wear their beautiful silver *tupos* at fiestas. Most women also carry a square or rectangular carrying cloth called an *ahuayo* (which means "weaving"). The *ahuayo* is similar in function to the Peruvian *lliclla.* Aymara and Quechua *ahuayos* are quite different in appearance; the Aymara ones are typically woven with many narrow, multicolored stripes and have only a few narrow pattern bands with figures *(saltas).*

While *campesinas* wear tire-rubber sandals *(abarcas* in Spanish; *wiscus* in Aymara), the city-dwelling *chola* wears shoes *(zapatos)* and sometimes hose *(calcetas). Cholas* (and *cholos*) usually wear underpants.

Other traditional garments include the *delantal* (a factory-made cotton apron worn by market vendors), the *tari* and the *estalla*. While I've collected *taris* and *estallas*, I've never seen them used. A *tari* is a small piece of cloth, patterned like the *ahuayo*, that's used only to carry coca leaves. (All the ladies I observed carried their coca leaves in plastic bags in their *ahuayos*.) The *estalla* is a small square bag used to carry dry food. *Ahuayos*, *taris* and *estallas* are usually handwoven from sheep's wool on horizontal ground looms and, like Peruvian *llicllas*, are four selvedge.

CONTEMPORARY AYMARA MAN'S DRESS: LA PAZ

Like *cholas*, more and more Aymara *cholos* living in La Paz are wearing factory-made clothing, which usually includes a pair of baggy, shapeless, wool pants (*pantalón*), a suit jacket (*saco*), a European-style shirt (*camisa*) and sometimes a wool vest (*chaleco*). The same type of clothing is worn in the countryside, although it's more often made from homespun *bayeta*.

The only traditional garments still worn today are the handknit hat with earflaps (*gorro* in Spanish; *llucho* in Aymara), poncho, belt (*faja* in Spanish; *wak'a* in Aymara) and coca pouch (*chuspa*). Ponchos are usually made from handspun sheep's wool in simple striped patterns. While city-dwellers have taken to wearing European-style leather belts with buckles, *campesinos* still wear handwoven belts and coca pouches, many of which are true works of art.

Finally, an Indian man wears a European-style brown or black felt hat, often over his *chullo*. A country Indian wears tire-rubber sandals (*abarcas* or *wiscus*) while a city-dweller wears either sandals or ordinary shoes.

Small boys up to five years of age, as well as all babies, are dressed in a wrap skirt called a *pfandilla*. The Aymara believe trousers would keep a child's legs from growing.

CONTEMPORARY QUECHUA WOMAN'S DRESS: YAMPARÁEZ PROVINCE

The Indian women of Yamparáez (Chuquisaca) wear distinctive clothing that's completely handwoven, except for the hat (*montera*), which is made from white wool and is covered with sequins and braid. Occasionally you'll see a woman wearing a man's *montera*. A woman's hair is worn in two braids that are fastened in back with a tie (*tula*). She wears a long, black *bayeta* dress with sleeves, covered by a black wrap skirt (*ak'su*) with a *pallay* border. The border patterns are woven in the area's traditional colors of yellow, orange, red, wine, dark green and light green, plus white for the ground weave. A wool belt is tied over

the skirt; it's usually about an inch wide and also has *pallay* patterns. A woman also wears one or two carrying cloths *(llicllas* or *ahuayos)* over her shoulders—one serves as a shawl and the other is used to carry a baby, firewood, etc. *Llicllas* are usually red or wine in color and have *pallay* patterns woven in traditional colors at each border and down the middle. Generally, *llicllas* are tied over the shoulders, but at fiestas women pin them shut with beautiful, antique, silver *tupos*. Finally, a woman wears *ojotos*, the tire-rubber sandals. Country Indians don't wear underpants.

All clothing, except the *bayeta* used for the dress, is woven on oblique or semivertical frame looms. *Llicllas* are woven on semivertical looms in two separate pieces and are then joined together with an embroidery stitch. They're edged with a beautiful tubular band *(ahuaquipita* in Quechua; *tiznu* in Aymara; *ribete* in Spanish)*, which completely baffled me until Adele Cahlander explained how it was made. One end of the warp is attached to a stake in the ground and the other end is held in the weaver's hand; the weft is threaded on a needle. As the band is woven it's simultaneously stitched to the edge of the *lliclla*. The *ak'su* is often edged in this manner also.

CONTEMPORARY QUECHUA MAN'S DRESS: YAMPARÁEZ PROVINCE

The colorful and distinctive dress of Indian men from Yamparáez is a mixture of Pre-Columbian and Spanish Colonial costume. The black suede hat known as a *montera* was probably inspired by the Spanish conquistadors' helmets. The shirt *(almilla)* is made from black *bayeta* in a plain weave, while the midcalf-length pants *(calzón)* are made from white *bayeta*. The *bayeta* for the shirt and pants is woven by men on floor looms, but all other textiles are woven on semivertical frame looms, usually by women. A man also wears a brown leather belt *(chumbi* or *chumpi)* with eyelets *(ojalillos)* that's doubled over so that it can hold money, as well as a coca pouch *(chuspa)* and tire-rubber sandals.

A man wears two to four ponchos. The first is a small one known as a *kunca unku* (see the illustration), which is derived from the Pre-Columbian man's tunic. Over the *kunka unku* a full-sized poncho is worn. The traditional poncho is woven in stripes of yellow, orange, red, wine, dark green and light green, arranged in that order. All ponchos have fringe *(flecadura)* the same colors as the poncho. *Flecadura* is woven separately and then sewn onto the garment. Not content with two ponchos, a man wears another small one called a *wasa unku* or *siki unku*, which is folded into a triangle over the back of his belt so that it hangs down over his bottom. Occasionally a fourth poncho is worn. This one

is full-sized and is either striped or solid black and is worn over the first full-sized poncho.

The Quechua in this province call their looms *ahuanas*, as do many Peruvian Quechua, and they also make lovely, warp-faced, *pallay* pattern bands, especially on *kunca unkus* worn at fiestas. These *unkus* are made in the traditional colors noted earlier in addition to white. All ponchos are woven in two four-selvedge pieces that are sewn together with a decorative embroidery stitch. All these traditional textiles are warp-faced and reversible.

CHIPAYA INDIANS

The Chipaya are believed by some Bolivian anthropologists to be the last living descendants of the people who built the great Tiahuanaco civilization on the south shore of Lake Titicaca between 400 B.C. and 1000 A.D. Like the Uru, with whom they have much in common, the Chipaya speak Puquina, a language unrelated to either Aymara or Quechua. The remaining 300 to 400 Chipaya now inhabit the salt flats around Carangas in the department of Oruro, a very isolated area. They raise llamas and grow a few things, primarily *quínoa*. Chipaya music and folklore has been strongly influenced by the Aymara. Their religion is also similar to that of the Aymara, and they worship *Pacha Mama* and a number of spirits *(mallku)* along with various Christian saints.

Like most Indians, the Chipaya spin and weave their own clothes. The men wear finely striped brown and white tunics *(iras)* which are sewn up the sides as were Pre-Columbian *unkus*.

Folk Art and Handicrafts

Beautiful handicrafts and folk art are produced throughout Bolivia, and it can be exciting to track them down. Fortunately for those of you who have neither the time nor the inclination for three-day truck rides to the middle of nowhere, many items find their way into markets and stores in La Paz, Cochabamba and Sucre, as well as some of the smaller cities.

Visiting museums is a good way to become more familiar with local folk art and handicrafts, and museum personnel are always willing to answer questions and explain things to you. In La Paz, the *Museo de Arte Popular* houses a collection of folk art, including musical instruments and some contemporary Indian costumes. There's an entire room devoted to dance in which you'll find an interesting collection of Aymara dance masks, including the *Diablada* mask and costume. The museum is located in the *Casa de los Marqueses de Villaverde,* at Calle Ingavi 921, near Calle Genaro Sanjines.

About four blocks to the northwest of the *Museo* is the *Casa de Murillo,* a Colonial house located on Calle Jaen off Calle Indaburo. After its restoration in 1948, this house was turned into a museum of folklore and history. In addition to the galleries of Colonial furniture and painting, the first floor galleries are devoted to the folk art and folklore of the department of La Paz, including traditional textiles, musical instruments and folk medicine.

In Sucre, the *Museo Colonial, Museo Antropológico* and *Galería de Arte Moderno* are all located in the same building at 401 Bolívar, near the corner of Calle Dalence. The *Museo Antropológico* includes exhibits of local Indian costumes, folk art and looms.

TEXTILES

Dyeing. Dyeing is women's work throughout Bolivia. As in Peru, aniline dyes predominate, and no local market is complete without its dye stand, where aniline powders are sold by the pinch. A brightly-dyed sample skein hangs by each tin of dye.

In Bolivia, if animal fiber isn't washed before it's spun, it's washed before dyeing to cut the grease, either with fermented urine or with a soap made from the leaves of the *agave (cabuya)* cactus.

The same three natural dyes and mordants used in Peru are used in Bolivia. In addition, the Quechua living in the provinces of Saavedra and Muñecas (La Paz) use other natural dyes, including the leaves from the Peruvian pepper tree *(molle)* for yellow and for mixing with other dyes, achiote and *achira* for red and indigo *(añil)* for blue. They also use alum as a mordant. The Aymara of the Lake Titicaca region use indigo *(quesña),* too, along with a metallic-salt mordant called *millu.*

Dyeing is often co-operative work, with women helping each other in turn. This kind of mutual help is called *aini* and dates back to Inca times.

For a discussion of spinning and plying techniques, see page 321.

Looms and Weaving. In Bolivia weaving is done on a number of different looms. These looms are used by both men and women, and who weaves what varies from community to community.

The horizontal ground loom is used throughout the country, usually to make large items, including *ahuayos, llicllas* and ponchos, which are almost invariably woven in two pieces that are sewn together edge to edge. *Ak'sus* are usually made in two pieces also.

The backstrap loom is used throughout Bolivia to weave ponchos, *ahuayos,* storage bags *(costales)* and *ak'sus,* but most often it's used to weave narrower textiles, such as belts, *chuspas,* small storage bags *(talegas)* and braid.

The semivertical (or oblique) frame loom is used extensively, especially in the Cochabamba Valley and in the department of Chuquisaca, which are both Quechua-speaking areas. This loom is very similar to the horizontal ground loom except that instead of being staked out on the ground, the loom bars are lashed to two long poles. When the loom is used, it's propped against a roof, wall or ceiling beam at an angle of forty-five to sixty degrees. It's used to make textiles ranging from wide items, such as carrying cloths, to smaller, narrower pieces, such as *chuspas.* The semivertical frame loom is popular because it's more comfortable to use than the horizontal ground loom.

Although the above three looms are the ones most commonly used in the highlands, several other looms are used, too. One of these is a vertical frame loom without heddles that's found in Tarija, in southern Bolivia; it's used to make saddle blankets in a technique that combines knotting and warp-wrapping.

In Villa Rivero, Cochabamba, enormous vertical-frame tapestry looms are used to make rugs. These looms are similar to semivertical and horizontal ground looms but are much larger, so that when the weaver (who starts weaving at the bottom) reaches the top, he has to climb a small ladder to a wobbly scaffold where he sits to complete his weaving.

Throughout the *altiplano* small toe looms, often with four or six heddles, are used to make straps, hatbands and the *ribete (tiznu* or *ahuaquipita)* which edges ponchos, *ahuayos* and *ak'sus.* One end of the loom is held taut in the weaver's hand and the other end is hooked over a stake in the ground or the weaver's toe—a completely portable loom.

In the Oruro area, Quechua men weave on a lap loom which is made from two long pieces of wood with smaller crossbars. These looms are used to make belts in a technique similar to soumak, in which the wefts are wrapped around the warps. The weavers don't wear these belts; they give them to their wives or girlfriends.

Finally, in the province of Oropeza (Chuquisaca), Quechua women use a ʏ-shaped loom made from the branch of a large tree. The loom is usually about six feet long and is used only for weaving belts. The horizontal ground loom is used to make larger, wider textiles, and the semivertical frame loom is used for *costales.*

All of the preceding looms are varations on looms that were already in use in Bolivia when the Spanish arrived.

You'll find that an astonishing variety of weave structures are used in Bolivia—far more than in Peru. These weaves have been identified, analyzed and explained so that you can learn them by Marjorie Cason and Adele Cahlander, who combine a love of the Andean Indian cultures with extensive technical knowledge. Their book, *The Art of Bolivian Highland Weaving* (New York: Watson-Guptill, 1976), is a classic work. Also see the general introductions to Bolivian weaving by Adelson and Takami and by Wasserman and Hill listed in the bibliography. If you're interested in Bolivian textiles, the above works are musts.

PONCHOS

As in Peru, Indians are gradually abandoning brightly-colored patterned ponchos for plain dark ones. A poncho commonly seen throughout Bolivia, especially on the *altiplano* and in the Cochabamba Valley, is either red, wine, black or brown in color, with several multicolored stripes on each side.

BELTS

Although some belt motifs, colors and techniques are widespread on the *altiplano*, others are so localized that you can immediately identify a person's village from the belt he or she wears. Belts (*fajas* in Spanish; *chumpis* in Quechua; *wak'as* in Aymara) are always warp-faced and reversible.

A typical woman's belt from the province of Saavedra (La Paz) is three inches wide and almost a yard long, in one-weft double cloth. The colors (white, red, wine and green) and the motifs, including a woman *Chuncho* dancer, birds, cat, dog and bull, are typical of this area. Alas, there's acrylic fiber as well as wool in the warp.

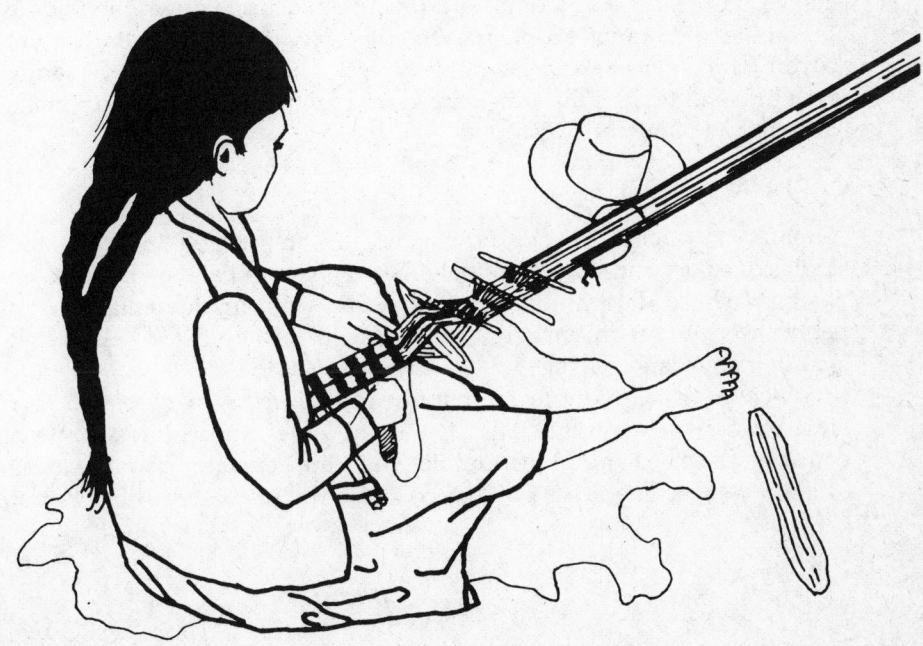

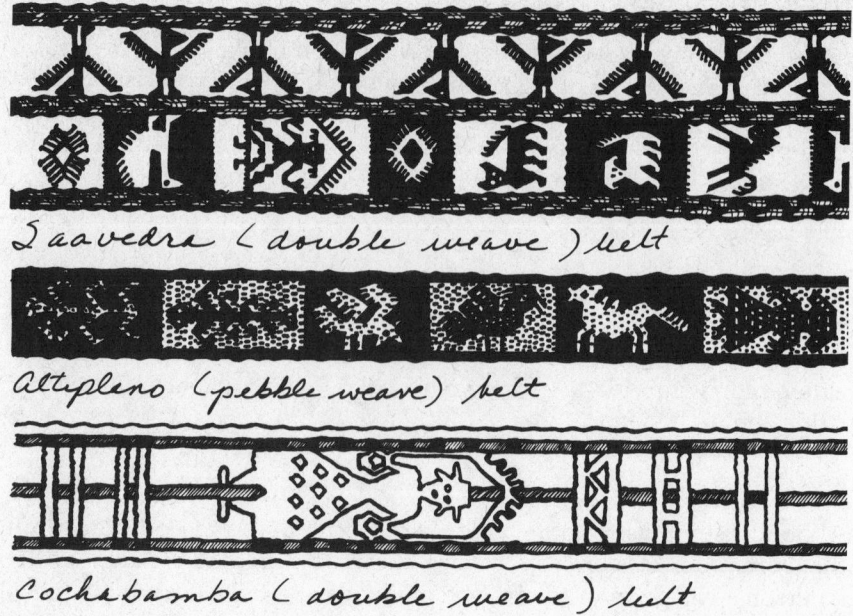

Saavedra (double weave) belt

altiplano (pebble weave) belt

Cochabamba (double weave) belt

Another type of belt is made of wool and comes from the *altiplano* south of La Paz. It's an inch wide and about twenty-eight inches long, with long narrow ties. It's done in colors of white, black, orange, green and pink.

A third belt is woven by Quechua women in the Cochabamba Valley. It's two inches wide and two yards long and is one-weft double cloth. The warp is yellow and white cotton, with a red stripe down the middle and a blue and orange stripe at each edge. Identical wool belts also are woven. The *Chuncho* dancer motif is typical. This type of belt frequently is cut into shorter lengths which are sewn together side-by-side to make satchels and shoulder bags.

CARRYING CLOTHS

Aymara carrying cloths *(ahuayos)* generally are striped in graduated shades of colors and have extremely narrow pattern bands with pick-up designs. These designs are usually woven in complementary-warp pebble weave. An intermesh weave structure is used for bands that include names and dates.

Quechua *ahuayos* (more commonly called *llicllas* or *quepin llicllas*, which means "carrying *llicllas*") usually have multicolored pattern bands on the sides and in the middle which are separated by large areas of plain weave. The most popular color for the plain area is black, but

I've seen *ahuayos* woven in every color of the rainbow. Many different weave structures are used for the pick-up bands, including one-weft double cloth, supplementary-warp weaves and several versions of complementary-warp weaves, including two- and three-color pebble weave, modified intermesh and more.

AK'SUS

Ak'sus, wrapped skirts worn in southern Bolivia, are made like *llicllas* and *ahuayos* but are longer and narrower in shape. As with other textiles, each particular village or region has its own style of *ak'su*. There's a wide variety of weaves, colors and motifs, but the plain-weave area is almost always black. Since an *ak'su* is worn over a *bayeta* dress, it needn't (and doesn't) wrap around the body completely. Often it's simply folded over the belt and is allowed to hang down in back like a decorative tail, but in cooler weather it's fastened up over one or both shoulders.

I bought a Quechua *ak'su* in Oropeza province (Chuquisaca) that has fantastic ornamental animals and imaginary beings along the bottom. The skirt is woven in a complementary-warp, uneven twill. Designs aren't planned ahead of time but evolve as the weaver goes along. The weaver may have several different animals taking shape across the piece, sometimes one inside another, but it all works out! The plain-weave areas of Oropeza *ak'sus* are brown or black, while the pick-up sections are usually pink or red combined with green, blue, black or brown. The delightful ornamental creatures also are woven into belts, *chuspas*, *ahuayos* and ponchos.

COCA POUCHES

Like belts, coca pouches (*chuspas*; also called *estallas* in the Cochabamba Valley) can help you identify a man's village. While a town or region

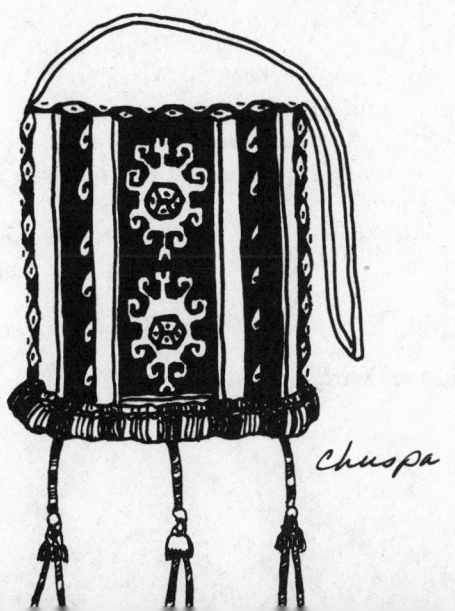

chuspa

has traditional colors, motifs and weaves, tremendous variety is found within this tradition. In fact, although I own a number of *chuspas* from the same village, no two are alike, and I've never seen two identical textiles anywhere in Bolivia.

A typical *chuspa* from Yamparáez province (Chuquisaca) is made primarily of red wool (the motif) and white cotton (the background) and has rainbow-colored tassels and bottom trim, which is typical of men's dress. The Yamparáez *chuspa* is about seven inches wide and six inches high and is often woven in a technique called modified intermesh. A common Yamparáez motif is horses, which are called Easter horses and symbolize the *khespicha* carousing that occurs on Good Friday (see Chapter Seventeen, "Fiestas, Music and Dance"). During Colonial times, Indians were forbidden to ride horseback, but several times a year (New Year's Day and possibly Good Friday) young Indian males rode horses in defiance of the law.

Another *chuspa* is smaller, about four inches by five inches, and comes from the *altiplano* south of La Paz. Its colors (yellow, pink, white and dark wine), size and the fact that it has no pocket are typical of this region.

Most *chuspas* have one or two tiny pockets or pouches *(sillus)* on the front. Since I'd read different explanations for the purpose of the pocket, I decided to ask the Indians what it's used for. Their answers included, "It's the *chuspa's wawa* (baby)," "It's the custom," "It's for money" and "It's for *lejia*."

The last two answers didn't make perfect sense since the tiny pocket isn't always sewn up the sides. No one gave one of the explanations I'd read, which was that the pocket was for the spirit of coca to ride in. It seems that the pocket is now simply *la costumbre* (the custom), although it was probably originally intended to hold *lejia*.

TAPESTRY RUGS AND BLANKETS

The small Cochabamba Valley town of Villa Rivero is the only tapestry-weaving area in Bolivia. Using vertical tapestry looms, artisans make beautiful rugs *(alfombras)* and blankets *(frazadas* or *cobijas)* from natural and dyed sheep's wool and natural-colored alpaca. These tapestries are sold in the Cochabamba market, so you needn't travel all the way to Villa Rivero to find them.

The artisans of Totora also weave wool blankets in bright colors and plaids, and these, too, are sold in the Cochabamba market.

UTILITARIAN TEXTILES

Many other fine textiles are woven, including large men's bags *(capachos)* and large and small storage sacks (*costales* and *talegas*) woven in natural-colored llama and alpaca. It's not uncommon to see pack trains in which *costales* loaded with thirty or forty pounds of potatoes are tied onto llamas with hand-braided llama or alpaca rope. These *costales* and rope are so finely woven that I always feel they should be in a museum rather than used for such mundane purposes. *Talegas* are used in markets and at herb stands, where they're filled with strange and astonishing things, from amulets to condor's claws.

When buying any of these traditional handwoven textiles, keep in mind the unbelievable amount of labor that went into them—from the shearing, spinning and dyeing to the weaving and finishing—and be sure to offer the artisans fair prices.

KNITWEAR

Bolivia is an excellent place to buy high-quality knitted clothing, including sweaters, vests, hats, ponchos, capes (*capas*) and shawls. These crafts combine indigenous motifs and skills with a commercial approach, as many of the items are made expressly for the tourist trade. Except for *chullos* and sweaters, most Indian clothing is woven, not knitted. Middle- and upper-class Bolivians wear some knitted clothing, especially *ruanas*, which are rectangular, poncho-like garments that are open down the front. One end hangs straight and the other end is thrown over the wearer's shoulder.

La Paz and Cochabamba are major knitting centers. Cochabamba is the site of the *Fotrama* cooperative, which was founded in 1960 by Father Gerard Ziegengeist, a Maryknoll priest from the United States. The cooperative operates a school and workshops in Cala Cala, a suburb of Cochabamba, where Indian women from the Cochabamba Valley can participate in a three-month course in cooking, reading, history, nutrition, knitting and floor-loom weaving. The co-op has ten teachers, who conduct all courses in Quechua, and a research division, which comes up with indigenous motifs for garments and rugs. After taking the course, Indian women work for the cooperative out of their homes, and *Fotrama* now has 600 weavers and knitters in the surrounding countryside.

The co-op also has its own alpaca ranch as well as a mechanized operation for washing, carding and spinning alpaca hair. The finished yarn is supplied to the co-op's weavers and knitters, and *Fotrama* keeps meticulous records of what's made and sold so that profits can be divided accordingly.

On the premises of the co-op itself there's a woodworking shop in which men make doors, wardrobes and collapsible chairs from cedar and mahogany, as well as a large weaving room where men and women weave ponchos, *ruanas* and pile-knotted rugs.

Fotrama has stores in La Paz, Cochabamba and Santa Cruz and is the only cooperative of its kind in Bolivia. The quality of both their weaving and knitting is superb.

Lots of fine knitted items for men, women and children can be found in markets in La Paz, Cochabamba and other cities. Most items are made from handspun alpaca, but some garments made from sheep's wool are available. Whenever you buy something in the market, be sure to try it on. As in Peru, occasionally you run across some very strangely proportioned clothes. Also be sure to check for slipped stitches and holes. If you have the time, you can have clothing custom-knit for you. It usually takes about a week or two. Agree on size, style, color and when you can pick it up; then leave a deposit and obtain a receipt. Bill and I were very satisfied with our custom-knit clothing.

HATS

Besides the hats already discussed, there are some other typical Bolivian hats.

The *ovejón* or *sombrero oveja* is made from felted white sheep's wool by Indians in Ucureña (Cochabamba). It's worn by both Indian men and women, especially in the Cochabamba Valley and in the department of Chuquisaca, which are Quechua-speaking regions.

The *chullo*, which was mentioned earlier, is worn throughout Bolivia (especially on the *altiplano*) by Quechua and Aymara men. The *chullo*

ovejón

phala chullo

chullo

wincha

chistera

cholara, c'nelara

pictured is made from sheep's wool in black, orange, pink, white and green and has plaited ties called *chacuña;* it comes from Yocalla (Potosí), a Quechua-speaking area. *Chullos* are also knit from natural-colored alpaca. In the province of Ingavi (La Paz), *chullos* are knitted with four needles in various colors of sheep's wool. One Ingavi *chullo* is called a *wiñay waynucho* (eternal youth) by Aymara young men; it's multicolored and has the year it was made knitted into the design. It's a matter of pride for a man to own this particular style of hat.

The *phala chullo* is handknit, usually from natural-colored alpaca or sheep's wool, and is made and worn by Quechua men in the province of Muñecas (La Paz). Some are dyed with aniline dyes.

A felted, white, wool hat with a stiff brim is made in Ancoraimes (La Paz) and is worn by the Quechua men and women of Muñecas (La Paz). The woman's hat is called a *cholara;* the man's a *c'nelara.*

You'll see a stiff white *chistera* (meaning "top hat") throughout the Cochabamba Valley. It's worn by *cholas* and represents a step up from the *ovejón*, which is only worn by country Indians. While *cholas* look down on *ovejones*, middle-class Bolivians make fun of *chisteras*, calling them such names as *tarros de yeso* (plaster jars).

Chisteras are made either from *paja* fiber or cotton thread. The *paja* hats come from three places: Peru, Ecuador and Santa Cruz, Bolivia. The thread hats are painstakingly worked with bobbins, and it takes a week of continuous labor to make one. Once the basic hat has been made it's soaked and shaped. The brim *(falda)* and crown *(capa)* are ironed and the hat is coated with *legua*, a mixture of cornstarch, ground chalk and glue. The hat is ironed, creased in the front and back of the crown, painted with a final coating of powdered chalk, zinc oxide, glue and bluing, and then ironed and brushed to a luster. Finally, a black ribbon *(toquilla)* is added. The hats are made in Cochabamba and surrounding towns, including Cliza, Tarata and Punata, and there are local variations in shape and shading, from yellowish to white. The shape of the ribbon varies from town to town and includes the *mariposa* (butterfly), *rosoncita* (little worm) and *botoncito* (little sprout). Women in the Punata area wear a black *bayeta* headcloth *(umpaño)* under the *chistera.*

The *wincha* (headband) is a direct carry-over from the Inca woman's headband and is worn by Quechua women in Bautista Saaverda province (La Paz). It's double-woven with pick-up patterns from fine cotton or handspun wool which has been dyed bright shades of yellow, blue, green and red, and is edged with European glass beads. Motifs include geometric designs, birds, horses and people. Acrylics are slowly reaching even the most remote areas, and I have one *wincha* that combines sheep's wool and acrylic fiber in the warp. Dyed alpaca is also used, and the colors include red, green and purple.

DOLLS

Although dolls (muñecas) are made in all the Andean countries, several of my favorites come from Bolivia, where dolls of various kinds pervade Indian life.

Bread-dough dolls are made and carried during Todos Santos (see Chapter Seventeen, "Fiestas, Music and Dance") and are placed on the table along with food, drink, sweets and offerings for the souls of the dead. There's an obvious connection between these dolls and the másapan dolls of Ecuador. In Yamparáez province, bread-dough dolls are called wawas y tuncas and in Santa Cruz, chapetones. Some of the very finest delicately-molded and painted dolls are made from bread crumbs (migas de pan) in Padilla (Chuquisaca). Dolls—or, more accurately, busts— called pasta lawas or lawa ttantas, made of wood, plaster or papier-mâché, are also used on Todos Santos by those who can afford to buy them.

On the altiplano, dolls are used in healing rituals. A straw doll is dressed in a sick person's clothes, taken outside and undressed; then the clothes are shaken out to "shake the illness away." For good measure, the doll is burned. In addition, the Callahuayas sell stone amulets (mullos or piedras de Charazani) in the shape of pregnant women for help in conceiving or for protection during delivery.

Dolls are also used in witchcraft. They're stuck with pins to bring harm to someone or sprinkled with menstrual blood as a love charm and are either left in the doorway or buried near the house of the person intended to receive the spell.

Among my favorite dolls are those dressed in typical costumes and those made for children. The Aymara word for "doll" is wawacchuqui, which means "baby to rock in the lap." Stuffed rag dolls (muñecas de trapo) are the most common, and in La Paz rag dolls are a prison craft. The chola ttejeta, or "chola sausage stuffed almost to bursting," is a rag doll, about a foot tall, that has horsehair braids and the complete costume of a La Paz chola, including the bowler hat.

Wooden dolls (muñecas de madera) are made in those regions with abundant wood, including Beni, Santa Cruz, Pando and Cochabamba. In the Cochabamba area, dolls are made from poplar, pine or willow and have movable arms. They're between five and ten inches tall and are popular toys among Indian children.

TARATA DOLL PURSES

The Cochabamba Valley town of Tarata specializes in knitted doll purses. In fact, as you come into town, you're beseiged by doll-sellers. The dolls are about a foot long and are handknit from brightly-dyed wool. A drawstring at the doll's collar allows you to use the doll for a purse. Although I thought these dolls were a recently developed tourist item, a friend has one that was given to her in the 1940s, so they've been made in the village for quite a while. They're knitted in the round (no side seams) with five needles.

MINIATURES

It's impossible to discuss Bolivian dolls without mentioning miniatures (*miniaturas*). The production of miniatures is a thriving Bolivian folk art because of the traditional *Alacitas* fairs (see Chapter Seventeen, "Fiestas, Music and Dance"). The basic concept is that any item you purchase in miniature at the fair will accrue to you in reality during that year. Fairs also provide an opportunity for people to simply display and collect these skillfully-made miniatures.

Miniature dolls include tiny versions of folk dancers, such as *Chatripullis* and *Kusillos*, as well as representatives of the various professions, including milkmaids, weavers, gardeners, fruit-sellers, bakers and so on. These dolls are made of dough or plaster of Paris and are brightly painted. They're made in and around La Paz.

Unique dolls called *muñecas de quissa* (dried-peach dolls) are made in Totora and Pojo for the Cochabamba and La Paz *Alacitas* fairs. These fringy, raggedy dolls are made from dried peach pulp and stand about eight inches high. Cloves are sometimes used for facial features.

Another common *Alacitas* doll known as *la negra* or *la marica* is a replica of an imported cupid which was sold at a La Paz *Alacitas* fair during the 1930s. The doll is made of plaster and is always painted black. It's dressed in a pleated paper skirt, a necklace and hat and is believed to bring good luck to its owner.

Besides dolls, *Alacitas* miniatures include tiny models of public buildings, such as legislative or governor's palaces, with perfect scale and exact detailing. There are also lots of tiny *totora*-reed and *ichu*-grass articles from Copacabana on Lake Titicaca, including baskets, flowers and *totora*-reed boats (*malacochaete-totoras*). The delicacy of the basketry work is amazing.

Also watch for *jueguitos de té*, which are miniature brass (*latón*) tea sets. They're made by jewelers or their apprentices in Umala (La Paz), Cochabamba, Sucre and Potosí.

COMBS

The Indian women of the Cochabamba Valley still comb their hair with handmade combs exactly like those used by their ancestors over a thousand years ago. The comb (*peine* in Spanish; *ñajcha* in Quechua) has teeth which are made from the wood of the *tocoro* tree. The teeth are lined up very close together and are lashed between two pieces of bamboo with cotton thread. This comb is also known as *el saca piojos*, "the lice-catcher," because its teeth are so close together that they catch lice in the hair. The *saca piojos* is sold in the Cochabamba market while its prototype is on display in that city's archaeology museum (see Chapter Fifteen, "Archaeology and Pre-Columbian Civilizations").

JEWELRY

In La Paz there are sidewalk jewelry stands run by Indian women who sell everything from old coins and jewelry to contemporary jewelry, cups *(keros)* and plates *(platos)*. Some of these items are silver—mostly the very old pieces—but nearly all of the new items have a high nickel content and very little silver, even though the ladies tell you they're *plata pura* (pure silver). Old Indian jewelry was made from silver coins, which were 900 parts silver, practically sterling. Most of the new street jewelry probably isn't even 100 parts silver. You simply have to develop a feel for silver unless you carry a metal-testing kit along, or buy silver in a reputable shop. Some nickel items sold on the street are rather nice and you might want to buy them anyway; just don't be misled into thinking they're silver. (See page 302 for further discussion on metal content and a listing of jewelry terminology.)

GUAYACÁN WOODCARVINGS

Guayacán is a tropical softwood that's commonly carved into bracelets, wine goblets, plates, salad bowls, cups, mugs and mortars and pestles. It's distinguished by its yellow or yellow-green color which shades into brown. It has a lovely grain and takes a good polish. The wood is used in Colombia, Ecuador and Peru as well as in Bolivia.

CHICHA TUBS

Enormous copper tubs for cooking *chicha* are sold in markets throughout the Cochabamba Valley. These homemade *peroles* are cast in clay molds

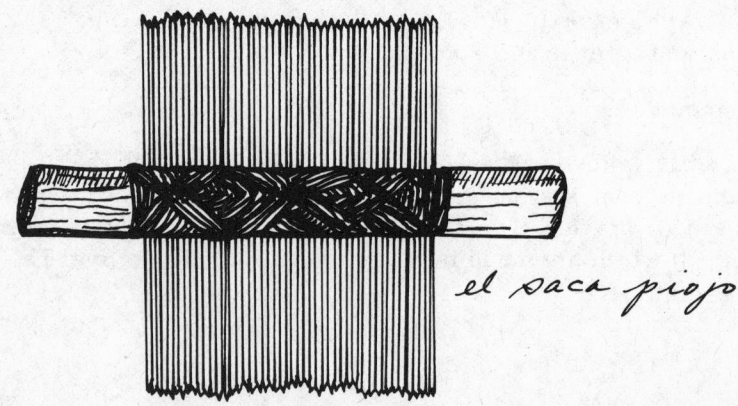

el saca piojo

in the ground. The copper is melted over an open fire, using bellows, and is poured into the mold. When the copper has cooled, *chicha* is sprinkled to *Pacha Mama*, the mold is broken and the tub is removed.

BASKETS

I've already mentioned miniature basketry. In almost every market you'll see large, one-handled market baskets *(cestas)* made of bamboo or cane. In addition to these, *Fotrama* sometimes carries baskets from other parts of Bolivia, including *yikas*, the bags made by the Mataco Indians of Bolivia's Chaco. *Yikas* are made from plant fiber by the knotless netting process and sometimes have designs created with natural dyes. Occasionally *Fotrama* sells tightly-netted carrying bags from the department of Santa Cruz. The fiber used to make these bags comes from the leaves of the wild pineapple and is dyed with aniline dyes.

WOODEN LOCKS

The Bolivian and Peruvian Quechua carve wooden locks *(cerraduras de madera)* for their houses. The tradition is quite old, possibly Pre-Columbian. When I visited the *Museo Histórico Regional del Cusco*, I saw an undated wooden lock, either Inca or Colonial, which was virtually identical to a lock I bought in Cochabamba.

The design is clever: inside the lock are movable wooden parts which can only be worked by a key carved especially to fit. When this key is inserted in the lock and lifted, the lock bar is released.

In the departments of Potosí and Chuquisaca the lock is carved in the shape of an armadillo shell *(quirquinchu)* and is called a *quirquinchu* or, in Chuquisaca, a *kaspi-llave*. This probably is related to the Aymara custom of hanging an armadillo shell in the house to scare away thieves; if a thief breaks in, it's said that he'll grow an armadillo's nose.

CERAMICS

Lots of pottery is made in the Cochabamba Valley and sold in the Cochabamba market. These glazed and unglazed ceramics consist of household items, such as cups, dishes, pots, candleholders, piggy banks, bulls, flower pots and miniature pots. Markets in outlying villages also carry enormous wide-mouthed pots *(virques)* used to ferment *chicha*.

If you're interested in folk pottery, there's an excellent book available which came to my attention just as this guide went to press. It's *South American Folk Pottery: Traditional Techniques from Peru, Bolivia, Chile, Ecuador, Venezuela, Colombia*, by Gertrude Litto (New York: Watson-Guptill, 1976). This beautifully written book includes many superb photographs and illustrations and is the most complete work published on this subject.

Markets

As you can see from the list of market days, you'll have plenty of opportunities to attend markets in Bolivia. In La Paz the Indian quarter is essentially one huge market; street after street is lined with vendors and kiosks. It's worthwhile spending a day roaming around all parts of this huge, continuous street fair.

CACERA RELATIONSHIP

You should know about *cacera* relationships because you might enter into one. Basically, it's a special relationship between a buyer and seller in Bolivian marketing that extends from the grower/producer through the middleman to the market vendor and the consumer. Each is someone's regular, preferred customer and, in turn, has regular preferred customers of his or her own. The preferred customer, or *cacera*, is sold the best produce at good prices. For example, if you're a *cacera* of the onion vendor, she'll set aside especially good onions for you and throw in a *yapa*, a little bit extra. When I walked through the market buying textiles, the ladies called, "*¡Cacerita, cacerita, compremi, compremi, pues!*" ("Little client, buy mine!"). I became the *cacera* of several women, whom I could always count on for high-quality weavings, and who would often tuck something special away for me to have first chance at buying. For the middleman and the market vendor, the *cacera* relationship is often based on credit; the merchandise isn't paid for until it's been sold to the next person down the line.

WITCHCRAFT MARKET

The La Paz witchcraft market (*mercado de hechicería* in Spanish; *laki'asina catu* in Aymara) is fascinating but requires some explanation. "Witchcraft" is a misleading word because to us it has negative connotations. The Aymara believe that the world is heavily populated with supernatural beings—some benevolent (*achachila*), some malevolent (*auka* or *supaya*) and some whose behavior depends on how they're treated. Offerings are made to all the spirits, from benevolent *Pacha Mama* to malevolent, cave-dwelling *supaya*. Each offering includes libations of *chicha*, alcohol or sweetened water; coca leaves; *lloq'e* (left-spun yarn) and a square block of llama fat covered with gold or silver leaf on which are placed little pairs of metal figurines. The llama-fat, figurines and coca leaves are burned. Also, no major offering to *Pacha Mama* is complete without a llama fetus. Since *Pacha Mama* presides over all first things, an offering *(challa)* is made to her when a new house is built or a new animal or truck is purchased. The Indians used to sacrifice living animals, but because they're poor and the animals are precious, they now use aborted fetuses instead. No Indian laborer will start work on a new skyscraper in La Paz until the *challa* has been performed and a llama fetus and other offerings have been buried under the cornerstone.

The Aymara also consult with diviners *(yatiri),* white magicians *(paqo),* black magicians *(laiqa),* herbal doctors *(qollasiri)* and the Callahuayas for a variety of purposes. Amulets *(conopas* or *illas)* (see page 336) are worn, carried in *chuspas* or buried in houses for protection.

The witchcraft market in La Paz carries llama fetuses and other ritual offerings as well as common remedies, such as chamomile for tea, which I always take for an upset stomach. It's a fascinating place to visit. Although other cities don't have separate witchcraft markets, there are witchcraft booths in local markets. In the Quechua-speaking department of Chuquisaca, there are stores *(qopa-boticas)* which sell folk medicine and witchcraft necessities.

"OLD THINGS MARKET"

Another fascinating part of any market is the *thantha catu,* which is Aymara for "old things market." (The Quechua also use this term.) Often it's an entire street lined with white sunshades *(quitasoles* in Spanish; *chiwiñas* in Aymara; *llantuchas* in Quechua).* The sunshades shelter booths piled high with second-hand things—from junk to antiques.

MARKET DAYS IN BOLIVIA

In Bolivia there are more terms for "market" than anywhere else. In Spanish the permanent market is called *el mercado;* in Quechua, *la cancha* (or in Chuquisaca department, *kkapach'eka);* in Aymara, *catu.* The weekly market where anyone may sell goods is called the *feria franca* or *feria,* while *tambo* refers to a small wholesale center in La Paz that specializes in produce from a certain area. Throughout Bolivia a *kiosko (chuisco* in Aymara*)* refers to a stand or booth.

The first day listed is the main market day.

Charazani (Villa General Perez) (La Paz) ‖ Sunday

Ayata (La Paz) ‖ Sunday

Mocomoco (La Paz) ‖ Sunday

Puerto Acosta (La Paz) ‖ Sunday

Sorata (La Paz) ‖ Sunday

Janko Amaya (La Paz) ‖ Thursday

Achacachi (La Paz) ‖ Sunday

La Paz (La Paz)
Mercado Artesanal (Artisans Market), off Plaza San Francisco ‖ every day

Mercado Negro (Black Market), calles Max Paredes and Graneros ‖ every day

Witchcraft and Herbal Cures Market, Calle Linares off Sagarnaga ‖ every day

Camacho Food Market, Avenida Camacho and Calle Bueno ‖ every day

Indian Street Market, Calle Buenos Aires and vicinity ‖ every day

Coroico (La Paz) ‖ Saturday and Sunday

Oruro (Oruro) ‖ Saturday and Wednesday

Huari (Oruro) ‖ Sunday

Potosí (Potosí) ‖ every day, especially Wednesday

Vitichi (Potosí) ‖ Sunday

Sucre (Chuquisaca ‖ every day, especially Sunday

Tarabuco (Chuquisaca) ‖ Sunday

Cochabamba (Cochabamba)
La Cancha, calles Sucre and 25 de Mayo ‖ every day

The streets around *La Cancha* south to Estación Cochabamba ‖ Saturday and Wednesday

Cliza (Cochabamba) ‖ Sunday

Tarata (Cochabamba) ‖ Thursday

Punata (Cochabamba) ‖ Tuesday

Quillacollo (Cochabamba) ‖ Sunday

Sacaba (Cochabamba) ‖ Sunday

Capinota (Cochabamba) ‖ Sunday

Vinto (Cochabamba) ‖ Tuesday and Friday

Coloni (Cochabamba) ‖ Sunday

Tiquipaya (Cochabamba) ‖ Friday

Totora (Cochabamba) ‖ Sunday

Cuente Lopez Mendoza (Cochabamba) ‖ Monday

Aiquile (Cochabamba) ‖ Sunday

Santa Cruz (Santa Cruz) ‖ every day

Fiestas, Music
and Dance

here's nothing like a good party and
South Americans really know how to throw them—on every scale. I'm
not talking about boring, official holidays like Washington's Birthday
or Veterans Day in the United States, but the occasions when South
Americans really celebrate—holidays equivalent to our New Year's
Eve, Fourth of July, Halloween, Thanksgiving and Christmas, as well
as birthdays, weddings and local events.

If you timed it right, you could spend your entire trip staggering from
one fiesta to the next. South Americans have so many holidays, and
they last so long (usually for at least three days), that the governments
in several countries have tried to curtail some of the celebrating on the
grounds that it seriously interferes with national productivity, such as
it is. One year Bolivia tried to limit the celebration of *Carnaval* to three
days, as hopeless a task as trying to get Americans to stay sober on New
Year's Eve. If giving up joyous fiestas is the price for increased productivity, I'm not sure it's worth it.

How to cash in on the good times? A Catholic calendar is an absolute
must, because many fiestas originally were Pre-Columbian celebrations which were incorporated into Catholic feast days, particularly
saints' days. Many of the saints' days are fixed, but other important
fiestas, such as *Carnaval* and *Corpus Cristi*, change from year to year.

363

Sometimes popular celebrations and saints' days are official national holidays, but not always. On national holidays almost everything in a country is closed, which is a pain in the neck for travelers, who are invariably looking for the bank or post office.

Fiestas throughout the Andes are traditionally celebrated with music, dancing, food and drink. If the fiesta is religious, there's usually a procession to or from the church and sometimes a mass (*misa*). Fairs (*ferias*) and international festivals are more commercial and often include large parades and exhibits.

Following the list of feast days and fiestas for each country is a discussion of the typical music and dance (*música y danza*) of that country, including the musical instruments, songs and dances you're most likely to encounter during your travels.

Colombia

FEAST DAYS AND FIESTAS

Colombia has a number of civic celebrations such as the film festival in Cartagena, the tennis festival in Barranquilla, the art festival in Cali and the orchid and textile festival in Medellín. Each town also celebrates the feast day of its patron saint, for whom the town is usually, but not always, named. Therefore, if you're in the vicinity of San Pedro on June 29, the Feast Day of Saints Peter and Paul, you can bet the people of San Pedro are going to tie on a good one and you may want to join them. In addition, the major Catholic holidays are celebrated all over the country.

The following list doesn't include all the official and unofficial holidays in Colombia since there's undoubtedly a fiesta somewhere every day of the year. Rather, it's a compilation of some of the more important fiestas which you may want to attend. Wherever you go, keep your ears open and ask other travelers, as well as residents, about local celebrations.

In this list, as well as those that follow, the name in parentheses following a town is the department or province in which the town is located.

January 1. *Año Nuevo*. New Year's Day.

January 5–6. *Día de los Negros* and *Día de los Blancos* (Days of Black and White). In Popayán and Pasto, people douse each other with water, grease and anything that's black on one day, and with water, flour and talc on the next. Locals either hide out or wear their oldest clothes.

January 6. *Día de los Reyes Magos* (The Epiphany). This fiesta commemorates the visit of the Three Kings (*Reyes Magos*) to the Christ Child. There are folk dances in Quibdó (Choco).

January, second week. Huge fair in Manizales, including *corridas* (bull-fights) and lots of dancing in the streets, bars, etc. Cafés are open all night.

February 2. Feast Day of the Virgin of *Candelaria* (Candlemas). On this feast day, candles and holy water are blessed for the year. In Cartagena there's a huge procession to the heights of La Popa, in which all the participants carry lighted candles.

February or March. *Carnaval* takes place the week before Lent and ends on Ash Wednesday, when people go to church to have ashes placed on their foreheads ("Dust thou art and to dust thou shalt return"). Lots of revelry, including water fights, street dancing, costumes and parties. The Caribbean and Pacific coasts are the places to go for *Carnaval* in Colombia. Barranquilla has a very famous *Carnaval*, and the Caribbean cities of Santa Marta and Cartagena also have especially good celebrations. On the Pacific, Buenaventura and Tumaco also have lively *Carnaval* festivities.

March. Film festival in Cartagena.

March. International Tennis Festival in Barranquilla.

March 19. Feast Day of Saint Joseph *(San José)*. Especially celebrated in the highlands.

March or April. *Semana Santa* (Holy Week) is the last week of Lent. It begins on Palm Sunday *(Domingo de Ramos)*, when palms are distributed in the churches, and ends on Easter Sunday *(Pascua)*. In Catholic countries, Holy Week is a serious event, with many religious processions. During this week, only religious movies are shown on television and in theaters. Thousands of people come to Popayán, which is famous for its Holy Week processions in which people carry statues of Christ, known as *El Maestro* (the patron of workers and guardian of the city), the fallen Christ and Our Lady of Sorrows. On Good Friday *(Viernes Santo)* there's an elaborate procession depicting the events of the crucifixion. In Silvia, the Guambiano Indians hold an impressive Holy Week procession.

April 4. Fiesta honoring Saint Isidore *(San Isidro)*. There's a procession in Río Frío (Magdalena) petitioning the saint to bring the rains.

May 1. Labor Day.

May, last week, and June, first week. International Orchid and Textile Festival, held in Medellín, the orchid capital of the world. There are *corridas*, art shows, street dances and concerts.

June. National Art Festival in Cali.

June 18–28. *Bambuco* (Colombia's national dance) festival in Neiva (Huila). Lots of music and folk dances as well as the coronation of the *bambuco* queen. This fiesta carries over to the feast days of Saint John and Saints Peter and Paul.

June 24. Feast Day of Saint John *(San Juan)*.

June 29. Feast Day of Saints Peter and Paul *(San Pedro* and *San Pablo)*. This fiesta and the Feast Day of Saint John are celebrated especially in the departments of Tolima and Huila.

June, last week. Ibague Festival. This festival, held in Ibague, is one of the largest annual folklore events in Colombia. Folk dances from all over the country are performed.

July. *Fiesta del Mar* (Sea Festival) in Santa Marta. All kinds of aquatic activities—regattas, water-skiing and such—as well as street dances.

July 16. Feast Day of the Virgin of Carmen. There are processions in Cartagena.

July 20. Colombia's Independence Day. The occasion for boring political speeches and military parades.

August 16. Feast Day of *San Roque*. Celebrated in Barranquilla.

August (date uncertain). Feast Day of Saint Anthony *(San Antonio)* in Guapi (Cauca) on the Pacific coast. Guapi is a community of blacks who have identified Saint Anthony with an African god. This fiesta is a good opportunity to hear *costeño* music (see "Music and Dance").

September 9. Feast Day of Saint Peter Claver *(San Pedro Claver)*, who lived in Cartagena and ministered to the black slaves in the seventeenth century. Processions are held in Cartagena.

October 4. Feast Day of Saint Francis of Assisi *(San Francisco de Asís)*. Major fiesta of the year in Quibdó (Choco). Celebrations start on September 26.

October 7. Feast Day of the Virgin of Chiquinquirá, the patroness of Colombia. Thousands of people make a pilgrimage to Chiquinquirá (Boyacá) for this festival.

November 1–2. *Todos Santos* (All Saints' Day) and *Día de los Muertos* (All Souls' Day). South American countries celebrate these two feast days with a weird mixture of Catholic and Pre-Columbian beliefs. The essence of the celebration is the belief that the dead return to earth on November 2, so people visit cemeteries with gifts of food and drink for the souls of the dead, and everyone parties all day. Sometimes altars with offerings are set up in individual homes.

November 11. Cartagena's Independence Day. The celebration in Cartagena includes street parties, parades, music and dancing.

December 8. *Fiesta de la Purísima Concepción* (Feast of the Immaculate Conception) and the beginning of the Christmas season in Colombia. People place candles in their windows, and blue-and-white (the colors of the Virgin) flags and banners are flown. In the Andes, *campesinos* light bonfires in honor of the Immaculate Conception. There's also a pilgrimage to the shrine of Our Lady of Chiquinquirá (Boyacá), as well as folk dancing in Condoto (Choco).

December 25. *Navidad* (Christmas) is celebrated through January 6, The Epiphany. There are parties *(novenas)* during the nine days preceding Christmas, and Christmas carols *(villancicos)* are sung at the *novenas*, on the streets and in churches. There are lots of fireworks, especially on Christmas Eve *(Nochebuena)*.

In the fourth century, the church established Christmas on December 25 in order to compete with the many pagan festivals celebrated at that time, including the Roman Saturnalia, the Scandinavian winter-solstice festivals, the Jewish Festival of Lights and the Mithraic Feast of the Invincible Sun. In South America, Christmas falls close to the summer solstice, a day on which many Pre-Columbian celebrations and harvest festivals are held.

As with most of Latin America, Christmas in Colombia is very much a religious celebration. Elaborate nativity scenes (called *pesebres, nacimientos* or *portales)* are common. The Christ Child *(el Niño de Diós)* is not placed in

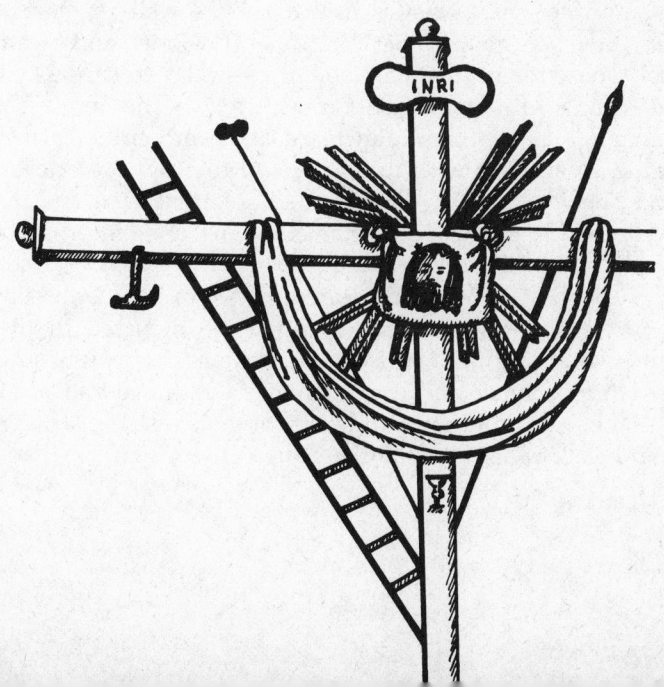

the manger until Christmas Eve. It's the Christ Child, not Santa Claus, who brings presents that night.

In Colombia there's an interesting Christmas custom called *aguinaldos gritados*, which usually takes place on Christmas Eve. Two friends agree on a meeting place and time, and then each round up a group of friends of similar height. Each group costumes itself identically, and any costume will do—it needn't have a Christmas theme. When the two groups meet, the leaders try to discover each other among the identically costumed friends. When one discovers the other, he shouts "¡Mis aguinaldos!" ("My presents!") and the losing leader has to hand over gifts or treat everyone to a party.

In the department of Cauca, in such cities as Popayán and Silvia, you'll find a Christmas custom called *chirimías*, the name of a group of Indian musicians who used to play a traditional flute by that name. The musicians now use a more modern reed flute and also play maracas, drums and triangles. They announce the presence of a masked-devil dancer, who collects coins from the audience, whips non-contributors with his tail and chases the children who come to watch. The exact origin of this custom is unknown, but it's probably Pre-Columbian.

December 28. *Fiesta de los Santos Inocentes* (Feast of the Holy Innocents). This fiesta commemorates the innocent children who were killed by the Romans in their attempt to slay the newborn King of the Jews. Folk dances and processions take place in Condoto and Quibdó (Choco).

MUSIC AND DANCE

The Pre-Columbian Indians of Colombia played a number of wind instruments, including simple reed flutes *(flautas)*, conch-shell horns *(futotos)* and ceramic whistles *(capadores)*, as well as maracas, rattles *(carracas)*, notched gourds *(guacharacas)* and wooden and ceramic drums *(bombos)*. These instruments are still in use today in various parts of the country, along with instruments introduced by the Spanish, including the guitar *(guitarra)*, mandolin *(bandola)*, tambourine *(pandereta)* and *dulzaina* (a small flute with four holes on the top side and two on the bottom). The *tiple*, which could be called Colombia's national instrument, is a twelve-string guitar with strings that are tuned in groups of threes. Brass bands are also very popular.

The *bambuco* is Colombia's national dance and is danced by couples holding white handkerchiefs. Although it originated in the Andean highlands, it shows a lot of Spanish influence. If you're interested in Colombian folk music and dance, there's an annual *bambuco* festival in Neiva that begins on June 18 and lasts for ten days. The *torbellino, pasillo, bunde* and *guabina* are also highland dances.

The *llanos,* or great plains of Colombia, are the equivalent of our Wild West—lots of cattle ranches and cowboys. Several dances are unique to the *llanos,* including the *corrido* (or *galerón*) and the *joropo,* a lively dance for couples. There's special music for the *joropo,* and when people hear it, they all get up and dance. Its rhythm is somewhat like that of a horse-back ride.

My favorite Colombian music is *costeño* (coastal) music, which has African rather than Spanish or Indian origins. It's related to Caribbean, reggae and Brazilian music and was brought to Colombia by black slaves. "*Costeño*" refers to music from both Colombia's Caribbean and Pacific coasts. Besides guitars and maracas, you'll hear single- and double-headed drums (*conunos* and *redoblantes*), xylophones with keys made from the wood of the *chonta* palm, bamboo flutes and long, tubular rattles filled with seeds (*guasás*).

In Cartagena we heard an impromptu *costeño* street concert consisting of men singing and playing guitars, maracas and drums. It was fantastic. You'll recognize *costeño* music by its strong, percussive rhythms and by the alternation of soloist and chorus, both of which are distinctly African.

Costeño dances include the *merengue, rumba, porro* and *cumbia.* The *cumbia* is danced by couples, with the man holding a candle, and you'll see it performed at *costeño* fiestas and parties.

You can buy recordings of *costeño* and other Colombian folk music while you're in Colombia. They make excellent mementos of your trip as well as good gifts for friends. One thing I regret about my last trip is that I didn't buy more records.

Ecuador

FEAST DAYS AND FIESTAS

Ecuador was once part of the Inca Empire and therefore celebrated traditional Inca feasts as well as many local, pre-Inca rituals. (For further background on Inca festivals, see page 406.) Many Pre-Columbian fiestas are still celebrated in Ecuador, especially in the Andes. While a fiesta may be enveloped in a thin veneer of Catholicism, this really doesn't fool anyone; the true meaning of the event is usually Pre-Columbian and often relates to agriculture and the cycle of the seasons.

The name "Ecuador" derives from the fact that this country is located at the equator, which circles the globe like a belt around the pregnant belly of Mother Earth. The Indians of the equatorial region were aware that the sun shines there for twelve hours every day of the year, with no variation in the length of the days and nights, unlike regions to the north and south. They believed they lived at the center of the world, as indeed they did. Sun-worship ceremonies are still held in the town of San Antonio de Lulumbamba (San Antonio de Pichincha on modern maps), which is located right on the equator.

The following list will acquaint you with some of the many fiestas and holidays celebrated in Ecuador. Indian fiestas usually last several days to a week, starting a day or two before the actual holiday and running a day or so past it, with non-stop drinking and dancing. The Indians' energy is prodigious. As with the list for Colombia, I haven't included all the official and unofficial holidays, but I've given you some idea of what's going on.

January 1. *Año Nuevo.* New Year's Day.

January 6. *Día de los Reyes Magos.* The Epiphany.

February 5. Feast Day of Our Lady of Holy Water in Baños (Tungurahua). Processions are held.

February or March. *Carnaval.* Festivities are held all over Ecuador, including parades, street dancing, water fights and masked balls. The Ambato Fruit Fair is also held during *Carnaval.*

March or April. *Semana Santa* (Holy Week). In Quito there's an enormous, spectacular Good Friday procession through the streets of the city, complete with flagellants and men dragging crosses, as well as what looks like the Ku Klux Klan in purple.

Sunday after Easter. *Quasimondo* or *Guasimondo* (Low Sunday). Celebrated in Salasaca with a dance that moves to Pelileo and back to Salasaca. The Indians tie bells (similar to the Inca *chanrara*) to their knees for this fiesta.

April. Fair Month in Riobamba.

May 1. Labor Day. There are interesting workers' parades in the major cities.

June 13. Feast Day of Saint Anthony *(San Antonio)* in San Antonio de Pichincha, which is located on the equator. The Indians hold a sun-worship dance that involves the symbolic capture and death of the chief as a sacrifice to the sun.

June 15. *Octavario Octava.* A fiesta in honor of *Santo Vintio* held in Salasaca. The Indians masquerade as deer, monkeys, bears and other animals.

Thursday in mid-June. *Corpus Cristi.* This fiesta is celebrated as a harvest

festival by the Andean Indians in Ecuador. In Pelileo the Salasaca Indians celebrate with costumes and dancing.

June 24. Feast Day of Saint John the Baptist *(San Juan Bautista)*. This fiesta falls just after the winter solstice, so all kinds of sun-worship festivities have been transferred to this day. It's one of Otavalo's major fiestas. Iluman (near Otavalo) has its own celebration, while the villages of San Rafael, Gonzales Suarez and San Pablo celebrate in Araque. There's also a celebration with music and dancing in San Antonio de Pichincha. Costumes imitating and satirizing whites are common at fiestas in the Otavalo area.

June 29. Feast Day of Saints Peter and Paul *(San Pedro* and *San Pablo)*. Fiestas related to harvest celebrations are held in many Andean towns.

July 25. Feast Day of Saint James *(Santiago)*. Celebrated in Gualaceo, near Cuenca.

August 8. Feast Day of the Virgin of Guapulo. Celebrated in Guapulo, a suburb of Quito.

August 19. Feast Day of *San Luis Obispo*. Elaborate celebrations, music and dancing in the town of San Rafael, near Otavalo.

September 8. Feast Day of the Virgin of Cisne *(La Virgen del Cisne)*. Processions and a fair are held in Loja.

September, first two weeks. *Fiesta del Yamor* in Otavalo. This is partly a thanksgiving festival for the harvest. Lots of music, dancing and pageantry, including a colorful procession re-enacting the arrival of the Inca.

September 24. *Fiesta de la Virgen de las Mercedes* (Feast Day of Our Lady of Mercy). Celebrated throughout the Sierra.

October 9–10. Guayaquil's Independence Day and *Día del Montuvio* (the name given to Ecuador's coastal people). Parades and the usual.

November 1–2. *Todos Santos* (All Saints' Day) and *Día de Difuntos* or *Día de los Muertos* (All Souls' Day). These two days honor the dead and are celebrated all over South America. The Indians bake little bread-dough figures of men and horses, offer them to the dead and then eat them. In Pre-Columbian Indian burials, food and drink were invariably included to feed the dead in the next life; so the modern *Día de Difuntos* festivities have a strong pre-Christian bias. Food, drink and wreaths are brought to the cemeteries and placed on graves.

November 3. *Día de Cuenca.* Music, dancing and celebrating in Cuenca.

November 21. Feast Day of the Virgin of El Quinche. Celebrated in El Quinche, in northern Ecuador.

End of November. *Fiesta de Capitanes* in Salasaca in honor of Saint Anthony *(San Antonio).*

December 1–6. Fair in Quito commemorating the founding of that city. There are bullfights throughout the fair. On December 4 there are street dances on Avenida Río Amazonas, and on December 5 there are street dances throughout the city.

December 24. *Nochebuena* (Christmas Eve). Costume pageants, caroling and midnight masses, especially in Quito and Guayaquil.

December 25. *Navidad* (Christmas). In Quito the holiday is celebrated through January 6, the Epiphany.

December 28. *Fiesta de los Santos Inocentes* (Feast of the Holy Innocents). Celebrated in Quito and Guayaquil.

December 31. New Year's Eve. The old year, in the form of a dummy of an old man, is symbolically burned at midnight. Other representations of the old year are also burned in the streets.

MUSIC AND DANCE

Whenever I attend fiestas I invariably want to know what's going on — what the musical instruments are, what kind of music is being played and

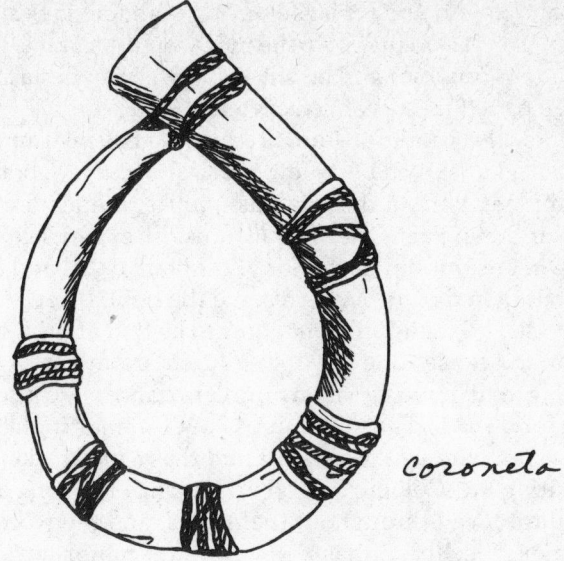

coroneta

what kind of dances are being performed (besides the general circle dance and staggering around the plaza). When you ask, you usually get a quick word in reply; but if you remember the word, you can look it up below.

Two kinds of music are usually played at fiestas in Ecuador: traditional, pre-Conquest Indian music and Spanish music. Anything that sounds wailing and somewhat eerie is Indian; this music is traditionally based on just five notes—a pentatonic scale. Music that sounds more familiar is generally Spanish-influenced.

You'll find that traditional instruments are still played at just about every Indian fiesta. These instruments include the panpipe *(rondador)*, gourd rattle *(chil chil)*, conch shell *(quipa)*, flute *(pinquillu)* and drum *(bombo)*. Instruments introduced by the Spanish include the guitar, violin *(violín)* and harp *(arpa criolla)*. After the Spanish introduced cattle into Ecuador, the Indians made a unique wind instrument from cow horns called a *coroneta*. Between sixteen and twenty horns are cleaned and joined, and then the joints are bound. The tone of the *coroneta* depends on the number of horns used.

The *rondador* dates back at least two thousand years. Its modern name comes from that of the night watchman in Colonial Ecuador who played the instrument on his rounds. A typical *rondador* is made of varying lengths and widths of bamboo tied together; the different lengths and diameters produce distinct tones. There are also many varieties. The five-fluted *rondador* is used during September equinox sun-worship ceremonies. The double *rondador* has a double row of pipes (between thirty and forty-four altogether) and is played during both religious and secular fiestas. The large *rondador* is probably the most common and is composed of six or eight flutes. You'll see and hear it at every Indian fiesta and dance, unless the brass bands take over completely.

In recent years, the beautiful Indian and Spanish instruments have often been replaced at fiestas by a new musical element—brass bands. No fiesta is complete without these bands—tubas, French horns, trumpets, clarinets and cymbals. The overall musical experience might be called "New Dimensions in Cacophony." About one band in fifteen sounds good, but then the musicians reserve the right to get drunk along with everyone else and their function seems to be that of providing some kind of rhythm and noise for everyone to lurch around to.

As for singing and dancing, many Indian dances are occasions to parody whites, and the Indians often dress in costumes imitating *blanco* dress. In two Indian dances, the *danzante* and the *guarande*, dancers wear masks representing Pre-Columbian gods. The *yaravi* is a song and dance that the Incas introduced throughout the Andes, and the words are still generally sung in Quechua. It has that beautiful, minor-key, haunting quality, which is difficult to describe but unforgettable once you've heard it. Other Indian songs and dances include the *abago*, *yumbo* and *sanjuanito*, which is Ecuador's national song.

Another musical tradition combines both Indian and Spanish elements into what is called *música criolla* (creole music). This includes the music for the *chileno*, *pasacalle* and *pasillo* folk dances. *Costeño* music, played by blacks, is also popular. Ecuadorian blacks are the descendants of slaves, and large communities of blacks are located on the Pacific coast and in the Chota Valley near the Colombian border. (For a more detailed discussion of the *costeño* tradition, see "Music and Dance" for Colombia.)

The best way to learn about all these songs and dances is to ask what is being performed. People are usually delighted to explain things to you and may even offer to teach you the dances.

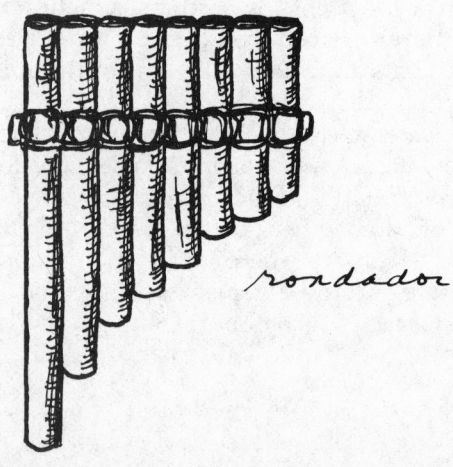

rondador

Peru

FEAST DAYS AND FIESTAS

There are a tremendous number of fiestas celebrated in Peru, especially in the Andean highlands, where seventy to eighty percent of the population is Indian. Not only is Peru the fourth largest country in South America, it's the heartland of the old Inca Empire, so many Pre-Columbian festivals are celebrated there, usually with Christian overtones.

Between Sundays and feast days, fully a third of the year is devoted to religious observances. It's estimated that the Pre-Columbian Indian population was ten times more productive than the Indians are today. Nevertheless, the practice of celebrating Christian feasts was a way to educate the Indians in Catholic doctrine, since every major event in the life of Christ and the feast days of the Apostles and major saints are celebrated.

What should you expect at a fiesta? First, although the actual saint's day or fiesta falls on a particular date, the celebrating invariably starts at least the day before *(la víspera)*. There are traits ubiquitous to every fiesta: some kind of procession to and from the church, a mass if there's a priest in the vicinity, music and dancing, fireworks *(voladores)* and lots of drinking and eating, sometimes with special food for the occasion. Much depends on the size of the town and the importance of the fiesta. Often there are brass bands, costumed dance groups *(comparsas)* and vendors selling coca leaves, food, drinks and handicrafts in the plaza.

You also can expect ritual drunkenness—literally. In the Inca Empire it was considered a religious act to become intoxicated, and at a certain point in the ceremonies everyone drank *chicha* until he or she dropped. Today the Indians follow this same pattern. Except for fiestas, I can't remember ever seeing a drunk Indian, although judging from the fiestas alone you'd think the entire population had an acute alcoholism problem. (There's some debate on this issue.)

Occasionally a fiesta is held on a market day or in conjunction with a large fair. In southern Peru there are huge fairs starting with the Feast Day of the Virgin of Carmen on July 16 and ending with the Feast of the Exultation of the Cross on September 14. This is the dry season, a time when transportation is good and the crops are ready for marketing, and thousands of Indians attend these fairs. They come from all parts of Peru and the Lake Titicaca region of Bolivia. It's like Easter and the Minnesota State Fair combined.

The Indians' involvement with the church is a lot looser than most Americans and Europeans are used to. For example, one day you discover that the raucous sounds of a brass band are coming from a church. The band leads a procession of drunks, followed by the *padre*, to a new

Toyota jeep that's decorated with flowers and streamers. After a few bottles of beer are broken over the jeep, the *padre* anoints the vehicle with holy water. This is the *challa*, the blessing of the truck. A *challa* is performed at the purchase of any new vehicle or animal and at the dedication of a new house, and is actually a ritual offering of liquor to *Pacha Mama*.

When there's no *padre* in the area, which is true for much of the Andes, the Indians do their own thing in church. While partying in a Catholic church seems strange to *gringos*, you have to understand that the Indians make less of a distinction than we do between the secular and the holy. Many things are holy to the Indians: the church, the saints, the *huaca* near the river, the mountain peaks, the earth itself. Their sense of the sacred is also more joyful. There's none of the feeling that in order to be religious you must be somber, serious and grim. (Praise the Lord and pass the *chicha*.)

The *minga* (also spelled *minka*) is a Quechua custom. It's basically a community work party that's organized to help build or roof a house or, less frequently, to bring in crops. The host, or person who receives the help, is obliged to provide *chicha* and food for his guest helpers. In Peru and Bolivia, the host also provides coca leaves. While no one is obliged to participate, members of the community invariably pitch in, both for the fun of it and because they may need a *minga* themselves one day.

In the Andean countries, as elsewhere in Latin America, fiestas are usually sponsored by an individual *(el mayordomo)* or a group. This sponsorship is called a *cargo* (burden), and the system was introduced by the Spanish. Sponsorship of a fiesta brings great prestige to a person and in many places is linked with holding local political office. A person can go deeply into debt sponsoring some of the larger fiestas (paying musicians, supplying decorations, fireworks, food, drink and coca leaves, etc.). In some Indian communities a person isn't considered a full adult member until he has married and has sponsored at least one fiesta. A *pasado* is a person who's filled all the obligations of the fiesta system, and he holds a position of status and respect.

In addition to public fiestas, there are the usual private parties, such as weddings, birthdays and baptisms. The Quechua and Aymara Indians also celebrate such occasions as a child's first haircut.

The following list includes just a sampling of the astonishing number of fiestas celebrated in Peru, especially in the Sierra. Just because one or two towns are listed for each fiesta doesn't mean there aren't festivities elsewhere; the celebrations noted here are simply the ones I happen to be familiar with. I've discussed the importance of a fiesta, its meaning and its relation to Pre-Columbian observances whenever possible. For more specific information on the traditional music and dance that are a part of these celebrations, see the "Music and Dance" section that follows the list of fiestas.

Note: The Catholic church has confused matters for the Indians as well as the rest of us by recently removing about forty saints from the calendar—saints who did not historically exist, such as Saint Christopher *(San Cristóbal),* the patron saint of travelers. The latest liturgical calendars no longer include a feast day for Saint Christopher, although, as you can imagine, the people of San Cristóbal still have a party in his honor every year on his (former) feast day. If you find a fiesta listed here but can't find the saint on your Catholic calendar, he or she may have been removed in the purge. This doesn't matter in the least to the people celebrating the fiesta; they're probably partying in honor of some long-forgotten Pre-Columbian deity anyway. Furthermore, many Indians probably don't know *why* they're celebrating; a fiesta on a certain day is simply *la costumbre* (the custom). These fiestas undoubtedly will continue as long as there's life on the planet.

January 1. *Año Nuevo.* New Year's Day is traditionally the time when Indian community leaders *(varayoks)* turn over their staffs of office (silver and wooden *varas*) to incoming officials during a ceremony and blessing of the *varas* in the local church.

January 1–6. *Fiesta del Año Nuevo.* New Year's Fiesta in Andahuaylas (Apurimac).

January 6. *Día de los Reyes Magos.* The Epiphany is celebrated in many towns, including Cuzco, Puno and Sicuani (Cuzco).

February 2. Feast Day of the Virgin of *Candelaria.* Candlemas is celebrated in churches throughout the highlands, including Ayacucho, Puno, Cuzco and Arequipa. There's a chapel for the Virgin of Candelaria in Canincunca (Cuzco).

February 24. Feast Day of Saint Matthew *(San Mateo),* Apostle and Evangelist.

February or March. The fiesta of *Cóndor Rachi* or *Arranque del Cóndor* in Cashapampa in the Callejón de Huaylas (Ancash). The highlight of this fiesta is the rather gruesome tearing apart of a captured condor. A live condor is hung upside-down and is charged by horsemen who strike it with their fists until it dies. One horseman finally grabs the bird by the throat and bites out its tongue. The origin of this event is uncertain although the condor was considered sacred by the Incas, who believed it to be a messenger of the gods because it appeared to fly so close to the sun. To the Spanish, the killing of a condor symbolized the killing of the Indians' gods.

February or March. *Carnaval,* the week-long fling before the beginning of Lent, is always one of the biggies. It's celebrated in all the Andean communities. The *Carnaval* in Abancay (Apurimac) is one of the more famous Peruvian folklore events. Other *Carnaval* celebrations are held in Cuzco, Callejón de Huaylas (Ancash), Andahuaylas (Apurimac) and Puno. Once again, water fights are common during *Carnaval,* so be wary. The Quechua word for *Carnaval* is *Pukllay taki* (Let's play).

March 8. Feast Day of *San Juan de Dios,* the patron saint of hospitals. In Puno on the afternoon of March 7, llamas loaded with firewood are marched through the streets while music is played. In the evening, there's a bonfire in the plaza and *Suri Sikuri* dancers perform. During the afternoon of the feast day itself the statue of San Juan de Dios is paraded through the streets and there's more *Suri Sikuri* dancing.

March or April. *Semana Santa* (Holy Week) is celebrated everywhere. Ayacucho has a famous celebration with processions on Monday, Wednesday and Friday in which the townspeople dress in black.

In Cuzco there's a famous procession on the Monday of Holy Week. In 1650 a statue of Christ called *El Señor de los Temblores* (Lord of the Earthquakes) was carried in a procession by the people of Cuzco, imploring Christ to end the earthquakes which had been devastating the city. Nowadays the statue is carried in a procession around the city. When it's returned to the cathedral the sign of the cross is made with the statue to the four directions. The Indians prostrate themselves (believing that at that moment Christ chooses those who are to die that year) and ask to be spared. You may want to participate in this ritual, particularly if you have any long bus rides ahead of you.

On Good Friday there's a procession in Puno, mourning the death of Christ. Early in the day there's a small fair on El Calvario Chico hill, near Puno, where miniature items are sold. The idea is that whatever is purchased in miniature on Good Friday will accrue to the buyer in real life during that year. This fair is similar to the *Alacitas* fairs in Bolivia (see page 289). Another Good Friday activity is to hang effigies of Judas (or obnoxious officials) in the streets.

In many places in Peru and Bolivia, Good Friday is a time of complete indulgence. Anything goes, including robbery and wife- and daughter-stealing. The belief behind this is that since Christ (God) is dead and won't be resurrected until Easter Sunday, He won't know about or be offended by anything that happens.

Sunday after Easter. *Quasimondo* (Low Sunday). There are many processions throughout Peru in which priests carry the Sacred Host, including a big procession in Ayachucho. In Huancayo (Junín), the Sunday market is a *Quasimondo* fair.

April 25. Feast Day of Saint Mark *(San Marcos)*, Apostle and Evangelist. This is a time when livestock are either branded or cut on the ear and body. The ears of female llamas are decorated with colored wool. Offerings are made to *Pacha Mama* in thanks for the fertility of the herd.

April 27. Feast Day of *Santo Toribio* in La Villa de Macate, located in the Callejón de Huaylas (Ancash). Santo Toribio de Mogrovejo was the Bishop of Peru and a champion of the Indians; he died in Zana, Peru, in 1606. According to the legend, Santo Toribio passed through La Villa de Macate when its spring had gone dry. When he struck the rocks near the spring with his staff three times, water began to flow. This miracle is re-enacted during a procession from the church to the spring.

May, first week. *Alacitas* fair in Puno. (For a description of Bolivian *Alacitas* festivals, see page 289.)

May 3. *Día de la Santa Cruz* (Day of the Holy Cross). In the Andes people paint and decorate the wooden crosses along the roads and near local churches. Household crosses are cleaned and taken to the church to be blessed. There's a fiesta in Puerto de Etén (Lambayeque) in honor of the cross. This fiesta comes at the beginning of the harvest, and people celebrate by erecting trees filled with fruit and gifts, which they dance around. The *aymorai* (also the Quechua name for the month) is sung by the harvesters, followed by the *haylli*, or *haycha*, a harvest song.

May 11–13. Fiesta in Cochas Chico (Junín) with music and dancing.

May 13. Feast Day of the Virgin of Fátima. Celebrated in Grau (Apurimac).

May 15. Feast Day of Saint Isidore *(San Isidro)*, the patron saint of agriculture. In Moche (La Libertad), the first two weeks of May are devoted to his feast. Each night the church's statue of San Isidro is taken to one of the *chacras* (fields) outside town, where it's left overnight to bless the field. An overnight vigil *(velada)* is held at each field, and an arbor is prepared for the statue, along with offerings of food. On May 14 the statue is returned to the church and there's a procession as well as music and dancing.

Thursday in mid-June. *Corpus Cristi*. This fiesta is celebrated all over the Sierra. In the Cuzco area the outlying towns of San Gerónimo and San Sebastián prepare the statues of their patron saints the day before and carry them to Cuzco in a procession. The saints are blessed and then carried into the cathedral for the night. On Thursday there's a High Mass, followed by a procession around the Plaza de Armas. This celebration dates back to 1571. Such traditional foods as *chiriuchu* and baked *achira* (see Chapter Twelve, "Food") are prepared and sold in Cuzco that day.

June 24. Feast Day of Saint John the Baptist *(San Juan Bautista)*. This saint's day falls around the winter solstice, the time of the ancient Inca Festival of the Sun *(Inti Raymi)*. The dual celebration of Christian and Inca festivals makes June 24 an important fiesta throughout the Andes.

Because Saint John baptized Christ, all waters are considered safe on his feast day and people bathe in streams and play with water. (If you're on the road, cover your belongings with plastic!) Furthermore, since Saint John is the patron saint of cattle- and sheep-breeders, cattle are branded on this day.

On the eve of this fiesta, Indians in Puno tell fortunes by dropping molten lead into cold water. The form the lead takes as it hardens is a clue to the future. On this same night, bonfires are lit all across the Andes, symbolizing the rebirth of the sun. It's a stunning sight.

In Cuzco the week before June 24 is devoted to the celebration of *Inti Raymi*. This has become a major tourist attraction, so if you plan to be in Cuzco that week make all transportation and hotel reservations well in advance. Folk groups from all over the Cuzco area perform during the week. On the feast day itself a procession and symbolic sacrifice to the sun are held at the fortress of Sacsayhuaman outside the city. This event is truly spectacular; it's as if Cecil B. De Mille were recreating the past glory of the Inca Empire, complete with rather tacky costumes.

Inti Raymi is celebrated with music, dancing and pageantry in many other towns in the Sierra besides Cuzco, including Antabamba (Apurimac) and Rajchi (Cuzco). Indians in the Andahuaylas and Apurimac valleys burn their old clothes on Saint John's Day in the belief that they're destroying poverty along with their clothes, as well as symbolizing the end of the harvest cycle.

June 24 is also the Day of the Indian *(Día del Indio)* and is celebrated in Lima with Indian dancing.

June 29. Feast Day of Saint Peter *(San Pedro)*, the patron saint of fishermen, and Saint Paul *(San Pablo)*. This feast day is celebrated in many places in the Sierra, but especially in the towns of Ollantayambo, San Pedro and San Pablo (Cuzco). At Chorillos (Lima), a fishing town, there's a procession of boats in the port, including a statue of Saint Peter carrying silver keys and silver fish. Saint Peter is also the patron saint of the Aymara town of Ichu (Puno), and a large fiesta is held in that town also.

July 6–8. Fiesta in the Callejón de Huaylas (Ancash) in honor of Saint Elizabeth. The July 6 celebrations have nothing to do with the saint but consist of the re-enactment of a naval battle fought against Chile in the War of the Pacific (1879–83).

July 16. Feast Day of the Virgin of Carmen. The Virgin of Carmen is the patroness of many towns and churches, and processions are held in her honor in these places. Her feast day falls in the Quechua month of *Anta Situa* (Earthly Purification), and on July 16 Pre-Columbian rites are held in the fields to cleanse the earth of impurities. This day also marks the beginning of the great fairs held in the Sierra in southern Peru.

An especially large fiesta takes place in Paucartambo (Cuzco), a town built on the site of an Inca *tambo* (roadhouse). The fiesta runs from July 15 through 17. On July 15 the statue of the Virgin is dressed and the church is decorated. There's a procession to the church, as well as music and dancing, and Indian dance groups come into town from the surrounding countryside. (For more on these costumes and dances, see the "Music and Dance" section that follows.) The party continues for the next two days, with lots more music, dancing, drinking and carrying on. The Paucartambo fiesta commemorates a Colonial uprising by the Chunchos, a tribe of jungle Indians who killed the people of that town and stole their statue of the Virgin (which still has the scar from an arrow in one eye). When the Spanish put down the rebellion, they found the statue on an island in the *Amaru Mayo* (river), which they renamed the *Río Madre de Dios*, after the Mother of God.

On July 16 there's also a fiesta and market in Pucara (Puno). Indians come from all over the Lake Titicaca area, including northern Bolivia. One of the highlights of this event is the racing and sale of horses from Chumbivilcas.

July 24. Fiesta in Huaráz (Ancash).

July 25. Feast Day of Saint James *(Santiago)*. Saint James is the patron saint of Spain, and the Spanish colonists carried his statue everywhere. He is always shown mounted on a horse and brandishing a sword. The Indians immediately saw Saint James as *Illapa*, the god of thunder and lightning, about to hurl a thunderbolt. Even today, lightning is worshipped by the Indians. Llamas are sacrificed in spots that have been struck by lightning, and any person who has been struck by lightning and lived is endowed with special powers and can become a *brujo*. The many fiestas in honor of Saint James are most certainly not because of his status as the Spanish patron saint, but because of his identification with *Illapa*. Numerous towns in the Sierra celebrate this fiesta, including Lampa (Puno). There's also a large fair and fiesta in Santiago de Pupuja (Puno).

In many places cattle and llamas are marked on the Feast Day of Saint James. First an offering is made to *Pacha Mama*, who's asked to protect the cattle and make them fertile, and often a prize animal of each sex is decorated. The ears of the animals are marked and the tails of the cattle are cut off. Occasionally a lamb is sacrificed to *Pacha Mama*. Following this, there's a party, with meat from the sacrificed lamb, *chicha*, music and dancing.

July 26. Feast Day of Saint Ann (*Santa Ana*). A large fair and fiesta are held in Pomata (Puno).

July 28. Peru's Independence Day. While this is an official national holiday, it's also an excuse for a fiesta in many places.

In Curahuasi (Apurimac), a Colonial custom is observed in which a bull is pitted against a condor (which is sometimes lashed to the bull's back). If the condor wins it's set free. Since the bird has a ten-foot wing spread, a sharp beak and talons, it stands a chance against the bull. In this contest, the condor represents the Indians and the bull represents the Spanish, so it isn't hard to guess who the populace cheers for.

During the last week of July, a fair takes place in Porvenir, a suburb of Lima, in honor of Peru's independence. The fair covers several city blocks and includes folk groups and handicrafts from all over Peru.

July 31. Feast Day of Saint Ignatius Loyola (*San Ignacio*), founder of the Jesuit order. Celebrated in Jesuit parishes.

August. August roughly corresponds to the Inca month of *Kapaq Situa* (General Purification). Beginning on August 2, various acts of penance are performed by the Indians, who believe the earth is alive during this month. *Ccoime* is the ceremony in which offerings are made to the living earth to protect the community.

August 1–2. Fiesta in Cochas Chico (Junín).

August 4. Feast Day of Saint Dominic (*Santo Domingo*), founder of the Dominican order. Celebrated in Arequipa, where there's a procession to the Plaza de Armas, as well as in Dominican parishes.

August 10. Feast Day of Saint Lawrence (*San Lorenzo*), who is connected with magical practices in Peru.

August 15. Feast of the Assumption (*Asunción*) of the Blessed Virgin. This is an important fiesta, and there are numerous celebrations in honor of

the Virgin, including those in Pampacucho (Cuzco), Grau (Apurimac) and the towns of San Bernardo, Umachiri, Cabana and Yunguyo in the department of Puno. It's also another major fair day throughout the Peruvian Sierra.

On August 15 the Virgin supposedly appeared at Tiobamba (Cuzco), and so an annual festival in her honor is held in that town. On this same day in Tiobamba the price of corn is set for southern Peru.

August 15 is also the anniversary of the founding of Arequipa. There's a week-long artisans' fair and folk festival there, with participating groups from all over Peru.

August 16. Feast Day of *San Roque*. A six-day festival is held in the village of San Gerónimo (Junín), near Huancayo. While the town is named after Saint Jerome, San Roque is actually its patron saint.

August 22. Feast of the Assumption *(Asunción)* of the Blessed Virgin in Rosapata (Puno). For some reason, the Assumption is celebrated in this town on August 22 rather than on August 15. It may have been the date of a long-forgotten pre-Conquest fiesta.

August 28. Feast Day of Saint Augustine *(San Agustín)*, founder of the Augustinian order. Celebrated in Augustinian parishes.

August 30. Feast Day of Saint Rose of Lima *(Santa Rosa de Lima)*, the patron saint of that city and the Americas. Processions take place in Lima. August 30 is also the Day of the Indian *(Día del Indio)*, celebrated with a fiesta in Arequipa.

September 8. Feast of the Nativity of the Blessed Virgin. This fiesta coincides with the Inca Festival of the Queen, *Koya Raymi*, which is also the Quechua name for the month. Since the Virgin is the patroness of Chincheros (Cuzco), a big fiesta is held in this town. The festivities center around the plaza and marketplace, which are located in front of the ruins of an Inca palace and an Inca stone wall that has twelve trapezoidal niches. This feast day is also celebrated in Cajamarca, where it's the biggest fiesta of the year. Thousands of Indians join in a procession to the Inca baths, and there are dancing and fireworks (really in celebration of *Koya Raymi*).

September 14. *La Exultación* (Feast of the Exaltation of the Cross), celebrated in many places. This is an important fiesta in Huaráz (Ancash) and also marks the end of the great fairs held in southern Peru during the late dry season.

September 24. *Fiesta de la Virgen de las Mercedes* (Feast Day of Our Lady of Mercy), celebrated in Arequipa.

September 30. Feast Day of Saint Jerome *(San Gerónimo)*, the patron saint of many villages.

October 4. Feast Day of Saint Francis of Assisi *(San Francisco de Asís)*, founder of the Franciscan order. Saint Francis is a very popular saint and his feast day is celebrated in Franciscan parishes and in many villages. Arequipa's fiesta is quite famous. On this day, statues of Saint Francis and Saint Dominic are paraded to the Plaza de Armas.

October 7. *Rosario* (Feast Day of Our Lady of the Rosary). October corresponds to the Quechua month of *Uma Raymi* (Festival of the Water). In parts of the Peruvian Andes, the rains begin in late October, when the first crops are planted. October is a rogation *(rogación)* month. Rogation masses are generally offered when the crops are in danger; however, because the beginning of the rain is absolutely vital to survival, throughout this month children weep at church doors and church bells petition God to send rain. This is reminiscent of the Inca practice of *huacayllicuy:* if the rains were late, groups of people dressed in mourning and went wailing through the streets, and dogs and llamas were tied to stakes without food and water in hopes that their cries would induce *Illapa* to have pity and send rain.

October 10. Feast Day of *San Francisco de Borja,* a Jesuit who was responsible for obtaining religious instruction for the Indians.

October 18. Procession of Our Lord of the Miracles *(El Señor de los Milagros)* in Lima. Our Lord of the Miracles is credited with halting the earthquakes which devastated Lima in the seventeenth century. He's also credited with miraculous cures, and those devoted to him wear purple in his honor. His church is decorated in purple throughout the month of October, and during the October 18 procession people wear purple and carry a copy of the painting of Our Lord from the Las Nazarenas church to the Plaza de Armas. A second procession takes place on October 28.

October 18 is also the Feast Day of Saint Luke *(San Lucas)*, Apostle and Evangelist.

October 21. Feast Day of Saint Ursula *(Santa Ursala)*, patron saint of the town of Hualcán (Ancash). This fiesta runs from October 19 through 25 and also honors Our Lord of the Afflicted and Our Lady of Perpetual Help. Saint Ursula is the patron saint of the harvest and health, and her feast day coincides with the planting of potatoes, *oca* and *ullucu*. Lots of processions, music, dancing and fireworks.

November 1–2. *Todos Santos* (All Saints' Day) and *Día de los Muertos, Todos los Muertos* or *Día de Difuntos* (All Souls' Day). These days in honor of the dead are celebrated by both Indians and non-Indians. On November 2, everyone carries food, drink and flowers to the cemetery, where they party. It's believed that the souls of the recently dead (those who died in the past few years) return to earth at this time and partake of the treats left for them. Altars are also prepared in homes. The Incas held a celebration honoring the dead at exactly this time of year, so the Inca and Christian rituals are now celebrated together.

November 3. *Día de Abancay.* Fiesta in Abancay (Apurimac).

November 5. *Día de Puno.* Fiesta in Puno commemorating the birth of the mythical first Inca, *Manco Capac*, and his sister/wife, *Mama Occlo*. There are several legends about their origin, but the one honored in Puno holds that *Manco Capac* and *Mama Occlo* were sent to the Island of the Sun *(Isla del Sol)* in Lake Titicaca by their father, the sun god, in order to instruct mankind in the arts of civilization. The couple carried a long, golden rod with them as they traveled across the *altiplano* and had been instructed to settle in the spot where they could sink the rod completely in the soil. They did this on the site of Cuzco. The fiesta in Puno includes stupendous costume dances, including the famous *Diablada*.

November 30. Feast Day of Saint Andrew *(San Andrés).* Celebrated in Kauri and Ccatcca (Cuzco).

December 4. Feast Day of Saint Barbara *(Santa Bárbara).* Procession in San Sebastián (Cuzco).

December 8. *Fiesta de la Purísima Concepción* (Feast of the Immaculate Conception). Celebrated in Kauri (Cuzco).

December 25. *Navidad* (Christmas). Mangers are set up in homes and churches on Christmas Eve. Many towns and villages celebrate a Midnight Mass. Gifts *(aguinaldos)* are exchanged after Midnight Mass or on Christmas Day.

December 27. Feast Day of Saint John *(San Juan),* Apostle and Evangelist.

December 28. *Fiesta de los Santos Inocentes* (Feast of the Holy Innocents). The Holy Innocents were the Jewish children killed by the Romans in their attempt to slay the newly-born King of the Jews. (The Christ Child was saved by the Holy Family's flight into Egypt.) In Peru this feast day is celebrated much like April Fools' Day; people play jokes and tell outrageous lies. Anyone who falls for the tales is called an *inocente.*

MUSIC AND DANCE

In Peru, as in Ecuador and Colombia, you'll frequently encounter brass bands *(cachimbos),* along with more traditional instruments. Inca instruments included the drum *(huankara),* tambourine or very small drum *(tinya)*, silver or copper bells *(chanrara)*, snail-shell rattles *(churu)*, pan-pipes *(antara, ayarichic* or *siku)* and several kinds of flutes *(flautas)*. These flutes vary in size and number of holes and include the notched flute *(quena)*, which usually has six finger holes and a thumb hole, and a smaller flute *(pinquillu)*, which has three holes. The *quena* and *pinquillu* are made from bamboo or cane which grows in the Yungas. The *piruru* is a tiny flute made from the wing bone of a condor. The conch shell *(pututu)* was used by the Incas as a trumpet and is still used in the Cuzco area, most notably at the Sunday mass at Pisac. It's blown when the Host is elevated and when the priest leaves the church after mass. All of these Inca instruments are still in use.

As in Colombia and Ecuador, many instruments were introduced by the Spanish, including the accordion *(acordeón)*, violin, guitar and harp. Peruvians also use the cow-horn *coroneta;* usually it's played on occasions concerned with cattle, such as ear-marking ceremonies and bullfights.

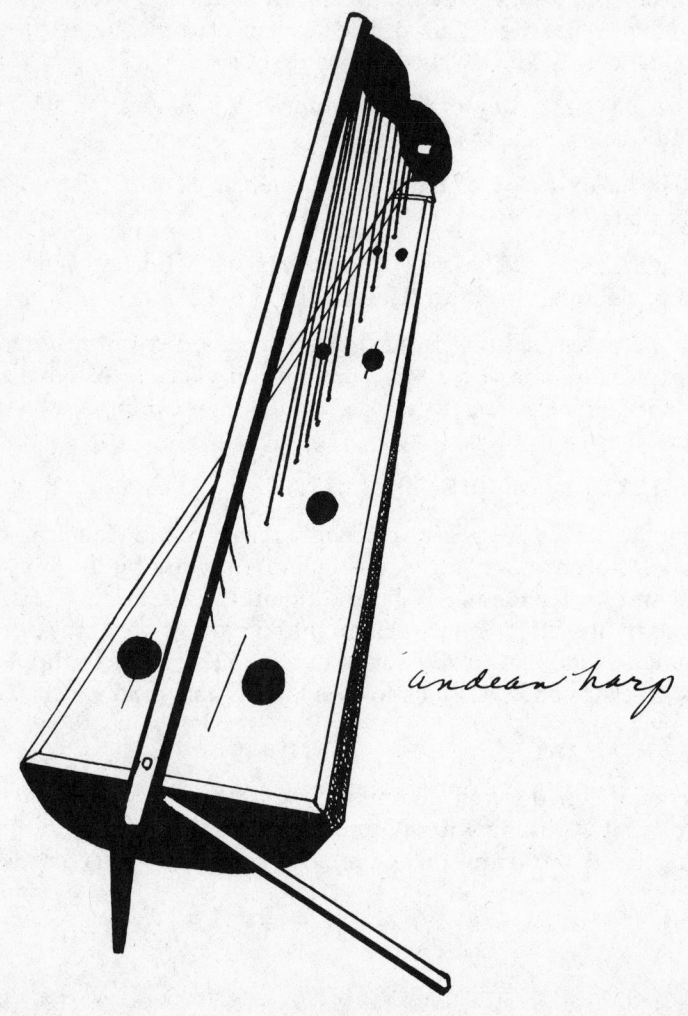

andean harp

There are also some amazing instruments that are unique to certain regions of Peru. The *clarín* is a long (more than ten feet), straight, cane instrument with a horn on one end that's played in Cajamarca. The *waraqu* is very similar, but is more than fifteen feet long and made of metal. It's played in the Ayacucho region only during *Carnaval*.

You'll also encounter lots of dancing at Peruvian fiestas. The *marinera* is a popular folk dance that just about everyone knows how to do. It's like knowing how to square-dance in the United States. The *marinera* is a courtship dance done by a number of couples, each holding a handkerchief, and is derived from the *cueca* or *zamacueca* (see "Music and Dance" for Bolivia). One folklore event I attended in Lima ended with the *marinera,* and the performers invited members of the audience on stage to dance with them. Up came college students, stylishly-dressed older people and an old Indian janitress, who'd been cleaning in the building. It's the custom for spectators to clap during the chorus; the rhythm is easy, so join in.

The Quechua have a rich tradition of music and oral poetry, and many songs and poems have been passed down through the centuries. The *huayño* and *yaraví* are traditional Indian dances and songs with words that usually are sung in Quechua. The *huayño* is danced by couples who hold hands and is composed of two parts—a slow-moving beginning called the *triste* and a lively ending called the *fuga* or *zapateo*. The music for the *yaraví* traditionally was played only on *quenas*. Two other popular Indian dances are the *k'aswa,* a general circle dance in which many people take part, and the *huifala,* a chain dance through the streets.

The Indians also do a number of dances which originated in Inca and pre-Inca rituals. These include the *aymatha,* a dance to ensure fertility in the fields, and the *choquela,* an Aymara dance performed in the communities of Ichu, Juli and Chucuito (Puno). The *choquela* is danced with poles simulating the fence used in a vicuña hunt. It's performed after the harvest to ensure abundant crops the following year. However, it's unlikely that you'll see these two dances performed.

Peruvian fiestas are especially fun because you have the opportunity to see literally dozens of different costume dances. Dances in which costumes and masks were worn were important to the Incas, and the concept is still amazingly popular, although there are interesting modern twists. Many costume dances parody whites, especially the *conquistadores*. Others portray animals or historic events. Sometimes the costumed dancers have specially choreographed dances; other times they simply dance the *huayño*. Generally, each dance group has a distinct costume and dance. Costumes are either owned or rented for the occasion. The dance groups I mention here are just some of those you'll find throughout Peru.

Caballerías ride horses and dress like *mestizos* or like Spanish gentlemen, complete with Napoleon-like hats. The group usually consists of three men who do considerable clowning. I saw *caballerías* who greatly amused the crowd at a fiesta in Cochas Chico.

Chilenos represent the Chileans who fought against Peru in the War of the Pacific (1879–83). These dancers wear old-fashioned, military-type costumes.

Chunchos represent jungle Indians and are common at the July 16 fiesta in Paucartambo. The costumes are almost impossible to describe and vary from group to group, but one outstanding feature is a headband with lots of tropical bird feathers that's somewhat like a Plains Indian's war bonnet.

Collas represent the Aymara warriors of the Lake Titicaca region.

Diabladas are seen at fiestas around Puno. The dance is Aymara and originated in Bolivia. The Indians around Lake Titicaca (especially the Aymara) don't relate to borders at all and cross between Peru and Bolivia constantly to visit relatives and attend fiestas. Puno is mainly Aymara and is quite different from Peruvian Quechua communities. (For more about the *Diablada,* see "Music and Dance" for Bolivia.)

The above groups usually include male dancers only.

Incas re-enact scenes from Inca history, including a procession of the Inca and the capture and death of Atahualpa. Inca dance groups usually include both men and women.

Llameros represent llama-herders and include both boys and girls carrying *hondas,* slings which are used in herding the animals.

Negritos represent black slaves. These groups sometimes wear masks.

Panaderos represent bakers. These dancers carry wheat, corn, baking pans and sometimes flour and water, which are thrown at the crowds.

Pallas were historically wives of the Inca. He was officially married to his sister, who was the head wife and queen *(koya),* but all children born to *pallas* were recognized as descendants of the Inca. In modern fiestas, *pallas* are women dancers who often dance at the beginning or end of a procession. In some areas, such as the Callejón de Huaylas, only widows can be *pallas.*

Suri Sikuris are male dancers who play the *siku* (panpipes). (See "Music and Dance" for Bolivia.)

Tercianos represent sufferers of malaria. These male dancers fall to the ground pretending to be stricken with fever and chills.

Waca groups parody bullfights. (See "Music and Dance" for Bolivia.)

A good way to learn about folk music and dance is to attend some folklore programs. In fact, don't leave Peru without attending at least one music and dance event. A folklore program is held in Lima every Monday night at the Teatro Felipe Pardo y Aliaga, in the Ministry of Education building in the Parque Universitario. Admission is less than a dollar and printed programs are given out to help you understand the dances. Folk dancers from all over Peru perform at these programs and the dancers I saw were excellent. Another folk music and dance program is held in Lima on Sunday afternoon at the Coliseo Amauta, which is located near San Marcos University.

In Huancayo there's a folk music and dance program following the Sunday market; it's held in the afternoon in the Coliseo Municipal, off the plaza by the Tourist Hotel. Admission is nominal and the program is well worth seeing. I was as intrigued by the costumes as I was by the music and dance.

Cuzco also has folk music events that are worth checking out. We were alerted to one by someone who came around to all the restaurants and handed out notices.

Finally, don't ignore traditional Western classical music. As with movies, tickets to cultural events are much cheaper than they are in the United States. While I was in Lima I heard the Northern Symphony of England at the Teatro Municipal for only a dollar, and my parents and I attended an excellent Baroque music concert in Arequipa performed by Peruvian college students. The student concert was held at the Santa Catalina convent in candlelight, and also cost about a dollar a person.

Bolivia

FEAST DAYS AND FIESTAS

Like Peru, Bolivia has a rich and interesting folk culture. Many fiestas are celebrated here, from Pre-Columbian agricultural rites to all the major Catholic holidays, plus some civic holidays unique to Bolivia, such as *Día del Mar*.

As with Colombia, Ecuador and Peru, the following list includes just a sampling of the enormous number of annual celebrations. The towns listed for each fiesta are places where I know there's a celebration—there may be festivities in many other localities as well.

January 1. *Año Nuevo* (New Year's Day). January 1 is also the *Fiesta de las Trucasiris* in Laja (La Paz) with music and dancing.

January 6. *Día de los Reyes Magos.* The Epiphany is celebrated in many places, including Trinidad (Beni), Tupiza (Tarija) and Sucre.

January 24–31. Annual *Alacitas* fair in the Plaza San Pedro in La Paz. *Alacita* is an Aymara word which means "Buy me" or "Buy from me." This fair is held in honor of *Ekkekko,* a Pre-Columbian god of prosperity

and good fortune. Traditionally, little statues of *Ekkekko* made of gold, silver, tin, clay or rock were kept in all Indian homes. The worship of *Ekkekko* was outlawed by the Spanish, who prohibited the Indians from making the tiny statues. In 1871, *Ekkekko* made a comeback during a fiesta to the Virgin of La Paz, which the Indians turned into an *Alacitas* fair.

The god *Ekkekko* is connected with the miniature objects sold at the *Alacitas* fairs. The idea is that whatever you purchase in miniature at the fair you will obtain in real life. Vendors sell tiny cars, airplanes, farm animals, houses, dishes, groceries and money. According to tradition, on the first day of the fair you must buy an *Ekkekko,* a rotund statue covered with household goods. And, if you buy miniature play money before noon on this same day, you'll never run out.

Ekkekko is also honored as the god of marriage. An Indian looking for a spouse keeps his statue in a special place in the house and offers gifts to it. *Ekkekkeros* are people who specialize in making *Ekkekko* statues, although the modern, plaster varieties with mustaches are made by brickmasons.

Alacitas fairs are held in several Bolivian towns at different times of the year. I attended the *Alacitas* fair in Cochabamba, which begins the third Sunday in October. Many of the miniatures were true works of art, and I was especially intrigued by the tiny kitchens, exact replicas of a Cochabamba *chola*'s kitchen, right down to the old-fashioned stove. There's also an *Alacitas* fair in Oruro sometime during the year and one in Tarija on July 26; there are two in Sucre (July 16 and 26) which are called *Calvario* (rather than *Alacitas)* fairs.

February 1–2. Feast Day of the Virgin Copacabana in Copacabana. This is an enormous Indian fiesta which attracts people from both the Bolivian and Peruvian sides of Lake Titicaca. Many Aymara dance groups perform and one group (the *Incas*) dramatically re-enacts the struggle between the brothers Huascar and Atahualpa for control of the Inca Empire. The image of the Virgin of Copacabana housed in the basilica was carved in 1576 by Francisco Tito Yupanqui, a descendant of the Inca Yupanqui. This statue is made of a very dark wood and is known as the Black Madonna.

Historically, Copacabana was a resting place for Indian pilgrims visiting the Inca shrine on the Island of the Sun (*Isla del Sol*) in Lake Titicaca. It's possible to rent a boat in Copacabana to visit the Inca ruins on the Island of the Sun. However, the Island of the Moon (*Isla de la Luna*), also located on Lake Titicaca, has been closed to travelers for several years since it serves as a prison for Bolivian political prisoners.

February 2. Feast Day of the Virgin of *Candelaria* (Candlemas). Processions and celebrations are held in many towns.

February or March. *Carnaval.* In Bolivia, *Carnaval* begins on the Sunday before Ash Wednesday and continues until the following Sunday, although Ash Wednesday is officially the beginning of Lent. Since *Carnaval* is the major fiesta of the year in Bolivia, there are exceptionally exciting celebrations, especially the festivities held in Oruro.

In La Paz, *Carnaval* is known as *Anata*, which means "Time of Play" in Aymara. On Sunday there's a parade down the Prado called *la entrada*, with distinctively costumed Aymara dance groups known as *comparsas*, including the famous *Diabladas* (see "Music and Dance"). The parade is led by *pepinos* (clowns). Monday and Tuesday are water-fight days and no one is exempt. Buckets of water are dumped off balconies, so be prepared. On Tuesday there's a *challa*, a ritual sprinkling of liquor to *Pacha Mama* which is usually confined to new homes, trucks, etc. In this case, the *challa* is performed for general prosperity and good luck.

Ash Wednesday is the beginning of *aptapis*, the season for corn, fruit and flowers (remember, this is summer in the Southern Hemisphere), and it's traditional to go to the country on this day. Booths with liquor and food for sale are set up behind the cemetery in La Paz.

Carnaval continues on Thursday, Friday, Saturday and Sunday, and on the last two days there's dancing on the Prado. These last two days are called *días de tentación* (days of temptation), perhaps because everyone is tempted to go on drinking and dancing. People wear torn clothes as an expression of their sadness that *Carnaval* is over, and *Carnaval* is "buried" on Sunday night.

Like La Paz, Sucre has *comparsas*, who parade and play music in the street, as well as masked groups, an *entrada* parade on Sunday and water bombs and balloons on Monday and Tuesday. Watch out for people throwing *cascarones*, which are egg shells with the insides blown out that have been refilled with perfumed or regular water.

In Tarabuco, near Sucre, *Carnaval* begins one week later, so you can attend festivities in both towns.

In Cochabamba, a Quechua-speaking area, *Carnaval* begins on Sunday, when decorated cars congregate at the main plaza for a parade, and continues with the traditional water-throwing on Tuesday and Wednesday and various public and private parties with lots of drinking and dancing.

In Potosí, Indian *comparsas* dance in the plazas and streets, and there are the inevitable water fights.

In Santa Cruz, people start carrying on several weeks before the fiesta officially begins. (This prompted the government to announce the year I was in Bolivia that *Carnaval* was to be limited to only three days that year, a totally useless proclamation.) Santa Cruz has parades, water fights, street dances and lots of eating and drinking. The town, which is located close to Brazil, has a lighter vibe than the *altiplano* and a very jolly *Carnaval*.

The tin-mining town of Oruro has the most famous *Carnaval* in Bolivia, attended by many Bolivian and foreign tourists because of its famous *Diablada* dance groups (see "Music and Dance"). The *entrada* parade is held on the Saturday before Ash Wednesday and agencies in La Paz arrange tours for this day only. If you plan to stay in Oruro overnight, make arrangements for lodging well in advance. *Comparsas* perform in the plazas throughout the week and there are handicraft exhibits as well.

Another Bolivian celebration held during *Carnaval* is *Jueves de Compadres* (*Taripaco* in Aymara), which is held on Thursday during the week of *Carnaval* and includes a mass in honor of godparents (*compadres*). Godparents are often of a higher social class than their godchildren and the ties are much closer than in the United States and Europe. The custom of *compadrazgo* is very widespread in Latin America, and in many cases the *compadres* become patrons of both the child and his or her family.

March 8. Feast Day of *San Juan de Dios*, the patron saint of hospitals. There are usually masses and processions in hospitals.

March 19. Feast Day of Saint Joseph (*San José*), the patron saint of carpenters. In Sucre there are fireworks (*la víspera*) the night before the fiesta and a mass and music the day of the feast, while in Oruro *Diablada* dances are performed at the San José mine. There's also a lot of music and dancing around Lake Titicaca.

March 19 is also Father's Day in Bolivia since Saint Joseph was the father of Christ.

March or April. *Semana Santa* (Holy Week). On Palm Sunday (*Domingo de Ramos*) in Sacaba (Cochabamba) the procession of *El Señor de Ramos*

(Christ of the Palms)—a wooden statue of Christ—takes place. In other towns, palms are passed out.

In the highlands, *khespicha* is practiced from the evening of Good Friday until Easter Sunday. As in parts of Peru, the belief is that since God is dead during these days, anything goes, including robbery and wife- and daughter-snatching. Fathers keep a close watch on their daughters and possessions lest they become *khespiado*.

In many places there are more traditional Catholic practices on Good Friday, such as the procession of penitents.

There are other interesting Quechua customs connected with Easter *(Pascua)*. One belief is that if Easter falls in March (rather than April, which is more common), it forbodes bad things: earthquakes, droughts and other natural disasters. In the province of Yamparáez (Chuquisaca) the Indians also celebrate Easter in honor of the Holy Spirit, whom they call *Taita Espíritu*. The old Inca commandments *Ama sua; ama llulla; ama quella* (Don't steal; don't lie; don't be lazy) are associated with Christ, the Holy Spirit and God the Father.

Throughout Bolivia there are special foods, beverages and folk music associated with Easter.

March 23. *Día del Mar* (Day of the Sea). There are speeches and parades all over Bolivia during which Bolivians demand the return of their seaport of Arica, which they lost to Chile in the War of the Pacific (1879–83).

March 25. Feast of the Annunciation, celebrating the appearance of the Archangel Gabriel to Mary, telling her she was to be the mother of Christ. Potosí celebrates with music and dancing, and *Diablada* dancers perform in Oruro.

March (date uncertain). Fiesta of *Romerías,* celebrated by the Indian community of Obrajes, a suburb of La Paz.

March or April (two weeks after Holy Week). Two-week local Indian fair in Challapata (Oruro). Animals for sale, food, drinking and some handicrafts.

April 15. Fiesta of the department of Tarija, with celebrations all over.

May 3. *Día de la Santa Cruz* (Day of the Holy Cross). On the night of May 2, crosses all over Bolivia are decorated with flowers and paper streamers, and throughout the country this fiesta is celebrated with a mixture of Pre-Columbian and Christian elements. In Inca times, May was the time of the corn harvest, which was celebrated with copious *chicha* drinking, and this custom has been incorporated into the *Día de la Santa Cruz* festivities.

In Valle Hermoso (Cochabamba), women who have many children and don't want any more make small rag dolls wrapped in colored yarn and deposit them in a small hole behind the main altar of the shrine to the Holy Cross to insure the miracle of no more children. Barren women collect these dolls in hopes that they will become pregnant. Tiny woolen animals (horses, pigs, hens, etc.) are also deposited behind the altar in hopes of increasing the flocks and herds. This shrine to the Holy Cross was formerly the site of a shrine to a small, sacred, miraculous stone. The stone has long since disappeared but the devotions to it have not.

Italaque (La Paz) is a town where *sikuri (zampoña)* musicians are trained. On May 3 the *Suri Sikuri* groups are tested. After eating and drinking, they must run to the top of a hill and back without stopping while playing their instruments. If anyone collapses, it's considered a bad omen for his group.

Santa Cruz de la Sierra was named after the Holy Cross, and its celebrations begin on May 2 with music and dancing in the barrio of Siete Calles.

There's also a huge fiesta in Copacabana, with people from all over Peru and Bolivia, a celebration in Tatala (Cochabamba) and music and dancing on El Calvario hill in La Paz.

June 8 (approximately). Feast Day of *El Señor del Gran Poder* in La Paz. Jesus the Most Powerful is the patron of the Aymara barrio of Gran Poder in La Paz, and this fiesta has become a big event. There's a parade *(la entrada)* with lots of music and *comparsas* which goes along Avenido Buenos Aires; don't miss this event if you happen to be in La Paz.

June 13. Feast Day of Saint Anthony *(San Antonio).* In Bolivia, Saint Anthony is the patron saint of people looking for spouses, and he is also the patron of those looking for lost articles. Because Saint Anthony's feast day is the thirteenth, anyone seeking a favor from him makes an offering in thirteens—thirteen candles, thirteen coins, etc. Celebrations are held in Sorata and Jesus de Machaca (La Paz).

Thursday in mid-June. *Corpus Cristi.* Celebrated in many places in the highlands with the usual music, dancing and drinking. Around Lake Titicaca, *Corpus Cristi* is the first day of threshing: first *quinoa* and then, later in the month, *haba* beans and barley. Thus, this holiday is also celebrated as a kind of harvest festival.

In La Paz religious statues are carried from churches in a procession honoring the Body of Christ. Fine Aymara music and dancing also mark the occasion.

In Sucre the main market is decorated with flowers, while *campesinos* in the area adorn their hats with the *corpus ttika,* a flower.

Late June (one week after *Corpus Cristi*). *Octavia*. The "octave" always takes place eight days after a feast day. In some parts of Bolivia there's a public procession of the Eucharist on the *Octavia* of *Corpus Cristi*.

June 24. Feast Day of Saint John the Baptist *(San Juan Bautista)*. Bill and I were in Cochabamba on the eve of this fiesta. From our hotel window we saw the hills dotted with bonfires—the Andes were ablaze, as if the stars had fallen and settled on the mountains. According to legend, Elizabeth had fires lit across Israel to announce to Mary that John had been born, but that's only a partial explanation of the origin of this fiesta. The fiesta falls just after the winter solstice during the Quechua month of *Inti Raymi* (Festival of the Sun), and for thousands of years bonfires have been lit on the mountains in Bolivia and Peru at the time of the solstice to bring back the sun and to light up the longest night of the year. On the feast day itself, there were torchlight parades and everyone set off firepoppers and firecrackers; the city was smoky for days.

La Paz, too, is ringed with bonfires on the eve of the fiesta, and there are parties all over in honor of Saint John.

Because Saint John the Baptist is associated with water, another tradition is for everyone to bathe on his feast day. As in Puno, the Aymara Indians tell fortunes by dropping molten lead or tin into buckets of water.

June 29. Feast Day of Saints Peter and Paul *(San Pedro* and *San Pablo)*. This feast day is celebrated in many places. Bill and I attended the celebrations in Achacachi and Huatajata on Lake Titicaca, where there were three days of music and dancing. The Aymara have many costume dances, and the one that tickled me the most was a little boy dressed like a United States Plains Indian, complete with war bonnet and tomahawk. In Huatajata it may have been possible to join the *huayño* circle dancing, but I was too busy filming to try. This feast day marks the end of harvesting on the *altiplano*, and during this cold, dry season (it's winter), potatoes and *oca* are made into *chuño* and *tunta*.

July 16. Feast Day of the Virgin of Carmen (called *Mamita Carmen)*, the patroness of Bolivia. I was in Cochabamba for this fiesta, too. There's a procession that includes military personnel, bands and a statue of the Virgin through Cochabamba to the church at the corner of calles Bautista and Ecuador. The parade passes under huge arches of greens carried by the Indians. There are also automobiles decorated with textiles, dolls and family silver. This symbolic offering dates back to an old Colonial custom called the *achura*, in which miners offered the best silver they had mined to their *patrón*. On July 16 and 17 masses are celebrated, and a little fair is held in the plaza in front of the church.

Since the Virgin of Carmen is the patroness of the country, which is officially Roman Catholic, there are processions in her honor throughout Bolivia. In La Paz a High Mass is celebrated in the basilica, and many government officials attend. Candles are lit in the Virgin's honor at the chapel on El Calvario hill.

In Sucre, there's a *Calvario* fair on July 16; a second *Calvario* fair takes place here on July 26. There's also music and dancing in Charazani (La Paz).

July 25. Feast Day of Saint James *(Santiago)*. As I mentioned earlier, Saint James is associated with *Illapa*, the Inca god of thunder and lightning. In Bolivia, Saint James is also the patron saint of many churches and villages, and on this day statues of him are taken to the church to be blessed. The fiesta is celebrated in many places on the *altiplano*, including Umala and Quime (La Paz), and Laja and Achocalla, which are near La Paz. As usual, *comparsas* perform at the festivities.

Saint James is the patron saint of Campo Grande (Tarija), and his fiesta is celebrated here on the Sunday closest to July 25. In Torotoro (Potosí), the fiesta is celebrated with a ritual fight *(tinku)* in which fists, clubs or slings are used. This is probably related to a custom still practiced in parts of Peru whereby neighboring groups have ritual battles once a year and abduct each other's women. The *tinku* is also held in Capinota (Cochabamba) on July 25.

The Feast Day of Saint Christopher *(San Cristóbal)*, one of the purged saints, is also celebrated on July 25. Saint Christopher is the patron saint of cab and truck drivers (called *chóferes* or *transportistas)* and also of travelers. In Sucre, a statue of the saint is carried in a procession from the Colegio Seminario church to the cathedral.

July 26. Feast Day of Saint Ann *(Santa Ana)*. In Bolivia, Saint Ann is the patron saint of the sick, who pray to her for health. She is also the patron saint of a barrio in the city of Sucre. In Sucre, her feast begins with fireworks held on the night of July 25 in front of La Recoleta convent's church. On the feast day itself, there's an afternoon *Calvario* fair that's much like an *Alacitas* fair. There's also an *Alacitas* fair in Tarija, a fiesta in the Cochabamba barrio of Cala Cala and a fiesta in Umala (La Paz).

August 1. *Señala*. This is a Quechua custom celebrating the increase in the sheep and goat herds. It's traditionally held in a sheep corral, complete with ritual buyers and sellers of the animals and a coca-leaf ceremony, followed by *charango* music and *chicha* drinking. This custom is related to ceremonies held in Peru which thank *Pacha Mama* for the fertility of the animals.

August 5–7. On August 5 and 6 a fiesta takes place in Copacabana which is part of an overall celebration in honor of the Virgin of Copacabana, observed in the entire department of La Paz. August 6 is also the anniversary of Bolivia's independence, so official ceremonies are mixed in with popular celebrations. Markets and public places are decorated in Bolivia's colors—red, green and yellow. On August 7 there's also a fiesta at Angostura (Cochabamba).

August 10. Feast Day of Saint Lawrence *(San Lorenzo),* the patron saint of San Lorenzo (Tarija), where a big fiesta takes place. The Quechua believe this day is ominous for fires and are therefore especially careful with them.

August 12. Feast Day of Saint Clare *(Santa Clara).* High Mass is celebrated in the convent of Santa Clara in Sucre. The traditional food of the day is chicken *empanadas,* which are sold at the convent and in bakeries.

August 15. Feast of the Assumption *(Asunción)* of the Blessed Virgin. There's dancing in Italaque (La Paz), and *Diablada* dances are performed at the Paria mine in Oruro. It's also the Feast Day of the Virgin of Urqupeña in Quillacollo (Cochabamba), with music, dancing and a fair.

August 16. Feast Day of *San Roque.* As I've said before, there's a patron saint for everything. In Bolivia, *San Roque* is the patron saint of dogs. All over Bolivia the skinny, mangy mutts are decorated with colored ribbons on this day.

August 24. Feast Day of Saint Bartholomew *(San Bartolomé).* Celebrated with practical jokes, though I don't know why. There are fiestas in Cohoni and Chulumani (La Paz).

August 30. Feast Day of Saint Rose of Lima *(Santa Rosa de Lima).* Saint Rose is the patron saint of Yotala (Chuquisaca), so a big fiesta takes place here in her honor. There's also Indian dancing in Kaata (La Paz).

September 8. Feast Day of the Virgin of Guadalupe (called *Mamita Guadalupe).* Also the Feast of the Nativity of the Blessed Virgin. Processions are held in many places, including Sucre and Tarija. There's also a fiesta in Mocomoco (La Paz).

September 10. Feast Day of Saint Nicolas *(San Nicolás).* Saint Nicholas is the patron saint of bakers, who don't work on this day but attend mass in honor of the saint.

September 14. Feast of the Exaltation of the Cross *(La Exultación* or *La Fiesta del Señor de la Vera Cruz).* In Oruro this feast day is celebrated with *Diablada* dancing at the Cala Cala mine. It's also celebrated in Laja (La Paz), Obrajes (a suburb of La Paz) and in Mizque (Cochabamba). In

Potosí a statue of Christ which has been credited with numerous miracles is venerated. The Uru of Lake Titicaca formerly held their major fiesta at the vernal equinox on September 23, but have changed the date of the celebration to September 14.

September 24. *Fiesta de la Virgen de las Mercedes* (Feast Day of Our Lady of Mercy). Celebrated on the *altiplano* and around Lake Titicaca.

October, first Sunday. *Rosario* (Feast Day of Our Lady of the Rosary); also a fiesta in honor of the patron saint of Entre Ríos (Tarija). This fiesta is in honor of a missionary priest killed by the Indians in 1735 and also honors the Virgin of Guadalupe. There's a mass and procession, with music and dancing. Some of the participants in the procession carry bows and arrows in honor of the martyred priest.

October 13. Feast Day of the Virgin of Fátima. Celebrated in the La Paz barrio of Villa Fátima.

October 20. Week-long fiesta in Coroico (La Paz), with *comparsas,* thirty-piece brass bands, *chicha* huts in the main plaza, etc. On the second to the last day, all the trucks in town are decorated with flowers and streamers and are blessed with holy water by the priest. Then the owners spray the trucks with beer and wine and drive them in a procession.

October 24. Feast Day of Saint Michael *(San Miguel)*. Celebrated in Tiquipaya (Cochabamba).

October 25. Feast Day of *San Crispín,* the patron saint of shoemakers. In Sucre there's a morning procession from the church of Santo Domingo. The statue of Saint Crispín is carried by shoemakers and shoe repairers.

November 1–2. *Todos Santos* (All Saints' Day) and *Día de Difuntos* or *Día de los Muertos* (All Souls' Day). On these two days, Christian and Pre-Columbian practices mix since, coincidentally, November was the month the Incas and Christians held ceremonies in honor of the dead.

Before the Spanish Conquest both the Quechua and Aymara believed that the spirits of the dead looked after the living. The deceased were buried with objects they had used during their lives and were offered food and drink to nourish them in the beyond. Sacrifices were offered to burial sites to ask favors and obtain protection. Today the Indians still believe that the souls of the dead return to earth on *Todos Santos* to visit and protect the family and to take the souls of those about to die. Wandering, lost souls also return. The Indians visit cemeteries on November 2 to place food and drink on relatives' graves. This is especially important for any family that has lost a member in the preceding three years. Special breads are baked, decorations are made and liquor is purchased.

The family sets up a table in the cemetery with offerings of food, drink, candles and flowers. Purple *chicha (chicha morada)* is traditionally made. Bands play and sometimes the Catholic priest (if there is one in the area) offers a mass in the cemetery for the souls of the dead. On the *altiplano,* Aymara girls and unmarried women dance with dolls or someone else's baby in their *ahuayos* (carrying cloths), hoping to attract the souls of dead children to insure their own future fertility.

Besides food and drink, the Aymara also make offerings of little reed boats (to help the souls of the dead travel across the lake), ladders (to help them climb out of purgatory), *quinoa*-bread llamas (to represent the dead person's herd) and so on. I spent part of *Día de Difuntos* at the cemetery in Arani, near Cochabamba, and it was quite a party; the whole town attended.

November 17. *Fiesta de la Virgen de Ámparo* in Sacaba (Cochabamba).

November 21. *Fiesta de la Virgen de los Remedios* (Feast of Our Lady of Perpetual Help). Masses are offered in churches and hospital chapels throughout Bolivia, where the sick ask to be cured. There's also traditional dancing in Sorata (La Paz).

November 22. Feast Day of Saint Cecilia *(Santa Cecilia),* the patron saint of musicians. Fiestas occur in Guaqui (La Paz), Sucre and Tarija, with lots of music and dancing.

November 30. Feast Day of Saint Andrew *(San Andrés).* November is springtime on the *altiplano,* and the eve of this fiesta marks the start of Aymara spring and fertility celebrations, including the *Kachua,* a dance and ceremony performed by adolescents (see "Music and Dance"). The best places to witness the *Kachua* are towns around Lake Titicaca, such as Pucarani (La Paz). Saint Andrew is also the patron saint of Taquiña (Cochabamba). This town is the site of the Taquiña Brewery, which provides free beer for the fiesta.

December 4. Feast Day of Saint Barbara *(Santa Bárbara).* Again, primarily an *altiplano* fiesta, as well as the second performance of the *Kachua.*

December 8. *Fiesta de la Purísima Concepción* (Feast of the Immaculate Conception). This date marks the third performance of the *Kachua.* The *Diablada* is performed at the Siglo xx mine in Oruro. There are also fiestas in Laja and Sapahaqui (La Paz).

December 8–15. Feast Day of the Virgin of Cotoca. This week-long fiesta celebrates the apparition of the Blessed Virgin to a woman in the town of Cotoca (Santa Cruz) in the eighteenth century. The Virgin is called *Virgencita Camba,* meaning "Little *Camba* Virgin." (*Camba* is the term used in Bolivia to describe a person from the eastern lowlands, while *colla* describes a person from the *altiplano* and Andean highlands.) The Virgin is often called *Mamita* throughout the Andes, and the image of the *Camba Mamita* is credited with miraculous cures. This manifestation of the Virgin is recounted in folk tales and folk music throughout eastern Bolivia. The fiesta is also celebrated in Recoleta and Sarco (Cochabamba).

December 13. Feast Day of Saint Lucy *(Santa Lucía)*. Celebrated mainly in *altiplano* towns such as Ancoraimes (La Paz), this feast day is the occasion for the fourth performance of the *Kachua*.

December 25. *Navidad* (Christmas). Throughout Bolivia during the week before Christmas, groups of costumed children sing carols *(villancicos)* and accompany themselves on musical instruments. They perform in the streets and in churches and go from door to door honoring the Christ Child in the nativity scene set up in each home. The carolers are given treats and money in return for their adoration of the Christ Child.

In La Paz *campesinos* take their sheep and llamas to Midnight Mass, called *Misa de Gallo* (Mass of the Rooster), at the Basílica de San Francisco. This is done in remembrance of the shepherds who brought their flocks with them to the manger when they came to adore the newborn Christ.

Christmas is also the occasion for the fifth performance of the *Kachua*.

December 28. *Fiesta de los Santos Inocentes* (Feast of the Holy Innocents). As in Peru, this is a day for tricks and practical jokes, much like our April Fools' Day. Anyone who falls for a trick is called an *inocente*.

MUSIC AND DANCE

I saw more music and dance in Bolivia than anywhere else in my travels. It's interesting that I most often saw traditional music performed on traditional instruments in folk music clubs *(peñas folklóricas)* in La Paz or at special folklore programs in Cochabamba. When I went out into the countryside to authentic Indian festivities, the music was invariably provided by unbelievably funky brass bands. The traditional instruments are still played in the countryside, but it depends on the occasion. I did hear Indians playing the *charango* in Tarabuco on market day, but I never heard the lonely Indian shepherd playing his flute on the hillside.

Traditional instruments are still played by both the Quechua and Aymara. The *pinquillu* is a *soqosa*-reed flute with a wooden mouthpiece and a small opening end. Like the old Peruvian *pinquillus*, these instruments were made from bone during Pre-Columbian times. There are at least twenty-five kinds of *pinquillus*; they come in four different pitches (from soprano to bass) which are played together. Two types of *pinquillus* are the *phuna* and the *khoana.*

The *pututu* is a bull's horn which is blown like the conch-shell *pututu* of Peru. The *khepa*, played in Tarija, is a *pututu* on the end of a long reed.

The *quena* is the same as the Peruvian flute of the same name—a notched bamboo flute with six holes (The bamboo comes from the Yungas.) The *quena* traditionally was played as a solo instrument and comes in various sizes and pitches. The *yaraví* is typical *quena* music.

The *tarka* flute is unusual because it's made of wood rather than reed or bamboo. It has six finger holes and, like the *pinquillu*, comes in four different pitches. *Tarkas* are sometimes squared off rather than round.

The *erque* is a wind instrument that's played in the Sucre and Tarija area. It's a long, wooden cylinder with a metal mouthpiece and is held vertically.

The *zampoña* is called an *antara, ayarichic* or *sikuri* in Quechua and a *siku* in Aymara. This is the familiar bamboo panpipe known as a *rondador* in Ecuador and an *antara* or *siku* in Peru. Most *zampoñas* span at least three octaves. They come in single and double rows and in five different sizes and pitches. The *bajón, malta, chuli* and *licu* are varieties of *zampoñas.*

Traditional *altiplano* instrumental music used the pentatonic scale exclusively and was never accompanied by singing. Furthermore, the instruments were never mixed; there would be a group of *zampoña*-players, one of *pinquillu*-players, one of *tarka*-players and so on. The only instrument used as an accompaniment was the drum (*bombo* in Spanish). There are two kinds of traditional highland drums—the *caja*, a small drum almost like a tambourine, and the *huankara*, a very large, double-headed drum. Extra rawhide or gut strings are stretched across the bottom of the *huankara* for extra sound, as they vibrate when the drum is beaten.

The *charango* is another common instrument, especially among the Quechua. This small, stringed instrument looks like a ukulele but has five pairs of strings and eight frets. It is sometimes made of wood but is more often made from an armadillo (*quirquinchu*) shell. The body and neck are usually carved from a solid block of wood (cedar, orange, willow or *mara*), and the face is either painted or inlaid with mother-of-pearl. *Charangos* are sold in the Cochabamba market and around Sucre, where the Tarabuqueños are especially fine *charango*-players. The towns of Aiquile, Quillacollo, Sacaba and Tarata, near Cochabamba, are places where *charangos*, mandolins, violins and guitars are made.

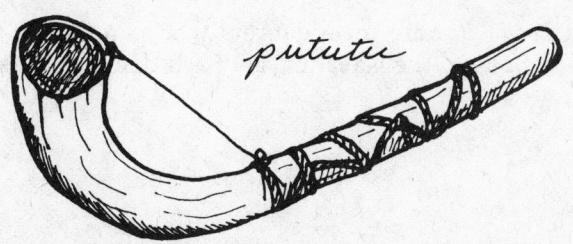

pututu

If you attend any fiestas on the *altiplano*, you'll see a noisemaker called a *qeru qeru* that looks like a tiny wooden barrel on a stick. When it's twirled in time to music it makes a grating, rasping sound.

The *chullu chullu* is another popular noisemaker. It's made of pieces of tin cans or beer-bottle caps which are strung on a piece of wire that can be either circular or held between the two branches of a Y-shaped stick. *Chullu chullus* are played in La Paz and Sucre at Christmas by costumed children who go from house to house playing and singing carols.

There are also a number of musical instruments unique to the Yungas and the jungle which you'll encounter if you travel into these areas.

One of the real treats of Bolivian fiestas is the opportunity to watch costumed dance groups *(comparsas)*. The best time for this is during *Carnaval* in Oruro or La Paz or during any of the celebrations in La Paz or around Lake Titicaca. While both the Quechua and Aymara perform costume dances, the Aymara have raised this folk art to new heights. The costumes are amazing—plaster masks, velvet cloth with braiding, beads, mirrors, sequins, metallic thread, feathers, coins, silver spoons, etc. The *Diablada* and *Morenada* costumes can weigh up to sixty pounds each and cost the dancer between $160 and $250! Like Peruvian *camparsas*, the Bolivian groups do specific dance steps to specific music. Occasionally they play their own instruments, but more often they're accompanied by a band.

The Bolivian folk dancers perform many of the same dances done in Peru. You'll see *Chunchos,* who dress like jungle Indians; *Pallas; Llameros;* and *Incas,* who re-enact scenes from Inca history, such as the civil war between the armies of Huascar and Atahualpa. Like the Indian dances in Ecuador and Peru, many Bolivian Indian dances parody the Spanish *conquistadores* or whites in general. Some *comparsas* include little kids as well as adults.

I mention here just a few of the fifty or sixty *comparsas,* but they are the ones you're most likely to see performed.

Auqui Auquis ("*auqui*" is Aymara for "old man") parody Spanish Colonial dandies; they wear huge, tall hats, carry canes and dance hunched over like old men.

The *ayarichi* is the name of a band composed of musicians who play *zampoñas (ayarichics)* and a huge drum *(huankara),* as well as the name of a dance. The *Ayarichi* dancers are Tarabuco Indians who live near Sucre, and the group is composed of both men and women. Instead of costumes, they wear their everyday clothes, which are extremely colorful.

Callahuayas or *Doctorcitos* are male dancers who parody the famous curers of northern Bolivia, the Callahuayas. Each dancer wears a knit purse covered with old coins across his breast and a hat adorned with flowers, and carries an open umbrella in the right hand and a bird's claw in the left.

Chatripulis get their name from the Aymara words *"chacha,"* meaning "man," and *"puli,"* meaning "angel." These "men angels" are costumed according to the Aymara conception of angelic dress. The *Chatripulis* I saw in Huatajata on the Feast Day of Saints Peter and Paul were wearing the typical costume—crowns with three ostrich *(suri)* plumes and tiered silver-lamé dresses. They could best be described as dancing Christmas trees.

The *Chiriguano* is a dance that predates the Spanish Conquest. It's a war dance in which the dancers wear jaguar-skin ponchos.

Chutas represent the highland *cholos,* and the dance is performed by couples. Each man wears a *chullo* (the typical *altiplano* knitted hat with earflaps), a short, ornate jacket and fancy pants which are split at the hem. (*"Chuta"* means "split" in Aymara). The women wear the typical Aymara fiesta dress, which consists of as many as eleven *pollera* skirts worn one over the other, a shawl *(manta),* a fancy embroidered blouse *(jubón)* and the familiar brown derby hat.

Cullahuas include both men and women. This dance was important during the period of Inca rule in Bolivia and was modified after the Spanish Conquest. Both sexes carry large distaffs and spindles, and they spin yarn as they dance. A modern brass band provides the music.

The *Diablada* is the most famous Bolivian *comparsa*. It dates back to medieval Spanish masques and tells the story of the battle between good and evil. The dance is dedicated to the *Virgen del Socavón* (Virgin of the Cave). *El Diablo* (the Devil) is associated with the spirits who own the minerals and dwell in the tin mines of Oruro, causing cave-ins and other misfortunes. These spirits are called *tíos* (uncles) and the miners make

Diablada mask

offerings to them. The *Diablada* begins with a salute to the Virgin, continues with the rebellion of the devils and ends with the victory of the Archangel Michael over the devils. It's all meticulously choreographed and performed.

The costumes worn by *Diablada* dancers are amazing and have given rise to an entire industry in Oruro and La Paz devoted to making these costumes and masks. The devil masks are made of plaster and are quite large and heavy. Each has a dragon over the forehead, horns, large ears and a grotesque mouth with pointed teeth and tusks. Each devil wears what looks like a suit of long white underwear covered with an elaborate breastplate, a kerchief for a cape, a loincloth, a belt covered with hundreds of coins and a pair of high-laced boots with spurs. Lucifer, the chief devil, wears an embroidered red-velvet cape. In the dance there's also a woman called a *china supay* (which means "female animal devil" in Aymara and Quechua) who wears the costume of a typical *chola* of forty years ago, including high-laced boots.

The best time to see the *Diablada* is during *Carnaval* in Oruro. *Diablada* groups composed of up to a hundred dancers each begin practicing in November for this celebration. They all participate in the *entrada*, the grand parade on the Saturday of *Carnaval*, and perform throughout the city during *Carnaval* week and on other occasions (see "Feast Days and Fiestas"). The *comparsas* compete for prizes for the best costumes and choreography. In La Paz, the best opportunity to see *Diabladas* and other dance groups is in June during the festival and parade of *Gran Poder*.

The *Kachua* is an Aymara spring and fertility dance—in a way, a kind of love or courting dance performed by adolescents. There's a ritual exchange of food, alcohol, coca leaves and sweets between the girls and boys. This is one of the few dances in which there's singing. First the girls take the lead while the boys play their *quenas*, and after a while the boys counter the girls' verses. Finally, both sexes begin dancing and the performance ends with a group snake dance. The *Kachua* is performed five times on specific dates, beginning on November 29, the eve of the Feast Day of Saint Andrew, which is the beginning of the Aymara calendar year.

Kusillos are clowns and buffoons who mime and crack jokes to entertain the spectators.

Lecheras are dancers dressed as milkmaids who represent the now-dying custom of milkmaids delivering milk door to door. They wear the same costume as female *Chuta* dancers and hold miniature milk cans.

The *Morenada* is a masked dance. The dancers represent *morenos*, black slaves who were brought to the Yungas by the Spanish. Their rattles represent the clanking of chains, and the extremely elaborate costumes poke fun at Colonial courtesans' dress.

Waca Takoris

Negritos represent blacks, also. The dance and its music are conspicuously Caribbean, as is *costeño* music. The dancers play drums, providing their own accompaniment.

Puli Pulis imitate birds. They wear wings made of green parrot feathers sewn onto cloth.

Suri Sikuris are impossible to miss. They're a group of *zampoña (sikuri)* musicians who wear enormously large, umbrella-like headdresses made from ostrich *(suri)* plumes.

All *Waca* dances are related to the bullfight and show Spanish influence. *Waca Takoris* represent bulls. Each man wears a plaster bull mask at his waist, and the women wear typical Aymara fiesta dress similar to the *Chutas. Waca Tintis* represent picadors. Each one wears a horse's head at his waist. *Waca Wacas* also dress like bulls, but this dance is related to ceremonial potato-planting and is said to have originated in Oruro. *Tinticaballos* accompany *Waca* dancers. They parody the *cuadrilla* portion of the bullfight and carry plaster saddles.

I'm waiting for a dance that parodies tourists. The costume would be a down jacket, blue jeans and dark glasses, and each dancer would carry several cameras, a camera bag and a notebook.

In addition to *comparsas*, there are two general kinds of folk dances you'll probably come across. One is the *huayño*, an *altiplano* dance that has spread all over Bolivia. It's become an anything-goes dance for either groups of separate couples or circles of individual people. I watched a *huayño* at Huatajata that consisted of many couples who held hands and moved in a circle. (Bolivian dances move counterclockwise, the direction of the movement of the sun in the Southern Hemisphere.) The men wore ordinary dress except for red wigs, to satirize whites, and the women wore the typical multilayered *pollera* skirts, fancy blouses, beautifully embroidered shawls and derby hats. The *huayño* went on for hours with couples continually dancing around in a circle. Some of the high-steppers had a woman on each arm, and other men carried *qeru qerus*. The dancers were accompanied by a brass band that played the same melody over and over again and struggled valiantly to keep up with the participants, who covered a lot of ground. Anyone with stamina (including travelers) could join in. The *takirari* is basically a lowland version of the *huayño*.

The other dance you should know about is the *cueca*. It's a Spanish dance derived from the *jota* and is danced by any number of couples holding handkerchiefs. The dance has four parts, and could be called Bolivia's national dance. The *bailecito* is very similar to the *cueca* but is a little more delicate. It's done by a group of two couples who form a square. During the climax, called the *zapateo*, the spectators clap to the dance's distinctive rhythm. In folklore events the *bailecito* is often just sung or played instrumentally, and the audience always claps during the *zapateo*.

As I said at the beginning of this section, I saw more music and dance in Bolivia than anywhere else. In La Paz the *peñas folklóricas* have very minimal cover charges and serve food and beer. The shows begin around 9 P.M. and run for about five hours. The acts range from excruciatingly bad amateurs to Bolivia's best folk artists, such as the excellent *charango*-player Ernesto Cavour. It's worth even the bad performances for the fun of seeing traditional music and dance. In Cochabamba there are folk music performances at the Palacio de la Cultura and at other theaters. These folk music events are well worth attending, and I urge you to see at least one program if the opportunity arises.

Inca Festivals

To understand the cycle of fiestas in Ecuador, Peru and Bolivia, you have to tune in to the religious celebrations of the Incas. These ancient rituals form the basis of modern festivities, which are now celebrated in Catholic trappings.

While the Incas believed in a creator god they called *Viracocha*, the primary god in their pantheon was Father Sun, *Inti Taita*. It's not hard to understand why the sun is worshipped in the Andes; nowhere else have I been so cognizant of the sun's presence—and absence. The sun is light, heat and life itself. Because the sun was the tribal god of the Incas and the Inca was believed to be the son of the sun, the Inca was also considered divine.

Besides the sun, the Incas worshipped many lesser gods and goddesses. In fact, with a nice feeling for the divine nature of all creation, the Indians worshipped just about everything—Mother Earth *(Pacha Mama)*, Mother Moon *(Mama Quilla)*, Mother Sea *(Mama Cocha)*, Father Thunder and Lightning *(Inti Illapa)*, mountain peaks, caves, rivers, rocks and plants. Any sacred thing or place was (and still is) called a *huaca*.

In Inca mythology *Inti Taita* married *Mama Quilla*, who presided over the lunar calendar and many festivals, especially those that have to do with agriculture. The celebration of Inca festivals was based on the agricultural, solar and lunar cycles.

In trying to understand the Inca calendar year, it's important to recognize the basic differences between it and our present-day Gregorian calendar. Since the Inca calendar was lunar, the Quechua months do not directly correspond to our solar months. The Inca year started in November or December, while ours begins in January. In addition, the Quechua and Aymara have always recognized only two "seasons." These are the wet or rainy season (in Quechua, *Paray Mita*; in Aymara, *Jallu Pacha*) and the dry season (in Quechua, *Rupay Mita*; in Aymara, *Lupi* or *Auti Pacha*). Also, since the South American seasons are the reverse of those in North America, you have to turn your concept of seasons around.

December is a summer month in the rainy season. Although December 22 is actually the summer solstice, all Indian summer-solstice celebrations have been moved to Christmas. For the Incas, the major festival in December was *Warachicuy*, an initiation ceremony for young Inca males. Young women who reached puberty also celebrated rites connected with their first menstruation.

During the remaining summer months (January, February, March and April), most fiestas were concerned with crops. Since this is the rainy season, essential for the maturation of crops, rituals were performed to ensure the crops' success. Among these were a ceremony celebrated in Cuzco to give thanks for water and the *Ayriwai* feast held in March or April in honor of the young corn.

May and June are harvest months as well as the beginning of the dry season. Then, as now, many festivals were held in connection with the harvest and transportation of crops, including *Aymorai*, a harvest festival, and *Inti Raymi*, the Festival of the Sun. Today these thanksgivings for the harvest are celebrated as saints' days and Catholic religious holidays. For example, Corpus Christi (mid-June), Saint John's Day (June 24) and the Feast Day of Saints Peter and Paul (June 29) are actually harvest and sun festivals that have taken on Christian overtones. June 24 is especially significant since it is very close to the winter solstice (June 22) and is celebrated as a major fiesta in the Andes today. The winter-solstice festival of *Inti Raymi* coincided with the appearance of the constellation Pleiades, worshipped by the Incas, and also involved the ritual ground-breaking for the coming year's planting.

During the dry, winter months of July and August, two significant festivals were celebrated. These involved the repair of terraces and irrigation canals and the assignment of *chacras* (fields) throughout the empire, based on the population of each area and a rotation system of planting (one year planted, five to eight years fallow). Near the end of August an early corn-planting took place. This planting was initiated with a ceremony performed by the Inca himself.

In September, the Incas planted potatoes and other crops and performed the ceremony of *Situa*, a purification in which all evils were expelled from the empire. This festival, also called *Koya Raymi* (Festival of the Queen), is now celebrated on September 8, the Feast of the Nativity of the Blessed Virgin. During October there was a ceremonial spinning of thread and a special brewing of *chicha* for the *Warachicuy* feast to be held in December.

In November, the Incas celebrated a feast in honor of the dead, and this feast has been incorporated into the Catholic All Saints' and All Souls' days on November 1 and 2. By the end of October or beginning of November the rains were supposed to begin; if they didn't, it meant famine. If the rains were delayed, a *huacayllicuy*, or petition for rain, was held. In this ritual, llamas were tied up without water in hope that their cries would cause the gods to send rain.

Not only have Christian feast days been added to Inca festivals, but Catholic saints and Christ have been identified with Inca deities. Christ is identified with *Inti Taita* (Father Sun). The Virgin Mary is associated with both *Mama Quilla* (Mother Moon) and *Pacha Mama* (Mother Earth). In many places the Virgin has been given *Pacha Mama*'s role as the patroness of agriculture and protector of crops and all living things. *Inti Illapa* (Father Thunder and Lightning) has become associated with Saint James, the patron saint of Spain. The Indians called the Spanish guns *Illapa*, so it's not surprising that they associated the Spanish patron saint with their former god.

QUECHUA MONTHS

Remember that these are lunar months; they don't correspond exactly to our solar months. Also note that the month and the principal feast held that month have the same name.

	English	Quechua	Meaning
Paray Mita (Rainy Season)	December	*Kapaq Raymi*	The Principal or Magnificent Festival
	January	*Quchuy Pokoi*	The Small Ripening
	February	*Quatun Pokoi*	The Great Ripening
	March	*Paukar Warai*	The Garment of Flowers
	April	*Ayriwai*	Dance of the Young Maize
Rupay Mita (Dry Season)	May	*Aymorai*	Song of the Harvest
	June	*Inti Raymi*	Festival of the Sun
	July	*Anta Situa*	Earthly Purification
	August	*Kapaq Situa*	General Purification
	September	*Koya Raymi* or *Situa*	Festival of the Queen
The Rains Begin	October	*Uma Raymi*	Festival of the Water
	November	*Ayamarqa*	Procession of the Dead

Leave-Taking

Today is the day of my departure,
today I will not go, I will go tomorrow.
You may see me leave playing a flute of fly bone,
carrying for banner a spider web,
my drum will be an egg of an ant,
and my cap! my cap will be a hummingbird nest.

PERUVIAN QUECHUA SONG

United States
Customs and Duty

Returning with Foreign Goods

Each returning American traveler is permitted to personally carry $400 worth of goods into the United States duty free. This $400 applies to the price you paid for the goods abroad. For example, if you paid $10 for a poncho in Ecuador it's valued as $10 worth of your $400 exemption, even though the same kind of poncho sells for $75 in fancy Los Angeles boutiques. You may want to save your receipts from South American purchases to show to United States Customs officials when you return. (If you're traveling by air, you'll be given a Customs declaration to fill out on the plane during your return flight.) And watch the cheating! You may get by with saying the $10 poncho cost only $9, but you won't convince them that it only cost $5. In the long run, it's better to be honest.

In January 1976, the United States instituted a new law called the Generalized System of Preferences (GSP), which was designed to help developing nations by eliminating duty on many of their products. (The items must be acquired in the country in which they were produced.) This law applies to Colombia, Peru and Bolivia, but not to Ecuador, which is a member of OPEC.

The new law sounded wonderful until I visited United States Customs and learned about the exceptions. For example, no clothing is included in the GSP, and clothing is certainly one of the main exports of the Andean countries. As of this writing, 155 exceptions to the GSP have been made. What it all boils down to is that you should expect to pay duty on everything you carry home above your $400 allowance. Then, if some items turn out to be duty free under the GSP, you'll be pleasantly surprised.

You'll find that United States Customs officials are honest and helpful. They tell you which souvenirs are duty free and help you pay the least amount of duty on the rest. When I returned to the United States through Miami I stated that I had several hundred dollars worth of treasures beyond my exemption. The Customs agent arranged it so that the items with the higher duty rates were included within my $300 (the then) allowance. She then estimated the duty on the remainder, and it came to about six dollars. You can help the agents by carefully listing on your Customs declaration each item, the country in which it was purchased, its price and content—for example, "Handwoven alpaca poncho, made and purchased in Bolivia, $15."

Important: you *can't* carry or ship into the United States any souvenirs that are "made from the furs, hides, shells, feathers, teeth, and flesh of animals threatened with extinction," including any products made from the more than 400 species of animals listed as endangered by the United States Fish and Wildlife Service. This includes such items for sale in South America as certain snakeskin purses and wallets; stuffed caimans, sea turtles and alligators, as well as products made from their skins; tortoise-shell products; and items made from bird feathers or jaguar, leopard or puma fur. For a complete list, write to the following:

> Division of Law Enforcement
> United States Fish and Wildlife Service
> Department of the Interior
> Washington, D.C. 20402

Shipping Foreign Goods Home

If you're shipping home a box of foreign goods, be sure to include an invoice stating what you paid for them so that Customs can estimate the duty. Include receipts if you can, although frequently this isn't possible since the Indians in the market don't issue them. (Even if you write the receipt yourself, a vendor may not sign it, since many of them can't read and are understandably reluctant to sign something they don't understand.) Always make out two identical invoices; place one inside the package and give the other to the shipper. If you're mailing the package, just enclose one invoice inside the package. A sample follows:

2 alpaca ponchos @ U.S. $20 each	$40.00
1 woven woolen purse @ U.S. $5.50 (receipt enclosed)	5.50
3 pairs of alpaca gloves @ U.S. $2 each pair	6.00
1 embroidered cotton blouse @ U.S. $10 (receipt enclosed)	10.00
TOTAL	$61.50

It's important to list the material content of each item since duty varies depending on the material, decoration and so on. Antiques, which are defined as items 100 years of age or older, are allowed into the country duty free. United States Customs publishes a pamphlet for travelers called "Customs Hints for Returning U.S. Residents—Know Before You Go," which gives all the details. It can be obtained free of charge from any United States Customs office or from the following:

> Superintendent of Documents
> United States Printing Office
> Washington, D.C. 20402

United States residents are permitted to receive one package of foreign goods worth twenty-five dollars or less, duty free, each day. If you're mailing a gift home, mark UNSOLICITED GIFT—VALUE UNDER $25 on the outside of the package.

If you're mailing gifts to more than one person, they can be consolidated in one package. The gifts must be individually wrapped with the value of the gift and the name of the recipient on each one. These can be put in a larger package marked UNSOLICITED GIFTS—CONSOLIDATED, along with the name of each person and the cost of each gift. The $25 exemption applies to each gift, not to the whole package, which can total more than $25.

Many people think that they can get all their foreign goodies into the United States duty free by sending $25 gift packages to every friend, relative and acquaintance. It sounds great until you realize that what is saved on duty is spent on postage and shipping. Also, be sure you don't send one person too many packages too close together, since they could all leave South America in the same shipment and arrive at United States Customs on the same day.

Two free brochures explaining the regulations—"U.S. Customs: International Mail Imports" and "A Gift: Are You Sure?"—can be obtained from United States Customs. Write to:

United States Customs
P.O. Box 7407
Washington, D.C. 20444

Bibliography

Recommended reading is listed in the text, by subject matter, on the following pages: archaeology, 254, 259–60, 262, 264; backpacking, 154; crafts, 286, 290, 292, 304, 349, 359; drugs, 245–46; fiction, 22; general reading, 21–22; guidebooks, 21, 57; health, 210; language, 25–26; poetry, 22–23; politics, 100. The following is an additional selected bibliography.

Adelson, Laurie, and Takami, Bruce. *Weaving Traditions of Highland Bolivia*. Los Angeles: Folk Art and Craft Museum, 1978.

Alvarado, Carlos A. Otarda. *Formas Decorativas Peruanas*. Huancayo, Peru: Talleres Gráficos de la ORAMS VI, 1973.

Américas. Washington, D.C.: Organization of American States, 1969–1976.

Anstee, Margaret Joan. *Bolivia: Gate of the Sun*. New York: Paul S. Eriksson, Inc., 1970, 1969–1976.

Anthony, Glynis. *Colombia: Land of Tomorrow*. New York: Roy Publishers, 1968.

Anton, Ferdinand, and Dockstader, Frederick J. *Pre-Columbian Art and Later Indian Tribal Arts*. New York: Harry N. Abrams, Inc., 1968.

Arciniegas, Germán. *Latin America: A Cultural History*. New York: Alfred A. Knopf, 1968.

——, editor. *The Green Continent: A Comprehensive View of Latin America by Its Leading Writers*. New York: Alfred A. Knopf, 1963.

Arguedas, Jose Felipe Costas. *Diccionario del Folklore Boliviano, Tomos I y II.* Sucre, Bolivia: Universidad Mayor de San Francisco Xavier de Chuquisaca, 1961.

Bates, Nancy Bell. *East of the Andes and West of Nowhere: A Naturalist's Wife in Colombia.* New York: Charles Scribner's Sons, 1947.

Baudin, Louis. *Daily Life in Peru Under the Incas.* New York: The Macmillan Co., 1962.

Beltrán, Miriam. *Cuzco: Window on Peru.* Second Edition, revised. New York: Alfred A. Knopf, 1970.

Bennett, Wendell C., and Bird, Junius B. *Andean Culture History: The Archaeology of the Central Andes from Early Man to the Incas.* Second Edition, revised. New York: American Museum of Natural History, 1960.

Bird, Junius B. "Handspun Yarn Production Rates in the Cuzco Region of Peru." *Textile Museum Journal.* Vol. II, No. 3. December 1965.

_____. *Suggestions for the Recording of Data on Spinning and Weaving and the Collecting of Material.* Berkeley: Kroeber Anthropological Society. No. 22. Spring 1960.

Bork, Albert William, and Maier, Georg. *Historical Dictionary of Ecuador.* Metuchen, N.J.: The Scarecrow Press, Inc., 1973.

Boyce, William D. *Illustrated South America.* Chicago: Rand McNally and Co., 1912.

Bray, Warwick. *The Gold of El Dorado.* London: The Times Newspapers Limited, 1978.

Brecher, Edward M., and the Editors of *Consumer Reports. Licit and Illicit Drugs: The Consumers Union Report on Narcotics, Stimulants, Depressants, Inhalants, Hallucinogens and Marijuana—Including Caffeine, Nicotine and Alcohol.* Boston: Little, Brown and Co., 1972.

Brundage, Burr Cartwright. *Lords of Cuzco: A History and Description of the Inca People in Their Final Days.* Norman, Okla.: University of Oklahoma Press, 1967.

Buechler, Hans and Judith Maria. *The Bolivian Aymara.* New York: Holt, Rinehart and Winston, Inc., 1971.

Bullrich, Francisco. *New Directions in Latin American Architecture.* New York: George Braziller, Inc., 1969.

Burland, C. A. *Peru Under the Incas.* New York: G. P. Putnam's Sons, 1967.

Candia, Antonio Paredes. *Artesanias y Industrias Populares de Bolivia.* La Paz, Bolivia: Ediciones ISLA, 1967.

_____. *La Danza Folklórica en Bolivia.* La Paz, Bolivia: Ediciones ISLA, 1966.

Caracciolo-Trejo, E., editor. *The Penguin Book of Latin American Verse.* Harmondsworth, England: Penguin Books, 1971.

Carpenter, Lawrence Kidd. *Ecuadorian Quichua: Descriptive Sketch and Variation.* Unpublished Ph.D. Dissertation, University of Florida at Gainesville, 1982.

Carter, William. *Bolivia: A Profile.* New York: Frederick A. Praeger, 1971.

Casteñada León, Luisa. *Vestido Tradicional del Peru.* Lima, Peru: Museo Nacional de la Cultura Peruana, 1981.

Chandler, Asa C., and Read, Clark P. *Introduction to Parasitology: With Special Reference to the Parasites of Man.* Tenth Edition. New York: John Wiley & Sons, 1961.

Cieza de León, Pedro de. *The Incas.* Edited by Victor Wolfgang von Hagen. First Edition. Norman, Okla.: University of Oklahoma Press, 1959.

Crow, John A. *The Epic of Latin America.* Third Edition, revised. Berkeley: University of California Press, 1980.

de Friedemann, Nina. "The Golden Gods of Colombia." *Craft Horizons.* Vol. XXXIV, No. 4. August 1974.

de Schauensee, R. Meyer. *The Birds of Colombia and Adjacent Areas of South and Central America.* Narberth, Pa.: Livingston Publishing Co., 1964.

Deuel, Leo, editor. *Conquistadors Without Swords: Archaeologists in the Americas.* New York: Schocken Books, 1974.

D'Harcourt, Raoul. *Textiles of Ancient Peru and Their Techniques.* Edited by Grace G. Denny and Carolyn M. Osborne. Seattle: University of Washington Press, 1962.

Disselhoff, Hans Dietrich. *Daily Life in Ancient Peru.* New York: McGraw-Hill Book Co., 1967.

——, and Linné, S. *The Art of Ancient America: Civilizations of Central and South America.* New York: Crown Publishers, Inc., 1960.

Dockstader, Frederick J. *Indian Art in South America: Pre-Columbian and Contemporary Arts and Crafts.* Greenwich, Conn.: New York Graphic Society Publishers Ltd., 1967.

Donnan, Christopher B. *Moche Art of Peru: Pre-Columbian Symbolic Communication.* Los Angeles: Museum of Cultural History, UCLA, 1978.

Donner, Florinda. *Shabono: A Visit to a Remote and Magical World in the Heart of the South American Jungle.* New York: Delacorte Press, 1982.

Donoso, Jose, and Henkin, William A., editors. *The TriQuarterly Anthology of Contemporary Latin American Literature.* New York: E. P. Dutton and Co., Inc., 1969.

Dorst, Jean. *South America and Central America: A Natural History.* New York: Random House, 1967.

Drum, Jim. "Andean Weaving Draws on the Past." *El Palacio.* Vol. 81, No. 4. Winter 1975.

Duguid, Julian. *Green Hell: Adventures in the Mysterious Jungles of Eastern Bolivia.* New York: The Century Co., 1931.

Dunning, John S. *Portraits of Tropical Birds.* Wynnewood, Pa.: Livingston Publishing Co., 1970.

Ebbing, Juan Enrique. *Aimara Gramática y Diccionario.* La Paz, Bolivia: Editorial Don Bosco, 1965.

Edschmid, Kasmir. *South America Lights and Shadows.* New York: The Viking Press, 1932.

Emery, Irene. *The Primary Structure of Fabrics: An Illustrated Classification.* Washington, D.C.: The Textile Museum, 1966.

Engl, Lieselotte and Theo. *Twilight of Ancient Peru: The Glory and Decline of the Inca Empire.* New York: McGraw-Hill Book Co., 1969.

Erquicia, Vincente Teran. *Chiwanwayus and Achankaras: Flowers of Quechua Legends.* Buenos Aires, Argentina: Ferrari Brothers Press, 1944. Unpublished English translation by Sandra Harrison.

Farfan, J.M.B. *Clave de la Lengua Quechua.* Lima, Peru: Imp. Palabre Libre (N.C.T.), 1940.

Fisher, Nora. *1500 Years of Andean Weaving.* Santa Fe, N.M.: University of New Mexico, 1972.

Flakoll, Darwin J., and Alegría, Claribel, editors. *New Voices of Hispanic America: An Anthology.* Boston: Beacon Press, 1962.

Flornoy, Bertrand. *The World of the Inca.* Garden City, N.Y.: Doubleday and Co., Inc., 1958.

Franck, Harry A. *Vagabonding Down the Andes.* New York: The Century Co., 1917.

Franco, Jean. *The Modern Culture of Latin America: Society and the Artist.* Harmondsworth, England: Penguin Books, 1970.

Gade, Daniel W. "The Llama, Alpaca and Vicuña: Fact vs. Fiction." *The Journal of Geography.* Vol. 68, No. 6. September 1969.

———. "The Guinea Pig in Andean Folk Culture." *The Geographical Review.* Vol. 57, No. 2. 1967.

———. "Red Dye from Peruvian Bugs." *The Geographical Magazine.* Vol. 45, No. 1. October 1972.

Galeano, Eduardo. *Open Veins of Latin America: Five Centuries of the Pillage of a Continent.* New York: Monthly Review Press, 1973.

Gasparini, Graziano, and Margolies, Luise. *Inca Architecture.* Translated by Patricia Lyon. Bloomington, Indiana: Indiana University Press, 1981.

Gerassi, John. *The Great Fear in Latin America.* Revised Edition. New York: Collier Books, 1965.

Getty, Nilda C. Fernandez, and Forsyth, Robert J. *Contemporary Crafts of the Americas.* Chicago: Henry Regnery Co., 1975.

Geyer, Georgie Ann. *The New Latins: Fateful Change in South and Central America.* Garden City, N.Y.: Doubleday and Co., 1970.

Gilbert, Alan. *Latin American Development: A Geographical Perspective.* Harmondsworth, England: Penguin Books, 1974.

Gille, Monif, M.D. *Infectious Disease in Obstetrics and Gynecology.* New York: Harper and Row, 1974.

Girault, Louis. *Textiles Boliviens: Région de Charazani.* Paris, France: Museé de L'Homme, 1969.

Goodell, Grace. "The Cloth of the Quechuas." *Natural History.* Vol. LXXVIII, No. 10. December 1969.

———. "A Study of Andean Spinning in the Cuzco Region." *Textile Museum Journal.* Vol. II, No. 3. December 1968.

Goodspeed, T. Harper. *Plant Hunters in the Andes.* Berkeley, Calif.: University of California Press, 1961.

Graham, John A., editor. *Ancient Mesoamerica: Selected Readings.* Palo Alto, Calif.: Peek Publications, 1960.

Gunther, John. *Inside South America.* New York: Pocket Books, 1968.

Hardoy, Jorge E. *Pre-Columbian Cities.* New York: Walker and Co., 1973.

Harner, Michael J., editor. *Hallucinogens and Shamanism.* New York: Oxford University Press, 1976.

Haywood, Charles. *Folk Songs of the World.* New York: The John Day Co., 1966.

Heath, Dwight B. *Historical Dictionary of Bolivia.* Metuchen, N.J.: The Scarecrow Press, Inc., 1972.

Holmberg, Allan R. *Nomads of the Long Bow: The Siriono of Eastern Bolivia.* Garden City, N.Y.: The Natural History Press, 1969.

Howes, Barbara, editor. *The Eye of the Heart: Short Stories from Latin America.* New York: Avon Books, 1973.

Huxley, Matthew, and Capa, Cornell. *Farewell to Eden.* New York: Harper and Row, 1964.

Indígena: News from Indian America. Berkeley, Calif.: 1974–1976.

Jacobs, Charles and Babette. *South America Travel Digest.* Tenth Edition. Los Angeles: Travel Digests, 1975.

Johnson, William Weber, and the Editors of Time–Life Books. *The Andean Republics: Bolivia, Chile, Ecuador, Peru.* New York: Time, Inc., 1965.

Jones, Julie. *Art of Empire: The Inca of Peru.* New York: The Museum of Primitive Art, 1964.

Katz, Friedrich. *The Ancient American Civilizations.* New York: Frederick A. Praeger, 1972.

King, Mary Elizabeth. *Ancient Peruvian Textiles from the Collection of the Textile Museum, Washington D.C./The Museum of Primitive Art, New York.* New York: The Museum of Primitive Art, 1965.

Kraigny, Frank W. *The Jungle Route.* New York: Orlin Tremain Co., 1940.

Kreig, Margaret B. *Green Medicine: The Search for Plants That Heal.* New York: Rand McNally & Co., 1964.

Krickeberg, Walter, and others. *Pre-Columbian American Religions.* New York: Holt, Rinehart and Winston, 1969.

Kubler, George. *The Art and Architecture of Ancient America: The Mexican, Maya and Andean Peoples.* Baltimore, Md.: Penguin Books, 1962.

———, and Soria, Martin. *Art and Architecture in Spain and Portugal and Their American Dominions: 1500–1800.* Baltimore, Md.: Penguin Books, 1959.

LaBarre, Weston. "The Aymara Indians of the Lake Titicaca Plateau, Bolivia." *American Anthropologist.* Vol. 50, No. 1, Part 2. January 1948.

Lackey, Maria J., editor. *Pan-American Cook Book.* Buenos Aires, Argentina: Talleres Gráficos J. Hays Bell, 1954.

Lanks, Herbert C. *By Pan American Highway Through South America.* New York: D. Appleton-Century Co., 1942.

Lara, René R. Camacho. *Atlas Escolar de Bolivia.* La Paz, Bolivia: Editores René R. Camacho Lara, 1958.

Lathrap, Donald W. *The Upper Amazon.* New York: Frederick A. Praeger, 1970.

Latin America: Intercultural Experiential Learning Aid. Provo, Utah: Language Research Center, Brigham Young University, 1976.

Lehner, Ernst and Johanna. *Folklore and Symbolism of Flowers, Plants and Trees.* New York: Tudor Publishing, 1960.

Lernoux, Penny. *Cry of the People.* New York: Penguin Books, 1981.

Lester, Kip, and McKeel, Jane. *Discover Bolivia: The First English Guidebook of Bolivia.* La Paz, Bolivia: Los Amigos del Libro, 1972.

Lingeman, Richard R. *Drugs from A to Z: A Dictionary.* Revised and Updated Second Edition. New York: McGraw-Hill Book Co., 1974.

Lothrop, S. K. *Treasures of Ancient America: The Arts of the Pre-Columbian Civilizations from Mexico to Peru.* Geneva, Switzerland: Albert Skira, 1964.

MacEoin, Gary, and the Editors of LIFE. *Colombia and Venezuela and the Guianas.* New York: Time, Inc., 1965.

Magnin, William, editor. *Peasants in Cities: Readings in the Anthropology of Urbanization.* Boston: Houghton Mifflin Co., 1970.

The Manual Industries of Peru. Report on a project of the Inter-American Development Commission, Washington, D.C., conducted by Truman E. Bailey, 1942–1946. New York: The Museum of Modern Art, no date.

Marrero, Levi. *Viajemos por America.* Caracas, Venezuela: Ediciones EDIME, 1969.

Martin, Edwina Tooley. *The Land of the Condor.* Bogotá, Colombia: Aedita Editores Ltda., 1963.

Masefield, G. D., Wallis, M., and Harrison, S.G. *The Oxford Book of Food Plants.* London, England: Oxford University Press, 1969.

Masters, Robert V. *Peru in Pictures.* Revised Edition. New York: Sterling Pub. Co., 1972.

Matthiessen, Peter. *The Cloud Forest: A Chronicle of the South American Wilderness.* New York: The Viking Press, 1961.

Mayorga, Cesar A. Guardia. *Diccionario Kechwa–Castellano, Castellano–Kechwa.* Quinta Edicion. Lima, Peru: Editora Los Andes, 1971.

McFarren, Ruth, and Prada, Teresa, editors. *Epicuro Andino: High Altitude Cooking.* Third Edition. La Paz, Bolivia: Cooperativa de Artes Gráficas E. Burillo, Ltda., 1973.

McIntyre, Loren. *The Incredible Incas and Their Timeless Land.* Washington, D.C.: The National Geographic Society, 1975.

Meggers, Betty Jane. *Ecuador.* New York: Frederick A. Praeger, 1966.

Meisch, Lynn Ann. "The Cañari People: Their Costume and Weaving." *El Palacio.* Vol. 86, No. 3. Fall 1980.

——. "Spinning in Ecuador." *Spin-Off.* Interweave Press. Vol. 4. 1980.

——. "The Weavers of Otavalo." *Pacific Discovery.* Vol. 33, No. 6. November–December 1980.

——. "The Ethics of Ethnographic Filmmaking." *Super-8 Filmaker.* Vol. 9, No. 3. May–June 1981.

——. "Paños: Ikat Shawls of the Cuenca Valley." *Interweave Technical Paper*. Vol. 1, No. 2. Spring 1981.

——. "Abel Rodas, the Last Ikat Poncho Weaver in Chordeleg." *El Palacio*. Vol. 87, No. 4. Winter 1981–82.

——. "Costume and Weaving in Saraguro, Ecuador." *The Textile Museum Journal*. Vols. 19–20. 1980–81.

Miller, Benjamin F., M.D. *The Complete Medical Guide*. Third Revised and Updated Edition. New York: Simon and Schuster, 1967.

Milne, Jean. *Fiesta Time in Latin America*. Los Angeles: The Ward Ritchie Press, 1965.

Moseley, Michael Edward. *The Maritime Foundations of Andean Civilizations*. Menlo Park, Calif.: Cummings Publishing Co., 1975.

Most, Harry, M.D., editor. *Health Hints for the Tropics*. Seventh Edition. Bethesda, Md.: The American Society of Tropical Medicine and Hygiene, 1975.

Mullins, Barbara. *Recetas de Tintes Naturales*. Miraflores, Peru: Instituto Centro de Arte, 1973.

Naranjo, Nicolas Fernandez. *Diccionario de Bolivianismos*. Tercera Edición. La Paz, Bolivia: Los Amigos del Libro, 1975.

Norton, Jonathan, and the editors of Time–Life Books. *Ancient America*. New York: Time, Inc., 1969.

Osborne, Harold. *South American Mythology*. Feltham, England: The Hamlyn Publishing Group, Ltd., 1968.

Paredes M., Rigoberto. *Mitos, Supersticiones y Supervivencias Populares de Bolivia*. Tercera Edicion. La Paz, Bolivia: Ediciones ISLA, 1963.

Pescatello, Ann, editor, *Female and Male in Latin America: Essays*. Pittsburgh, Pa.: University of Pittsburgh Press, 1973.

Petterson, Richard. *Folk Art of Peru*. Claremont, Calif.: Richard Petterson, 1968.

Phelan, John Leddy. *The Kingdom of Quito in the Seventeenth Century*. Madison: University of Wisconsin Press, 1967.

Prado, Benjamin Torrico. *Indigenas en el Corazon de America: Vida y Costumbres do los Indigenas de Bolivia*. La Paz, Bolivia: Los Amigos del Libro, 1971.

Radin, Paul, *Indians of South America*. Garden City, N.Y.: Doubleday, Doran & Co., Inc., 1942.

Ranier, Peter W. *Green Fire*. Garden City, N.Y.: Blue Ribbon Books, 1944.

Read, Piers Paul. *Alive: The Story of the Andes Survivors*. New York: Avon Books, 1974.

Richardson, Miles. *San Pedro, Colombia: Small Town in a Developing Society*. New York: Holt, Rinehart and Winston, Inc., 1970.

Rodman, Selden. *South America of the Poets*. Carbondale, Ill.: Southern Illinois University Press, 1972.

——. *The Colombia Traveler: A Complete History and Guide*. New York: Hawthorn Books, 1971.

_____. *The Peru Traveler: A Concise History and Guide.* New York: Meredith Press, 1967.

Rowe, Ann Pollard. "Weaving Processes in the Cuzco Area of Peru." *Textile Museum Journal.* Vol. IV, No. 2. December 1975.

_____. *Warp-Patterned Weaves of the Andes.* Washington, D.C.: The Textile Museum, 1977.

Rowe, John Howland. "What Kind of Settlement Was Inca Cuzco?" *Ñañpa Pacha.* No. 5, 1967.

Salvador, Mari Lyn. "Molas of the Cuna Indians." *A Report from the Center for Folk Art and Contemporary Crafts.* Vol. 1, No. 3. 1975.

Sandeman, Christopher. *A Wanderer in Inca Land.* London, England: Phoenix House, 1948.

Sanderson, Ivan Terence. *Ivan Sanderson's Book of Great Jungles.* New York: Julian Messner, 1965.

Sasser, Elizabeth S. *Architecture of Ancient Peru.* Lubbock, Texas: The Texas Tech Press, 1969.

Sawyer, Alan R. *Tiahuanaco Tapestry Design.* New York: The Museum of Primitive Art, 1963.

Schery, Robert W. *Plants for Man.* Second Edition. Englewood Cliffs, N.J.: Prentice-Hall, Inc., 1972.

Schetky, EthelJane McD., editor. *Dye Plants and Dyeing—A Handbook.* Brooklyn, N.Y.: Brooklyn Botanic Garden, 1964.

Shapiro, Samuel. *Invisible Latin America.* Boston: Beacon Press, 1963.

Shoumatoff, Alex. *The Rivers Amazon.* San Francisco: Sierra Club Books, 1978.

Sitwell, Sacheverell. *Golden Wall and Mirador: Travels and Observations in Peru.* Cleveland, Ohio: The World Publishing Co., 1961.

Stein, William W. *Hualcan: Life in the Highlands of Peru.* Ithaca, N.Y.: Cornell University Press, 1961.

Steward, Julian H., editor. *Handbook of South American Indians, Volume 2, The Andean Civilizations; Volume 5, The Comparative Ethnology of South American Indians.* New York: Cooper Square Publishers, Inc., 1963.

Steward, Julian H., and Faron, Louis C. *Native Peoples of South America.* New York: McGraw-Hill Book Co., Inc., 1959.

Stuart, George E. and Gene S. *Discovering Man's Past in the Americas.* Washington, D.C.: National Geographic Society, 1969.

Sumwalt, Martha Murray. *Colombia in Pictures.* New York: Sterling Pub. Co., 1970.

Taullard, Alfredo. *Tejidos y Ponchos Indígenas de Sudamerica.* Buenos Aires, Argentina: Editorial Guillermo Kraft Ltda., no date.

Tidball, Harriet. *Peru: Textiles Unlimited, Parts I and II.* Shuttle Craft Guild Monographs Twenty-five and Twenty-six. Santa Ana, Calif.: HTH Publishers, 1969.

Toor, Frances. *Three Worlds of Peru.* New York: Crown Publishers, 1949.

Torre, B., Joaquin Gómez de la. *Motivos Indígenas Ecuatorianos.* Quito, Ecuador: C.I. Artes Gráfica C. Ltda., 1971.

Vargas, Victor Angles. *Machupijchu: Enigmática Ciudad Inka.* Lima, Peru: Industrial Gráfica, S.A., 1972.

Verger, Pierre, and Valcárcel, Luis E. *Indians of Peru.* Lake Forest, Ill.: The Pocahontas Press, 1950.

Vlahos, Olivia. *New World Beginnings: Indian Cultures in the Americas.* Greenwich, Conn.: Fawcett Publications, 1970.

von Hagen, Victor W. *The Golden Man: The Quest for El Dorado.* London, England: Book Club Associates, 1974.

Waldo, Myra. *The Art of South American Cookery.* Garden City, N.Y.: Doubleday and Co., 1961.

Wasserman, Tamara E., and Hill, Jonathan S. *Bolivian Indian Textiles: Traditional Designs and Costumes.* New York: Dover Publications, 1981.

Wauchope, Robert, editor. *They Found the Buried Cities: Exploration and Excavation in the American Tropics.* Chicago, Ill.: University of Chicago Press, 1965.

Webb, Kempton E. *Geography of Latin America.* Englewood Cliffs, N.J.: Prentice-Hall, Inc., 1972.

Weil, Thomas E., and others. *Area Handbook for Bolivia.* Second Edition. Washington, D.C.: U.S. Government Printing Office, 1974.

_____. *Area Handbook for Ecuador.* Washington, D.C.: U.S. Government Printing Office, 1973.

_____. *Area Handbook for Peru.* Washington, D.C.: U.S. Government Printing Office, 1972.

Whitney, Caspar. *The Flowing Road: Adventuring on the Great Rivers of South America.* Philadelphia, Pa.: J. B. Lippincott Co., 1912.

Wilbert, Johannes. *Survivors of Eldorado: Four Indian Cultures of South America.* New York: Frederick A. Praeger, 1972.

Willey, Gordon R. *An Introduction to American Archaeology. Vol. II, South America.* Englewood Cliffs, N.J.: Prentice-Hall, Inc., 1971.

Woodcock, George. *Incas and Other Men.* London, England: Faber and Faber, 1959.

Young, Bob, M.D., and Young, Mary, R.N. *How to Stay Healthy While Traveling.* Northridge, Calif.: Young Publishing Co., 1972.

Zeballos, M., Luis. "Trajes Regionales del Departmento del La Paz." *Archivos del Folklore Boliviano.* No. 2. La Paz, Bolivia: Dirrección Nacional de Antropología, 1966.

Zimmern, Nathalie. *Introduction to Peruvian Costume.* Brooklyn, N.Y.: The Brooklyn Museum, 1949.

Zumbühl, Hugo. *Tintes Naturales.* Huancayo, Peru: Kamaq Maki, 1979.

Index of Place Names

An index of Spanish and Indian words used in the text appears starting at page 431.

Index of Spanish
and Indian Words

This index is alphabetized according to the Spanish alphabet, which has three more letters than the English: *ch*, following *c*; *ll*, following *l*; and *ñ*, following *n*.

Feedback

Correspondence and feedback of all kinds are welcome: comments, criticisms, corrections, updates, accolades, adventure stories, dinner invitations . . . Send them to El Dorado, 5528 York Avenue South, Minneapolis, Minnesota 55410. Anything used in future editions of the guide will be credited to you and the winners of the most mindboggling transportation tales and "the worst hotel I ever stayed at" stories will receive letters of condolence from me. Thanks.   *L.M.*